After Terrorism

After Terrorism

The US–Japan Alliance in the
Post-9/11 Security Dilemma

RYUJI HATTORI

Published by State University of New York Press, Albany

An open access version of this book has been made available thanks to the generosity of Ryuji Hattori.

EU GPSR Authorised Representative:
Logos Europe, 9 rue Nicolas Poussin, 17000, La Rochelle, France
contact@logoseurope.eu

For information, contact State University of New York Press, Albany, NY
www.sunypress.edu

Library of Congress Cataloging-in-Publication Data

Name: Hattori, Ryuji, author.
Title: After terrorism : the US–Japan alliance in the post-9/11 security
    dilemma / Ryuji Hattori.
Description: Albany : State University of New York Press, [2026]. | Includes
    bibliographical references and index.
Identifiers: ISBN 9798855805208 (hardcover : alk. paper) | ISBN 9798855806915
    (epub) | ISBN 9798855805222 (PDF) | ISBN 9798855805215 (pbk. : alk. paper)
Further information is available at the Library of Congress.

Contents

Illustrations

Abbreviations

ABM	anti-ballistic missile
ADC	Air Defense Command
AIA	Afghan Interim Administration
APEC	Asia-Pacific Economic Cooperation
ASDF	Air Self-Defense Force
AU	African Union
BJOCC	Bilateral Joint Operations Coordination Center
BMD	ballistic missile defense
CPA	Coalition Provisional Authority
CSD	collective self-defense
CVID	complete, verifiable, irreversible dismantlement
EU	European Union
DPRK	Democratic People's Republic of Korea
FOIP	Free and Open Indo-Pacific
FRF	Futenma Replacement Facility
G8	Group of Eight (Summit)
GHQ	General Headquarters
GPR	Global Posture Review
GSDF	Ground Self-Defense Force
HEU	highly enriched uranium
HFO	heavy fuel oil
IAEA	International Atomic Energy Agency

IOM	International Organization for Migration
ISG	Iraq Survey Group
JICA	Japan International Cooperation Agency
JSDF	Japan Self-Defense Forces
KEDO	Korean Peninsula Energy Development Organization
LDP	Liberal Democratic Party of Japan
MCAS	Marine Corps Air Station
MD	Missile Defense
MEF	Marine Expeditionary Force
Mini-SSC	Mini Security Subcommittee
MOD	Ministry of Defense of Japan
MOFA	Ministry of Foreign Affairs of Japan
MSDF	Maritime Self-Defense Force
NPT	Nonproliferation Treaty
NATO	North Atlantic Treaty Organization
NSC	National Security Council
NSS	National Security Strategy
ODA	Official Development Assistance
OEF	Operation Enduring Freedom
OIF	Operation Iraqi Freedom
OND	Operation New Dawn
PSI	Proliferation Security Initiative
Quad	Quadrilateral Security Dialogue
RCC	Revolutionary Command Council
SACO	Special Action Committee on Okinawa
SCC	US–Japan Security Consultative Committee
SDF	Self-Defense Forces
SOFA	Status of Forces Agreement
UFC	Uniting for Consensus
UN	United Nations
UNDP	United Nations Development Programme
UNGA	United Nation General Assembly

UNHCR	United Nations High Commissioner for Refugees
UNMOVIC	United Nations Monitoring, Verification and Inspection Commission
UNSC	United Nations Security Council
USMC	United States Marine Corps
UNSC	The United Nations Security Council
WFP	United Nations World Food Programme
WMD	Weapons of Mass Destruction
WTO	World Trade Organization

Introduction

The US–Japan Alliance in the Bush–Koizumi Era

After Terrorism

Historical military conflicts often provide profound insights into alliance dynamics and strategic miscalculations. The United States' involvement in the Vietnam War (1955–1975) is often regarded as its most significant military miscalculation of the 20th century, and Japan's participation in the Second Sino-Japanese War (1937–1945) and the Pacific War (1941–1945) holds an analogous distinction. While contemporaneous understandings of these conflicts were limited, retrospective analysis reveals a more complex narrative.

When now considering the 21st century, one must examine whether the American invasion of Iraq, initiated in early 2003, and the policies that followed may be deemed the greatest blunder for these two world powers. A thorough analysis of available intelligence and strategic planning documents suggests that many of the challenges encountered were foreseeable. The US and Japan may have been adversaries during the Pacific War, but their relationship had undergone a profound transformation by the time of the 2003 Iraq War. They had established a robust alliance, as illustrated by Japan's support for US military operations in Afghanistan in 2002.[1]

It is striking that, 60 years after being characterized by American legislators and commentators as "mad," "sublimely insane," and "irrational" in the wake of the Pearl Harbor attack, Japan engaged in a cooperative partnership with the US under the leadership of the Bush and Koizumi administrations. The close relationship that developed between the George W. Bush administration (2001–2009) and the Jun'ichirō Koizumi administration (2001–2006) reached its zenith in the aftermath of the September 11, 2001, terrorist attacks in the US.

Japan does not seem to have played a large role in Bush's vision of his foreign policy prior to taking office. It is perhaps not surprising that the book he published prior to his inauguration in January 2001 largely omits Japan, instead focusing on his positions regarding non-aligned regimes such as Iraq and North Korea.[2] This book suggests that the incoming Bush administration intended to pivot US foreign policy from a framework of deterrence and containment toward a strategy emphasizing prevention and preemption against any challengers to US global hegemony. Consequently, it is significant that, as a candidate, Bush criticized then-President Bill Clinton's foreign policy, which prioritized trade negotiations and agreements aimed at opening foreign markets to American goods, asserting that "China is a [strategic] competitor, not a strategic partner."[3]

The early leadership profiles of Bush and Koizumi reveal that both leaders had had similarly limited foreign diplomatic experience prior to taking office in 2001. An often overlooked characteristic of Koizumi's leadership was an inclination to be a free thinker, which led him to eschew relying solely on briefings prepared by the Ministry of Foreign Affairs (MOFA).[4] This was notably evident in his diplomatic engagements with the US throughout his tenure. In addition to endorsing the Bush administration's military intervention in Iraq, Koizumi also supported the deployment of the Japan Ground Self-Defense Force (GSDF) to Samawah in southern Iraq and instructed the Japan Air Self-Defense Force (ASDF) to provide logistical support to US operations in the region. These military reinforcements built on earlier directives issued in response to the commencement of the Afghan War in late 2001, during which Japan's Maritime Self-Defense Force (MSDF) provided refueling assistance to vessels of the US and the North Atlantic Treaty Organization (NATO). The close relationship between Japan and the US gave rise to numerous concerns, particularly in light of the criticism the US faced from various global leaders regarding the legitimacy of the 2003 Iraq War, which many argued had exacerbated instability across the Middle East. These actions contributed to a deterioration of global trust in the US.

Unprecedented challenges were created for US–Japan relations when the Iraq War converged with North Korea's nuclear ambitions. In the same year that the US invaded Iraq, North Korea (DPRK—the Democratic People's Republic of Korea) formally withdrew from the Nuclear Nonproliferation Treaty (NPT), an agreement it had entered into in

1985. The subsequent revelation that North Korea had been stockpiling nuclear material not only complicated geopolitical dynamics in Asia but also illuminated the challenging decisions that Bush and Koizumi had faced in the lead-up to this pivotal event. This was not the first occasion on which North Korea had threatened to withdraw from the NPT; earlier threats had been alleviated through negotiations during the Clinton administration. The US and Japan had attempted to manage the second withdrawal threat through the Agreed Framework (1994–2002), albeit with diminished success. By this time, American attitudes toward peacekeeping had evolved, particularly in light of claims regarding evidence of North Korea's uranium enrichment capabilities, leading the Bush administration to exhibit ambivalence toward the existing agreement.

Moreover, the Iraq War had significantly undermined international trust in the US due to criticism over its initial misinformation, unilateral military action, ineffective postwar management, human rights violations, contributions to the escalation of terrorism, and civilian casualties. These developments underscored the critical importance of accurate intelligence, international cooperation, and meticulous post-conflict management in sustaining global credibility. Consequently, the responsibility of mediating nuclear peace between North Korea, the US, and regional states fell to the Koizumi administration, which had participated in the Six-Party Talks since 2003. Japan collaborated in this endeavor with China, the Republic of Korea, and Russia.

The unique strategic context of the Bush–Koizumi partnership emerged during a pivotal transition in the global order. The Bush–Koizumi era commenced a decade after the dissolution of the Soviet Union in 1991, during a period characterized by US-led unipolarity. The significance of revisiting US–Japan relations and diplomacy in Asia during this era can be encapsulated in five key points.

First, following the Bush administration's withdrawal from the Anti-Ballistic Missile Treaty, missile defense (MD) emerged as a contentious issue between the US and Japan in 2002.

Second, in addition to marking a pivotal moment for the US, the Iraq War brought the issue of collective self-defense (CSD) to prominence (as articulated in the UN Charter, Article 51). For Japan, the actions of the US in this context served to globalize the US–Japan alliance, attracting increased international attention and broadening the scope of the alliance. Japan's earlier misstep during the Gulf War—its engagement in what was termed "checkbook diplomacy"—initially cast the nation in a negative light; however, this legacy ultimately evolved to enable Japan to assume a more significant role in security matters.[5] Koizumi faced the challenge of identifying alternative legal justifications for reinterpreting the Japanese Constitution to permit CSD, thus extending security collaboration beyond the Far East, enhancing involvement in global peacekeeping, and strengthening the integration of Japanese military forces.

Third, North Korea's nuclear program and missile launches persisted as major concerns throughout Asia.

Fourth, the United Nations (UN) had played a limited yet consistent role in attempting to mediate disputes arising from the situations in Iraq and North Korea.

Fifth, although China was experiencing growth in its national power, it remained weaker than the US and, to some extent, cooperated with the US and Japan on North Korea. Despite the Hu Jintao administration's endorsement of the notion of a "peaceful rise" for China, it was not until 2009–2010 that Chinese foreign policy adopted a more hardline stance.[6] Nevertheless, China exhibited reluctance to support Japan's strong advocacy for certain UN reforms; consequently, Japan's positions on these matters aligned closely with those of the US.

The evolving power dynamics between the US, China, and Japan present critical implications for the future Indo-Pacific security architecture. In analyzing the transition from US unipolarity to a potential bipolar structure characterized by a New Cold War between the US and China, or a multipolar system featuring the US, China, and Russia as dominant powers in the 2020s, it is instructive to examine how the US and Japan have responded to China's ascendance. Ultimately, the US–Japan relationship of the Bush–Koizumi era serves as a paradigm for Indo-Pacific relations in the 21st century.

Addressing these matters, this study investigates the evolution of US–Japan relations and the foreign policy perspectives of both nations through the analysis of previously unpublished diplomatic documents. This book primarily approaches these issues through the lens of foreign diplomacy, with a specific emphasis on the US military and the Japanese Self-Defense Forces (SDF). While provocative and informative, previous studies have either lacked a sufficient documentary foundation or overestimated Japan's role in international politics. Furthermore, many of these studies have presented an incomplete view of Koizumi's foreign policy; on one hand, he is depicted as a decisive leader, as exemplified by his audacious decision to visit North Korea, while on the other, he is characterized as a dogmatic leader lacking a coherent strategy who permitted the US involve Japan in the Iraq War.[7]

The structural constraints on Japan's foreign policy capacity became increasingly evident during the Bush–Koizumi era. Japan's diplomatic role during this period reflected the inherent tensions between alliance management and regional engagement. This study argues that Japan's position within the US-led security framework was a complex one, as it endeavored to balance its alliance obligations with regional diplomatic initiatives toward North Korea and China, while simultaneously seeking to moderate aggressive US military postures through diplomatic channels. Nevertheless, Japan's standing within the international order has been adversely affected by its alliance with the US and the latter's propensity for engaging in high-risk conflicts. Since the 1990s, Japan has primarily occupied a peripheral role in Middle Eastern affairs, attributable to its "unique war-renouncing constitution, as well as policy proscriptions on nuclear weapons and defense spending."[8] These constitutional and policy constraints, while restricting Japan's military capabilities, have fundamentally influenced its approach to international security and alliance management.

Three Methodological Approaches

Asian regional security experienced considerable transformations in the early 2000s as Japan aimed to recalibrate its diplomatic role. In this study, I conduct a document-based analysis of the Koizumi administration's foreign policy positions on Asian security. The research incorporates insights derived from records made accessible by Japan's MOFA under the Information Disclosure Law of 2001, as well as materials obtained from the Digital National Security Archive in Washington, DC.[9] It is widely recognized that President Bush characterized North Korea, Iran, and Iraq as an "axis of evil." These primary documents will demonstrate that Koizumi's policies toward Iraq and North Korea were interconnected, albeit in a distinct manner. Some analysts contend that Japan's support for the Iraq War served as a strategic maneuver to garner American support for its North Korea policy. I will further develop this hypothesis through documentary evidence and will contextualize it with actions taken at the UN and Group of Eight (G8) summits.[10] The declassified documents from the Act have proven to be a necessary yet previously unexplored resource for elucidating these issues, as well as for interpreting Koizumi's behavior and intentions.

Modern policy analysis requires multiple analytical frameworks to capture complex political phenomena. In this study, I aim to provide a comprehensive analysis of Japan's positions and the US–Japan alliance by taking three methodological approaches.

First, I acquired documents from the MOFA under the Information Disclosure Law.[11] Although certain sections of these documents remain classified, such as statements made during summit discussions, portions offering significant insights into the diplomatic efforts and activities conducted during the Iraq War and the attempts to address the North Korean situation were disclosed. In this work I will also analyze the perspectives and actions of key figures, including Koizumi, Chief Cabinet Secretary Yasuo Fukuda, Deputy Chief Cabinet Secretary Shinzō Abe, and Foreign Minister Yoriko Kawaguchi. The discussions between Bush and Koizumi, as well as the minutes of ministerial-level meetings and telegrams exchanged between Tokyo and Washington, will be particularly crucial, as they illustrate the globalization of the US–Japan alliance.

Second, I will analyze the policy process and the perceptions of policymakers through a variety of sources, including memoirs, newspapers, magazine articles, and official documents obtained through Freedom of Information Act requests, as well as instances of misperception. This approach underscores the significance of contextualizing these documents. As Robert Jervis articulates, historical documents—even if "all documents are preserved and opened for public inspection"—cannot provide a complete picture of "motives, calculations, beliefs, and goals" in decision-making processes.[12] Operating under intense pressure, foreign policy organizations rarely document their full reasoning and positions. This reflects the reality that policymakers' job is "to make decisions, not to lay out a record for future scholars."[13] If leaders are compelled to make decisions under duress, using skewed information and constrained by time, the influence of desires, wishful thinking, fears, perceptions, and misperceptions becomes paramount; individuals often perceive what aligns with their preconceptions.[14] As Johann Wolfgang von Goethe aptly wrote, "A man is not deceived by others; he deceives himself."[15]

Third, I conducted a range of interviews to enhance the understanding of US–Japan relations during the Bush–Koizumi era. Among the personal interviews were dialogues with Masahiro Akiyama (administrative vice-minister of defense from 1997 to 1998), Terusuke Terada (ambassador to South Korea from 2000 to 2003), Kensaku Hōgen (ambassador to Canada from 2001 to 2005), and Masaki Orita (ambassador to the UK from 2001 to 2004 and a special envoy for UN reform from 2005 to 2006).[16]

The three above approaches facilitated the exploration of the following fundamental questions: 1) What factors contributed to Japan's misconceptions regarding weapons of mass destruction (WMD) in Iraq? 2) How did the international community perceive and respond to Japan's support for the Afghanistan and Iraq wars? 3) Did Koizumi's perception of Japan's policy toward the US change as a result of his visits to North Korea and that regime's threats to withdraw from the NPT? 4) How did Japan assess its prospects for becoming a permanent member of the United Nations Security Council (UNSC) and what were the reasons for its eventual failure to attain full recognition as a significant player within this group?

The Global Alliance Security Dilemma

In examining the multifaceted challenges faced by the US–Japan alliance in the early 21st century, sophisticated analytical frameworks are required to capture both regional dynamics and global strategic imperatives. This study integrates a globalized security paradigm with a structural analysis of the fundamental components of Japan's security to elucidate the significance of the Iraq War, North Korean issues, UN policy, and G8 summits. The analysis employs three primary theoretical frameworks: the global alliance security dilemma, the asymmetry of the alliance, and the dual-structured security dilemma. Historically, these issues have been addressed in isolation.

Japan pursued a peaceful resolution to its disputes with North Korea even as it simultaneously endorsed the US's use of force in Iraq. The contradiction in these two policies is representative of what this study characterizes as Japan's unresolved "global alliance security dilemma." The global alliance security dilemma pertains to the complexities that emerge when an alliance between nations evolves beyond its initial geographic or functional parameters, thereby generating an expanded set of responsibilities and risks for the participating entities. In the context of the US–Japan alliance, this dilemma is particularly salient in relation to Japan's involvement in international military operations, such as the Iraq War, which surpass the alliance's traditional emphasis on regional security within the Far East. This extension into global security affairs compels Japan to balance the apprehension of potential entrapment in conflicts instigated by its more powerful ally with the risk of abandonment should it fail to offer full support for those engagements. These apprehensions engender two concerns central to the security dilemma: entrapment and abandonment.

The fundamental distinction between this "global alliance security dilemma" and the more conventional "alliance security dilemma" is empirical rather than theoretical and speaks specifically as to whether the scope of an alliance extends beyond the stipulations outlined in the treaty creating that alliance. The alliance security dilemma typically pertains to regional issues or the specific provisions of an alliance, emphasizing the tensions involved in maintaining a close alliance while mitigating conflicts that may arise as a consequence. Conversely, the "global" iteration of this dilemma broadens these considerations to encompass international matters, wherein an alliance's engagement in global conflicts—such as the Iraq War—transcends its original regional mandate, thereby complicating decision-making processes for the weaker ally. Before exploring the complexities of the global alliance security quandary, it is essential to establish a definition of alliances and global alliances.

The conceptual foundation of alliance theory requires careful examination of how scholars have defined and characterized interstate security partnerships. In *Alliance Politics*, Glenn H. Snyder articulates that "alliances are formal associations of states for the use (or non-use) of military force, in specified circumstances, against states outside their own membership."[17] While this definition is accurate, it is overly restrictive for describing global alliances in this context. For instance, Japan's support for the Iraq War transcended "the Far East," which constitutes the geographic scope of the US–Japan alliance as delineated in Article 6 of the US–Japan Security Treaty. In fact, Japan's formal decision-making criteria were informed by several UN resolutions, including a ceasefire resolution adopted more than a decade prior to the Iraq War. Consequently, the definition of global alliances should encompass broader informal policies that are not constrained by treaty provisions. In this study, I adopt Stephen M. Walt's definition: "An alliance (or alignment) is a formal (or informal) commitment for security cooperation between two or more states, intended to augment each member's power, security, and/or influence."[18] This broader conceptualization better captures the complex reality of contemporary alliance relationships that frequently operate beyond their original geographic and functional parameters.

Having established a working definition of alliances, we must next examine the fundamental tensions that shape alliance behavior and decision-making. The notion of the "alliance security dilemma," characterized by the dual anxieties of "abandonment" and "entrapment," remains salient; as Snyder posits, "The risk of abandonment can be reduced by strengthening one's commitment to, hence value to, the ally, but this increases the risk of entrapment." However, Snyder's analysis primarily focused on Europe, and few scholars have broadened their investigations to incorporate other regions. This gap can be attributed, in part, to a scarcity of fact-based and empirical research that examines the Iraq War, North Korea, and UN policy as interrelated cases, particularly as Japan did not serve as a non-permanent member of the UNSC during the Koizumi administration (with the exception of 2005–2006). The relationship between Japan's support for the Iraq War and its policy toward North Korea has been questioned over the years, making it imperative to reexamine this connection in light of newly uncovered official documents.[19]

In this study, I argue that the global alliance security dilemma emerged in Japan due to the US–Japan Security Consultative Committee (SCC, commonly referred to as "2+2"), the absence of independent Japanese intelligence, and Japan's desire to address its "Gulf War Trauma"[20] (i.e., Japanese policymakers' concerns about being perceived as free riders, in an illustration of what Ernest May termed the "misuse of history"[21]) manifesting as an effort to globalize the US–Japan alliance. Furthermore, I contend that Koizumi's attempts to mitigate the dilemma by visiting North Korea and promoting UN reform were ultimately unsuccessful and, in fact, exacerbated the situation. In addition to analyzing the personal preferences of Koizumi and other key figures, I will provide an integrated interpretation of Japan's foreign policy. By tracing the SCC since its establishment following the 1960 revision of the US–Japan Security Treaty, we can analyze its role by applying the concept of the global alliance security dilemma from a macroscopic perspective. By 1990, the US had come to be represented at the SCC by the Secretaries of State and Defense, reflecting its greater importance.

Asymmetry of the Alliance

The second theoretical framework analyzes the intrinsic asymmetry in the US–Japan alliance. No alliance partner can assert equivalence with the US in the context of international relations, as the inherent power dynamics necessitate an intrinsically asymmetrical relationship. Japan's association with the US exemplifies this dichotomy. As articulated by James D. Morrow in the "autonomy-security trade-off model," alliances are characterized by a trade-off between autonomy and security, suggesting that "asymmetric alliances should be easier both to form and to maintain than symmetric alliances; in an asymmetric alliance, the stronger partner gains autonomy and provides security to the lesser partner."[22] In this framework, the weaker partner possesses limited autonomy due to its dependence on the stronger partner for security. Conversely, if the weaker partner were to achieve full autonomy, the stronger partner's ability to ensure security would be compromised.

Asymmetric bilateral alliances, such as America's alliances with Japan and South Korea in the Indo-Pacific, are more likely to encounter security dilemmas. For instance, the US Department of Defense oversees a global portfolio of bases and installations distributed across 45 countries, with the majority of its assets located in Germany, Japan, and South Korea, totaling 194, 121, and 83 sites, respectively.[23] This unparalleled military presence, which no other country can match, creates an inherent power asymmetry that can intensify security dilemmas, as allies must navigate between the benefits of US protection and the challenges of managing autonomy within such an unequal partnership. The Indo-Pacific region also notably lacks a multilateral alliance analogous to NATO; the existence of such a multilateral alliance serves to diffuse rather than focus mutual distrust between nations.[24]

Taking only major imbalances into consideration, the asymmetries in the US–Japan alliance can be classified into at least eight distinct categories.

First, while the US alliance system is multifaceted, encompassing agreements and treaties with NATO, Australia, New Zealand, and South Korea, Japan has only true ally: the US. Consequently, the US's asymmetric alliances in the Indo-Pacific region can be analogously described as a hub-and-spoke system in which the US serves as the central hub.

Second, while American military expenditures are the highest in the world, Japan has been able to benefit from allocating significantly less funding toward national defense. This strategic choice has enabled Japan to devote more resources to its economic development. It is noteworthy that economic cooperation is explicitly addressed in Article 2 of the US–Japan Security Treaty.

Third, American military power, including in the areas of advanced information and intelligence-gathering capabilities, surpasses that of Japan. While Japan has focused on using its limited military capabilities for self-defense, none of its other allies possess military strength comparable to that of the US. This dynamic has led to the two nations' relationship being frequently compared to that of a "spear and shield." Japan lacks nuclear weapons and, as such, relies on the US for long-term deterrence, including nuclear deterrence. While the US can deter undesirable behavior through punitive measures, Japan can only offer deterrence through denial; there thus exists a considerable dependence on the US as an enforcer.

Fourth, despite its official designation as the "Treaty of Mutual Cooperation and Security," Article 6 of the US–Japan Security Treaty stipulates that the US bears a responsibility to defend Japan, while Japan has no reciprocal obligation to protect the US. This framework contrasts with the mutual defense arrangements characterized by NATO and the US–South Korean alliance. Nevertheless, the events of September 11, 2001, revealed the vulnerabilities of the US as a target; they also underscored that Japan, as the junior partner in the alliance, would be compelled to align with American foreign policy in such situations. Notably, the administration of Shinzō Abe (2006–2007; 2012–2020) amended its interpretation of the Japanese Constitution in 2015 to permit Japan to exercise its CSD rights.

Fifth, Article 6 of the US–Japan Security Treaty permits the US to deploy its forces in Japan for both national defense and the security of the Far East. In this sense, the presence of American military forces in Japan confers significantly greater advantages to the US than it derives from its forces in South Korea, whose mission is primarily focused on the defense of that nation; this is accepted in exchange for American deterrence.

Sixth, US forces stationed in Japan have been deployed to locations beyond the Far East, thereby operating outside the specific provisions outlined in Article 6. These locations have included Singapore, the Indian Ocean, Afghanistan, the Persian Gulf, and Iraq.

Seventh, the Agreed Minutes pertaining to Article 3 of the US–Japan Status of Forces Agreement stipulate that the US not only maintains control over the facilities of its bases in Japan but also retains the authority to act independently in nearby regions when deemed necessary, in accordance with Article 6 of the Security Treaty.[25]

Eighth, the Exchanged Notes Regarding the Implementation of Article 6 of the US–Japan Security Treaty assert that prior consultation with Japan is required before deploying American forces from Japanese bases to overseas locations. Nevertheless, the US has consistently failed to consult Japan prior to such deployments, rendering this consultation framework ineffective.

Of these eight imbalances, only the second and fourth are in Japan's favor.

Table I.1 Asymmetries in the US–Japan Alliance

	Asymmetry	Relevant Article(s) of the Security Treaty	US	Japan	Advantage
1	Hub-and-spoke	N/A	Hub	Spoke	US
2	Economic efficiency	2	Vast military budget	Limited military budget/focus on economy	Japan
3	Military power/deterrence	5, 6	Overwhelming/deterrence by punishment	Limited military capabilities/deterrence by denial	US
4	Duty to defend	5	Duty to defend Japan	No duty to defend the US	Japan
5	Far East	6	Uses US forces in Japan for the security of the Far East	Permits the US to use US forces in Japan for the security of the Far East	US
6	Beyond the Far East	Outside the provisions of Article 6	Uses US forces in Japan for security beyond the Far East	Permits the US to use US forces in Japan for security beyond the Far East	US
7	US bases in Japan	SOFA, pursuant to Article 6	Control (including areas in the vicinity of bases)	Limited control (including areas in the vicinity of bases)	US
8	Prior consultation	Exchanged Notes regarding the implementation of Article 6	Has never consulted Japan prior to troop dispatch	Dysfunctional prior consultation system	US

The asymmetrical nature of the US–Japan alliance has led to competing narratives and criticisms from both nations regarding the fairness and burden of the partnership. The perception that the US considers Japan a free rider in the alliance was particularly prevalent during Donald Trump's first term. Conversely, Japan perceives the American military presence on its territory as a burden, as the stationed troops are tasked with the security of the Far East, which extends beyond Japan's national borders. Strong sentiments within the US that other NATO members are free riders have led to threats of withdrawal from the organization, especially during the Trump administration. Multilateral alliances, such as NATO, may be more prone to the issue of free riding compared to bilateral alliances, as they afford smaller, less powerful nations a voice and incorporate complex decision-making processes among larger organizations.[26] Smaller or middle powers can exercise a degree of influence over the US, albeit a limited one, due to the possession of certain bargaining chips.[27]

Additional evidence is necessary to assess the validity of the Japanese perspective, which I argue is significantly influenced by the asymmetrical dynamics of the bilateral alliance. More information is also required to address fundamental questions regarding how and when the issues involving Iraq and North Korea became interconnected, as well as whether or not Japan has sought to dissociate from this linkage. Although the alliance security dilemma has been present since the late 20th century, dating to the signing and subsequent revision of the Security Treaty, it was not until the onset of the 21st century that the dilemma surrounding the US–Japan alliance transcended the Far East and assumed a global dimension.

Being an ally does not necessarily imply that an alliance is without friction; some European allies of the US like France and Germany opposed the Iraq War, for example. For the US–Japan alliance to be regarded as a security dilemma, this must be applicable within the context of Asian international security. Reinterpreting the concept as a global alliance security dilemma is therefore a legitimate consideration. For Japan, this primarily pertains to the fear of becoming entrapped in undesirable conflicts involving its American ally, which extend beyond the geographical confines of the Far East. This concern contrasts with the necessity to mitigate the risk of US abandonment in the event of hostility from Japan's immediate neighbors.

But it is important to recognize that the US is not entirely free from obligations associated with the US–Japan global alliance security dilemma, even if the constraints on it are considerably less binding than those on Japan. The dilemma for the US arises from the need to take Japanese perspectives (such as its emphasis on peaceful solutions to North Korean issues) into account even when they conflict with American policy so as to avoid Japanese disapproval of conflicts in regions beyond the scope of the Security Treaty. These limitations serve a dual purpose: They enable Japan to reassess its CSD stance while also compelling the US to reconsider its aggressive or bellicose behavior. These factors are some of the costs associated with the security of the US–Japan global alliance.

Represented in this manner, the dilemmas faced by Japan and the US are asymmetric: Japan's dilemma exists within the spectrum of "entrapment" and "abandonment," while the US dilemma is primarily concerned with the dual issues of "consideration" and "disapproval." The American dilemma seems considerably less pressing; had the US disregarded Japanese demands on North Korea, it is plausible that Japan would have opposed the Iraq War, but the US would likely have proceeded with its decision to invade Iraq despite the lack of Japanese support.

The Iraq War serves as a notable illustration of how weaker states in a unipolar world face the risk of becoming entrapped within coalitions led by an unparalleled power, potentially incurring unforeseen costs should the judgment of the unipolar state prove to be erroneous.[28] Generally, unbalanced alliances give rise to asymmetric dilemmas. To mitigate the risk of abandonment, weaker states often find themselves compelled to incur higher costs and possess diminished bargaining power. Weaker allies contribute to both the defense and autonomy costs of the alliance; the former encompasses cost-sharing and burden-sharing, while the latter pertains to sovereignty constraints and garrison costs.[29] In scenarios where contingencies arise due to the actions of a powerful ally, the burden-sharing obligations of a weaker ally may surpass the parameters outlined in their alliance treaty, thereby engendering a global alliance security dilemma.

The Dual-Structured Security Dilemma

The third theoretical framework under which I examine the US–Japan alliance is that of the "dual-structured security dilemma," which analyzes how alliance dynamics intersect with adversarial relationships. The intricate interplay between alliances and adversaries in international relations has been a long-standing focus of inquiry for scholars and policymakers alike.

In the context of East Asian security dynamics, the interactions among the US, Japan, and China constitute a particularly complex case. Glenn Snyder's contributions to alliance theory offer a valuable framework for elucidating these multifaceted relationships. In his analysis, Snyder posits that "allies are dealing with their adversaries at the same time they are dealing with each other. The alliance and adversary games proceed simultaneously and complement each other in various ways."[30] Accordingly, he identifies a "composite security dilemma" that encompasses both an "alliance game" and an "adversary game"; in the latter, characterized by adversarial relations, an increased commitment to an alliance can provoke adversaries and escalate tensions.[31]

While the US–Japan alliance experiences an alliance security dilemma, the relationship between the US–Japan alliance and China (and, by extension, North Korea) presents an additional fundamental security dilemma: the potential for any opposition by the US–Japan alliance to China to result in that country strengthening its military. The existence of this dual-structured security dilemma within the US–Japan–China triangle is significant. The concept of the dual-structured security dilemma pertains to a scenario in which an alliance or security framework encounters two concurrent challenges: one related to internal alliance dynamics and the other arising from interactions with external adversaries. Within the context of the US–Japan–China asymmetric triangle, this concept elucidates the dual pressures experienced by the US–Japan alliance. Internally, within the alliance, there exists the risk of abandonment or entrapment. Externally, opposition to adversaries such as China may elicit military responses from those adversaries, thereby exacerbating regional tensions.

The complexities of this dual-structured security dilemma are particularly pronounced in East Asia, as it necessitates the management of both the internal dynamics of the US–Japan alliance and the external challenges posed by China's military and political ascendance. This framework adds an additional layer of difficulty to policymaking, as actions taken within the alliance may inadvertently escalate conflicts with external powers. This dual-structured security dilemma poses a unique challenge for policymakers and strategists by necessitating a delicate balancing act between upholding alliance commitments and avoiding unnecessary provocations that could escalate tensions. Given the importance of this dynamic in influencing regional security, this study will investigate the complexities of this dual-structured security dilemma within the US–Japan–China asymmetric triangle. By examining its manifestations and implications,

I aim to contribute to a more nuanced understanding of the intricate security landscape in East Asia and potentially inform more effective policy approaches.

Chapter Organization

This book provides a comprehensive examination of the US–Japan alliance and Asian diplomacy, with a particular emphasis on pivotal events occurring during Koizumi's tenure as prime minister of Japan from 2001 to 2006. In the initial chapter, I analyze the globalization of the US–Japan alliance in the wake of the 9/11 terrorist attacks. Notably, this period also marked the 60th anniversary of the San Francisco Peace Conference and the conclusion of the Treaty of San Francisco or the Treaty of Peace with Japan. Diplomatic dialogues between Koizumi and Bush began at Camp David and continued at the G8 summit in Genoa. With the start of the Afghan War, Koizumi expressed his support for the US and enacted the Anti-Terrorism Special Measures Law to assist. The US–Japan Mini-SSC also convened to deliberate on the framework for cooperation. Following a meeting in Brussels, the US and Japan reached an agreement to co-chair an international conference on reconstruction assistance in January 2002 in collaboration with the European Union (EU) and Saudi Arabia.

In chapter 2, I examine the International Conference on Reconstruction Assistance to Afghanistan, held in Tokyo in January 2002. Koizumi appointed Ogata Sadako, former United Nations High Commissioner for Refugees (UNHCR), as his special representative at the conference. He also published an article in *Newsweek* that same month in which he articulated Japan's preferred role in Afghanistan; this emphasized providing assistance to reconstruction efforts over participation in military operations. His administration also announced the Ogata Initiative aimed at assisting Afghan refugees. In this chapter I also analyze the context that led Bush to label North Korea, Iran, and Iraq as forming an "axis of evil" in his State of the Union address in January 2002, as well as his subsequent visit to Japan a month later to discuss Iraq and North Korea.

When Koizumi again met with Bush at the United Nations General Assembly (UNGA) meeting in September, he emphasized the importance of international cooperation. But he adopted an approach to North Korea in stark contrast to that of the US, traveling to the DPRK, meeting with General Secretary Kim Jong-il, and signing the Pyongyang Declaration.

Days later, Bush issued the National Security Strategy of the United States of America, which incorporated the policy commonly referred to as the Bush Doctrine: the assertion that the President would not hesitate to launch preemptive strikes against any nation deemed a threat to US security. That same year, the United Nations Security Council (UNSC) unanimously passed Resolution 1441, authorizing inspections for WMD in Iraq. Shortly thereafter, North Korea announced the reactivation of its nuclear program. At an SCC meeting, the issue of North Korea was linked with concerns regarding Iraq, thereby presenting Japan with a complex global alliance security dilemma.

The third chapter is organized into two sections. In the first, I examine North Korea's withdrawal from the NPT in 2003. After North Korea's declaration that it was in possession of nuclear weapons, Bush exerted considerable pressure on Chinese President Jiang Zemin to take action, leading to the US and China initiating the Six-Party Talks with South Korea, North Korea, Japan, and Russia. In the second section of the chapter, I address the Iraq War. While Japan's policy toward North Korea sought to find a peaceful resolution, Koizumi opted to support the Iraq War to maintain American deterrence against North Korea. These contrasting strategies underscored Japan's security dilemma within the context of its global alliances. The US–Japan alliance gained additional global significance following discussions between Bush and Koizumi at Bush's private residence in Crawford, Texas. Further discussion of Iraq and North Korea occurred at the G8 Summit in Evian, France. To facilitate the overseas deployment of the SDF, the Koizumi administration enacted the Act on Special Measures Concerning Humanitarian Relief and Reconstruction Work and Security Assistance in Iraq. Bush also made an unofficial visit to Japan, during which Koizumi highlighted the significance of the "US–Japan alliance in the world." The Koizumi administration would subsequently authorize the deployment of the SDF to Iraq.

The fourth chapter focuses on significant events that transpired in 2004. The SDF were deployed to Samawah, Iraq, while Koizumi undertook a second visit to North Korea, which resulted in the repatriation of five Japanese citizens who had been abducted decades earlier. Notably, the ongoing Six-Party Talks were not disrupted by this diplomatic engagement. Nevertheless, these developments indicated Japan's increasing reliance on the US, not only for security against North Korea but also for assistance in addressing the abduction issue. During the second round of the Six-Party Talks in Beijing, US Assistant Secretary of State James Kelly asserted the necessity of North Korea complying with the "complete, verifiable, irreversible dismantlement" of its nuclear program. He also sought to persuade North Korea to acknowledge its intentions to produce highly enriched uranium, something that it had consistently and vehemently denied. The third round of talks concluded with the release of an ambiguous chairman's statement rather than a joint communiqué. In contrast, the UNSC unanimously adopted Resolution 1546, which had been presented by the US and the UK, facilitating the transfer of sovereignty from the Coalition Provisional Authority to the Iraqi Interim Government. The Iraq Survey Group's investigations yielded no evidence of the presence of WMD in Iraq at the onset of the Iraq War in 2003, a troubling revelation for both American and Japanese leaders. Interestingly, declassified MOFA documents reveal that neither US Secretary of State Colin Powell nor Japanese Foreign Minister Nobutaka Machimura referenced this issue during their talks in Tokyo.

In chapter 5, I examine the 2005 security dialogue between the US and Japan, with a particular emphasis on the SCC and UNSC reform. The consultations of the SCC are significant in two respects. First, despite the absence of substantiating evidence for the justifications for the Iraq War and the ongoing instability within the country, the SCC reframed the US–Japan alliance in a way that extended its influence globally, beyond the treaty-defined parameters of the Far East. Second, while advocating for greater transparency from China regarding its military capabilities and intentions, the SCC also called on China "to play a responsible and constructive role regionally as well as globally." As the UN celebrated its 60th anniversary in 2005, the Koizumi administration, in concert with the governments of Germany, India, and Brazil (collectively referred to as the "G4"), proposed a draft resolution that would permit these members to achieve permanent membership in an expanded Security Council. This was opposed by the Bush administration, however, signaling that, despite Koizumi's close relationship with Bush, the US position on this issue remained steadfast and unchanging.

In chapter 6, I comprehensively cover the withdrawal of the SDF from Iraq, Koizumi's 2006 visit to the US, and North Korea's missile tests. During Koizumi's final visit to the US, he and Bush issued a joint statement titled "The Japan-U.S. Alliance of the New Century," which characterized the US–Japan partnership as "one of the most accomplished bilateral relationships in history." The two leaders engaged in close collaboration in response to North Korea's missile tests, resulting in the unanimous adopting of UNSC Resolution 1695 to condemn the launches. This resolution was passed during the G8 summit in St. Petersburg, and Bush and Koizumi notably chose to eliminate references to Chapter 7 of the UN Charter from the resolution to secure approval from both China and Russia.

In the conclusion, I elaborate on the interpretations offered in each chapter and synthesizes the implications of the post-9/11 US–Japan alliance and Asian diplomacy through the lens of the global alliance security dilemma. I contextualize this analysis by examining the interconnected cases of the War in Afghanistan, the Iraq War, Northeast Asian issues, UN policy, and G8 summits. Moving beyond the period covered in the earlier chapters into the 2020s, it becomes clear that Japan's security dilemma is not confined solely to its relationship with the US but also encompasses its interactions with China and North Korea. This dual-structured security dilemma is pivotal to understanding the dynamics of the US–Japan–China asymmetric triangle and the broader landscape of East Asian international politics.

Chapter 1

9/11 and the Afghanistan War

2001

Terrorist Attacks

Inauguration of the Koizumi Administration

Unlike the US, where presidents serve one or two fixed four-year terms, the Japanese political system allows considerable variation in the duration of prime ministerial terms. This was particularly evident at the onset of the 21st century, when Yoshirō Mori assumed the role of prime minister in the spring of 2000 following the illness of Keizō Obuchi. Mori's administration would prove short-lived, lasting only 387 days. In contrast, his successor, Jun'ichirō Koizumi, would go on to govern for five years and five months, making him the second-longest-serving prime minister of Japan in the 21st century after Shinzō Abe.

On April 26, 2001, Koizumi established his first government.[1] He appointed Yasuo Fukuda as chief cabinet secretary, Makiko Tanaka as foreign minister,[2] and Gen Nakatani as director-general of the Defense Agency. Fukuda was the eldest son of former prime minister Takeo Fukuda (1976–1978), for whom Koizumi had previously worked as secretary. The day after taking office, Koizumi initiated a call to President George W. Bush. During their initial conversation, Koizumi emphasized Japan's status as a US ally, and Bush responded that he was "very heartened by [his] statement."[3]

High-level diplomatic exchanges with the US early in Koizumi's tenure reinforced the two nations' alliance. On May 8, less than two weeks

21

after Koizumi took office, Deputy Secretary of State Richard L. Armitage paid a courtesy call to the Prime Minister's Office, during which he presented a personal letter from Bush. The letter emphasized that "The U.S.-Japan alliance is the cornerstone of peace in Asia" and plays a vital role in ensuring regional stability and prosperity.[4] He expressed gratitude for Koizumi's public support of their partnership and proposed expanding their strategic discussions to address regional and global security matters. Looking ahead, Bush wrote that he hoped they could "broaden our strategic dialogue" and announced that Armitage would visit Tokyo to consult on missile defense (MD) and deterrence strategies.[5]

In the presence of Chief Cabinet Secretary Fukuda and Deputy Chief Cabinet Secretary Shinzō Abe, Koizumi emphasized to Armitage that "The US–Japan relationship is the foundation of Japan's diplomacy."[6] While also affirming Japan's commitment to maintaining good relations with China, South Korea, and Russia, he stressed that strengthening US–Japan ties was essential for these broader diplomatic efforts. Koizumi firmly rejected the minority view in Japan that deteriorating relations with the US could be compensated for through other international relationships, declaring that "the enhancement of our relations with the US directly correlates with the improvement of our relations with other nations."[7] In response to Bush's comments on MD, Koizumi remarked, "I hope that Japan and the US will exchange ideas and expand our areas of cooperation in the future."[8] As he discussed the significance of relations with the US for Japanese foreign policy, Koizumi also noted, "I represent Yokosuka, where the US Navy is stationed."[9] He had grown up close to the American naval base in Yokosuka, and this likely fostered a strong attachment to the US. That his father, Jun'ya Koizumi, had once served as director-general of the Defense Agency may have also contributed to this affinity.

First Discussions at Camp David

On June 30, 2001, Koizumi arrived at Camp David for his inaugural US–Japan summit, accompanied by Deputy Chief Cabinet Secretary Abe. This first meeting between Koizumi and Bush addressed several pressing bilateral issues, establishing foundational themes for US–Japan relations under their leadership. In his address to Bush and National Security Advisor Condoleezza Rice, Koizumi commemorated the 50th anniversary of both the San Francisco Peace Treaty and the US–Japan Security Treaty. He emphasized the significant contributions of then–Prime Minister Nobu-

Table 1.1. Major Actors During the Bush–Koizumi Era

	US				Japan			
Position	President	National Security Advisor	Secretary of State	Secretary of Defense	Prime Minister	Chief Cabinet Secretary	Minister of Foreign Affairs	Director-General of the Defense Agency
2001	Clinton/ Bush	Berger/Rice	Albright/ Powell	Cohen/ Rumsfeld	Mori/ Koizumi	Fukuda	Kōno/ Tanaka	Saitō/ Nakatani
2002	Bush	Rice	Powell	Rumsfeld	Koizumi	Fukuda	Tanaka/ Kawaguchi	Nakatani/ Ishiba
2003	Bush	Rice	Powell	Rumsfeld	Koizumi	Fukuda	Kawaguchi	Ishiba
2004	Bush	Rice	Powell	Rumsfeld	Koizumi	Fukuda/ Hosoda	Kawaguchi/ Machimura	Ishiba/ Ohno
2005	Bush	Rice/Hadley	Powell/Rice	Rumsfeld	Koizumi	Hosoda/ Abe	Machimura/ Asō	Ohno/ Nukaga
2006	Bush	Hadley	Rice	Rumsfeld	Koizumi/ Abe	Abe/ Shiozaki	Asō	Nukaga/ Kyūma

Source: Created by the author.

suke Kishi (1957–1960), Abe's grandfather, in revising the treaty in 1960. Now regarded as "Kishi's greatest accomplishment," this was a challenging endeavor undertaken in the face of considerable public opposition.[10]

Koizumi also reflected on the resolute position his father had adopted as chairman of the Foreign Affairs Committee, a stance that garnered him esteem from his peers despite their opposition over the treaty. He concluded by addressing the idea of greater Japanese independence from the US, arguing, "the relationship between Japan and the US is fundamental; the better that relationship is, the better our relationship with other countries will be."[11] Bush responded by stating, "The best foreign policy starts with our allies. This summit is a chance to demonstrate—not only to our two countries, but to the world at large—that the leaders of these two powerful nations are willing to collaborate."[12]

The proximity between Marine Corps Air Station Futenma and the local population had been a long-standing source of discontent in Okinawa, and there had been extensive discussion of relocating it (likely to Henoko, on the northern tip of the island). When Koizumi broached the subject, noting that "Okinawa has raised the issue of the 15-year expiration date, and there have been requests to relocate Marine training to Guam or the Philippines," Bush responded, "I will have the State and Defense Departments work closely with Japan. The deadline for use is a difficult issue, and I would like to consult with you on the Futenma relocation."[13]

In discussing MD, Koizumi made Japan's military posture clear, stating that "Japan's national security policy is predicated on the premise that it will be exclusively defensive in nature."[14] He justified Japan's interest in the area by noting that "these are missiles rather than offensive weapons," making it "precisely the kind of issue that falls under our exclusively defensive security policy."[15] He drew a clear distinction between research and implementation, asserting that "the question of the development and deployment of such missiles should be considered separately from their research," and emphasized that Japan's commitment to MD needed to align with its strictly defensive national security posture.[16]

Following these discussions, the US and Japan issued a joint statement underscoring the "critical" role of US military forces in ensuring regional stability and expressing American gratitude to Japan for its ongoing support.[17] Both leaders agreed on the importance of addressing concerns related to the US forces stationed in Japan and placed a particular focus on the efforts of the Special Action Committee on Okinawa (SACO) to mitigate the burdens faced by Okinawans and thereby strengthen the US–Japan alliance. They also recognized the increasing threat posed by the prolif-eration of WMD and ballistic missiles and highlighted the necessity of "a comprehensive strategy" that encompassed a range of defense measures and diplomatic initiatives, including arms reduction.[18]

What insights can be gleamed from Koizumi's first US–Japan summit? 2001 marked the 50th anniversary of two pivotal agreements signed by Prime Minister Shigeru Yoshida (1946–1947, 1948–1954): the San Francisco Peace Treaty and the US–Japan Security Treaty. But rather than focusing on Yoshida's legacy, Koizumi chose to instead emphasize the contributions of Nobusuke Kishi (1957–1960), the leader who oversaw the latter treaty's revision in 1960. In doing so, he deliberately aligned himself with men like Kishi, Takeo Fukuda, and Shintarō Abe (d. 1991)—Kishi's son-in-law and father of Shinzō Abe.

Through this political positioning, evident from the onset of his meetings with Bush, Koizumi signaled an intention to pursue a more assertive role within the alliance. But Kishi had articulated a clear vision as prime minister and chosen to conduct a diplomatic mission to South-east Asia before visiting the US for the first time. Largely owing to his reliance on the US, Koizumi lacked comparable strategic depth and a well-defined Asia policy. Significantly, while Koizumi's administration would see US–Japan relations flourish, Japan's relations with both China and South Korea deteriorated markedly under his leadership, primarily due to his controversial annual visits to Yasukuni Shrine, where Class A war criminals are enshrined alongside Japan's war dead.[19]

US–Japan Status of Forces Agreement and the G8 Summit

A high-profile incident in the summer of 2001 led to renewed scrutiny of the US–Japan Status of Forces Agreement (SOFA). On June 29, during Koizumi's visit to the US, an American airman sexually assaulted a woman in Chatan, Okinawa. The Okinawan Prefectural Police secured an arrest warrant for the airman on July 2; due to the stipulations of the SOFA, however, his extradition to Japanese authorities did not occur until July 6.[20] During this interval, US Ambassador to Japan Howard Baker commu-nicated to Foreign Minister Tanaka that he would permit the extradition, and this decision was subsequently formalized by the US–Japan Joint Committee in accordance with the SOFA.[21]

Discussion of SOFA issues took a backseat during the 2001 G8 sum-mit, held in Genoa from July 20 to 22. While both Bush and Koizumi were in attendance, the environment was not conducive to a thorough discussion of bilateral issues. Instead, the summit was primarily focused on the state of the global economy in the wake of the bursting of the dot-com bubble. Koizumi unequivocally asserted his commitment to improving the Japanese economy, emphasizing that it "would not grow without reform."[22] Bush and other attendees concurred, a position that was reflected in the G7 statement, which noted the continued decline in Japan's economic activity and in prices. This statement recommended that Japan's monetary policy persist in injecting substantial liquidity and emphasized the urgent need for comprehensive reforms in both the financial and corporate sectors to establish a foundation for more robust economic growth in the medium term. It also expressed approval of Japan's recent reform initiatives and acknowledged their potential contribution to achieving these objectives.[23] Notably, the statement was attributed to the G7 rather than the G8, as Russian President Vladimir Putin was not included.

Following the formal summit discussions, Koizumi emphasized Japan's agenda of economic reform to the international media. At a press conference, he explained his remarks concerning the Japanese economy and identified this as one of his principal accomplishments at the summit.[24] The G8 leaders also issued statements on a range of regional issues, including military involvement in Macedonia, the situation on the Korean Peninsula, and developments in the Middle East. They expressed shared concerns about North Korea and reaffirmed their support for implementation of the Agreed Framework. They anticipated that North Korea would act on "its announced moratorium on missile launches" and provide a constructive response to "international concerns over security, non-proliferation, humanitarian and human rights issues."[25] Such a response was deemed critical for alleviating regional tensions and facilitating North Korea's greater integration into the international community. Implementation of the Agreed Framework was overseen by the Korean Peninsula Energy Development Organization (KEDO), created in October 1994. The initial agreement stipulated that North Korea would cease its nuclear operations in exchange for 500,000 tons of heavy oil annually from the US, with the US ultimately committing to provide North Korea with two light-water reactors contingent on North Korea's agreement to dismantle its nuclear facilities. However, implementation of the Agreed Framework fell apart following the emergence of suspicions regarding North Korean uranium enrichment in October 2002.

The SOFA issue resurfaced during the high-level diplomatic discussions between US and Japanese officials held shortly after the G8 summit. When Secretary of State Colin Powell visited Japan on July 24, Koizumi raised the matter, noting that the Foreign Affairs Committee of Japan's House of Representatives had passed a resolution calling for the agreement to be revised. He had previously indicated that Japan's SOFA was no less favorable than those the US had concluded with NATO, Germany, and South Korea, and that improvements needed to be made in its implementation rather than its content. He nevertheless cautioned Powell that, should issues involving American military personnel continue, "the domestic situation is such that we will have to consider revising the Agreement."[26]

Powell responded by acknowledging that the four-day duration between request and execution for detention transfer might be slower than optimal. He concurred with Koizumi's assessment that "now is not the time to revise the US–Japan SOFA" and assured him that discussions aimed at improving the agreement's implementation would be ongoing.[27] As the summer drew to a close, Okinawa and the SOFA had emerged as the most pressing issues for US–Japan relations. Regrettably, this situation would soon change with the global upheaval that followed the events of September 11, 2001.

9/11 as the Origin of the Global Alliance

The diplomatic focus on SOFA would soon be dramatically overshadowed by the most catastrophic terrorist attack in American history. On September 11, 2001, two hijacked aircraft were deliberately flown into the World Trade Center towers in New York City. A third hijacked plane crashed into the Pentagon, the headquarters of the Department of Defense, resulting in significant structural damage, while a fourth crashed into an open field in Somerset County, Pennsylvania. As Bush was visiting an elementary school in Florida at the time of the attacks, Vice President Dick Cheney assumed command of the White House.[28] The 9/11 attacks elicited profound feelings of disbelief, grief, and shame among American policymakers. Their emotional response was exacerbated by a desire for retribution and a sense of guilt from the disaster transpiring on their watch, as well as intelligence reports that subsequent attacks could be imminent.[29]

The Koizumi administration responded to the attacks by establishing a task force within the Prime Minister's Office and convening a Security Council meeting on September 12. Acting under Koizumi's leadership, the council affirmed its commitment to "provide the assistance and cooperation to the US necessary to counter terrorist incidents," stressing that it was important to work together with the US and other relevant countries to prevent similar events in the future.[30] Koizumi postponed a planned visit to Southeast Asia on the grounds that "The terrorist attacks are an unprecedented calamity and a grave challenge to democracy" and that he needed to take the lead in the Japanese response.[31]

Significantly, his administration also determined that "it might be reasonable to study the issue of CSD" in light of the situation, a development notable for the potential constitutional implications.[32] The reaction of the Koizumi administration in the wake of the attacks not only marked a decisive moment in US–Japan alliance relations but also signaled a new willingness to reconsider Japan's traditional security constraints in the face of emerging global threats. Bush noted in his memoirs that "Junichiro Koizumi, prime minister of the nation that struck America at Pearl Harbor, called the events of September 11 'not an attack against just the United States but an attack against freedom and democracy.'"[33]

The controversy over alleged American pressure on Japan to demonstrate visible support in the aftermath of 9/11 shows just how complex US–Japan diplomatic communications could be at the time; there continues to be a widespread misconception that American officials employed the phrase "show the flag" to this end. The September 18 evening edition of the *Mainichi Shimbun* carried two pieces of information related to US–Japan cooperation. First, it reported that Deputy Secretary of State Richard Armitage had instructed Japanese Ambassador Shunji Yanai that Japan needed to "show the flag," apparently in reference to the MSDF transporting supplies and fuel to US military bases on the Indian Ocean. It also quoted Koizumi as having asserted that Japan should voluntarily engage in anti-terrorism activities rather than merely acquiesce to American requests, stating, "This time it is not so much about the U.S. as it is about how Japan will proactively respond to terrorism. The Constitution's preamble states that Japan wishes to occupy an honorable position in the international community."[34]

On the following morning, *The New York Times* reported that Armitage had urged Japan to provide "visible forms of participation" in the escalating anti-terror campaign, and news agencies quoted him as saying that "Japan must show the flag" rather than merely provide financial contributions.[35] The phrase is notably absent from declassified MOFA documents, however, and Yanai himself later stated that while Armitage "definitely did not use the phrase," he acknowledged that "it is true that his words held those kinds of expectations."[36]

Perceptions of the attacks within the Prime Minister's Office and MOFA were significantly influenced by the phenomenon characterized as "Gulf War Trauma," the apprehension that Japan would once again be perceived as acting as a "free rider" as it had during the 1991 Gulf War. Although Japan had extended significant financial assistance at that time, its failure to contribute personnel or resources had led to substantial international criticism and comparisons of the country to a single-purpose "ATM." Yanai made these concerns explicit at a September 18 press conference, remarking that "Japan's $13 billion in financial assistance was not appreciated internationally. In light of the lessons of the Gulf War, logistical support by the SDF is one area in which we can contribute effectively."[37] As noted by the late Yukio Okamoto, a special advisor to the cabinet who liaised with key American officials in Washington including Rice, Armitage, Deputy Secretary of Defense Paul Wolfowitz, and Joint Chiefs of Staff Chairman General Richard Myers, "not permitting a repeat of the Gulf War situation" was seen as an imperative by American leaders as well.[38]

Koizumi soon announced a series of measures in response to 9/11, beginning with a basic policy under which Japan committed to actively combating terrorism as a matter of national security. The announced measures included robust support for the US, collaboration with other nations globally, and the implementation of swift, comprehensive, and practical actions to demonstrate Japan's resolve. More specifically, in response to UNSC Resolution 1368, the Japanese government would promptly take "measures necessary for dispatching the SDF" to provide support, including medical assistance, transportation, and logistical services to US forces and other allies in response to the attacks.[39] It would enhance the security of US military facilities and other critical locations within its territory, dispatch SDF vessels for intelligence gathering, and strengthen international cooperation, particularly in the realms of information sharing and immigration control.

The government also planned to provide humanitarian, economic, and other necessary assistance to neighboring and affected countries, including emergency economic aid to Pakistan and India, which were collaborating with the US during this crisis. Assistance to displaced persons, potentially including humanitarian aid from the SDF, would be provided as deemed necessary. Finally, Japan stated its intention to implement appropriate measures to prevent disruptions in international and domestic economic systems arising from the evolving situation. This included enacting the "measures necessary for dispatching the SDF" in accordance with UNSC

Resolution 1368. As the widely anticipated American retaliatory strikes would be justified under the principle of self-defense, Japanese participation via the SDF would be tantamount to exercising CSD, something explicitly prohibited by the Japanese Constitution. As such, Koizumi framed Japan's engagement in the fight against terrorism as "Japan's own security issue" and referenced the UNSC resolution rather than the US–Japan Security Treaty as the legal foundation for acting.[40] It is worth noting, however, that while the resolution, swiftly passed the day after the attacks, condemned the acts of terrorism, it did not explicitly authorize the use of force.

Were these moves to dispatch the SDF constitutional? This was clearly a concern the Koizumi administration wanted to address. At the press conference where he announced these "specific measures," Koizumi noted that, "as is written in the preamble of the Constitution of Japan, Japan desires to occupy an honored place in international society."[41] He also underscored his commitment to Article 9, emphasizing that he would "give due regard to the fact that Article 9 of the Constitution renounces the use of force as a means of settling international disputes."[42] He additionally commented that, as Japan provided the "utmost assistance and cooperation in concert with the United States and other countries concerned," he would keep in mind "what kind of assistance will not constitute an integral part of the use of force."[43] Koizumi thus used the preamble to justify his actions and claimed that the SDF, in accordance with Article 9's limitations, would not engage in the use of force. As would become clear later, however, distinguishing between combat and non-combat zones in the areas where the SDF was dispatched would prove to be extremely difficult.

While the Koizumi administration formulated this policy independently, it is evident that American pressure played a significant role in shaping its direction. Although Koizumi may have used the UNSC resolution as a pretext, as a practical matter, the approach he adopted closely aligned with the principles of CSD and can be traced back to the origins of the globalization of the US–Japan alliance. In a later interview, Chief Cabinet Secretary Fukuda cited the "bitter experience" of the Gulf War as a pivotal factor in the Koizumi administration's decision to deploy the SDF.[44] While the government of Toshiki Kaifu had provided $13 billion during the Gulf War, its reversal of its decision to dispatch the SDF had caused its contribution to face widespread criticism from the international community, including the US. This "Gulf War Trauma" served as a distant catalyst for the Koizumi administration's decision to send the SDF, a decision it followed through on with the passage of the Anti-Terrorism Special Measures Law in October. It was compelled to adopt a more proactive stance in contributing to international anti-terrorism efforts to mitigate the criticism and stigma that Japan had encountered a decade earlier. Its actions here represented a major shift in Japan's post–World War II security policy and set the stage for further debates over the SDF's role in international affairs.

Koizumi at Ground Zero

The practical implementation of Japan's response to 9/11 began to take shape through a series of high-level initiatives and bureaucratic reforms spearheaded by key administration officials. Koizumi's vision for Japan's role in the global response became clearer during his high-profile diplomatic mission to New York mere weeks after the attacks. On September 24, Koizumi visited Ground Zero in New York City and met with UN Secretary-General Kofi Annan, to whom he expressed his desire for "the United Nations to play an active role in promoting the deterrence and prevention of terrorism."[45] He affirmed Japan's commitment as a member of the international community to collaborating with the secretary-general, emphasizing that "terrorism is a global problem and should be addressed on a worldwide scale."[46] Annan responded by stressing the importance of avoiding a religious framing of the conflict, as "perpetrators of terrorism do not represent the Islamic community."[47] He also emphasized the critical need for humanitarian assistance to Afghanistan, both to demonstrate that the country itself was not being targeted and to secure Japan's support in these efforts.

While Koizumi's meeting with Annan had focused on humanitarian assistance to Afghanistan, his discussions at the White House with Bush on the following day took a markedly different direction. Referencing a recent phone conversation with British Prime Minister Tony Blair, he told Bush that they had reached a consensus on the necessity of collaborative efforts to combat terrorism, and that Blair had asked him to convey the UK's intention to maintain close communications with Japan to Bush. Acknowledging the UK's capacity to engage in combat operations alongside the US—an effort that Japan aimed to enhance—Koizumi emphasized that "For both of our nations, our alliance with the US is our most important relationship."[48]

Koizumi expressed a desire to harmonize the US–Japan alliance with the Anglo-American alliance and use this as a new foundation for bolstering the US–Japan alliance, a sentiment he had already conveyed to both Bush and Blair in previous conversations. Koizumi also reflected on the significant shifts that the attacks had brought to the global landscape, highlighting the increasingly ambiguous nature of safety in non-combat zones. He committed Japan to supporting the US to the fullest extent possible short of direct engagement in hostilities and noted new legislation being drafted to facilitate this support. He acknowledged the limitations of the SDF due to their non-combatant status but stressed their capabilities in providing medical assistance, supporting refugees, gathering intelligence, and transporting supplies.[49]

For his part, Bush emphasized the long-term nature of the counter-terrorism effort. Declaring terrorism "a threat to freedom," he made clear that, while immediate action was necessary, they also needed "to establish a framework for how the US, Japan, and the international community will continue to confront this issue until it is eradicated."[50] He reassured Koizumi that Japan's inability to engage in combat alongside the US would not undermine the value of their alliance. When Koizumi asked whether Bush could present compelling evidence of Osama bin Laden's culpability to the international community, Bush replied, "All men like him are destroyers of freedom. This is a battle between good and evil."[51] Koizumi sought as much advance notification of the impending military action in Afghanistan as possible, as "it is essential that Japan cooperate quickly," and Bush agreed that it would be given.[52] While Koizumi's approach was primarily focused on the legal and logistical dimensions of the alliance, as well as the implications of any potential military engagement, Bush adopted a more ideological and moralistic perspective. Despite these differences, both men valued the US–Japan alliance and acknowledged the significance of a collaborative, long-term strategy for addressing the issue of terrorism.

After these crucial diplomatic exchanges in Washington, the Koizumi administration moved swiftly to translate its international commitments into concrete domestic policy measures. Upon his return, Koizumi promptly drafted legislation for the Anti-Terrorism Special Measures Law and the necessary amendments to the SDF Law. As he did so, Deputy Chief Cabinet Secretary Abe worked to garner support for the proposed measures within the ruling Liberal Democratic Party (LDP). He also conducted study sessions with uniformed SDF personnel at the Prime Minister's Office and communicated their concerns to Koizumi.

That Abe was directly engaging with SDF personnel provoked irritation within the Internal Bureau of the Defense Agency, the customary guardians of civilian control in Japan. This bureau, composed of bureaucrats seconded to the Agency, traditionally functioned as an intermediary between uniformed SDF personnel and political leaders. Abe, however, believed that civilian control meant that politicians, rather than internal bureaucrats, should be the ones overseeing the SDF. Koizumi subsequently incorporated Abe's reports on feedback from SDF officers in the field into his statements and answers given to the Diet, Japan's national legislature.[53]

The War in Afghanistan

Operation Enduring Freedom

The US's decision to launch military operations in Afghanistan marked a critical moment that would test Japan's newly established commitments to its ally. On October 7, 2001, shortly after 8:30 p.m., Secretary of State Powell placed a crucial call to Koizumi in which he informed him on behalf of Bush that US military operations in Afghanistan were imminent. He outlined plans for targeted aerial strikes concentrated in sparsely populated regions, to be followed by humanitarian aid distribution. Powell explained that, while the president would personally call within the next four to five hours, he had wanted to provide advance notice to avoid catching Koizumi off guard.[54] Koizumi responded by telling Powell that "Japan strongly supports the US, and I hope you will communicate that to President Bush as well."[55] While the Bush administration was characterized by a predominance of unilateralism, Powell favored a multilateralist approach and actively sought collaboration with foreign nations.[56] Simultaneously, Deputy Secretary of State Armitage notified Japanese Ambassador Yanai about the impending US attacks on terrorist "training centers."[57]

At around 9:30 p.m. local time on October 7, American and British forces initiated military operations in Afghanistan, targeting al-Qaeda terrorist training facilities and Taliban regime military installations. Bush then delivered a televised address in which he formally designated the operation as Operation Enduring Freedom (OEF). The launch of OEF triggered an immediate and comprehensive effort by the Japanese government to demonstrate its alliance commitments. At 2:54 a.m. JST, Koizumi convened a press conference in which he articulated his "strong support for the actions" undertaken and announced the establishment of Japan's Emergency Task Force on Terrorism.[58]

Later that evening, shortly after 11:00 p.m., Koizumi held a second press conference to declare that the task force had met, and that decisions had been reached regarding "emergency response measures to prevent and eradicate acts of international terrorism." He laid out the following seven measures: 1) enhancing security protocols to safeguard the population within Japan; 2) ensuring the protection of Japanese nationals abroad and facilitating evacuation assistance; 3) expediting the enactment of the Anti-Terrorism Special Measures Law; 4) preparing for the implementation of refugee assistance as well as humanitarian, economic, and other aid to affected countries; 5) reinforcing efforts to enhance systems for monitoring terrorist financing; 6) safeguarding the stability of both the Japanese and global economic systems against the threat of terrorism; and 7) promptly and accurately disseminating necessary information to the citizens of Japan.[59] These comprehensive measures demonstrated Japan's determination to fulfill its alliance obligations while also addressing both domestic and international security concerns.

The contrast between the response to the Gulf War and 9/11 reveals how Japan's crisis response mechanisms had evolved over the course of a decade. During the Gulf War, MOFA had collaborated with the Ministry of Finance on initiatives to facilitate Japan's contribution to the war effort; these proposed initiatives were then submitted to and approved by the Prime Minister's Office. Now, a decade later, the heads of the relevant ministries and agencies convened at the Prime Minister's Office to deliberate on actions. Koizumi served as the SDF's supreme commander, while Deputy Chief Cabinet Secretary Teijirō Furukawa played a pivotal role in the administrative operations of the Prime Minister's Office.[60] Some scholars raised concerns regarding the American and British forces military operations in Afghanistan. Kiichi Fujiwara, professor at the University of Tokyo, cautioned that, while bin Laden and the Taliban were already "isolated in the Muslim world," the airstrikes could be perceived as "state terrorism against Muslim society at large," potentially "fostering new forms of terrorist activity."[61]

Undeterred, Koizumi remained firmly committed to supporting Japan's alliance partner as he navigated the complex post-9/11 political and security landscape and notably refrained from questioning the legitimacy of the US-led military operations. In stark contrast to the Iraq War that would follow, Japan, NATO, Russia, and China were all in agreement on the Afghan War. His administration enacted three terrorism-related bills, including the Anti-Terrorism Special Measures Law, on October 29. This legislation, which would be effective for two years, stipulated that SDF activities would be subject to post hoc parliamentary approval, and permitted SDF personnel to use weapons when deemed necessary for their protection.[62]

The new laws empowered the SDF to provide logistical support in non-combat zones to coalition members and to bolster security at US military bases in Japan. These increased SDF responsibilities were regarded as significant not only for combating terrorism but also for strengthening the US–Japan alliance. The US State Department voiced strong approval of the new legislation and expressed appreciation for Japan's considerable contributions in humanitarian and economic assistance, as well as its efforts in refugee relief within the region. It applauded "Prime Minister Koizumi's strong support and political leadership" on counter-terrorism initiatives, specifically acknowledging his commitment to enhancing Japan's participation in resolving international security challenges.[63]

The Bush administration cultivated coalition partnerships with 69 countries, with Britain, Canada, Germany, Australia, France, and Italy playing key roles in addition to Japan.[64] As such, Japan's participation may not have been prominent from an American perspective. Nonetheless, Japan's enactment of the Anti-Terrorism Special Measures Law represented a pivotal moment for the nation. The earlier Emergency-at-Periphery Law had limited SDF deployment to areas adjacent to Japan, prohibiting deployment to distant regions such as the Middle East or the Indian Ocean. Consequently, the Koizumi administration's decision to expand the SDF's scope effectively internationalized the US–Japan alliance, extending it beyond Japan's territorial boundaries and into international waters. The intersection of terrorism, American pressure, and Koizumi's policy decisions culminated in a global US–Japan alliance. A significant concern, however, was that his administration was prioritizing support for the US over counterterrorism efforts and peace-building initiatives.

The Mini-SSC and the Framework for Coordination

High-level bilateral discussions were initiated through specialized committees to facilitate bilateral cooperation under the new Anti-Terrorism Special Measures Law. The Mini Security Subcommittee (Mini-SSC), convened in Tokyo on November 1, featured prominent participants including Christopher J. LaFleur (principal deputy assistant secretary of state for East Asian and Pacific affairs), Peter Brookes (deputy assistant secretary of defense for Asian and Pacific affairs), Chikahito Harada (deputy director-general, North American Affairs Bureau, MOFA), and Kōhei Masuda (deputy director-general, Defense Bureau, Defense Agency), among others. The Mini-SSC served as a meeting of the deputy director-general/

deputy assistant secretary-level officials within the US–Japan Security Subcommittee. After the Japanese delegation presented the procedures established by Japan's new anti-terrorism law, the two parties discussed the framework for US–Japan coordination. The consensus they reached is illustrated in figure 1.1.

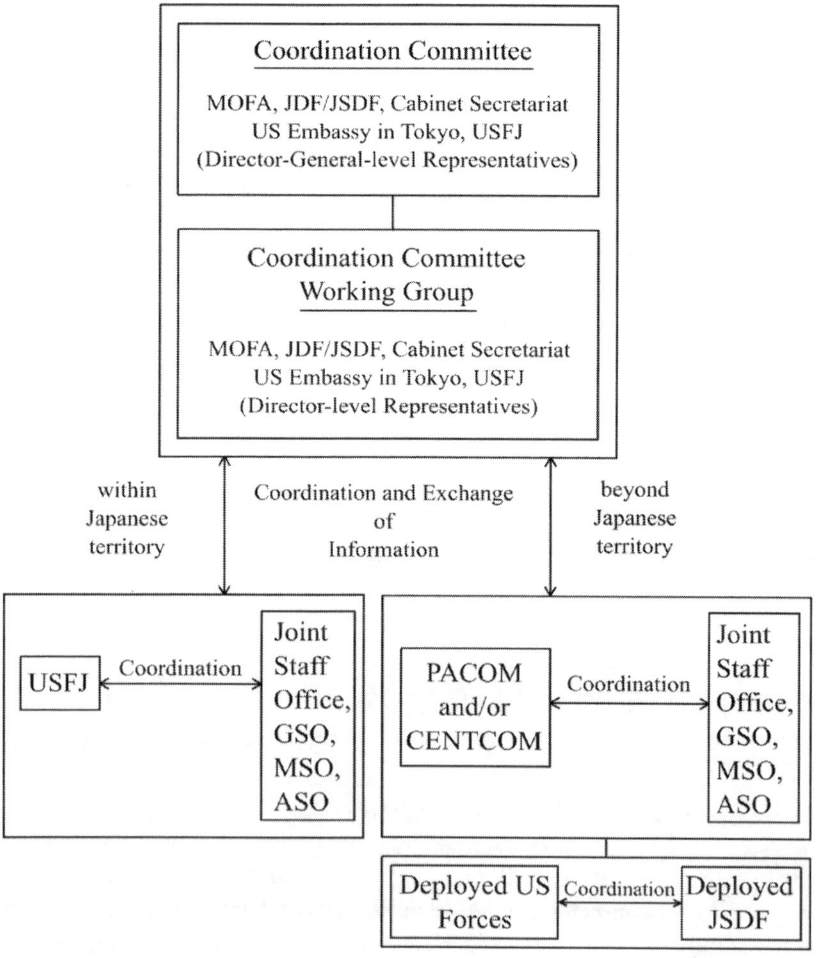

Figure 1.1. Framework for Support Coordination for US Forces Under the Anti-Terrorism Special Measures Law. *Source:* Tanaka to Katō, November 2, 2001, fax no. F25557, MOFA documents disclosed under the Information Disclosure Law, 2019-119-20.

The high-ranking officials of the Mini-SSC also discussed MD, the status of US forces in Japan, and emerging conflicts on the Korean Peninsula and in Indonesia. Raising the issue of Futenma and its relocation, Japanese officials emphasized that they were continuing to monitor local sentiment and highlighted the need for sustained bilateral consultations on the matter. Their American counterparts expressed anticipation for tangible progress.[65] Jurisdiction over US military personnel in Japan was also covered, and the importance that both the SOFA and established criminal justice procedures were adhered to was stressed, as well as the need for the ongoing negotiations to enhance these procedural frameworks to be expedited.[66]

With bilateral coordination mechanisms established at the Mini-SSC, Japan moved swiftly to implement its maritime contributions to OEF. On November 9, two MSDF destroyers and an accompanying replenishment ship departed from Sasebo en route to the Indian Ocean for the purpose of conducting an information-gathering mission. The Japanese embassy had briefed State and Defense officials on the deployment on November 6 and 7, and coordination over the mission also involved personnel from the US Marine Corps, US Pacific Command, and the MSDF in Honolulu.[67] On November 25, an additional three vessels were dispatched to transport supplies to Diego Garcia, a British territory in the Indian Ocean that functioned as a logistical support base for American and British military forces. The Koizumi administration's action to deploy the SDF overseas in support of foreign military operations represented an unprecedented development for Japan's postwar security policy.

Assistance to Afghanistan and Its Reconstruction

The military campaign in Afghanistan ushered in a new era of governance and expanded international support for the country's reconstruction. The Taliban regime disintegrated in early December. On December 5, a few days prior to the fall of the capital of Kabul, representatives of various Afghan factions met in Bonn, Germany, and reached an agreement on establishing a transitional government. That same day, Foreign Minister Tanaka formally declared that "Japan will continue to support the efforts of Afghan factions and the UN to create a lasting peace and will cooperate with relevant countries and organizations to contribute to real stability in Afghanistan."[68] On December 7, Richard Haass, director of Policy Planning at the State Department, and James Dobbins, American special representative to the Afghan opposition, announced at a press conference that the US and Japan had co-chaired an administrative-level conference focused on reconstruction efforts. He further indicated that following a meeting in Brussels, the International Conference on Reconstruction Assistance would convene in January 2002, co-chaired by the US, the EU, Japan, and Saudi Arabia.[69] On December 22, 2001, Hamid Karzai was inaugurated as chairman of Afghanistan's new interim government in Kabul. Vice-Minister for Foreign Affairs Shigeo Uetake attended the inauguration ceremony and formally recognized the new Afghan government.[70]

Japan's approach to combating international terrorism encompassed several vital strategies: diplomatic efforts focused on building global unity against terrorism through the deployment of special envoys, personal communications, and participation in international meetings; cooperative support under the Anti-Terrorism Special Measures Law, including logistical assistance and the resupplying of warships; efforts to strengthen international legal frameworks and implement financial measures aimed at preventing and eliminating terrorism; substantial aid to Afghan refugees, including the provision of essential supplies and pledging financial support through various channels; recognition of Afghanistan's interim government and the commitment of significant resources to the country's reconstruction; and economic assistance to neighboring countries like Pakistan, India, Uzbekistan, and Tajikistan to bolster regional efforts against terrorism.[71]

These comprehensive strategies demonstrated Japan's commitment to global security and its decision to take a proactive role in the international fight against terrorism. By adopting a multifaceted approach—ranging from diplomatic initiatives to financial measures, from refugee assistance to regional support—Japan positioned itself as a key player in global counter-terrorism efforts. This not only showcased Japan's dedication to international peace and stability but also highlighted its capacity to leverage the various tools of foreign policy and international cooperation in pursuit of a common objective. But while Japan's military involvement was significant, it was predominantly restricted by constitutional limitations to providing logistical support. This limited its effectiveness in more direct counter-terrorism operations.

Conclusion

In the aftermath of 9/11, Japan was faced with a global alliance security dilemma as the Koizumi administration was pressured to provide support to US military actions beyond the geographical boundaries delineated in the US–Japan Security Treaty. This dilemma was exacerbated by the "Gulf War Trauma," the psychological impact of the international criticism that Japan had received in 1991 due to its failure to provide more than financial support during the Gulf War. To avoid a repeat of its prior experience, Japan swiftly enacted the Anti-Terrorism Special Measures Law, enabling the SDF to provide logistical support for US forces in Afghanistan. But while Chief Cabinet Secretary Fukuda and MOFA emphasized international cooperation, their focus on alliance management also revealed Japan's struggle to balance its alliance obligations with its constitutional constraints.

The asymmetry of the US–Japan alliance was readily evident in the early response to 9/11. Koizumi's early meetings with Bush, Armitage, and Powell demonstrated Japan's dependent position, with Koizumi repeatedly emphasizing that the US–Japan relationship was "fundamental" to Japan's diplomacy. The asymmetric nature was further highlighted in the framework for military cooperation established at the Mini-SSC, under which Japan's role was primarily reactive to US initiatives. Japan's lack of independent intelligence capabilities also meant that it was heavily reliant on the US for assessments of the terrorist threat and strategic planning in Afghanistan.

It was as Japan attempted to navigate its alliance commitments and regional relationships that its dual-structured security dilemma began taking shape. As Japan strengthened its military cooperation with the US through the Anti-Terrorism Special Measures Law, it simultaneously had to consider how this could affect regional stability in Asia, particularly China's response. This awareness of regional sensitivities is evident in Japan's careful attempt to frame its support for US operations as being based in UNSC Resolution 1368 rather than its bilateral security treaty. Its delicate balancing act between deepening alliance cooperation and regional diplomatic relationships was also evident in the SCC meetings.

As will be seen in chapter 2, these dynamics would intensify as the Bush administration articulated its "axis of evil" doctrine and confronted North Korea's nuclear program. The December 2002 SCC meeting would prove crucial in formalizing the connection between Japan's North Korea policy and its support for US military actions, further complicating its global alliance security dilemma. This evolving situation would demonstrate how Japan's strategic choices became increasingly constrained as regional security challenges became intertwined with its global alliance obligations, setting the stage for more complex challenges in the US–Japan relationship.

Chapter 2

American Doctrine, Japanese Support

2002

Koizumi and Kim Jong-Il

Japan's Leadership in Afghanistan's Reconstruction

The year 2002 opened with the International Conference on Reconstruction Assistance to Afghanistan, which convened in Tokyo in January. Shortly afterward, Prime Minister Koizumi's insistence on visiting Yasukuni Shrine, where many Japanese wartime leaders are enshrined, damaged diplomatic relations with other Asian countries, particularly with China and South Korea. In September, he traveled to Pyongyang to meet with General Secretary Kim Jong-il to address the resumption of North Korea's nuclear weapons development and the long-standing issue of the North Korean abduction of Japanese citizens. Koizumi's engagement with Pyongyang presented significant complications from the American perspective, given the North Korean nuclear weapons program. During this same period, President George W. Bush announced the Bush Doctrine in the US, escalating tensions with Iraq. The linkage between security concerns regarding North Korea and the imminent conflict in Iraq, facilitated by the US–Japan alliance, represented a critical turning point for Japan. The global alliance security dilemma arising from the US–Japan SCC became crucial for Japan; it found itself compelled to rely on the US for the implementation of its North Korea policy and to endorse American military actions in Iraq.

Let us start with the January conference in Tokyo. In October 2001, MOFA had raised to the US the idea of hosting a conference on the reconstruction of Afghanistan, and Koizumi had appointed Sadako Ogata as a special representative of the prime minister to oversee this initiative in November. During her inaugural address to the conference, Ogata recounted her appointment by Koizumi to lead Japan's reconstruction efforts in Afghanistan and its distinctly personal nature. Koizumi, known for his independent leadership style, had chosen to discuss the appointment with her in a private, one-on-one meeting, an approach that had a significant impression on her.[1] Ogata's commitment to Afghanistan stemmed from a profound sense of responsibility. She had identified Afghanistan as the largest global source of refugees upon becoming UNHCR in 1991 and saw her efforts toward the nation as her "unfinished business."[2]

During a preparatory conference on Afghan reconstruction held in Washington in November 2001, Ogata stressed that the international community—spearheaded by Japan and the US—would persist in its engagement with Afghanistan. The extensive network, experience, and trust that Ogata had cultivated during her tenure at the UNHCR were evidenced in the international conference held in Tokyo on January 21 and 22, 2002. She was notably successful in securing the attendance of numerous governmental and UN leaders, many of whom were established acquaintances of hers. She had conducted assessments of Kabul and Herat (the third-largest city in Afghanistan) in advance of the conference and compiled a comprehensive report on them for the Japanese government.[3] This report, focusing on themes of "reconstruction and politics" as well as "humanity and reconstruction," effectively established the thematic framework for the conference.[4]

MOFA was represented at the conference by Deputy Minister for Foreign Affairs Shōtarō Ōshima and Director-General of the Middle Eastern and African Affairs Bureau Toshinori Shigeie. Ōshima was authorized to disclose the financial contributions that Japan would be putting toward reconstruction, and in his preliminary discussions with the US State Department and the Spanish Foreign Ministry (Spain held the presidency of the EU), he indicated that Japan would be committing $500 million over the span of the next two and a half years, with $250 million earmarked for disbursement in the first year. These figures had been made in accordance with directives from Koizumi.[5]

Koizumi published an opinion piece in the January 21, 2002, issue of *Newsweek* entitled "Starting from Scratch . . . Again" in which he drew compelling parallels between Japan's own wartime devastation and subsequent recovery and Afghanistan's reconstruction needs. Drawing on his own personal experience with the destruction of Tokyo in 1945 when he was three years old, he emphasized the profound contrast between contemporary Japan's development and the widespread devastation and acute poverty of its postwar condition. He cautioned that "the international community must avoid the temptation to accept a halfway solution for [Afghanistan]."[6] His article further asserted that Japan, as host of the Afghan Reconstruction Conference, would actively collaborate with the interim government in Kabul to devise a comprehensive plan covering health, education, demining, and refugee resettlement and that it would also coordinate with NGOs to ensure that these aid efforts were directed at the grassroots level. He concluded with an appeal to the international community to "work together to give Afghanistan the same chance my country received half a century ago."[7]

In writing this article, Koizumi ostensibly aimed to rationalize the non-military nature of Japan's support for Afghanistan to the international community by framing its response within the context of its pacifist constitution. His article sought to elicit international backing for Afghanistan's reconstruction by referencing Japan's own historical experiences and emphasizing the humanitarian contributions it was prepared to make. In doing so, however, he failed to address the substantial differences between Japan's postwar reconstruction—the presence of a tradition of democracy and a well-established bureaucracy—and the contemporary circumstances in ravaged Afghanistan. That Japan had successfully recovered from its defeat in the Pacific War did not imply that Afghanistan was capable of being reconstructed in a similar fashion. Whatever its failings, however, the article served as the immediate precursor to the international conference in Tokyo.

International Conference in Tokyo

The International Conference on Reconstruction Assistance to Afghanistan, held at the New Takanawa Prince Hotel in Tokyo on January 21 and 22, exclusively featured participants at the ministerial level and higher.[8] The conference was co-chaired by Japan, the US, the EU, and Saudi Arabia, and delegates from 61 countries and 21 international organizations participated, including UN Secretary-General Kofi Annan. Other notable attendees included Hamid Karzai, chairman of the Afghan Interim Administration

(AIA), other representatives from the interim government, US Secretary of State Colin Powell, and Secretary of the Treasury Paul H. O'Neill. Ogata served as the Japanese co-chair.[9]

In his address to the conference, Koizumi emphasized that Japan's aid would be directed toward promoting peace, national reconciliation, and human development in Afghanistan. He underscored the significance of having Afghan leadership in the nation's reconstruction process and asserted that Japan's contributions would be multifaceted, encompassing support for refugee resettlement, education, medical and healthcare services, and women's empowerment. He also highlighted the critical importance of on-the-ground security to the success of these initiatives, with a particular emphasis on demining efforts.[10] He then announced Japan's planned contribution of $500 million; compared to the amounts pledged by other individual governments, Japan's promised contribution to reconstruction was second only to that of the US.[11]

It is significant that the key figures at the conference were Karzai and Ogata, Koizumi's emissary, rather than Koizumi himself. Notably, the longest speech at the conference (more than 30 minutes long) was given by Karzai.[12] In it, he articulated his aspirations for Afghanistan, portraying a thriving and secure nation. He placed emphasis on the establishment of a reliable state with a capable and transparent accountable to its citizens and the international community. His plan included the development of a robust private sector and a vibrant civil society supported by democratic institutions so that "the rule of law and transparent systems would eventually allow us to realize the potential of our own natural and human resources."[13] He further stressed Afghanistan's commitment to attracting foreign direct investment as a means of generating sufficient revenue to gradually diminish dependence on international assistance. This vision for a "new Afghanistan" positioned it as a catalyst for regional economic prosperity and geopolitical stability.[14]

In her opening statement, Ogata underscored two foundational principles. First, she highlighted the necessity of reinforcing the political process initiated by the establishment of the Afghan Interim Authority (a result of the Bonn Agreement reached under UN auspices, particularly the efforts of the UN secretary-general's special representative, Lakhdar Brahimi). Second, she argued that "there should be a seamless transition from ongoing humanitarian assistance to recovery and reconstruction."[15] She stressed that, while the day's discussions would be centered on Afghanistan's reconstruction, it was imperative that the vital short-term relief and rehabilitation initiatives already in progress could not be forgotten, as "unless immediate needs are adequately met, we have less possibility of tackling the tasks that lie ahead, beyond relief and rehabilitation."[16]

The conference's summary of conclusions delineated the critical national reconstruction priorities for the AIA: enhancement of administrative capacity with a particular emphasis on salary payments and government administration; prioritization of education, especially for girls; improvement of health and sanitation; development of infrastructure, including roads, electricity, and telecommunications; reconstruction of the economic system with a focus on the currency system; and the advancement of agriculture and rural development, including food security, water management, and the revitalization of irrigation systems. The summary acknowledged the indispensable role of the UN and specifically commended Brahimi's efforts to promote peace and stability in Afghanistan. It stressed the importance of supporting his initiatives and recognized the United Nations Development Programme's role in spearheading the early recovery efforts. The conference's participants responded to the vision for reconstruction outlined by Karzai by committing to assisting the Afghan populace, announcing pledges and contributions for 2002 exceeding $1.8 billion, with some providing in-kind support and others extending multi-year commitments totaling over $4.5 billion. In doing so, they emphasized the necessity of prompt disbursement of the funds to address the AIA's immediate financial needs in the coming months.[17]

Ogata characterized the conference as "a great success," and Treasury Secretary O'Neill expressed gratitude for her leadership.[18] Bush wrote in his memoirs that "Prime Minister Junichiro Koizumi of Japan hosted an international donors' conference in January 2002. . . . Japan launched an initiative to disarm and demobilize warlords and their militias."[19] It is unsurprising that Bush lauded Japan's pivotal role in the reconstruction of Afghanistan, given its significant contributions. Its advocacy for and successful conclusion of the conference fortified its presence within the international community. Japan had sustained a close administrative relationship with the US from November 2001, effectively leveraging bilateral coordination while securing commitments from other nations at the high ministerial level. This was commendable. The AIA had only been operational for a single month at the time of the conference, however, and the extent to which the US–Japan reconstruction initiative would contribute to stability in the still volatile region remain uncertain.[20]

The initial success of the Tokyo conference laid the groundwork for Japan's sustained involvement in Afghanistan's reconstruction through targeted initiatives and strategic partnerships. When Karzai assumed the presidency of the Afghan Transitional Administration in June 2002, six months later, Ogata attended his inauguration as an observer. During this same period, the Koizumi administration announced the Ogata Initiative, a strategic plan aimed at supporting refugees. Active until April 2005, this prioritized the repatriation of refugees from designated areas, notably Kandahar and Mazar-i-Sharif, to their original homes. Japan contributed a total of $98.49 million to the initiative through various international organizations including the UNHCR, the United Nations Children's Fund (UNICEF), and the World Food Programme (WFP). The Japan International Cooperation Agency (JICA) also collaborated with the Ogata Initiative, playing a pivotal role in the recovery efforts by establishing liaison offices in Kabul and other locations.

While the Ogata Initiative achieved its primary objective of supporting refugee repatriation and reconstruction, it experienced challenges in coordinating the various international organizations involved in the effort. Ogata later acknowledged the initiative's effectiveness in delivering continuous assistance but also noted that UN agencies often operate independently and competitively, and that the bureaucracy inherent to international organizations had impeded collaborative efforts. She had recognized these hurdles when proposing the initiative and had hoped to unite these agencies under a broader framework to facilitate more efficient assistance but acknowledged that resistance to interagency cooperation had still impeded their collaborative potential. Ultimately, she conceded, "I cannot assert that we were successful in this regard."[21]

"Axis of Evil"

Evolving geopolitical tensions further exacerbated the difficulties of international coordination, particularly as the US shifted its focus toward perceived threats from specific nations. A week after the conclusion of the reconstruction conference in Tokyo, Bush delivered a State of the Union address on January 29. In this speech, he articulated two fundamental points on counterterrorism. First, he asserted that while US military operations successfully dismantled the terrorist training infrastructure in Afghanistan, similar installations continued to operate in numerous countries—at least 12 by contemporary estimates. A clandestine network of terrorist organizations, including Hamas, Hezbollah, Islamic Jihad, and Jaish-e-Mohammed, maintained operations across diverse geographical terrains, ranging from remote wilderness areas to densely populated urban centers. Second, he portrayed North Korea, Iran, and Iraq as constituting "an axis of evil," a nexus of hostile powers actively pursuing armaments that endangered global stability.[22] The address contended that these states' development of WMD represented an escalating menace and raised the specter of such armaments being transferred to terrorist organizations or utilized to coerce the US and its international allies. A failure to confront these threats, Bush argued, could have devastating consequences.

The Bush administration's counterterrorism strategy of 2002 marked a significant shift from a framework of international cooperation to a more unilateral approach centered on specific state actors. This evolution created divisions among global leaders. In his memoirs, Bush recounted his discussions on Iraq with world leaders that year. He emphasized that many leaders, including John Howard of Australia, José María Aznar of Spain, Jun'ichirō Koizumi of Japan, Jan Peter Balkenende of the Netherlands, Anders Fogh Rasmussen of Denmark, and Aleksander Kwasniewski of Poland shared his view of the threat, as did others in Central and Eastern Europe. Others did not. Vladimir Putin, for instance, did not consider Saddam a threat, likely due to Russia's economic interests in Iraqi oil. France, represented by Jacques Chirac, advocated for comprehensive weapons inspections but expressed reluctance regarding the use of military force. Bush contended that Chirac's approach lacked the credible threat necessary for effectiveness. He also found Chancellor Gerhard Schröder of Germany to be one of the most challenging leaders to understand.[23]

Bush's controversial phrasing in the State of the Union address would have lasting diplomatic repercussions that his administration had not fully anticipated. But while "axis of evil" would go on to become one of the most frequently quoted terms of his presidency, the imprudent language resulted from an inadvertent misstep. In her memoirs, Condoleezza Rice observed that, despite the significant attention it garnered, the content behind it was standard. The phrase, introduced by a speechwriter, had been intended to underscore the peril associated with regimes possessing WMD and the potential for these weapons to be transferred to terrorist organizations. Rice recalled it receiving minimal focus during the speechwriting process. She and Stephen Hadley, assistant to the president and deputy national security advisor, had contemplated whether the use of "evil" was excessively strong, but they had not given much consideration to the word "axis" or the potential for the phrase to be misinterpreted as implying an alliance among rogue states. She wrote that "the President was not saying that the three nations were in formal alliance," and that the Pentagon and State Department had both reviewed the speech without raising any significant objections.[24] Her account is exculpatory, partly attributing responsibility to the speechwriter.

Whatever the intentions of the administration, the phrase "an axis of evil" startled observers both domestically and internationally. An internal MOFA report on the speech indicated that Bush had "shown off his counterterrorism achievements and expressed his determination to continue the war on terror."[25] On the whole, it was "more of a 'war speech' than had been anticipated."[26] Of the three nations identified, it was Iraq that would increasingly become the focal point of attention. A few weeks following the speech, Bush visited Japan to discuss that nation and North Korea.

BUSH'S VISIT TO JAPAN

The February 2002 summit between Bush and Koizumi reflected both the personal rapport and strategic considerations that defined US–Japan relations in the post-9/11 era. The increasingly close relationship between the two leaders was evident in their greeting upon Bush's arrival in Tokyo on February 18. During the exchange, Koizumi invited Bush to address him as "Jun," to which Bush replied that he preferred that Koizumi to call him "George."[27] Only a select group of advisors, including Secretary of State Condoleezza Rice and Deputy Minister for Foreign Affairs Toshiyuki Takano, were present at the meeting. Koizumi also remarked during the exchange that he "understood the words 'an axis of evil' to be an expression of the president's strong determination to stand against terrorism."[28] After reiterating his gratitude to Japan for hosting the reconstruction conference, Bush said, "This visit gives us an opportunity to reaffirm our solidarity in the fight against terrorism."[29] He further stated, "There's a good reason that I chose to visit Japan, where you are prime minister, first in my Asian tour. The US–Japan relationship is not only extremely important for the US, but for the world as a whole."[30] That an American president would emphasize the significance of relations with Japan is noteworthy given the US's historical and strategic ties to Western Europe.

Bush then turned the discussion to North Korea. He emphasized that "the US and Japan need to work together on North Korea. I would like you to share the information that your country has on North Korea with us."[31] Koizumi was enthusiastic about reevaluating relations with North Korea and noted that "North Korea has abducted Japanese citizens, and they have not yet been returned."[32] When Koizumi indicated that he would consult closely with the US and South Korea on the normalization of diplomatic relations with North Korea, Bush repeatedly requested intelligence sharing, stating that "Japan plays an important role here."[33] We can see here a globalization of the US–Japan alliance in response to the presence of an "axis of evil."

It was, in fact, China, with its close relations with North Korea, on which Bush's multilateral diplomacy placed its greatest hopes in this area, and he solicited Koizumi's perspective regarding his impending visit there.[34] Koizumi stressed the importance of China's increasing interdependence with the international community, as exemplified by its membership in organizations such as the World Trade Organization (WTO) and its upcoming hosting of the 2008 Olympics, not only for China itself but also for global stability. He argued that China's "great potential," as demonstrated by substantial Japanese corporate investment there, meant that its enhanced international engagement was likely to serve both regional and global interests.[35]

Elsewhere, Bush's diplomatic priorities appeared to have favored relations with Russia over those with China, as evidenced by his emphasis on transformative bilateral engagement with Moscow. He notably characterized Russo-American relations as undergoing a post–Cold War metamorphosis "from those of the Cold War to those of the 21st century."[36] The administration's strategy centered on incorporating Russia into the international community of democratic, market-oriented states—a policy intended to mitigate Russian perceptions of external threats. In response to proliferation concerns from states such as North Korea and Iraq, the Bush administration initiated a significant shift in strategic doctrine by withdrawing from the Anti-Ballistic Missile (ABM) Treaty in favor of pursuing Missile Defense Initiatives. It also engaged in negotiations for a new bilateral framework aimed at substantially reducing nuclear arsenals, with the explicit objective of finalizing such an agreement prior to the president's scheduled visit to Russia in May.[37] Koizumi, however, refrained from invoking any grand strategy toward Russia, merely stating that "it is also crucial that the US and Russia have a friendly relationship with regard to counterterrorism."[38]

Prior communications from Bush to Koizumi provide further context. On December 13, 2001, Bush had formally notified Koizumi via letter of the US decision to exit the 1972 ABM Treaty, with the withdrawal set to take effect six months from the date. He elaborated that the nature of global threats had undergone significant transformation since the Cold War, as shown by the events of September 11. These emergent threats included the potential for WMD to fall "into the hands of terrorists and rogue states," and this necessitated a comprehensive approach that involved the enhancement of non-proliferation and counter-proliferation strategies as well as the development of new deterrence and defense capabilities.[39]

Bush emphasized the concern regarding nations such as North Korea and Iran acquiring long-range missile technology as a means to deliver WMD. His use of the term "rogue states" in his official letter to Koizumi is significant, particularly as it named North Korea and Iran alongside various terrorist groups. Given Japan's reliance on the US for deterrence against North Korea, Koizumi had little option but to concur with Bush's designation of Iran and North Korea as "rogue states." The Japanese government expressed its appreciation for the advance notification of the US withdrawal from the ABM Treaty and demonstrated support for American defense policy.[40] As will be discussed in chapter 3, the Koizumi administration subsequently decided to implement a US-developed ballistic missile defense (BMD) system in Japan to address missile threats from North Korea and other sources.

"George, You Are So Unilateralist"—the Kananaskis G8 Summit

While Bush's Iraq policy encountered criticism from certain allies, he also garnered substantial support from pivotal partners. The most robust endorsement of his hardline stance on Iraq came from British Prime Minister Tony Blair. Bush wrote in his memoirs that "If we had to remove Saddam from power, Tony and I would have an obligation to help the Iraqi people replace Saddam's tyranny with a democracy."[41] In April 2002, Blair traveled to Crawford, Texas, where he and Bush engaged in discussions regarding coercive diplomacy as a strategy for addressing the threat posed by Iraq. He proposed pursuing a UNSC resolution that would present Saddam Hussein with a definitive ultimatum: Permit the return of weapons inspectors to Iraq or face serious consequences. While Bush harbored reservations about the efficacy of the UN, he expressed a willingness to consider Blair's suggestion.[42]

International cooperation and tensions related to security threats were prominently addressed at the G8 summit held in Kananaskis, Canada, on June 26 and 27. The summit's discussions focused on countermeasures against WMD and terrorism, resulting in the issuance of two key statements: "The G8 Global Partnership against the Spread of Weapons and Materials of Mass Destruction" and "The G8 Global Partnership: Principles to Prevent Terrorists, or Those That Harbour Them, from Gaining Access to Weapons or Materials of Mass Destruction."[43] Although not formally a party to these statements, Koizumi became the first Japanese prime minister to directly address the issue of North Korean abductions, positioning it alongside the concerns regarding WMD; previous prime ministers had only alluded to this matter indirectly, referring to it as a "humanitarian issue."[44] In a private meeting, Koizumi requested that Russian President Vladimir Putin communicate Japan's stance on the abductions to North Korea, to which he agreed. Throughout the summit, Koizumi persistently raised the issue in nearly every discussion, irrespective of whether it had been included in the agenda prepared by the Japanese foreign ministry.[45]

The summit also exposed deep divisions between traditional allies on matters beyond those involving security, such as development policy in Africa. It served as a notable illustration of the Franco-American rivalry, as well as Japan's unequivocal support for the US. When Bush proposed conditioning aid to Africa on the implementation of anti-corruption measures and other reforms, French President Chirac commented, "George, you are so unilateralist," to which Bush retorted, "America did not colonize African nations. America did not create corruption. And America is tired of seeing good money stolen while people continue to suffer. Yes, we are changing our policy, whether you like it or not."[46] Reflecting on the exchange in his memoir, Bush wrote that "My friend Prime Minister Koizumi of Japan flashed a slight smile and gave me a subtle nod of approval."[47] This exchange at Kananaskis highlighted the growing alignment between the US and Japan on development policy, in contrast to the tensions with European allies like France.

"International Collaboration Is Essential"— The Bush–Koizumi Talks in New York

Diplomatic engagement between the US and Japan intensified over the late summer as the Bush administration endeavored to cultivate international support for its policy toward Iraq. Deputy Secretary of State Armitage visited Japan on August 27 and met with Koizumi and Director-General of the Defense Agency Gen Nakatani. Japan held to the position that its existing legislation, including the Anti-Terrorism Special Measures Law, would not permit cooperation in the event of American military action against Iraq.

Consequently, Japan would make independent determinations as required based on the prevailing circumstances in Iraq.[48] This dialogue would continue at the UN in September, when both leaders gave speeches addressing Iraq.

When Bush delivered an address to the UNGA criticizing Iraq's violations of UNSC resolutions on September 12, Koizumi was in attendance, and the two met afterward. While Bush was inclined toward acting unilaterally, Koizumi emphasized the importance of global collaboration, referencing the Gulf War as a pertinent example. He noted that the Iraqi invasion of Kuwait had elicited widespread international condemnation, allowing effective coordination among multiple nations under American leadership. The matter was ultimately resolved through the diplomatic efforts of Bush's father to assemble a broad international coalition. Referencing Bush's address, Koizumi highlighted the emphasis Bush had placed on Iraq's violations of UN resolutions, asserting, "international collaboration is essential, and we should make another effort, focusing on the UN."[49] Bush seemed to acknowledge this perspective, responding, "I do know that international cooperation is significant. You are my best friend among the world's leaders, and we know what the other is thinking."[50]

Koizumi gave his own address to the UNGA on September 13 in which he reinforced his commitment to multilateral action. He emphasized the importance of adopting a new UNSC resolution to compel Iraq to permit WMD inspectors. At a press conference afterward, he elaborated on Iraq and also announced his intention to hold a summit with North Korean leader Kim Jong-Il on September 17, during which the issues of WMD, nuclear armament, and the abduction of Japanese citizens would be discussed.[51] Through these complex diplomatic interactions, Japan demonstrated a nuanced approach to balancing its alliance obligations with its commitment to multilateral cooperation, while maintaining its sovereign prerogative in foreign policy decisions amid escalating tensions over Iraq.

The Japan–DPRK Pyongyang Declaration

Koizumi's visit to Pyongyang involved meticulously coordinated institutional arrangements building upon Japan's calculated diplomatic approach to regional security challenges. He prepared for his trip in collaboration with Hitoshi Tanaka, director-general of MOFA's Asian and Oceanic Affairs Bureau, and Kenji Hiramatsu, director of the Northeast Asia Division.[52] Tanaka provided Ambassador to South Korea Terusuke Terada with "vague hints" regarding the upcoming visit during a trip to Seoul, but he did not disclose any of the behind-the-scenes negotiations to the Japanese embassy there.[53] Terada only learned of Koizumi's visit shortly before the Japanese government formally announced it. Tanaka exercised meticulous control over the dissemination of information, and it was not until August 21 that Tanaka presented a draft of the Japan–DPRK Pyongyang Declaration to Vice-Minister for Foreign Affairs Yukio Takeuchi, Director-General of the Foreign Policy Bureau Shōtarō Yachi, Director-General of the North American Affairs Bureau Ichirō Fujisaki, and Director-General of the Treaties Bureau Shin Ebihara.[54]

The selective sharing of information pertaining to these sensitive diplomatic preparations shows the administration's careful management of both domestic and international relationships. During the nearly year-long secret negotiations with North Korea conducted through Tanaka and Hiramatsu, Koizumi let Chief Cabinet Secretary Fukuda and Foreign Minister Kawaguchi know of his intention to visit North Korea, but he did not notify Abe, his deputy chief cabinet secretary. The Bush administration was also unaware of this development until Koizumi confidentially informed Armitage during the latter's August visit to Tokyo.[55]

While Bush expressed understanding regarding the visit, the US government harbored suspicions that Japan would negotiate a deal with North Korea concerning the abduction issue and normalize diplomatic relations without addressing the nuclear allegations. These American concerns regarding Koizumi's intentions were arguably unwarranted, however, and the visit to North Korea entailed considerable risk. Koizumi did not receive any information on the safety of the abductees until the day he met with Kim Jong-il, leaving him in a weakened position to leverage the abduction issue as a bargaining tool for normalization. He also lacked intelligence regarding the quantity of ballistic missiles possessed by North Korea.[56] The Bush administration maintained a skeptical posture toward North Korea, and certain members expressed disapproval of Koizumi's visit. Despite this skepticism, the personal rapport between Koizumi and Bush proved effective, ensuring that the US did not obstruct the negotiations.[57]

On September 17, Koizumi became the first Japanese prime minister to visit North Korea. The historic talks between Koizumi and Kim Jong-il yielded significant diplomatic breakthroughs on both bilateral grievances and regional security concerns. Accompanied by Abe, Koizumi aimed to encourage North Korea to engage in a dialogue with the US, South Korea, and other concerned nations to address regional security issues. While there were security concerns shared among all Northeast Asian nations, there was also an issue unique to Japan: An undetermined number of Japanese citizens had been abducted by North Korean agents in the late 1970s and early 1980s. Kim issued an apology for the abductions, acknowledging the abduction of 14 Japanese individuals, and revealed that eight of these had died, five were alive, and one remained missing. Kim assured Koizumi that he would facilitate the return of the remaining abductees and informed him that the moratorium on missile launches would extend beyond 2003. When Koizumi proposed the possibility of Six-Party Talks involving the US, South Korea, China, and Russia as a means of fostering trust in the region, Kim expressed a willingness to participate.[58]

Although the details provided by North Korea regarding the abductees were more tragic than Japan had anticipated, Koizumi chose to continue pursuing normalization, and the summit culminated in the signing of the Japan–DPRK Pyongyang Declaration.[59] This declaration, endorsed by both leaders, announced the resumption of discussions aimed at normalizing relations. It also included a formal Japanese apology for its colonial rule, a commitment to fostering economic cooperation post-normalization, an agreement to abstain from actions that could jeopardize each other's security, a commitment to promoting multilateral dialogue to address nuclear and missile issues, and an extension of North Korea's moratorium on missile launches beyond 2003.[60]

At the subsequent press briefing, Koizumi outlined two fundamental messages that he had communicated to Kim. First, he had expressed Japan's earnest readiness to engage in normalization talks with North Korea. In doing so, however, he had emphasized the necessity for North Korea to genuinely address the abduction issue, security concerns, and other unresolved matters for these discussions to progress. Second, Koizumi had highlighted the importance of maintaining a dialogue with the international community to ensure peace and security in Northeast Asia, including ongoing discussions with the US and South Korea. He specifically urged North Korea to "make a decision on the abduction and security issues."[61] Koizumi's juxtaposition of these two issues naturally raises questions about their interrelation within Japan's policy toward North Korea.

Japan–DPRK Normalization Talks and the Abduction Issue

Following the historic summit and declaration, Japan moved quickly to establish a concrete framework for advancing diplomatic normalization with North Korea while maintaining focused on the abduction issue. The relevant ministers met on October 9 to establish Japan's basic policy for the normalization negotiations. Under the adopted policy, talks would resume on October 29 and 30 in Kuala Lumpur, Malaysia, with the abduction issue designated as the highest priority on the agenda. The relevant ministries and agencies would also open security consultations with North Korea aimed at resolving a range of security concerns of paramount importance to Japan and the international community such as the nuclear and missile issues.[62]

The Japanese government intended to act cautiously during the talks, grounding the discussions in the principles and spirit of the Pyongyang Declaration so as to evaluate North Korea's sincerity. Prior to visiting Pyongyang, Koizumi had asserted that "there will be no normalization of diplomatic relations without the resolution of the abduction issue," and this approach was maintained in the basic policy.[63] The linkage of the abduction issue with regional security concerns kept Japan in alignment with the US and South Korea, but it meant pursuing goals that were fundamentally distinct in nature: The former was a purely bilateral issue while the latter was a multilateral one.

The five abductees were repatriated to Japan on October 15 via a chartered aircraft, and this represented a partial diplomatic breakthrough. But the ongoing dispute regarding the fate of the other victims strained relations and affected the broader regional security discussions. There were widespread doubts in Japan about the veracity of this assertion as well as suspicions that there had been additional victims beyond the 14 citizens acknowledged by North Korea. Particular noteworthy was the case of Megumi Yokota, who was only 13 years old at the time of her abduction. North Korea asserted that she had committed suicide and produced ashes that were purportedly hers. Subsequent laboratory testing to verify this claim proved inconclusive, however, and her parents remained resolute in their belief that she was still alive somewhere within the country. The abduction issue was vigorously championed by prominent conservative members of Koizumi's party, including Abe, making it difficult for him to back down on the matter. Failure to resolve the abduction issue posed a potential threat to the Six-Party Talks that Koizumi had helped bring about in Pyongyang.[64] Consequently, it was not until August 2003 that the inaugural session of those talks would convene in Beijing.

North Korea's Nuclear Development and the US–Japan Relations

North Korea's nuclear ambitions and evolving diplomatic dynamics presented unforeseen challenges for Japan's diplomatic initiatives, complicating

Koizumi's strategies toward both Pyongyang and Washington. Given the outcome of his visit to North Korea in September 2002, few had anticipated he would return in May 2004, but this subsequent visit was deemed necessary following North Korea's admission to the US in October 2002 that it was developing nuclear weapons. As international scrutiny of the nuclear program intensified, resolution of the abduction issue appeared increasingly improbable.[65] It seems that Koizumi had made miscalculations in his approaches toward both the US and North Korea. On September 19—just two days after the release of the Pyongyang Declaration—he requested that Bush dispatch an American delegation to North Korea but received a lukewarm response.[66]

When Bush did send James Kelly, assistant secretary of state for East Asian and Pacific Affairs, to North Korea in early October, it was revealed that North Korea was advancing its uranium enrichment program. North Korean officials also notified US representatives that they had abrogated the 1994 agreement with the US mandating the cessation of all nuclear weapons development. This resulted in the Bush administration adopting a hardline stance toward the country in an effort to thwart its acquisition of nuclear weapons. For Japan, the disclosure that North Korea had already violated the Pyongyang Declaration, coupled with the increasing rigidity of the American position, rendered subsequent negotiations with North Korea considerably more challenging.[67]

The US had first notified Japan of North Korea's nuclear program on September 12, shortly before Koizumi departed for Pyongyang. The US, Japan, and South Korea had chosen to keep this information confidential. Koizumi interpreted North Korea's admission to Kelly in early October as a miscalculation, given that he had intended to leverage the Pyongyang Declaration to curtail North Korea's nuclear program. On October 16, the State Department announced that North Korea had acknowledged its program. The next day, a Japanese diplomat involved in North Korean affairs told a reporter that the dual challenges of the abductions and nuclear weapons made "the negotiations difficult" and suggested that the US government's announcement had been intended to caution Japan against pursuing diplomatic progress too quickly.[68]

Faced with the reality that North Korea had violated the Pyongyang Declaration merely half a month after its signing and that the regime intended to negotiate exclusively with the US on the nuclear issue, Koizumi was now compelled to reconcile his belief that his visit to North Korea had improved the situation on the Korean Peninsula with the possibility that it may have been a misjudgment.[69] These misgivings were further bolstered by the North Korean claim that the return of the five abductees to Japan had only been meant to be temporary, and that Japan had agreed that they would be sent back to North Korea; its failure to do so supposedly constituted a breach of that agreement.[70]

It is essential to acknowledge that Japan closely aligned its policy toward Iraq with that of the US as a means of advancing its North Korea policy. The linkage between the two is substantiated by statements from Abe, who had participated in Koizumi's 2002 visit as deputy chief cabinet secretary. In an interview given before his assassination, Abe indicated that Bush's characterization of Iraq, Iran, and North Korea as an "axis of evil" had a profound psychological impact on North Korea and that "North Korea was scared of President Bush."[71]

Bush's initiation of the Iraq War had a profound psychological impact on North Korea and prompted the regime to seek diplomatic engagement with Japan to mitigate the possibility of conflict with the US. Recognizing the leverage this gave, the Koizumi cabinet discerned that North Korea was unlikely to undertake significant diplomatic moves without substantial pressure from the US. It consequently saw no alternative but to align with and support Bush's Iraq policy to advance its agenda for North Korea. This strategic calculation had global implications, broadening the scope of the US–Japan alliance well beyond the confines of the Far East (the geographic limits delineated in the US–Japan Security Treaty). Although US forces stationed in Japan had been previously deployed outside of the region, the Iraq War represented a pivotal moment: the first full-scale deployment of the SDF overseas and the consequent unprecedented globalization of the US–Japan alliance.

The Bush Doctrine

Preemptive Action Against Terrorism

The Bush administration's post-9/11 foreign policy strategy was formalized in a seminal national security document that fundamentally redefined the US's approach to global threats. On September 20, 2002, three days after Koizumi's visit to North Korea, Bush submitted a document entitled "The National Security Strategy of the United States of America" to Congress. Prepared by the National Security Council (NSC), this inaugural report

Table 2.1 Timeline of the Disarmament and Nonproliferation Regime

2002	September	Koizumi's first visit to North Korea (Pyongyang Declaration)
2002	October	North Korea acknowledges uranium enrichment program to the US delegation
2002	December	North Korea deports the International Atomic Energy Agency (IAEA) inspectors
2003	January	North Korea declares withdrawal from the NPT
2003	August	First round of the Six-Party Talks (Beijing)
2004	February	Second round of the Six-Party Talks (Beijing)
2004	May	Koizumi's second visit to North Korea
2004	June	Third round of the Six-Party Talks (Beijing)
2005	February	North Korea declares the indefinite suspension of its participation in the Six-Party Talks and its resumption of nuclear weapons production
2005	September	Fourth round of the Six-Party Talks, first meeting (Beijing)
2005	November	Fifth round of the Six-Party Talks (Beijing)
2006	July	North Korea launches ballistic missiles
2006	July	The UNSC adopts Resolution 1695 on North Korea
2006	October	North Korea declares that it has conducted a nuclear test
2006	October	The UNSC adopts Resolution 1718 on North Korea
2006	December	Fifth round of the Six-Party Talks, second meeting (Beijing)
2007	March	Sixth round of the Six-Party Talks, first meeting (Beijing)
2007	July	Sixth round of the Six-Party Talks, representatives meeting (Beijing)
2007	September	Sixth round of the Six-Party Talks, second meeting (Beijing)

Source: MOFA, *Nihon no Gunshuku/Fukakusan Gaikō* [Japan's Disarmament and Nonproliferation Diplomacy], May 2008, 247–49, www.mofa.go.jp/mofaj/gaiko/gun_hakusho/2008/pdfs/shi2_17.pdf (partially modified).

from the Bush administration articulated the administration's position on the necessity of conducting preemptive strikes to safeguard the US against potential attacks; this would come to be frequently referred to as the "Bush Doctrine."[72]

The document asserted that while the US would consistently seek the support of the international community, it would not hesitate to act unilaterally if deemed necessary to exercise its "right of self-defense" by preemptively targeting terrorists in order to prevent harm to the American populace and the nation.[73] The report acknowledged that it had taken nearly a decade to fully comprehend the nature of this new threat. In light of the objectives of "rogue states" and terrorist groups, the US could no longer rely solely on a reactive approach as it had in the past. The difficulties associated with deterring potential aggressors, the immediacy of contemporary threats, and the severe potential consequences associated with adversaries' choices of weaponry implied that waiting for enemies to strike first is not a viable strategy.

While recognizing China's military advancements, the report argued that China's pursuit of advanced military capabilities, which could pose a threat to its neighbors in the Asia-Pacific region, represented an antiquated approach that would ultimately impede its quest for national prominence. It posited that China would eventually recognize that true greatness could only be achieved through "social and political freedom."[74] It asserted that "the United States seeks a constructive relationship with a changing China" and acknowledged areas of successful cooperation, such as the ongoing war on terrorism and efforts to maintain stability on the Korean peninsula.[75] The new grand strategy being crystallized in Washington diverged from the earlier US post–Cold War order characterized by stable relationships and an open world economy.

The new paradigm established by the Bush administration was rooted in an anti-terrorism stance that dictated the US role within this framework. Scholar G. John Ikenberry identified seven core elements of Bush's grand strategy: American military dominance, innovative threat assessment methodologies, the rejection of Cold War–era deterrence strategies, preemptive intervention capabilities, a diminished emphasis on international frameworks, unrestricted responses to perceived threats, and a minimal focus on global stability.[76] He contended that this unilateral approach, divorced from established international norms, posed a significant risk of escalating global antagonism and undermining US interests. This prescient analysis, published prior to the formal articulation of the Bush Doctrine, accurately forecasted the administration's strategic direction.

The fundamental premise underlying President George W. Bush's strategic doctrine can be discerned through careful analysis of his memoirs. In the aftermath of the September 11 attacks, Bush developed a strategy for national protection that emphasized the transformative power of freedom, as exemplified in countries such as South Korea, Germany, and Eastern Europe. His relationship with Koizumi served as a salient example of this approach. Koizumi was among the first world leaders to offer support following the attacks, marking a significant shift given the historical context between their respective countries and families. Notably, Bush's father had fought against Japan as a Navy pilot during World War II, while Koizumi's father had served in the Japanese government during the same conflict. Bush wrote, "something big had changed since World War II: By adopting a Japanese-style democracy, an enemy had become an ally."[77] This statement is particularly poignant as Japan had previously experienced a democratic system—referred to as "Taishō Democracy"—from the time of the Russo-Japanese War until the 1920s.

The Allied occupation of Japan can thus not be considered the sole catalyst for the establishment of democracy in the country following the war. While the US ousted many politicians and high-ranking officials during its occupation, the General Headquarters (GHQ) retained the existing bureaucracy and many of its officials. Notably, Hayato Ikeda and Eisaku Satō, two future prime ministers who played significant roles in the development of Japan's party politics, were among these bureaucrats.[78] In the case of Iraq, however, the US excluded all members of the Ba'ath Party from the governing apparatus. Bush's omission of these critical differences in his memoirs reflects a significant misunderstanding; to assume that a nation lacking democratic traditions could be democratized through war and occupation was a deeply flawed perspective that demonstrated a disregard for historical context. Consequently, Bush's reference to Japan in this context was inappropriate. Nevertheless, John Dower's book *Embracing Defeat: Japan in the Wake of World War II* was reportedly "required reading in the Bush White House."[79]

Bush's oversimplified interpretation of Japan's democratization and its applicability to Iraq encountered considerable resistance from Japanese officials who recognized the fundamental distinctions between the two contexts. In a conversation with Vice-Minister for Foreign Affairs Takeuchi, Koizumi asserted, "I cannot support a pre-emptive strike [by the US against Iraq]."[80] Through Ryōzō Katō, ambassador to the US, the

Koizumi administration communicated to the Bush administration that America's occupation policy toward Japan in the late 1940s significantly diverged from its approach to Iraq in the early 2000s. In Katō's words, "Japan's situation was quite different from that in Iraq; it had not only a wealth of human resources but also a long tradition of democracy and practical experience."[81] However, only a limited number of individuals, such as JCS Chairman Gen. Richard Myers—who had extensive experience in Japan—agreed with Katō's assessment. Consequently, there was minimal motivation within the US government to conduct thorough research into an appropriate occupation policy for Iraq. This failure to acknowledge the distinct differences would be to its great detriment.

CHINA: COLLABORATOR OR THREAT?

On China, the Bush Doctrine presented a nuanced perspective characterized by both optimism and caution. The US National Security Strategy posited that China's pursuit of advanced military capabilities represented a regressive strategy that might undermine China's ambitions for national prominence. The strategy suggested that China would ultimately come to recognize that the adoption of "social and political freedom" was essential for achieving true greatness.[82] Given this, the US should seek to cultivate a positive and evolving relationship with China. While the Bush Doctrine recognized China's "advanced military capabilities that can threaten its neighbors in the Asia-Pacific region," it also acknowledged, "We already cooperate well where our interests overlap, including the current war on terrorism and in promoting stability on the Korean peninsula."[83] The Bush administration therefore seems to have anticipated that China would act as a collaborator in its initiatives to combat terrorism and viewed "rogue states and terrorists" as a greater threat than China.

The October 2002 summit between Bush and Chinese President Jiang Zemin underscored their differing approaches to international security, particularly with respect to terrorism, North Korea, and Iraq. Meeting with Bush in Crawford, Texas, on October 25, Jiang emphasized his position that his commitment to combating terrorism was commensurate with that of the US. But while he agreed that denuclearization of the Korean peninsula was imperative, he stressed that the issues concerning North Korea should be addressed through peaceful means. And when Bush sought Chinese support for a new UNSC resolution on Iraq, Jiang expressed his opposition to the use of military force by quoting Sun Tzu: "The supreme art of war is to subdue the enemy without fighting."[84] Although segments of the US and Japanese governments—particularly within the Department of Defense—perceived China's expanding military and economic capabilities as a potential threat, neither Bush nor Koizumi shared this perspective. Koizumi aimed to foster a complementary economic relationship with China, especially following its accession to the WTO.[85] For its part, China remained cautious regarding the proliferation of the "China threat" theory in the US and Japan.[86]

UNSC RESOLUTION 1441 AND THE POSSIBILITY OF WAR AGAINST IRAQ

There was considerable support for military intervention against Iraq within the US government, and Bush was poised to take such a step unilaterally. Nevertheless, acting on the counsel of Secretary of State Powell and other advisors, he requested that Iraq clarify its intentions regarding WMD when addressing the UNGA on September 12.[87] On November 8, the UNSC unanimously adopted Resolution 1441, which addressed WMD inspections in Iraq.[88] This resolution was a dilution of a proposal initially put forth by the US and the UK, as it incorporated the "two-stage approach" advocated by France, Russia, and China, rather than providing explicit authorization for the use of force.[89] The Koizumi administration endorsed the resolution and, through Foreign Minister Kawaguchi, issued a statement on November 9 that strongly urged Iraq to recognize the significance of its adoption.[90] The pivotal issue was whether Resolution 1441 granted authorization for the use of force in the event of Iraqi noncompliance, or whether such action necessitated the passage of a new resolution. Japan's UN Policy Division supported the assertion made by the US representative at the UN that the Security Council would need to reassess the situation in such a case.[91]

Bush, however, alluded to the potential for unilateral military action absent a subsequent UNSC resolution. Following the adoption of Resolution 1441, he delivered an address at the White House in which he asserted that "the outcome of the current crisis is already determined: the full disarmament of weapons of mass destruction by Iraq will occur. The only question for the Iraq regime is to decide how. The United States prefers that Iraq meet its obligations voluntarily, yet we are prepared for the alternative."[92] At this juncture, it is likely that Bush seems to have anticipated that it was unlikely that he would obtain an additional resolution authorizing the use of force.[93] It had not been until the afternoon of November 7, just one day prior to the vote, that France had communicated to the US that it intended to support Resolution 1441—a delay attributed to apprehensions regarding the potential for military action. Similarly, Russia only informed the US of its decision to endorse the resolution shortly after 9 a.m. on the day of the vote.[94]

In December 2002, the Bush administration opted against initiating military action against Iraq for the time being. On December 9, Armitage made a courtesy call to Koizumi at the Prime Minister's Office and conveyed a message from Bush: "I appreciate the leadership you have shown, and I am grateful for your friendship."[95] Koizumi responded by acknowledging the criticism directed at the close US–Japan relationship from certain opposition parties. Nevertheless, he asserted that key figures in governance—including himself and officials from both the Prime Minister's Office and the Ministry of Foreign Affairs—believed "there has never been a time when there was greater trust in the US–Japan relationship or a deeper understanding of the importance of the US–Japan alliance."[96]

Koizumi also commented on the experience gained from a year of support operations conducted under the Anti-Terrorism Special Measures Act and how the SDF, the public, and experts had all gained an increased understanding of the need for improved protection capabilities for SDF operations. In response to these security needs, Japan had decided to deploy an Aegis-equipped destroyer to support operations in the Indian Ocean. Armitage remarked that the decision to deploy the Aegis ship was indeed extraordinary and reflected Japan's role in the international community. He did not address the matter of the future situation in Iraq.[97]

Armitage then visited Foreign Minister Kawaguchi at MOFA and expressed his appreciation for Japan's response to the war on terror, including the deployment of the Aegis ship. He told those at the ministry that the US had not yet reached a decision regarding military action against Iraq and would first examine the 10,000-page report submitted by the country in its defense. Kawaguchi indicated that the Japanese government would be dispatching a three-person delegation, including Senior Vice-Minister for Foreign Affairs Toshimitsu Motegi, as special envoys to the Middle East to urge Iraq to dismantle its WMD and comply with the UN resolutions.[98]

Armitage's meeting with Defense Agency Director-General Shigeru Ishiba also provided substantial insights into Japan's evolving geopolitical stance. Ishiba reiterated Japan's commitment to fulfilling its international responsibilities and indicated that the government was actively assessing potential roles for Japan in the event of military intervention in Iraq. He underscored the significance of Japan's "proactive" engagement while also noting that such involvement was contingent on US-led military action becoming "unavoidable."[99] To this end, he also highlighted the necessity of continued coordinated international efforts and that Japan had high hopes that the US would exercise leadership in fostering consensus within the UNSC. Armitage responded by conveying the US position and stressing that military conflict was not an inevitable outcome. While he placed the onus for a peaceful resolution firmly in "Saddam Hussein's hands," he contended that effective disarmament would necessitate a credible threat of military force and that the international community could only realize its objective of Iraqi disarmament through the demonstration and application of "military pressure."[100]

Armitage and Ishiba's conversation, with its exploration of the potential for war against Iraq and the need for consensus within the UNSC, was the most substantive meeting of Armitage's visit. Should the US initiate military action in Iraq, Japan—ultimately reliant on the US for its security—would be compelled to extend its support. The prospect of war in Iraq therefore presented a global dilemma for Japan, which favored a peaceful resolution to the North Korean nuclear issue. The origin of this global alliance security dilemma can be fully understood by examining the US–Japan SCC meeting a few days later.

SCC as the Origin of the Global Alliance Security Dilemma

Alongside the situation in Iraq, North Korea's nuclear development also constituted a pressing international issue in the winter of 2002, as the North Korean government announced its intention to resume its nuclear program on December 12. The next day, Koizumi instructed Kawaguchi to collaborate with the US and South Korea in devising a response.[101] Kawaguchi and Ishiba thus decided to raise the issue at the US–Japan SCC meeting held in Washington on December 16. This was the first meeting of the SCC since September 2000, as the previous session planned for September 2001 had been canceled due to 9/11. While the meeting had been intended to focus on Iraq, the North Korean announcement caused that issue to rapidly rise to the forefront of the agenda.[102] Kawaguchi, Ishiba, Secretary of State Powell, and Deputy Secretary of Defense Paul Wolfowitz were in attendance (with Wolfowitz standing in for Secretary of Defense Rumsfeld due to illness).

This SCC meeting represented a pivotal moment for both the Bush and Koizumi administrations. Although Japan continued to seek negotiations with North Korea, including discussions related to the abduction issue, North Korea had altered its approach and displayed a preference to negotiate exclusively with the US. Japan found itself reliant on the US to sustain its North Korea policy and acquiescing to American actions concerning

Iraq. This state of affairs illustrates the origin of Japan's unresolved global alliance security dilemma. Following the meeting, the SCC released a joint statement affirming that both countries would enhance their cooperation should further action against Iraq become necessary. The statement also criticized North Korea's nuclear program while pledging to resolve the issue through peaceful means. Over the course of these discussions, the US and Japan clarified their collaborative efforts on these two significant issues and sought to strengthen their cooperative framework on WMD.[103]

Ishiba briefed Koizumi and his cabinet on the course of the SCC meeting on December 19 after returning to Japan. The cabinet then endorsed the meeting's outcomes, most notably the mutual commitment between the US and Japan to collaborate in the "war on terror" and a unified stance against North Korea's ongoing nuclear proliferation.[104] The meeting represented a pivotal moment, reinforcing the robustness of the US–Japan security alliance and fostering greater trust between the two nations in an increasingly dynamic global landscape. Under Koizumi's leadership, the cabinet formalized the interconnectedness of Japan's policies toward Iraq and North Korea, institutionalizing this linkage as an official component of Japanese foreign policy.

The issues pertaining to North Korea were tied to those concerning Iraq at the SCC, resulting in Japan's unresolved global alliance security dilemma. This linkage reflected a reciprocal arrangement under which the US would exert pressure for a peaceful resolution to the North Korean issue in exchange for Japanese support of US policy in Iraq. Even if Japan could characterize this as a strategy, however, it was a passive one, arising from the confluence of the two international conflicts. The Koizumi government prioritized North Korea, and there are no indications that it critically examined the legitimacy of the use of force against Iraq. Many declassified MOFA and Ministry of Defense (MOD) documents on Iraq merely reiterated arguments put forth by the US.[105]

Thus, as a byproduct of North Korea's declaration of the resumption of its nuclear program, a system was put into place under which Japan could not decline to support the American use of force in Iraq. While the close relationship between Japan's approaches to Iraq and North Korea has been discussed in prior scholarship, the origin of this relationship has not yet been rigorously examined through empirical evidence. This study breaks new ground by positing that the SCC meeting in December 2002 served as a seminal moment in shaping Japan's global security dilemma. This argument is substantiated by analyzing previously undisclosed documents from MOFA and MOD obtained under the Information Disclosure Law.

Table 2.2 Main US–Japan Government Consultative Bodies on Security Issues

Body	Attendees from Japan	Attendees from US	Purpose	Basis
US–Japan Security Consultative Committee (SCC or 2+2)	Foreign Minister; Defense Agency Director-General	Secretary of State; Secretary of Defense*	Consideration of issues that form the basis of and relate to security matters that help promote understanding between the governments of Japan and the US and contribute to increased cooperation in the area of security	Correspondence between the prime minister and the US secretary of state on January 19, 1960, grounded in Article 4 of the Security Treaty and other legislation
US–Japan Security Subcommittee (SSC)	Not specified**	Not specified**	Exchange of opinions on security issues of mutual interest to Japan and the US	Article 4 of the Security Treaty and others
Subcommittee for Defense Cooperation (SDC)†	Director-General, North American Affairs Bureau, Foreign Ministry; Director-General, Defense Bureau; Director-General, Defense Operations Bureau, Defense Agency; Representative of the Joint Staff Office‡	Assistant Secretary of State; Assistant Secretary of Defense; Representatives of the US Embassy in Japan, US Forces Japan, the Joint Chiefs of Staff, and US Pacific Command	Research and consultation on forms of US–Japan cooperation such as guidelines for consistent joint responses between the SDF and the US military in an emergency	Established in the 16th meeting of the SCC on July 8, 1976, as a subsidiary body of the SCC; later reorganized as a US–Japan vice-minister-level council on June 28, 1996

Body	Attendees from Japan	Attendees from US	Purpose	Basis
US–Japan Joint Committee (meets every two weeks in principle)	Director-General, North American Affairs Bureau, Foreign Ministry; Director-General, Defense Facilities Administration Agency; others	Chief of Staff, US Forces Japan; US ministers and councillors to Japan; others	Consultation on implementation of the Status of Forces Agreement	Article 25 of the SOFA

Source: Defense Agency, *Nihon no Bōei: Bōei Hakusho* [Defense of Japan: Defense White Paper] (Gyōsei, 2003), 122.

*Before December 26, 1990: US ambassador to Japan and US Pacific Command commander.

**Meets as appropriate with administrative-level officials from both countries, such as those at the vice-minister and director-general level.

†Established as a meeting of representatives at the deputy director-general and vice-minister levels upon reorganization on June 28, 1996.

‡The Director-General of the Defense Operations Bureau of the Defense Agency was added on September 23, 1997.

Conclusion

The US–Japan alliance evolved significantly over the course of 2002, with the global alliance security dilemma becoming particularly evident following the December SCC meeting. This pivotal meeting explicitly linked Japan's concerns about North Korea's nuclear program with the impending Iraq War, creating a situation where Japan felt compelled to support US military action in Iraq to secure American cooperation on North Korean issues. Declassified MOFA documents reveal that this meeting marked the origin of Japan's unresolved global alliance security dilemma. This dilemma intensified after North Korea announced its intention to resume its nuclear program, placing Japan in an increasingly difficult position where it had to balance its desire for a peaceful resolution to the North Korean situation against pressure to support American military intervention in Iraq.

The inherent asymmetry of the US–Japan alliance was readily apparent throughout 2002, particularly in Japan's lack of independent intelligence capabilities and heavy reliance on US information regarding both Iraqi WMDs and North Korean nuclear developments. Despite Koizumi's historic visit to Pyongyang and the signing of the Japan–DPRK Pyongyang Declaration, Japan remained fundamentally dependent on US support for addressing both security concerns and the abduction issue. Even in moments of apparent diplomatic autonomy, such as Koizumi's North Korea initiative, Japan's actions were constrained by the need to maintain US support. This dependency was further highlighted by Japan's acceptance of US claims about Iraqi WMDs without independent verification.

The dual-structured security dilemma emerged more clearly in 2002 as Japan navigated not only its relationship with the US but also its regional relationships, particularly with China. While China was seen as potentially useful for managing North Korean issues (as seen from Bush's pressure on Chinese President Jiang Zemin), Japan had to carefully balance its alliance obligations to the US against regional dynamics in Asia. The Bush Doctrine's articulation of a more aggressive US foreign policy stance, including the concept of preemptive strikes and the designation of an "axis of evil," created additional complications for Japan in managing its regional relationships while still maintaining its alliance commitments.

These dilemmas would intensify significantly in 2003 with the outbreak of the Iraq War and North Korea's withdrawal from the NPT. The foundations laid in 2002—particularly the linking of Iraqi and North Korean issues at the SCC meeting and Japan's increasing dependence on US intelligence and security guarantees—would fundamentally shape Japan's response to these challenges. The patterns established in 2002—the simultaneous Japanese pursuit of peaceful solutions to regional issues and support for US military actions—would face severe tests as the security situation in both Iraq and North Korea continued to deteriorate.

North Korean Issues and the Iraq War

2003

The Six-Party Talks

NORTH KOREA'S WITHDRAWAL FROM THE NPT

North Korea's withdrawal from the Nuclear Nonproliferation Treaty (NPT) and the 2003 Iraq War presented significant international challenges that placed Japan in a strategic predicament. Japan's reliance on the US for deterrence and countermeasures caused it to be confronted by a complex dilemma: On the one hand, it hoped for a peaceful resolution to North Korea's nuclear proliferation; on the other, it needed to avoid alienating its ally, the US, by opposing its advocacy for military action in Iraq. At the same time, the US had to accommodate Japan's concerns to some extent in formulating its policy toward North Korea in order to secure Japan's support for the Iraq War. This reciprocal alignment of policies facilitated the expansion of the US–Japan alliance beyond the Far East, transforming it into a global partnership.

In this chapter, I examine North Korea's withdrawal from the NPT and the Six-Party Talks and then offer an analysis of the Iraq War and Japan's response. I emphasize the influence of the North Korean situation on the global alliance security dilemma and scrutinize the decision-making process that led the Koizumi administration to endorse the Iraq War. The events of the G8 summit in Evian underscored the Bush administration's intention to operate within a unipolar system, independent of international consensus. Due to constitutional limitations, Japan opted to deploy the Self-Defense Forces (SDF) to a nominally "non-combat zone" in Iraq, although the definition of such a zone remained ambiguous. Koizumi also promoted additional avenues for cooperation with the US, namely the implementation of a US-developed BMD system and the reduction of Iraq's debt.

It is essential to examine events dating back to March 12, 1993, to fully understand the context for North Korea's 2003 withdrawal from the NPT.[1] On that date, Pyongyang issued a high-level governmental statement declaring that it was "no longer able to fulfill its obligations under the Nuclear Nonproliferation Treaty" and was withdrawing to safeguard its "supreme interests."[2] The DPRK maintained that its position would remain unchanged "until the United States stops its nuclear threats" and the International Atomic Energy Agency (IAEA) secretariat "returns to the principles of independence and impartiality."[3] It also informed the UNSC that its withdrawal would take effect on June 12, three months later. One day before this was to come to pass, however, North Korea announced that it would suspend its withdrawal pending the conclusion of negotiations with the US in New York. Afterward, the DPRK began to moderate its public posture toward IAEA inspections, implicitly accepting American assurances that these inspections did not pose a nuclear "threat."[4] Then, on October 12, 1994, it reaffirmed its intention to remain a party within the framework of the US–DPRK agreement, under which North Korea committed to freezing its nuclear program in exchange for energy assistance.[5]

On January 10, 2003, the North Korean government again announced that it would withdraw from the NPT. According to North Korean officials, "Following the arrival of the Bush administration, the United States has listed the DPRK as part of an 'axis of evil,' adopted opposition to the DPRK as national policy, singled it out as a target for preemptive nuclear attack, [and] openly declared nuclear war."[6] This announcement stated that the prior withdrawal declaration made in March 1993 had only been temporarily suspended and would now take effect immediately. Foreign Minister Kawaguchi's speech gave the Koizumi administration's response: "Japan will strongly urge North Korea to immediately retract its decision and take prompt action to dismantle its nuclear development program."[7] When Secretary of State Powell told Kawaguchi that he "would like the US and Japan to remain in close contact on our future response," Kawaguchi concurred, noting that Japan planned "to hold close discussions with other concerned countries through the prime minister's visit to Russia and my visit to South Korea."[8]

In the meantime, Bush also exerted considerable pressure on Chinese President Jiang Zemin. On the same day as the North Korean announcement, he told Jiang, "If North Korea's nuclear weapons program continued, I would not be able to stop Japan . . . from developing its own nuclear weapons."[9] This statement was a tactical maneuver; Japan was not actually pursuing nuclear weapons and had not sought US permission to acquire them. In February, Bush informed Jiang, "If we could not solve the problem diplomatically, I would have to consider a military strike against North Korea."[10] In communicating to China that military action was a potential option, he circumvented Japan, which favored a peaceful resolution. This underscored the divergence between American and Japanese positions on North Korea, and it also ultimately contributed to the beginning of the Six-Party Talks six months later.

The Six-Party Talks

North Korea not only withdrew from the NPT but also went on to suggest that it might be in possession of nuclear weapons. Nevertheless, China sought to avoid having the issue being taken up by the UNSC. In what would become a precursor to the Six-Party Talks, representatives of the US, China, and North Korea convened in Beijing from April 23 to April 25 to discuss North Korea's nuclear program and the associated security concerns.[11] On April 30, a North Korean foreign ministry spokesperson stated that Bush's designation of the country as part of the "axis of evil" had "forced [North Korea] to take action and [we] have had no choice but to equip ourselves with the necessary deterrent," implying that it possessed nuclear weapons.[12] The statement concluded by urging the US to reassess its policies toward North Korea, emphasizing that "the denuclearization of the Korean Peninsula is entirely dependent on American policy."[13]

For Japan, North Korea's declaration meant that achieving a comprehensive resolution to the nuclear issue as outlined in the Japan–DPRK Pyongyang Declaration was no longer possible. The existence of North Korean nuclear weapons exacerbated Japan's global alliance security dilemma, as it had supported the initiation of the Iraq War a month earlier despite Iraqi denials that it was not stockpiling WMD and the failure of the US government to prove these to be false. And yet, it now had to convince the US to pursue a peaceful resolution to North Korea's possession of WMD. These two issues were inherently interconnected; Japan's ongoing endorsement of the Iraq War was a compensatory measure for its North Korean policy. The hope for achieving a peaceful resolution to the North Korean problem would now be in the hands of the Six-Party Talks.

Chinese involvement in these talks was critical, as the nation served as North Korea's economic lifeline and could therefore exert considerable influence. Previously reluctant to address North Korean issues, China under its new leader Hu Jintao sought to enhance its relations with the US in the hopes of ensuring that is rise as a responsible world leader would be a peaceful one.[14] Both China and Japan aimed to prevent tensions in Iraq from escalating and potentially spilling over into Northeast Asia. Unlike Japan, however, China took the stance that the abduction issue should not be included on the agenda for the Six-Party Talks. During a mid-August visit to Japan, Minister of Foreign Affairs Li Zhaoxing met with LDP Secretary-General Taku Yamasaki and emphasized that "the nuclear issue (the denuclearization of the Korean Peninsula) is the main topic [of the talks]; the abduction issue should be resolved through bilateral discussions between Japan and North Korea."[15] Yamasaki then informed Koizumi that he had been "told that the Six-Party Talks were all about the nuclear issue and that the abduction issue was only a 'trifling detail' for China."[16] It was far from "trifling" for Koizumi, however.[17] The Bush administration had been a key player in the formation of the talks and believed that China would be cooperative. In his memoirs, Vice President Cheney highlighted China's apprehensions about regional destabilization, particularly the potential for a nuclear-armed North Korea to incentivize Japan and other nations to "follow suit." He saw this as a significant Chinese consideration in its nuclear diplomacy pertaining to the Korean Peninsula.[18]

The inaugural session of the Six-Party Talks was held in Beijing from August 27 to 29. The participants included Assistant Secretary of State James Kelly, Russian Deputy Foreign Minister Alexander Losyukov, South Korean Vice Minister of Foreign Affairs and Trade Lee Soo-hyuk, Japanese Director of the Foreign Ministry's Asian and Oceanic Affairs Bureau Mitoji Yabunaka, North Korean Vice Minister of Foreign Affairs Kim Yong-il, and Chinese Vice Minister of Foreign Affairs Wang Yi.

At the first meeting, Kelly expressed that the North Korean nuclear issue should be addressed through peaceful means and conveyed his willingness to discuss North Korea's security concerns in subsequent discussions, contingent upon a verifiable and irreversible commitment from North Korea to dismantle its nuclear program. Losyukov also stressed the importance of denuclearization on the Korean Peninsula. Lee asserted that he would pursue a diplomatic resolution to the nuclear issue and made note of South Korea's continued provision of economic assistance to North Korea for humanitarian purposes. Yabunaka called for a comprehensive approach that would tackle both the abduction and nuclear issues. Kim, however, insisted on the establishment of a non-aggression pact and the normalization of diplomatic relations with the US as prerequisites for halting nuclear weapons development; he did not address the abduction issue in his remarks. Wang came closest to the North Korean position in contending that the denuclearization of the Korean Peninsula and guarantees for the North Korean regime should be addressed simultaneously. In summarizing the discussions as the host of the talks, he emphasized the need to continue efforts aimed at peacefully resolving the nuclear issue while notably also omitting any mention of abductions.[19]

China, North Korea, South Korea, and Russia all viewed the abduction issue as a bilateral concern between Japan and North Korea, something inappropriate for Japan to raise in the context of the talks. During the proceedings, Kim approached Yabunaka and accused Japan of violating a bilateral agreement by not returning the five abductees to North Korea after their visit to Japan. Japan's advocacy for a comprehensive solution that included the abduction issue hindered the ability of the other nations to utilize economic support as leverage for advancing security discussions. As if to reinforce this point, the North Korean delegation stated following the session that North Korea would "continue to strengthen [its] nuclear deterrence capabilities."[20] But while it recognized that a comprehensive solution addressing both the abduction and security matters would be intricate and could impede the progress of the Six-Party Talks, Japan remained attuned to domestic sentiment. And Koizumi was instrumental in articulating Japan's position. North Korea's view of nuclear issues as something to be negotiated unilaterally with the US compelled Japan to increasingly depend on the US in this area, significantly influencing its support for the Iraq War. Nevertheless, while Bush may have felt differently, Hu and South Korean President Roh Moo-hyun were committed to a "peaceful resolution" to the North Korean nuclear issue, something that aligned with Japan's objectives.[21]

The Iraq War

"I Stand by You, and You Stand by Me"

The issues concerning North Korea were not the sole challenges facing the US and Japan in 2003; the commencement of the Iraq War would be the most prominent event of the year, and arguably one of the most notable of the 21st century. Even though Iraq had accepted UNSC Resolution 1441 on November 13, 2002, and agreed to permit inspections by the United Nations Monitoring, Verification and Inspection Commission (UNMOVIC) and the IAEA, the US, the UK, and Spain prepared a new resolution that would have sanctioned the use of force under Chapter 7 of the UN Charter.[22] According to Bush's memoirs, "Years of intelligence pointed overwhelmingly to the conclusion that Saddam had WMD. . . . The only logical conclusion was that he was hiding WMD. And given his support of terror and his sworn hatred of America, there was no way to know where those weapons would end up."[23] Ultimately, the Bush administration would retract this resolution due to opposition from France, Russia, China, and non-permanent member Germany, all of whom advocated for the continuation of the UNMOVIC and IAEA inspections.[24]

Even prior to the delivery of Secretary of State Powell's infamous speech to the UNSC on Iraqi WMD in Iraq on February 5, 2003, Bush was unequivocal in his belief that military action was inevitable. In his memoirs, Powell recounts a pivotal moment in the lead-up to the war; Bush called a private meeting in the Oval Office on January 30 in which he indicated that it was time to present the case against Iraq to the UN. Powell wrote that, even though the National Security Council had never formally convened to deliberate this momentous decision, Bush "had crossed the line in his own mind."[25] While there were some internal disagreements on specific details, the intelligence community maintained a unified stance that Saddam Hussein possessed and was actively developing WMD.

Bush designated February 5 as the date for Powell's presentation to the UN—a speech that would prove to play a key role in shaping the trajectory of the conflict. In his account of the events leading to that presentation, Powell provides a revealing critique of Vice President Cheney's role in the process. He reveals that the initial presentation was crafted by Cheney's chief of staff, Scooter Libby, rather than by the NSC staff as might have been expected. And that Rice later disclosed to him that this had been Cheney's idea, and that he had convinced Bush to have Libby frame the material—in Powell's notable words—"as a lawyer's brief and not as an intelligence assessment."[26] This approach to presenting intelligence would prove highly consequential for both the domestic and international discourses surrounding the conflict. Powell expressed regret over the inaccuracies in the intelligence on Iraq, stating that "If we had known there were no WMD, there would have been no war."[27]

While the internal deliberations and intelligence assessments of the US government reveal significant complexities and later regrets, Japan expressed support for Bush's decision. As it did so, it knew little of the internal dynamics of the US government and the risks pertaining to its intelligence on WMD. On March 17, Bush delivered a televised address in which he cautioned Iraq that military action would be required if Hussein did not pursue a peaceful resolution. Later that day, Koizumi held a press conference in which he endorsed military intervention in Iraq, stating, "I support the American policy. . . . Some have argued that there are no resolutions in place that authorize the use of force, but I believe that a series of UN resolutions—including 1441 adopted last November, 678, and 687—could serve as grounds for the use of force."[28]

The resolutions referenced by Koizumi may not have constituted an adequate legal basis for the use of force in Iraq, however. Resolutions 678 and 687 pertained to the Gulf War and its ceasefire, while Resolution 1441 merely provided Iraq with "a final opportunity to comply with its disarmament obligations," warning that it would "face serious consequences as a result of its continued violations of its obligations."[29] Resolution 1441 did not include language analogous to that found in Resolution 678, which had authorized "Member States co-operating with the Government of Kuwait, unless Iraq on or before 15 January 1991 fully implements, as set forth in paragraph 1 above, the foregoing resolutions, to use all necessary means to uphold and implement resolution 660 (1990) and all subsequent relevant resolutions and to restore international peace and security in the area."[30] The US and UK argued that Iraq's failure to demonstrate that it no longer possessed WMD indicated that the terms of the ceasefire established in Resolution 687 had expired and that the authorization for force contained in Resolution 678 had been reinstated. Japan did not conduct an independent analysis of this reasoning, nor did it consider the alternative interpretation of China, France, and Russia that Resolution 687 had effectively revoked the authorization provided in Resolution 678.[31]

The final moments before the outbreak of hostilities demonstrate not only the close coordination between US and Japanese officials but also how Koizumi used the lens of regional security to strategically frame Japan's support for the war. On March 19, Armitage notified Vice-Minister for Foreign Affairs Yukio Takeuchi that military action would begin in ten minutes.[32] Takeuchi immediately briefed Koizumi. The next day, Bush delivered a televised address announcing the beginning of the Iraq War. Koizumi held a press conference following Bush's address in which he stated that "[The US] is the only country that has declared that an attack on Japan would be considered an attack on the US. That itself is a significant deterrent to any country that might want to attack Japan."[33] A reporter asked Koizumi which country he was referring to but did not receive a clear answer. But given that Koizumi later commented that "We must work closely with the US and South Korea to prevent North Korea from unleashing an unprovoked attack," it can be inferred that he was referring to North Korea.[34]

In the days that followed, Koizumi would emphasize the importance of the US–Japan alliance and the seriousness of the North Korean threat when speaking on Iraq at press conferences and the Diet, to a significantly greater extent than had been anticipated by Japanese officials. This reveals how the US–Japan alliance provided the framework for Koizumi to see his support for the Iraq War as intricately linked to North Korea.[35]

Koizumi garnered immediate appreciation from senior US officials by promptly undertaking several decisive administrative actions in an effort to formalize Japan's stance and implement concrete policy measures in response to the outbreak of hostilities. After his initial press conference, Koizumi convened an emergency meeting of the cabinet and reaffirmed Japan's support for military action. Addressing the group, he emphasized Japan's prior commitment to pursuing a peaceful resolution to "Iraq's weapons of mass destruction" through international channels and Iraq's pattern of defiance, citing 17 violations of UNSC resolutions over the previous 12 years.[36] He argued that Iraq had consistently rejected opportunities for peaceful resolution. Significantly, he framed Japan's endorsement of military action as having been done "in consideration of its national interests, and as a responsible member of the international community"—in other words, as a strategic necessity.[37]

I must stress that Koizumi cited WMD as the primary justification for Japan's support of the war, and I will argue shortly that when he emphasized Japan's "national interests," this implicitly included the American deterrence of North Korea. Koizumi established the Iraq Problem Countermeasures Headquarters, which he led, to explore strategies for protecting Japanese citizens residing in and around Iraq, strengthening counterterrorism measures, ensuring a steady supply of oil, and providing humanitarian aid to refugees and neighboring countries.[38] Bush called Koizumi shortly after the beginning of the war to express his gratitude for Japan's support, and said, "I stand by you, and you stand by me"—a sentiment rarely articulated by an American president during wartime.[39] Both Rumsfeld and Armitage also expressed their appreciation to him.[40]

"NORTH KOREA IS OBSERVING": THE GLOBAL ALLIANCE SECURITY DILEMMA

The complexity of the relationship between Japan's support for the Iraq War and its strategic concerns about North Korea became increasingly evident over the course of a series of diplomatic exchanges and internal policy deliberations. Koizumi's initial position had been that the US should enact a new UNSC resolution to follow up on Resolution 1441, and he had dispatched envoys to both the US and the nonpermanent members of the Security Council to encourage collaborative efforts to help facilitate this goal. On February 22, Koizumi met with Powell in Tokyo and emphasized that "international cooperation and a good reason" were necessary prerequisites for military action.[41]

Japan was closely aligned with the UK in this effort, with Prime Minister Tony Blair appreciating Koizumi's diplomatic outreach to other nations. Masaki Orita, Japanese ambassador to the UK, worked with David Manning, foreign policy advisor to the prime minister, at the time and later wrote that "Japan and Britain were in the same situation in that they needed to converse with the US What Blair articulated was akin to Koizumi's assertions."[42] While Bush would ultimately withdraw the proposed new resolution and proceed with military action against Iraq without it, he valued Koizumi's support for the war. Koizumi's conduct during this period raises several pertinent questions: Why did Koizumi opt to support the Iraq War despite having advocated for a new resolution? Was this alignment with US policy connected to Japan's approach to North Korea? Did the Koizumi administration possess accurate intelligence regarding WMD in Iraq? Later accounts from LDP Secretary-General Yamasaki and Chief Cabinet Secretary Fukuda shed significant light on the answers to these questions. Yamasaki, who was well-versed in defense policy, had previously served as director-general of the Defense Agency during the Sōsuke Uno administration in 1989.

A series of high-level discussions and diplomatic exchanges in early 2003 elucidate Koizumi's decision-making progress for supporting the Iraq War, particularly the role played by North Korea. On February 22, he told Yamasaki, "I believe supporting the US is the only viable approach to address the situation in Iraq; North Korea is observing how Japan and the United States respond."[43] This statement explicitly shows that Koizumi's support was a strategic response to the North Korean threat. The next day, Yamasaki met with Powell in Tokyo and explained, "We will await the report from Executive Chairman Blix and UNMOVIC regarding WMD in Iraq until March 7. If military intervention is intended, a new UN resolution will be necessary."[44] Powell countered that "there is no longer any doubt that Iraq possesses WMD. Should a new UN resolution prove unattainable, we will proceed based on the authority of UN Resolutions 678 and 1441."[45] On February 26, Yamasaki relayed this information to Koizumi, who responded that he would "determine Japan's position on support on or after March 7," and that this would involve "notifying the US, the NSC, the Liaison Meeting of the Government and Ruling Parties, and the cabinet."[46]

On March 7, UNMOVIC reported that it had been unable to find any evidence of the continuation of Iraq's WMD programs, while also noting that it still possessed only limited information and that the Iraqi government should have provided additional documentation on its arms disposal efforts. On March 11, Koizumi informed the leaders of the ruling parties that Bush had reached out to him to request his support for the military intervention and that he had given it; the leaders of both the Komeito and the New Conservative Party (the LDP's coalition partners) expressed their agreement with this decision. After discussing the matter with opposition leaders on March 13, Koizumi secured approval from the Ruling Parties' Liaison Committee on Iraq–North Korea Affairs and the LDP General Council on March 18. He released an official statement affirming his support for military action on March 20.[47]

Notably, the Ruling Parties' Liaison Committee on Iraq–North Korea Affairs served as a cohesive institutional platform for deliberating policies related to both nations, highlighting their interconnected nature within the framework of Japanese strategic thought. The committee was established on March 12 in response to a proposal from Tarō Asō, chairman of the LDP Policy Research Council, with Yamasaki as its chair. The committee's primary objective was to prevent the proliferation of WMD by formulating a framework for implementing new legislation to facilitate postwar reconstruction efforts (in the case of Iraq) and to respond swiftly to developments in North Korea.[48] The committee illustrated the reality of the alliance, wherein Iraq and North Korea were utilized as strategic bargaining chips between the US and Japan. With its formation, the ruling parties had explicitly linked the two countries. In discussing the committee's mandate, Yamasaki stressed that the parties were "aware of the need to prevent the development of WMD," again highlighting their central role in Japan's justification of its support.[49]

But while the committee's formation suggested a coordinated policy response to the situation, later statements by a prominent figure within the Japanese government would provide a very different evaluation of Japan's approach to the situation in Iraq. Yasuo Fukuda, chief cabinet secretary at the time, remarked in an interview a decade later that "Koizumi was very interested in preventing a war. He endeavored to persuade President Bush to pursue a Security Council resolution passed with unanimous consent. Had that resolution been adopted, Iraq would have exhibited greater flexibility."[50] In seeking assistance from Japan, the Bush administration has insisted on the existence of WMD in Iraq. In another interview, Fukuda noted that "Japan did not have enough information to overturn the American view. That was the biggest problem."[51]

There were divisions within the Japanese government over how to approach the impending conflict. While the Prime Minister's Office was hesitant about a military engagement, MOFA appeared to accept the inevitability of armed intervention and emphasized the primacy of US–Japan relations. The Prime Minister's Office orchestrated diplomatic missions to European and Middle Eastern nations, aiming to "prevent the situation from escalating."[52] These efforts reflected the office's strategic vision of "unifying those in the international community who were skeptical or hesitant" about military intervention.[53] As critically noted by Fukuda, MOFA's approach was "inadequate" by comparison, with its institutional predisposition toward preserving the US–Japan alliance seemingly constraining its pursuit of diplomatic alternatives.[54] This tension between the Prime Minister's Office's desire for more robust peace initiatives and MOFA's apparent resignation to military action exemplified the complex dynamics within Japan's foreign policy apparatus during this critical period. Although Fukuda contended that the Prime Minister's Office was more inclined than MOFA to utilize diplomacy to avert war, that office—under the leadership of Koizumi and Fukuda—had already resolved to support the US and the UK should they choose to engage in military action against Iraq. On March 17, the day after Bush presented Iraq with an ultimatum, Koizumi declared his intention to support the US and UK if they resorted to force.[55]

Koizumi's rapid endorsement of military intervention following the outbreak of war reflected intricate strategic calculations. According to Fukuda, Japan's leadership acknowledged its limited capacity to influence American decisions regarding military action and that preventing the conflict was "not feasible."[56] Under Koizumi, the government prioritized the preservation of the US–Japan alliance and the personal diplomatic relationship that had developed between the two leaders. An additional strategic consideration was Japan's ongoing reliance on the US for regional security, as Fukuda explicitly noted that "there was the matter of North Korea; we continued to hope for American deterrence in that context."[57] He further remarked that while Iran and North Korea represented fundamentally distinct issues, the US administration seemed poised to "utilize the situation in North Korea as leverage over Japan to secure our consent for the war in Iraq."[58] In his view, American officials would naturally exploit any available strategic advantage and exhibited a "certain degree of resoluteness" in their diplomatic approach to ensure Japanese compliance.[59]

Fukuda's candid assessment suggests that Japanese officials were acutely aware of this diplomatic pressure point within the bilateral relationship. The decision to support military action transcended considerations of the US–Japan security partnership and the containment of North Korea. A critical factor in Japanese decision-making was its reliance on American intelligence regarding weapons of mass destruction in Iraq. As Fukuda notably articulated, Japan's endorsement was fundamentally "predicated on that information."[60] The Japanese government found itself in a position of complete dependence on intelligence from US and UN sources, without any independent verification capabilities. This information asymmetry created a problematic dynamic in which potential misinformation could obscure accurate threat assessment. As such, the validity of the primary casus belli—the presence of WMDs—was impossible for Japan to verify independently. Fukuda employed a particularly evocative metaphor to describe this predicament, comparing Japan to a "Daruma doll," a traditional Japanese doll that lacks all limbs and would therefore be severely constrained in its capacity to act autonomously.[61] This metaphorical paralysis extended to institutional levels, with even MOFA acknowledging its inability to provide independent verification of the WMD claims. Despite the absence of independent information sources, however, "Koizumi's political instinct was to convey support for the war as soon as the decision to initiate it was made. Ultimately, he proved to be correct."[62]

Fukuda thus acknowledged that Japan's rapid support for the war helped enhance its regional influence and bolstered the diplomatic relationship between Koizumi and Bush. But his retrospective analysis also reveals three fundamental deficiencies in Koizumi's strategic decision-making framework. First, Japan lacked the necessary resources to make independent decisions and instead relied on inaccurate information on WMD provided by the US. Second, the Koizumi administration adopted strengthening the US–Japan relationship as its primary criterion for evaluating this decision, neglecting the perspectives of American allies such as France and Germany who were critical of the war. Third, Japan faced a structural vulnerability that compelled it to depend on American deterrence for its security. Fukuda advocated for the use of force against Iraq as a means of ensuring that the US would deter North Korea. This rationale, however, suggested that Japan would be obligated to support all American military engagements, irrespective of their legitimacy. And while Japan's stance on North Korea favored a peaceful resolution, its position regarding Iraq was decidedly less amicable.[63] Taken as a whole, the situation highlights Japan's unresolved global alliance security dilemma, and the actions taken represents a negative legacy of the Koizumi administration.

RHETORIC IN CRAWFORD: "THE US–JAPAN ALLIANCE IN THE WORLD"

Following the initial hostilities in Iraq, Japan attempted to balance its concerns about North Korea with support for the reconstruction of Iraq. But substantial challenges would arise for the US-led post-conflict governance of the country, creating conditions that would influence the parameters of Japan's potential military deployment and its broader alliance commitments. The US and the UK established the Coalition Provisional Authority (CPA) on May 12, with Bush appointing Lewis Paul Bremer III as its director for reconstruction. The CPA incorporated the US Office of Reconstruction and Humanitarian Assistance, previously led by retired Lt. Gen. Jay Garner. In his eagerness to establish a democratic framework, Bremer deprioritized the restoration of infrastructure. Efforts to rebuild Iraq stagnated as he prohibited former military personnel from Saddam Hussein's regime—estimated at 300,000 individuals—from participating in reconstruction and also barred the 1.5 million members of the Ba'ath

Party, the ruling regime prior to the conflict, from holding positions of governance. And as the situation for Iraqi citizens did not significantly improve, public sentiment gradually grew critical of the US. This was exacerbated by US military operations in Fallujah, a stronghold for Sunni extremists in central Iraq. The lack of understanding regarding the historical and geopolitical significance of the city resulted in the destruction of numerous mosques, which alienated Muslim opinion. Consequently, various extremists fled Fallujah and established terrorist bases in Mosul and other northern Iraqi cities.[64] Despite Bremer's extensive career in foreign policy and counterterrorism, it was evident that he lacked expertise regarding the Middle East.[65]

On May 22, the UNSC adopted Resolution 1483, which included provisions for humanitarian assistance and reconstruction efforts in Iraq.[66] The Koizumi administration expressed its intention to deploy the SDF to Iraq to assist in rebuilding infrastructure and providing logistical support for American and British forces. However, as will be demonstrated in the upcoming discussion, the execution of these intentions proved to be more complex than initially anticipated.

The evolving dynamics of US–Japan relations culminated in a pivotal summit when Bush invited Koizumi to his private residence in Crawford, Texas, to engage in discussions on Iraq, North Korea, and other pertinent issues on May 22 and 23.[67] During the Crawford summit, Koizumi expressed strong approval for the bilateral alliance, specifically praising American initiatives in missile defense and nuclear arms reduction. He emphasized that MD constituted a critical component of Japan's defense strategy and asserted that bilateral collaboration in this domain would bolster the "credibility of the Japan–US alliance."[68] To underscore Japan's commitment, he pledged to accelerate its assessment of MD programs. Bush welcomed Koizumi's stance, stressing the American resolve to "work with Japan to confront the threat of WMD and the missiles that deliver them."[69] Demonstrating a strategic understanding of regional military deployments, Koizumi highlighted the concentration of American military installations in Japan, commenting that his hometown hosted "the largest US naval base in the East."[70] He recognized that Okinawa bore a disproportionate burden, housing "75 percent of American military bases."[71] While acknowledging the strategic significance of US force positioning in Japan, Koizumi advocated for the consolidation of military bases to mitigate the administrative and social pressures faced by Okinawa. Bush briefly indicated a "willingness to cooperate" on the issue; but there is nothing to suggest that the two leaders engaged in a detailed discussion of it.[72]

Turning to Iraq, Bush asserted that it was "very significant [for Japan] to make visible contributions wherever possible."[73] Koizumi reaffirmed Japan's commitment to the reconstruction of Iraq but also made sure to assert Japan's diplomatic autonomy. He stressed that Japan would "take the initiative" in determining how to contribute, rather than acquiescing to directives from Washington.[74] Concerning military support, Koizumi proposed deploying ASDF C-130 transport aircraft for humanitarian missions to Iraq's neighbors but also clarified that such operations would have to operate within the framework of existing Japanese law. He viewed this proposal as exemplifying Japan's proactive approach to "playing a positive role in the reconstruction of Iraq" within its legal parameters.[75] The scope of this proposal was limited to the nations adjacent to Iraq due to the constraints of the existing International Peace Cooperation Act; new legislation would be needed to authorize SDF aircraft to transport supplies directly to Iraq. He implied that he would pursue such new legislation and deploy the SDF to Iraq, remarking, "I want us to make a contribution worthy of Japan's national power."[76] While Koizumi assured Bush that Japan would cooperate with the US, he was aware of the legal barriers. This situation exemplifies Koizumi's prime minister–driven approach to making policy; some LDP members expressed reservations, but the matter had yet to be comprehensively debated in the Diet.

The two leaders also discussed the situation in North Korea. Trilateral talks involving the US, China, and North Korea had been held in late April, during which North Korea acknowledged, for the first time, its possession of several nuclear weapons. Bush expressed his disappointment at the progress made so far but also noted that China's evolving role as a responsible actor represented a "significant breakthrough."[77] Notwithstanding the limitations of the discussions, he remained optimistic that a peaceful resolution would be reached, although he stressed that such a resolution would require "strong action."[78] While emphasizing the importance of maintaining strategic flexibility, Koizumi advocated for distinct approaches to the situations in Iraq and North Korea. He acknowledged that a variety of policy options should remain under consideration but also took care to stress that "a peaceful resolution" was critical.[79]

In addressing the North Korean situation, Bush underscored the necessity of multilateral engagement, both bilaterally with South Korea and Japan, as well as through the broader five-party negotiations. He emphasized maintaining a cohesive diplomatic front while adopting an uncompromising stance on "nuclear weapons and drugs."[80] Bush expressed optimism regarding the potential for achieving "a peaceful resolution" through these diplomatic channels.[81] Koizumi reinforced this multilateral approach by emphasizing the imperative for coordinated action among "the three nations"—Japan, the US, and South Korea.[82] Expressing solidarity with Japan, Bush affirmed unequivocal American support on the abduction issue, emphasizing the necessity of "ascertaining the whereabouts of every single Japanese citizen" taken by North Korea.[83] Koizumi expressed his appreciation for Bush's support.

The two leaders' statements highlight a nuanced distinction between their strategies toward North Korea. While Koizumi regarded a "peaceful solution" as an intrinsic necessity, Bush asserted that that would require "strong action."[84] Koizumi emphasized that the response to North Korea had to be fundamentally different from that applied to Iraq. Bush's statement that he had "complete confidence in achieving a peaceful resolution" thus served to benefit Koizumi's position.[85] When Koizumi articulated that "dialogue and pressure are necessary for a peaceful solution," Bush agreed.[86] Koizumi committed to "further strengthening the enforcement of regulations on North Korea's illegal activities."[87] It was actually Deputy Chief Cabinet Secretary Abe, who accompanied the prime minister on the visit, who insisted on the necessity of exerting "pressure" on North Korea. The phrase "dialogue and pressure" would subsequently become a central tenet of Japan's approach to achieving a peaceful resolution. Bush and Koizumi also reached a consensus on the five-nation talks and the issue of abductions.

Finally, Koizumi turned to UN reform, contending that it was "important to enhance the authority of the UN following Iraq."[88] He noted that Japan contributed the second highest share of dues after the US and significantly more than the combined contributions of the four non-US permanent members of the Security Council. Even so, the Enemy State Clause remained in effect and that Japan was not even a non-permanent member of the Security Council. In light of these circumstances, Koizumi advocated for reforms aimed at strengthening the UN and expressed Japan's commitment to collaborate with the US in various capacities to achieve this objective.[89] Bush gave only a brief and noncommittal response, noting that he "completely understood" Koizumi's position and proposing future discussions on the matter, signaling a lack of American engagement with the proposed UN reform agenda.[90]

In any case, Bush's invitation to Koizumi to visit Crawford Ranch, his vacation home, exemplified the nature of their diplomatic relationship. Speaking to reporters afterward, Abe characterized the meeting as a milestone event coinciding with the sesquicentennial of Japanese–American relations. He emphasized that this historical context underscored the evolution of bilateral ties into what he described as a "truly global" partnership that he referred to as "the Japan–US alliance in the world."[91] This framing positioned the relationship as one of international, rather than merely regional, significance. Abe's deliberate inclusion of the term "global" and his articulation of the phrase "the Japan–US alliance in the world" are significant, as they served to justify Japan's support for US efforts in Iraq, which was clearly beyond the Far East as delineated in Article 6 of the Security Treaty. This indicated that Japan was evolving into a "normal country" capable of deploying the SDF overseas when aligned with US interests, signifying that the US–Japan relationship had matured into a global alliance.[92] Following the end of the Cold War, the US was perceived as the sole superpower; it found itself unable to sustain the international order independently, however, and increasing disagreements with its European allies raised American expectations of Japan.

A Unipolar System Without Consensus: The G8 Summit in Evian

Shortly after the Crawford summit ended, a major diplomatic gathering of world leaders exposed the international division over Iraq. A G8 summit was held in Evian, France, from June 1 to 3; it addressed critical issues pertaining to the global economy and Africa, and it hosted discussions on Iraq and North Korea. Unlike the summit of a year earlier, no communiqué was released following its conclusion. Instead, French President Jacques Chirac, the summit's chairman, issued a summary of the leaders' discussions.[93] This included a number of significant points about Iraq. There was a collective endorsement of the unanimous adoption of UNSC Resolution 1483, as well as a consensus that the focus should shift toward peacebuilding and reconstruction in Iraq. The objective was Iraq as a fully sovereign, stable, and democratic nation, at peace with its neighbors and experiencing positive progress. The announcement by the UN of a preparatory meeting for an international conference on Iraq's reconstruction was also positively received. As for North Korea, the nuclear issue was addressed in the context of non-proliferation. Support was expressed for the peaceful efforts of various parties to comprehensively resolve the North Korean nuclear situation and related issues, including unresolved humanitarian concerns such as abductions.[94]

The timing and context of the summit shaped its limited discussion of Iraq reconstruction. Convened only 10 days after the adoption of UNSC Resolution 1483, it occurred at a moment when numerous nations, including Japan, were actively seeking avenues to address the Iraqi reconstruction predicament. Consequently, the discussions refrained from exploring detailed specifics. In contrast, the chair's summary of the North Korean discussions explicitly referenced the abduction issue. Koizumi had previously addressed this matter at the Kananaskis summit a year earlier, but this marked the first instance in which it was specifically acknowledged in a G8 chair's summary. This was a notable diplomatic achievement for Japan.

During the summit's substantive discussions, key leaders showed contrasting approaches to regional security challenges. The agenda for June 2 included discussions on North Korea and Iraq. Bush stated that the proliferation of WMD was intolerable and expressed appreciation for China's commitment to North Korean denuclearization, as well as its collaborative attitude. In his address, Koizumi emphasized that North Korea required a distinct approach compared to Iraq. While acknowledging North Korea's antagonistic posture toward both Japan and the US, he expressed optimism regarding a peaceful resolution, citing the constructive involvement of China and Russia, both of which maintained positive relations with North Korea. He noted the "willingness to collaborate" on the part of the US, contingent on North Korea's cessation of nuclear development.[95] Koizumi also highlighted Japan's ongoing concern regarding the "egregious abductions" issue, suggesting that North Korea acknowledged that Japanese cooperation depended on a comprehensive resolution of both the nuclear and abduction matters.[96] Accordingly, Koizumi posited that, in contrast to Iraq, a peaceful resolution to the North Korean issue was imperative, while emphasizing that the abduction issue remained unresolved. He also expressed support for the recently announced "UN-led preparatory meeting" (scheduled for June 24) that would focus on reconstruction assistance for Iraq.[97]

Despite the absence of WMD discoveries in Iraq, neither French President Chirac nor German Chancellor Gerhard Schröder pursued that issue at the summit.[98] But neither leader supported the US's unipolar system. France's invitation to developing nations, including China and several African countries, to participate in the summit exemplified its multipolar perspective. According to France, the global order could not be dictated solely by the G8; the perspectives of developing countries also warranted consideration. Simultaneously, Bush's departure from the still-underway summit to engage in Middle East peace negotiations in Egypt was unprecedented and symbolized the growing rift between the United States and France.[99]

"Boots on the Ground": The Act on Special Measures in Iraq and the Neoconservatives

The discussions on regional security challenges at the Evian Summit were succeeded by notable advancements in Japanese domestic security legislation. On June 5, the Koizumi administration enacted three legislative measures pertaining to responding to potential military aggression, including the Armed Attack Situations Response Act, which aimed to prepare Japan for possible involvement in wartime scenarios. In 1977, Asao Mihara, director-general of the Defense Agency in the Takeo Fukuda government, had commissioned a study on contingency legislation; such legislation was again referenced at a meeting between Prime Minister Yoshirō Mori and Bush in March 2001 in the context of reinforcing the US–Japan alliance. The Koizumi administration expedited the drafting of the legislation in the wake of the September 11 attacks. Significantly, a shift in Japanese public opinion, prompted by revelations concerning North Korea's advancements in nuclear and missile technology, led to a rare consensus among both ruling and opposition parties regarding the proposed legislation.[100] Following the enactment of the three bills, the government proceeded to establish a new statute permitting the SDF to participate in the reconstruction efforts in Iraq. Although MOFA expressed a strong desire to deploy the SDF, the Defense Agency was more cautious, citing concerns related to national security.[101]

As Japan deliberated over its legal framework for SDF deployment, developments in Iraq signified progress toward the establishment of democratic governance. On July 13, the Iraqi Governing Council was established, comprising 25 members selected by the CPA, including the leaders of each major political faction. Bush welcomed the Council's formation as a crucial advancement in Iraq's transformation. He framed it as a transition from authoritarian governance to self-determination, emphasizing the objective of creating a "free and democratic Iraq."[102] He expressed optimism about collaboration with the Council to realize the vision of a prosperous nation coexisting peacefully with its neighbors. The Council was granted the authority to appoint ministers, approve budgets, and form a constitutional preparatory committee. Following the adoption of a new constitution, Iraq's new government was to be elected democratically for the first time. However, persistent attacks on American soldiers in Baghdad indicated that the country's situation remained precarious. The two eldest sons of former president Saddam Hussein were killed in a US military operation on July 22, and by July 25, 16 countries beyond the US and the UK had deployed security forces to Iraq, including Australia, South Korea, and Saudi Arabia. Another 18, such as Thailand and Ukraine, were in the process of planning similar deployments. Although Japan had not yet decided whether to deploy the SDF, it had pledged financial support of up to $100 million for the efforts in Iraq.[103]

Following the above developments in Iraq's governance structure and the escalation of international military commitments, Japan sought to formalize its contributions to the reconstruction effort. The Koizumi administration called a session of the Diet on July 26 to pass the Act on Special Measures Concerning Humanitarian Relief and Reconstruction Work and Security Assistance in Iraq, which would authorize the deployment of the SDF. The State Department expressed its satisfaction with the move. Koizumi's justification for the SDF's deployment was predicated on the assertion that they would be stationed exclusively in "non-combat zones," thus allowing for their deployment without engaging in the use of force; "non-combat zones" was a term specifically devised by the government to circumvent potential violations of the Japanese Constitution. Should the SDF provide logistical support in combat zones, such action would be construed as Japan exercising its right to collective self-defense, a practice explicitly prohibited by the Constitution. Koizumi had elicited derisive laughter during a party leader debate on July 23, however, when he responded, "I have no idea" to Democratic Party of Japan President Naoto Kan's question, "Where are the non-combat zones and where are the combat zones?"[104]

Due to the unity of the ruling parties, the Act on Special Measures in Iraq was enacted in approximately one month, alongside the Anti-Terrorism Special Measures Law. To facilitate bureaucratic guidance, regular consultations were held with LDP Secretary-General Taku Yamasaki, Komeito Secretary-General Tetsuzō Fuyushiba, and New Conservative Party Secretary-General Toshihiro Nikai. In conjunction with the Bush–Koizumi relationship, the trust among these three individuals constituted a critical pillar of the Koizumi administration. Assistant Chief Cabinet Secretary Kyōji Yanagisawa noted that Yamasaki, Fuyushiba, and Nikai had each experienced "Gulf War Trauma," the anxiety that Japan would face criticism similar to that which had resulted from its decision not to deploy the SDF during the Gulf War.[105] In a parliamentary democracy, the cooperation among ruling parties significantly influences the outcomes of governmental operations.

While internal party dynamics and "Gulf War Trauma" influenced Japan's domestic response to Iraq, American officials were also applying substantial pressure on Japanese leadership to ensure military participation in reconstruction efforts. Armitage urged Yamasaki and others to deploy the SDF to Iraq, invoking the expression "boots on the ground."[106] This phrase was initially coined by Deputy Secretary of Defense Paul Wolfowitz and was subsequently used by US Ambassador to Japan Howard Baker during his meetings with Chief Cabinet Secretary Fukuda and other Japanese leaders.[107] Identified as one of the "neoconservative Wilsonians,"[108] Wolfowitz advocated for the use of military force as a means to promote democratization and had been contemplating an attack on Iraq since the onset of the Afghan War. Under the guidance of Rumsfeld and Cheney, other neoconservatives, such as Under Secretary of State for Arms Control and International Security John Bolton, Under Secretary of Defense for Policy Douglas Feith, and Assistant Secretary of Defense for International Security Affairs Peter W. Rodman, played significant roles in the events leading up to the Iraq War. Rumsfeld and Wolfowitz erroneously believed that the reconstruction of Iraq would proceed smoothly.[109]

But while neoconservative officials such as Rumsfeld and Wolfowitz had anticipated a seamless reconstruction process, Powell's retrospective assessment offered a significantly different perspective on Iraq's post-invasion trajectory. In his memoirs, Powell reflects on the unstable conditions in Iraq following the fall of Baghdad. He notes that despite the toppling of Hussein's regime and the initial declaration of victory, the situation had rapidly devolved into chaos. He emphasizes the failure to establish control and authority, particularly in Baghdad, and points out that the expectation that Iraq would swiftly transition into a stable, democratically led nation was not realized. Instead, "a raging insurgency engulfed the country."[110] He observes that some senior administration officials underestimated the insurgents, dismissing them as mere "dead enders" who were expected to dissipate quickly; this expectation proved to be misguided.[111] Powell underscores that it took three years for the severity of the deteriorating situation to be fully recognized, which ultimately led to the decision to deploy additional troops in an effort to address the escalating crisis.

Concerns over the situation in Iraq and the implications of the Bush Doctrine were shared by government officials and American political scientists alike. Robert Jervis highlighted a fundamental contradiction between Bush's initial campaign rhetoric, which advocated for "a more humble foreign policy," and the later assertiveness embodied in the Bush Doctrine.[112] He concluded that "Avoiding this imperial temptation will be the greatest challenge that the United States faces."[113] Both senior administrative officials and scholarly observers increasingly acknowledged the inherent tensions between the US's articulated principles and its expanding military role in the reconstruction of Iraq.

Bush's Visit to Japan

International cooperation for Iraq's reconstruction gained momentum in October with the implementation of formal policy initiatives. The UN, the US, Japan, and other nations were compelled to deliberate on strategies for the reconstruction of Iraq, leading the UNSC to unanimously adopt Resolution 1511 on October 16. The resolution's principal components were articulated in paragraphs 13 and 14, which concentrated on the establishment of a multinational force.

Paragraph 13 stressed security and stability as essential prerequisites for the success of the political process and for the UN's effective contribution. It authorized the formation of a multinational force under a unified command to undertake all necessary actions to sustain security and stability in Iraq. This mandate included the establishment of conditions conducive to the implementation of a defined timeline and program, as well as the protection of the UN Assistance Mission for Iraq, the Iraqi Governing Council, interim institutions, and crucial humanitarian and economic infrastructure. Paragraph 14 urged member states to extend support under this UN mandate, which encompassed the provision of military forces to contribute to the multinational force referenced in paragraph 13.[114] The Koizumi administration issued a statement through Foreign Minister Kawaguchi reaffirming Japan's commitment to the reconstruction of Iraq. This noted that Japan had already pledged an immediate grant of $1.5 billion on October 15 and further emphasized Japan's proactive and autonomous approach to sustaining its support for Iraq's rebuilding efforts. The statement also outlined Japan's intention to offer assistance in accordance with its capabilities, adhering to the guidelines established by the Iraq Reconstruction Assistance Special Measure Law.[115]

The adoption of Resolution 1511 was followed by a significant bilateral meeting that strengthened US–Japan cooperation over the reconstruction of Iraq. On October 17, Bush conducted an unofficial visit to Japan to meet Koizumi en route to the Asia-Pacific Economic Cooperation (APEC) conference in Bangkok. Although the two leaders had met at Bush's private residence in May, this marked Bush's first visit to Japan since February 2002, nearly 20 months prior. The Bush administration was facing significant challenges in the reconstruction of Iraq following the conclusion of the war, and Bush expressed his "gratitude for Japan's support for reconstruction."[116] Koizumi's response was noteworthy, as he emphasized the necessity of addressing critical issues, including the fight against terrorism and the reconstruction of Iraq, by implementing "the Japan–US alliance in the world."[117] He also said, "I will demonstrate the strength of 'the Japan–US alliance' by tackling the challenges in Afghanistan, Iraq, and North Korea."[118] For Koizumi, supporting the reconstruction of Iraq served not only as way of showing Japan's commitment to international efforts but also as a strategic means to advance a North Korea policy favorable to Japan; he thus categorized both issues under the framework of the global US–Japan alliance.[119]

The leaders' dialogue then shifted to addressing shared concerns over North Korea's nuclear program and the issue of abductions. When Bush asserted that "the abduction issue is also an important matter when regarding North Korea," Koizumi expressed gratitude for the involvement of the US representative in raising this issue during the August Six-Party Talks.[120] When Bush's described China as "the key to the North Korean problem," Koizumi highlighted his previous diplomatic engagement with President Hu in St. Petersburg, during which they had "agreed to cooperate on North Korean issues."[121] He emphasized that "China has also played a significant role in the Six-Party Talks" and referenced the forthcoming bilateral meeting with China at the APEC summit.[122] Importantly, while Koizumi maintained differences with China on historical issues, he acknowledged the significance of China's role in shaping North Korean policy, a sentiment that was also shared by Bush. When Koizumi spoke of the need to "combine pressure and dialogue" in addressing the situation in North Korea, Bush responded affirmatively: "We are willing to work out a peaceful solution."[123] The pursuit of a "peaceful solution" to this issue was Koizumi's enduring objective.

The discussion transitioned to addressing long-standing concerns regarding US military installations in Japan, with particular emphasis on Okinawa. Koizumi highlighted the disproportionate presence of US forces in Japan, noting that 75 percent were stationed in Okinawa, and expressed a desire to address this issue to strengthen the US–Japan alliance. He also recognized the differences between the Japanese and American legal systems, particularly in cases involving American service members, as well as the divergent perspectives on the SOFA. He acknowledged that Ambassador Baker was acutely aware of these challenges but highlighted the need for more careful consultation among administrators in these cases.[124] Bush merely agreed to work closely with him on the issue, however. When Koizumi requested that Bush "give direction from within the US government," Bush responded, "I've already done [that]. Senior Director [James F.] Moriarty [at the NSC] is well aware of this [issue]."[125] Koizumi did not assertively pursue this matter, and his reaction to Bush was not strongly indicative of an eagerness to address the issue of US bases in Okinawa. When Bush proposed that the US and Japan collaborate on MD, Koizumi responded positively: "I believe that MD is also important from the perspective of Japan's exclusively defense-oriented policy."[126] Indeed, he had previously indicated in a May meeting with Bush that he would consider the issue; this would ultimately lead to a cabinet decision on the topic in December that also took North Korea and other nations into account.

Moving to Dispatch the SDF to Iraq

In the wake of these high-level bilateral discussions, Japan initiated concrete measures to deploy the SDF to Iraq. On November 14, Defense Secretary Rumsfeld met with Koizumi in Tokyo. Koizumi conveyed Japan's support for the use of force in Iraq and indicated the country's readiness to provide substantial assistance for the reconstruction efforts. Highlighting a key challenge for Iraq's postwar reconstruction (and a significant way in which that country's experiences differed from Japan's), he also noted that while "Japan continued to have a Diet" that functioned under General Douglas MacArthur after World War II, "Iraq does not have such a parliament."[127] He further contended that facilitating the successful reconstruction of Iraq would align with "Japan's national interest."[128] Rumsfeld reiterated the US's unwavering commitment to achieving victory in Iraq. While the meeting did not address the potential deployment of Japanese military forces to Iraq or the status of US forces stationed in Japan, the Department of Defense was cognizant of Japan's plans to dispatch at least 150 personnel by December, with an additional contingent of approximately 550 expected to follow in January or February of 2004.[129]

Rumsfeld's visit to Tokyo also focused on North Korea and regional security matters. The following day, he met with Defense Agency Director-General Shigeru Ishiba and emphasized to him that the US had not entered into any recent agreements with North Korea. He reassured his Japanese counterpart that the US would refrain from any agreements that might compromise its commitment to defend Japan against external threats. Ishiba conveyed his confidence in US policy and briefly addressed Japan's decision to deploy the SDF to Iraq.[130] During his visit, Rumsfeld conducted inspections of US military bases in Yokosuka, Yokota, Atsugi, Kadena, and Futenma; engaged in discussions with Okinawa Governor Keiichi Inamine; and instructed his subordinates to contemplate the realignment of US bases within the prefecture. However, the Koizumi administration prioritized troop deployment to Iraq at this point, relegating the issue of base realignment to a secondary concern.[131]

The assassination of two Japanese diplomats on November 29 starkly illustrated the deteriorating security situation in Iraq. The diplomats were en route from Baghdad to a conference addressing reconstruction efforts in northern Iraq when they were killed by unidentified terrorists.[132] But this incident did not deter the Koizumi administration from deciding on December 9 to deploy the SDF to Iraq. On December 18, Koizumi approved the implementation guidelines submitted by Ishiba in accordance with the Act on Special Measures in Iraq; these stipulated that the deployment would extend until December 14, 2004, and that the SDF would operate in non-combat zones, such as Samawah.[133]

The government's decision to dispatch the SDF was influenced by the situation in North Korea. On December 8, the day before the Koizumi administration's formal decision, Torkel L. Patterson, a senior advisor at the US Embassy in Japan, cautioned Yamasaki that "any shakiness in the

Bush–Koizumi relationship would disrupt the military balance in East Asia and could harm the future of the Six-Party Talks."[134] His comments were predicated on the belief that the alliance was interconnected with the SDF deployment and issues pertaining to North Korea, which was reflected in the government's decision-making process. A MOFA official revealed that Japan's Iraq policy was primarily driven by strategic calculations regarding North Korea, not Iraq itself. By backing "the US, which faced isolation concerning the Iraq issue," Japan sought to obtain American support for its positions related to North Korean concerns.[135] This strategic alignment constituted the principal motivation for Japan's endorsement of the US–UK military intervention in Iraq. MOFA also facilitated efforts to prevent neoconservatives, particularly Wolfowitz, from assuming control over North Korean policy, thereby enabling Powell and Armitage to retain influential roles within the administration. The deployment of the SDF was consistent with Japan's endorsement of the Iraq War and support for the Powell-Armitage faction's approach toward North Korea.

While Japan's Iraq policy was driven by strategic concerns regarding North Korea, Koizumi struggled to present a clear public justification for the SDF deployment. His inability to clearly articulate his rationale for the deployment at the press conference following the December 9 cabinet decision proved to be problematic. He failed to provide a convincing justification for this significant shift in security policy, which entailed sending the SDF into a war zone.[136]

Avoiding direct discussion of Article 9 of the Japanese Constitution, Koizumi instead emphasized the principle of international cooperation outlined in the Constitution's preamble. He highlighted Japan's obligation to serve as a reliable ally to the US, its sole ally. However, this position overlooked the broader international context; only 37 of the over 190 UN member states had deployed troops to Iraq. Of the G8, while the US, UK, Italy, and Canada had committed forces, France, Germany, and Russia had not. The Koizumi administration did not permit the SDF advance team to depart until December 26, a decision perceived by the US as excessively cautious, especially given that Japan had already sent survey teams to Iraq nearly 10 times. The US, who performed the role of caretaker for the team, grew increasingly frustrated. However, the Koizumi administration's postponement of the SDF's deployment can be regarded as prudent. With an LDP presidential election scheduled for September and a general election in November, the delay prevented it from becoming an electoral issue. Despite the delay, the government was cognizant of the symbolic importance of joining the international coalition in 2003, the same year that the war had started, and successfully achieved that goal.[137]

The purpose of Japan's repeated and meticulous pre-departure surveys was to identify a suitable "non-combat zone" as laid out by the Act on Special Measures in Iraq. This was defined as an area where no armed conflict would occur and where the constitutional prohibition on the use of force abroad would not be violated. The "non-combat" nature of Samawah—the area where the SDF was ultimately deployed—would prove to be more theoretical than actual; I will examine the conflicts there in chapter 6. Nevertheless, this fiction allowed Koizumi to make his well-known assertion that "the SDF is located in a non-combat zone."[138]

Detention and Interrogation of Saddam Hussein

There was a major development in Iraq as Japan finalized its preparations for the SDF deployment: the capture of Saddam Hussein. CPA Administrator Bremer announced the capture on December 13, and on the following day Koizumi expressed optimism about what this meant for Iraq's future. While also noting the event's importance for Iraq's security situation and rebuilding efforts, he emphasized his desire to see the Iraqi people use this moment to work toward establishing "free and democratic Iraq."[139] Koizumi doubled-down on Japan's commitment to assist Iraq, pledging maximum support for the establishment of an Iraqi-led government and the nation's reconstruction process. He emphasized the objective of creating "a government by the Iraqi people for the Iraqi people" and indicated that Japan would engage in diplomatic efforts to foster international collaboration.[140] Foreign Minister Kawaguchi similarly characterized the capture of Hussein as a pivotal event that could provide "new momentum" for Iraq to transcend "the oppression of the last quarter of a century," viewing it as a chance for Iraqi unity and national reconstruction.[141]

The Japanese government officially declared its intention to maintain and enhance its assistance for Iraq's reconstruction process, and committed to pursuing diplomatic initiatives aimed at securing "effective international cooperation" to support reconstruction efforts.[142] Bush attempted to arrange a phone call to Koizumi later on the 14th, but this could not be scheduled. Afterward, Koizumi sent a message to Bush expressing empathy for Bush's position while reiterating his own commitment to the reconstruction efforts in Iraq. He underscored the importance of their "relationship of trust" as a foundational element of his dedication to supporting Iraq's rebuilding initiatives.[143]

While celebrated by Japanese leaders as a pivotal moment for Iraq's future, the capture of Saddam Hussein also provided unexpected insights into the former Iraqi leader's final years in power that contradicted earlier assumptions. For Bush, the revelations that emerged from the interrogation of Saddam Hussein were likely surprising. John Nixon, CIA officer who investigated Hussein, reported that foreign policy decisions in Iraq had increasingly been made by hard-liners such as Vice President Taha Yasin Ramadan, Revolutionary Command Council (RCC) Vice Chair Izzat Ibrahim al-Duri, and former Foreign Minister Tariq Aziz.[144]

Nixon observed that, in his final years, Saddam became less involved in governance and more focused on personal interests, primarily writing. This shift had been noted in various reports but was not communicated to US policymakers until after the war. Saddam's lack of attention to governmental affairs and the absence of a coherent defense strategy for Iraq constituted significant issues. Nixon also critiqued CIA Director George Tenet for his eagerness to align with the White House, surrounding himself with agreeable staff and pressuring analysts to emphasize favorable reports even if they were based on weak evidence. Misconceptions between Bush and Hussein were not accidental; rather, they were the result of the CIA's proclivities. Nixon expressed profound regret regarding the war's devastating costs, both in financial terms and in terms of human lives, noting that these sacrifices had ironically led to an Iraq that was "infinitely more chaotic than Saddam's Ba'athist Iraq."[145] Hussein was executed in Baghdad on December 30, 2006, after being sentenced to death for the massacre of Iraqi Shiites in 1982 at a trial by the Iraqi Special Tribunal, presided over by Iraqi judges.

Two Cooperative Policies

Koizumi undertook two significant cooperative initiatives with the US as the year drew to a close. First, on December 19, the Koizumi administration resolved to implement a US-developed BMD system as a countermeasure against missile threats from North Korea and other nations. By enhancing their existing Aegis-equipped destroyers and Patriot surface-to-air guided missiles, along with improving their integrated operational capabilities, Japan would be able to establish a national BMD system. The government emphasized that the BMD system constituted a purely defensive mechanism designed to protect the lives and property of Japanese citizens from ballistic missile attacks. The administration also justified the decision to proceed with the system's development by noting that, in the absence of viable alternatives, this system was in perfect alignment with Japan's exclusively defense-oriented military policy.[146] The government's decision explicitly excluded use of the system to defend against missiles targeting third-party countries, which would have contravened the government's interpretation of the Constitution and the restrictions on CSD. From the perspective of the Bush administration, however, Japan's introduction of an MD system was part of a broader US missile defense strategy for the Asia-Pacific region, which also encompassed South Korea and Australia. As such, the overarching objective was to globalize the US–Japan alliance by integrating it into this MD network.

Second, when US Special Presidential Envoy James A. Baker III visited Japan and paid a courtesy call on Koizumi on December 29, Baker expressed optimism about reducing Iraq's debt. Baker had traveled throughout Europe before arriving in Japan, as many of the creditor nations associated with the Paris Club were located there. He had successfully secured an agreement to alleviate Iraq's debt and sought to persuade Japan, another significant creditor, to follow suit. In their meeting, Koizumi conveyed his recognition of the necessity to collaborate with other nations as a major creditor country and expressed Japan's readiness to forgive substantial Iraqi debt, emphasizing the nation's "global leadership role" in Iraq's reconstruction.[147] But he stipulated that this commitment was contingent on analogous actions from other Paris Club creditors, who would also need to concur with comparable debt reduction terms. While Koizumi acknowledged that debt reduction was essential, he also saw fostering a global understanding of "America's goodwill" in the context of the war as being of equal importance.[148] He expressed his belief in the sincerity of American intentions, but he also pointed out that leaders from countries such as France, Germany, and Russia held different perspectives. He stressed the importance of attaining the understanding of these nations, as well as from Arab countries, as to America's motives and goodwill, asserting that this was even more critical for the successful reconstruction of Iraq than the matter of debt reduction.

To further this objective, Koizumi appointed former prime minister Ryūtarō Hashimoto as an envoy to Europe, with the task of informing French President Chirac and German Chancellor Schröder of Japan's intentions. Koizumi undertook additional diplomatic initiatives in early 2004 to expand international cooperation and promote the discussions surrounding debt reduction. In February, he dispatched Special Advisor Yukio Okamoto to France and Germany, where they reached an agreement to establish a Japanese–French–German coordinating committee aimed at facilitating Iraq's reconstruction.[149] But even as Koizumi spoke of Japan's "global leadership role" in rebuilding Iraq, this assertion was premised on an optimistic belief that France, Germany, and Russia would eventually recognize "the American cause and its goodwill."[150] Nevertheless, it appeared improbable that the major European nations (with the exception of the UK) would exhibit the same level of understanding as Japan. As demonstrated in table 3.1, Japan continued to provide substantial assistance to the US anyway. Thus, while Koizumi pursued a diplomatic balancing act between European engagement and Japan's commitments to the US alliance, his concrete policies consistently reflected steadfast support for American objectives in Iraq.

Conclusion

2003 made Japan's strategic challenges in its alliance with the US evident, particularly when viewed through the lens of the global alliance security dilemma. Japan faced the difficult decision of supporting the US invasion of Iraq while simultaneously contending with North Korea's withdrawal from the NPT and its declared nuclear capabilities. The Koizumi administration endorsed the Iraq War largely to ensure continued American deterrence against North Korean threats, demonstrating how Japan's regional security concerns influenced its participation in conflicts far beyond its traditional sphere of interest. This decision highlighted the fundamental nature of the global alliance security dilemma, through which Japan found itself compelled to support American military actions, even when they lacked clear justification, to maintain alliance solidarity and security guarantees against regional threats.

The inherent asymmetry of the US–Japan alliance played a central role in shaping Japan's decisions. Japan's heavy dependence on US intelligence and security guarantees was evident in its acceptance of American claims about Iraqi WMDs without independent verification. While Japan contributed significant economic and logistical support through the deployment of the SDF to Samawah, it possessed limited leverage in shaping US

Table 3.1. Overview of Main Responses to the 9/11 Terrorist Attacks in the US

Date	US/Overseas	Japan	Self-Defense Forces
2001-09-12	UNSC Resolution 1368 adopted		
2001-09-19		"Japan's measures in response to the simultaneous terrorist attacks in the United States"	
2001-10-05		Bills for Anti-Terrorism Special Measures Law and amendment of the Self-Defense Forces Act submitted to the Diet	
2001-10-06			SDF aircraft dispatched carrying aid for Afghan refugees
2001-10-08	US and UK begin bombing Afghanistan		
2001-11-02	First Japan–US Coordination Committee meeting*	Anti-Terrorism Special Measures Law enacted	
2001-11-09			MSDF warships dispatched to collect information
2001-11-16	Second Japan–US Coordination Committee meeting (2001-11-14)	Cabinet adopts Basic Plan Regarding Response Measures Based on the Anti-Terrorism Special Measures Law**	
2001-11-20		Implementation guidelines for Basic Plan adopted**	

continued on next page

Table 3.1. Continued.

Date	US/Overseas	Japan	Self-Defense Forces
2001-11-25			MSDF warships dispatched for aid and assistance to victims (through 2001-12-31)
2001-11-29			Use of SDF aircraft in logistical operations for US bases in Japan begins
2001-11-30		Diet gives approval to above SDF activities	
2001-12-02			Supplying of US Navy warships begins
2001-12-03			Use of SDF aircraft in international logistical operations begins
2002-05-10	Third Japan–US Coordination Committee meeting		
2002-12-05			Aegis destroyer *Kirishima* dispatched
2003-03-20	US, UK, and others begin military action against Iraq		
2003-03-25			Area of operations changed
2003-05-01	Fourth Japan–US Coordination Committee meeting		
2003-10-10		Anti-Terrorism Special Measures Law amended	

Source: Adapted from Defense Agency, *Nihon no Bōei: Bōei Hakusho* [Defense of Japan: Defense White Paper] (Gyōsei, 2004).

* See figure 1

** The Basic Plan and its implementation guidelines were continually amended throughout the period covered by this table.

strategic decisions. This asymmetric relationship was further demonstrated when Japan supported the Iraq War despite lacking concrete evidence of WMDs, primarily to maintain US support for addressing the North Korean threat. The SCC meeting in December 2002 institutionalized this asymmetric dynamic by explicitly linking Iraq and North Korean issues, effectively constraining Japan's diplomatic autonomy.

The dual-structured security dilemma manifested as Japan navigated both its alliance commitments and regional security challenges. Internally, within the alliance, Japan had to assess the risks of entrapment versus abandonment, aligning closely with US actions while remaining cautious about being drawn too deeply into US-initiated conflicts. Externally, Japan's enhanced military cooperation with the US, particularly through the SDF's deployment to Iraq, risked provoking regional neighbors, especially China and North Korea. This dual challenge was particularly evident in Japan's efforts to maintain a peaceful approach to North Korean issues while simultaneously supporting military action in Iraq, illustrating the complex balancing act required to manage security dilemmas on multiple fronts.

As I will discuss in chapter 4, these themes would intensify as Japan deployed the SDF to Samawah and engaged more deeply in the Six-Party Talks on North Korea. The decision to designate Samawah as a "non-combat zone" would test the limits of Japan's constitutional constraints and alliance commitments, while continued participation in diplomatic initiatives would highlight the ongoing challenge of balancing regional stability with alliance obligations. My examination of these developments in chapter 4 will further illuminate the constraints and contradictions inherent in Japan's position within both its alliance with the US and the broader regional security landscape.

Chapter 4

The Struggle over Iraq and North Korea

2004

Samawah, Okinawa, Beijing, and Pyongyang

THE SDF IN IRAQ

Japan's unprecedented deployment of the Self-Defense Force to Iraq in 2004 served as the most practical manifestation of the globalized US–Japan alliance, heralding a notable evolution in the scope and nature of the countries' bilateral security cooperation and Japan's international military engagement. The Ground Self-Defense Force (GSDF) participated in reconstruction activities in Samawah, designated as a "non-combat zone," for a period of two and a half years; they provided medical assistance, supplied water, and worked to restore public services. Japan also continued to play a role in the reconstruction of Afghanistan. Japan's support for the Iraq War was predicated on the expectation that US forces stationed in Japan would serve as a deterrent against the North Korean threat. However, the unilateral redeployment of US forces from Japan to Iraq, conducted without prior consultation with Japanese authorities, diminished Japan's military potential in the Asia-Pacific region. Koizumi made a second visit to North Korea to address the issues of abduction and nuclear proliferation. Despite his efforts, his focus on the abduction issue—both domestically and on the international stage—and his desire to achieve a simultaneous resolution to both issues through the Six-Party Talks complicated the process of addressing the North Korean problem.

The result was Japan becoming increasingly dependent on the US for both its security and the resolution of the abduction issue. Meeting with Bush, Koizumi emphasized Japan's aspiration to become a permanent member of the UNSC. This request was significant, given the UN Charter's mandate for maintaining international peace and security and promoting global harmony. However, the US, which opposed reforms to the UN, recalibrated the US–Japan alliance within the broader context of the global reorganization of its military forces. Furthermore, the failure to uncover WMD in Iraq undermined Koizumi's support for the Iraq War and adversely affected his political standing in Japan.

The historic deployment of the SDF to Iraq was brought about through a meticulously coordinated series of military and diplomatic initiatives, beginning with key developments in early 2004. On February 8, approximately 60 members of a GSDF advance unit arrived in Samawah in southern Iraq to support humanitarian and reconstruction efforts. A month later, on March 3, an ASDF C-130 transport aircraft delivered aid supplies, including medical equipment, to an airfield near Nasiriyah in southern Iraq. In conjunction with the deployment of the SDF, MOFA dispatched approximately five diplomats to Samawah to facilitate coordination between the GSDF and the CPA, as well as with local organizations.[1]

Over the course of approximately two and a half years, 5,600 GSDF personnel engaged in humanitarian and reconstruction activities in Samawah, closely collaborating with the MOFA liaison office there. Members of the Task Support Unit were rotated every six months, while members of the Reconstruction Support Unit were replaced every three months. The Task Support Unit was responsible for coordinating with administrative agencies in Samawah, as well as with MOFA, whereas the Reconstruction Support Unit was tasked with implementing the actual support activities. The number and duration of SDF deployments, GSDF activities, and incidents in Samawah are detailed in tables 4.1, 4.2, and 4.3. The GSDF's involvement specifically encompassed medical care, water supply, public facilities, job creation, and capacity building for government agencies. During the course of these operations, personnel were exposed to artillery shells and unexploded rockets located in and around the GSDF camp in Samawah.[2] This situation illustrates that, despite operating in a designated "non-combat" zone, they were nonetheless subjected to the dangers inherent in armed conflict.

Table 4.1. SDF Unit Deployment Record

Branch	Unit	Size	Period of Deployment
GSDF	Task Support Unit (1st Contingent)	100	2004-01-16–2004-08-07
GSDF	Task Support Unit (2nd Contingent)	100	2004-06-26–2005-01-29
GSDF	Task Support Unit (3rd Contingent)	100	2005-01-08–2005-07-26
GSDF	Task Support Unit (4th Contingent)	100	2005-06-25–2006-01-29
GSDF	Task Support Unit (5th Contingent)	100	2006-01-07–2006-07-25
GSDF	Iraq Evacuation Force	100	2006-06-26–2006-09-09
GSDF	1st Iraq Reconstruction and Support Group (IRSG)—2nd Division (ID) (Asahikawa, Hokkaido)	500	2004-02-21–2004-05-31
GSDF	2nd IRSG—11th ID (Sapporo, Hokkaido)	500	2004-05-08–2004-09-05
GSDF	3rd IRSG—9th ID (Aomori, Aomori)	500	2004-08-08–2004-12-12
GSDF	4th IRSG—6th ID (Higashine, Yamagata)	500	2004-11-13–2005-03-05
GSDF	5th IRSG—10th ID (Nagoya, Aichi)	500	2005-02-05–2005-06-04
GSDF	6th IRSG—3rd ID (Itami, Hyogo)	500	2005-05-07–2005-08-27
GSDF	7th IRSG—4th ID (Kasuga, Fukuoka)	500	2005-07-30–2005-11-20
GSDF	8th IRSG—8th ID (Kumamoto, Kumamoto)	500	2005-10-22–2006-02-26
GSDF	9th IRSG—1st ID (Nerima, Tokyo)	500	2006-01-29–2006-06-03
GSDF	10th IRSG—12th Brigade (Shintomura, Gunma)	500	2006-05-07–2006-07-25
ASDF	Iraq Reconstruction Support Airlift Wing (IRSAW; 1st Contingent)	200	2003-12-26–2004-04-23
ASDF	IRSAW (2nd Contingent)	200	2004-03-17–2004-07-22
ASDF	IRSAW (3rd Contingent)	200	2004-06-11–2004-10-16
ASDF	IRSAW (4th Contingent)	200	2004-09-15–2005-01-22
ASDF	IRSAW (5th Contingent)	200	2004-12-16–2005-04-23
ASDF	IRSAW (6th Contingent)	200	2005-03-14–2005-08-28
ASDF	IRSAW (7th Contingent)	200	2005-07-12–2005-12-24
ASDF	IRSAW (8th Contingent)	200	2005-11-07–2006-04-22
ASDF	IRSAW (9th Contingent)	200	2006-03-08–2006-08-26
ASDF	IRSAW (10th Contingent)	210	2006-07-10–2006-12-25
ASDF	IRSAW (11th Contingent)	210	2006-11-08–2007-04-21
ASDF	IRSAW (12th Contingent)	210	2007-03-12–2007-08-25
ASDF	IRSAW (13th Contingent)	210	2007-07-09–2007-12-22

continued on next page

Table 4.1. Continued.

Branch	Unit	Size	Period of Deployment
ASDF	IRSAW (14th Contingent)	210	2007-11-12–2008-04-19
ASDF	IRSAW (15th Contingent)	210	2008-03-10–2008-08-23
ASDF	IRSAW (16th Contingent)	210	2008-07-14–2008-12-23
ASDF	Iraq Reconstruction Support Withdrawal Task Force	130	2008-12-06–2009-02-14
MSDF	Ōsumi-class tank landing ships (Kure)	150	2004-02-14–2004-04-08
MSDF	Murasame-class destroyer [escort] (Yokosuka)	170	2004-02-16–2004-04-08

Source: Cabinet Secretariat, "Iraq ni okeru Jindō Fukkō Shien Katsudō oyobi Anzen Kakuho Shien Katsudō no Jisshi ni kan suru Tokubetsu Shochihō ni motozuku Taiō Sochi no Kekka" [Results of Response Measures Based on the Act on Special Measures Concerning the Implementation of Humanitarian and Reconstruction Assistance Activities and Security Assistance Activities in Iraq], July 2009, MOD documents disclosed under the Information Disclosure Law, 2021.4.2–HonHonB15.

Notes: All personnel numbers are approximate. ASDF figures indicate the number of personnel deployed to Kuwait. Approximately 60 members of the Iraq Reconstruction Support Withdrawal Force were transferred from IRSAW (16th Contingent).

Table 4.2. Activities of and Results Obtained by GSDF Units

Activity Type	Details	Outcome	Results
Medical	*Provided guidance and advice on diagnostic and treatment methods to Iraqi physicians and other medical personnel *Provided medical technology guidance using medical instruments such as ultrasound diagnostic equipment provided by ODA *Provided guidance on transport techniques to ambulance crews in the Al Muthanna Governorate *Provided guidance on methods of managing pharmaceuticals in medical supply storage centers	Medical Technology Guidance offered 277 times (2004-02-19–2006-07-09)	*Post-partum infant mortality rate at Samawah Maternity Hospital was reduced by approximately one-third from before Japanese assistance and the establishment of a basic medical care foundation *Emergency medical capabilities improved

Activity Type	Details	Outcome	Results
Water Supply	Purified water from canals near residential districts and supplied water to water trucks. The water purification facility established by the ODA near the residential district began operating on 2/4/2005.	Approximately 53,500 tons of water were supplied (enough for 11,890,000 people) (2004-03-26–2005-02-04)	A stable supply of purified water became available
Restoration and Maintenance of Public Buildings	Repaired structural features (walls, floors, electrical facilities) in the Al Muthanna Governorate	36 schools (2004-03-25–2006-07-12)	Approximately one-third of schools in the Al Muthanna Governorate were repaired, improving the region's educational environment
Restoration and Maintenance of Public Buildings	Repaired and repaved residential roads used by local residents	31 locations, approx. 80 km (2004-03-30–2006-07-13)	Repairs and maintenance of major roads that are vital to life in the local area, leading to improved mobility
Restoration and Maintenance of Public Buildings	Other facility repairs and maintenance: *Medical facilities (Primary Health Center [PHC]) *Children's care centers and low-income residences in Samawah *Uruk water purification facility; Al-Rumaitha water purification facility *Cultural sites (e.g., Uruk archaeological site and Olympic stadium)	66 locations (2004-06-15–2006-07-12)	Improvement of the daily life environment in the Al-Muthanna Governorate

continued on next page

Table 4.2. Continued.

Activity Type	Details	Outcome	Results
Job Creation	*Use of local businesses in the effort to repair and maintain public facilities *Employment of local residents in jobs (e.g., interpreters and garbage collectors) in encampments	Daily maximum employment of approximately 1,100 people. Total employment of approximately 490,000 people.	
Training at Administrative Organizations	As a result of coordination with the relevant governorate administrative bureaus: *The needs of the relevant administrative bureaus were identified and plans for operations were drawn up *The Al Muthanna Governorate Construction and Development Council was established		The capabilities of the relevant administrative bureaus in the Al Muthanna Governorate improved

Source: Cabinet Secretariat, "Iraq ni okeru Jindō Fukkō Shien Katsudō oyobi Anzen Kakuho Shien Katsudō no Jisshi ni kan suru Tokubetsu Shochihō ni motozuku Taiō Sochi no Kekka" [Results of Response Measures Based on the Act on Special Measures Concerning the Implementation of Humanitarian and Reconstruction Assistance Activities and Security Assistance Activities in Iraq], July 2009, MOD documents disclosed under the Information Disclosure Law, 2021.4.2–HonHonB.

Table 4.3. Incidents at GSDF Samawah Encampment and in the Surrounding Area

Date	Details
2004-04-07	Discovered evidence indicating mortar ammunition impact at locations (one at each location) several hundred meters and approximately 1 km to the northeast of the encampment.
2004-04-29	Detected sounds of explosions twice in the vicinity of the encampment. Discovered evidence indicating mortar ammunition impact at two locations outside the encampment.
2004-08-10	Detected sounds of explosion. Discovered evidence indicating mortar ammunition impact at three locations outside the encampment.

Date	Details
2004-08-21	Discovered one unexploded rocket outside the encampment.
2004-08-23	Discovered evidence indicating mortar ammunition impact at two locations outside the encampment.
2004-08-24	Discovered evidence indicating mortar ammunition impact at one location outside the encampment.
2004-10-22	Discovered one rocket in an empty lot outside the encampment.
2004-10-31	Discovered evidence suggesting that a shell thought to be a rocket had pierced a storage container inside the encampment.
2005-01-11	Discovered one unexploded rocket in an empty lot inside the encampment.
2005-07-04	Detected several sounds that suggested shells in flight or shell impacts. In an empty lot inside the encampment, evidence of a shell impact thought to be a rocket was found in one location. Outside the encampment, four locations were found with evidence suggesting shell impacts thought to be the result of rockets.
2005-11-07	Detected the sound of shell launches and flight. To the southwest outside the encampment, evidence was discovered suggesting the possibility of the impact of one shell thought to be from a rocket.
2005-12-12	Detected the sound of shell launches and flight. To the west outside the encampment, evidence was discovered suggesting the possibility of one shell thought to be from a rocket.
2006-03-29	Detected the sound of flight of a shell of indeterminate type and evidence suggesting the possibility of one shell impact outside the encampment.
2006-07-15	Detected the flash and sound of the explosion of a shell of indeterminate type.

Source: Cabinet Secretariat, "Iraq ni okeru Jindō Fukkō Shien Katsudō oyobi Anzen Kakuho Shien Katsudō no Jisshi ni kan suru Tokubetsu Shochihō ni motozuku Taiō Sochi no Kekka" [Results of Response Measures Based on the Act on Special Measures Concerning the Implementation of Humanitarian and Reconstruction Assistance Activities and Security Assistance Activities in Iraq], July 2009, MOD documents disclosed under the Information Disclosure Law, 2021.4.2–HonHonB15.

The "Move" of US Forces in Japan to Iraq

Japan supported the Iraq War primarily to ensure the continuation of American security commitments and nuclear deterrence in response to escalating threats in Northeast Asia, particularly those posed by North Korea's advancing nuclear and missile programs. Whether Japan's military assistance in Iraq effectively contributed to bolstering, or at minimum maintaining, US military capabilities in addressing these security challenges is questionable, however, with analysis suggesting that it did neither. Instead of reinforcing Japanese defenses, the US reduced its military presence in Japan by transferring 3,000 Marines from Okinawa to Iraq in February, causing a nearly 20 percent decrease in the USMC presence in Okinawa. It was particularly atypical for such a significant number of Marines to be deployed from Okinawa for an extended period. Notably, although the US had ostensibly been planning this deployment to Iraq for over a year, the details were only disclosed when the Okinawan prefectural government inquired about the status of American forces. Six months later, an additional 2,200 Marines were transferred from Okinawa to Iraq.[3] As the USMC forces were relocated beyond the confines of the Far East, it is evident that this move was not solely intended to support Japan or function as a deterrent against North Korea and China. This action thus constituted a violation of Article 6 of the US–Japan Security Treaty, particularly as it occurred without prior consultation with the Japanese government.

The Japanese government adopted a permissive stance toward these unilateral US troop movements, however, eschewing any diplomatic confrontation over the absence of any prior consultation. Remarkably, MOFA took no action, classifying it as an operation that fell outside the scope of "combat operations from Japan to a third country" and therefore not subject to prior consultation under the existing protocols.[4] The SOFA Division of MOFA informed the *Okinawa Times* that "the U.S. forces are being moved for operational reasons" and that "prior consultation is necessary when bombers carrying munitions attack other countries directly; however, in this instance, they will be relocated to other Middle Eastern countries. This is not a scenario where consultation is required."[5] The ministry's US–Japan Security Treaty Division also asserted that the Marine deployment to Iraq was a "move" rather than a "military combat operation" as delineated in the Exchanged Notes to Article 6 of the US–Japan Security Treaty, thereby exempting it from prior consultation. However, given that the transferred USMC forces' involvement in Operation Iraqi Freedom was well publicized, MOFA's assertion that the deployment did not qualify as a "military combat operation" lacked persuasiveness.[6] In fact, the impression given was that MOFA was articulating the position of the US military, which sought to avoid having the deployment subjected to prior consultation.

When compelled to discuss these troop movements in a governmental forum, Japan's official response was intentionally ambiguous and exhibited a deferential attitude toward US military autonomy. Foreign Minister Kawaguchi told the House of Representatives' Committee on Security that "I had been given advance notice that 3,000 Marines currently in Okinawa would be deployed to Iraq. . . . We are not aware whether or not they will return to the US, Japan, or Okinawa after their mission in Iraq is completed. In any case, we are not in a position to comment on US military operations."[7] She also added, "We have heard from the US military that they will implement various temporary measures to prevent any decline in the deterrence provided to Japan."[8]

Kawaguchi notably refrained from commenting on specific measures and did not address Japan's role in the response. As indicated in table 4.4, US forces in Japan constituted the second largest contingent of troops stationed outside the US that participated in the conflict in Iraq, trailing only those in Germany and significantly outnumbering those in Italy, the UK, South Korea, and Turkey.[9] Given the number of Marines deployed to Iraq, some American observers, such as Kurt M. Campbell, senior vice president of the Center for Strategic and International Studies, suggested that alternatives to Henoko should be considered as replacements for Futenma Air Station. However, following his appointment as the Obama administration's assistant secretary of state for East Asian and Pacific Affairs, Campbell revised his position and endorsed Henoko as the most viable solution.[10]

The impact of the US military operations in Iraq extended significantly beyond troop deployments, influencing various military installations throughout Japan and engendering serious local concerns regarding involvement in the conflict. Okinawans expressed unease about the potential for being drawn into the conflict, which signified that Japan had become involved in the hostilities in Iraq.[11] The US military personnel dispatched to Iraq from Japan were not exclusively from Okinawa, however; they also originated from Yokosuka and Misawa. At the onset of the Iraq War, aircraft from the Yokosuka-based carrier *USS Kitty Hawk* conducted bombing operations over Iraq, while cruisers and destroyers stationed in Japan launched Tomahawk missiles. Marines from Okinawa were deployed to Iraq aboard the *USS Essex*, an assault landing ship based in Sasebo, and subsequently participated in the Battle of Fallujah, an operation that resulted in significant civilian casualties. And a large CH-53D transport helicopter, stationed at Futenma Air Station, crashed on the grounds of Okinawa International University, adjacent to the base, during sortie training for the Iraq War. Despite these incidents, the Japanese government maintained that it was unconcerned about the "move" of US forces within Japan during the Iraq War. This stance remained consistent even after the Democratic Party of Japan, led by Yukio Hatoyama, won control of the government in 2009.[12]

These wartime deployments and Japan's acquiescent response illuminated fundamental tensions within the regional security objectives of the US–Japan alliance and highlighted the superficiality of the slogan "the US–Japan alliance in the world" given North Korea's recent admission to developing nuclear weapons. Nevertheless, whether this "move" actually diminished deterrence against North Korea and China remains subject to debate. If North Korea and China recognized the potential for US forces in Japan to act independently from Japanese approval, their perception of threat would likely be increased rather than diminish. Japan's strategic reliance on the US presented a dual-structured security dilemma: Securing US deterrence against regional threats like North Korea also risked provoking China. This issue reflects not only the inherent asymmetry in the alliance but also the broader regional implications for Japan's defense and diplomatic strategy. I will further explore this dynamic in the conclusion to this book to underscore the complexities of the US–Japan alliance in Northeast Asia's shifting security landscape.

Table 4.4. Number of US Troops Stationed Outside the US in Operation Iraqi Freedom (OIF), Operation New Dawn (OND), and Operation Enduring Freedom (OEF), by Country

	Germany	Italy	Japan	UK	South Korea	Turkey
September 2005	8,300	3,000	1,700	700	300	1,400
September 2006	21,100	1,100	2,000	1,000	400	(ND)
September 2007	15,800	2,400	3,000	600	0	(ND)
September 2008	16,000	600	3,400	600	100	(ND)
September 2009	9,000	450	2,700	450	(ND)	(ND)
September 2010	10,510	2,520	3,530	530	(ND)	(ND)
September 2011	21,890	720	2,480	800	(ND)	(ND)
March 2012	5,150	250	3,170	570	(ND)	(ND)

Source: Strategic Information Analysis Office, the Defense Intelligence Division and the Japan–US Defense Cooperation Division, the Bureau of Defense Policy, "Number of U.S. Troops Stationed outside the U.S. in Operation Iraqi Freedom (OIF), Operation New Dawn (OND), and Operation Enduring Freedom (OEF) from Their Respective Destination Countries," March 17, 2015, MOD documents disclosed under the Information Disclosure Law, 2021.4.2–HonHonB14–12.

Note: ND = No data.

Reconstruction of Afghanistan and Iraq

As Japan's role in Iraq highlighted the complexity of its alliance dynamics, the country continued to make significant contributions to another major US-led initiative in the War on Terror: the reconstruction of Afghanistan. A pivotal moment in Afghanistan's transition occurred on January 26, 2004, when the nation adopted a new constitution under the leadership of interim President Hamid Karzai. This constitutional framework laid the foundation for Afghanistan's first direct presidential election, a significant advancement in the country's democratic development.[13]

On March 31 and April 1, a conference on Afghanistan was convened in Berlin, with representatives from 65 countries in attendance. Japan was represented by JICA President Sadako Ogata as prime minister's special representative. She also co-chaired the meeting alongside officials from Germany, Afghanistan, and the UN. US Secretary of State Powell also participated in the conference. In addition to acknowledging the adoption of the new constitution, the conference addressed several security challenges and committed to providing $8.2 billion in support over the following three years. During this period, Japan was advancing the "Ogata Initiative," a comprehensive local development plan formulated in collaboration with the UN,[14] encompassing the provision of temporary housing equipment through UN agencies (e.g., UNHCR and UNICEF) as well as the development of essential infrastructure and measures to counter landmines.[15]

The Bush administration regarded Japan's reconstruction efforts in Iraq and Afghanistan positively, and this was apparent in high-level diplomatic engagements, particularly during Vice President Cheney's meeting with Koizumi in Tokyo on April 12, 2004, in which he expressed his "deep appreciation for Japan's commitment to nation-building in Iraq," and specifically lauded "the Japanese SDF's work in Samawah."[16] In turn, Koizumi contextualized Japan's involvement within a broader global security framework, emphasizing that "it is important for the world as a whole to not allow terrorists to have WMD" across multiple regions, including Iraq, Afghanistan, and North Korea.[17] His response was deliberately intended to connect these nations through their shared concerns over the proliferation of WMD.

In her memoirs, Rice specifically emphasized the crucial contributions of Japan and South Korea in enhancing coalition operations in the southern and northern regions of Iraq, respectively, through their involvement in humanitarian missions and the training of Iraqi security forces. She noted that, for Japan, this operation represented "the first 'overseas' mission for Japan in the post-World War II period."[18] Coalition partners were deeply offended when critics dismissed their contributions as inconsequential, and American officials found it particularly troubling when military action against Saddam was characterized as unilateral, especially given that 33 different countries ultimately provided troops to support operations in Iraq throughout 2003.[19] The legitimacy of the coalition effort was further challenged when, in April 2004, revelations regarding the abuse of Iraqi prisoners of war by American soldiers at Abu Ghraib elicited profound shock worldwide, including in Japan and other coalition countries, particularly after military officials corroborated the authenticity of photographs broadcast by the American news program *60 Minutes*.[20]

CVID AND HEU: THE SECOND ROUND OF THE SIX-PARTY TALKS

As reconstruction efforts progressed in Iraq and Afghanistan, diplomatic initiatives continued to be taken to address North Korea's nuclear program. The second round of the Six-Party Talks convened in Beijing from February 25 to 28. Assistant Secretary of State James Kelly, representing the US, insisted that North Korea comply with the "complete, verifiable, irreversible dismantlement" (CVID) of its nuclear program. These countries also sought to persuade North Korea to acknowledge its intention to produce highly enriched uranium (HEU), but North Korea consistently denied this allegation. Although China had hoped to issue a joint statement, the disagreement over these issues meant that this particular round of discussions culminated only in a chairman's statement.[21] Competing priorities were the primary challenge in achieving CVID through the Six-Party Talks. While the talks' framework was designed to eliminate nuclear capabilities, North Korea's positions revealed more profound anxieties. The Chinese released a statement emphasizing that "CVID alone is not enough" and that "each party has its own concerns, including the DPRK's security concerns."[22] Most critically, Pyongyang's fundamental need for its "security concerns" to be "discussed and addressed" emerged as a significant impediment to reaching a meaningful agreement.[23]

The second round of Six-Party Talks in February 2004 revealed significant obstacles to achieving consensus, particularly around CVID requirements and North Korea's persistent denial of HEU production. The downgrade from a joint statement to a chairman's statement, coupled with

China's inability to persuade North Korea, perplexed the delegations from the other five participating nations. Throughout the talks, North Korea consistently rejected proposals for a joint statement and undermined China's role as chair.[24] According to Kelly, "China has been active as a participant and makes clear it will not accept nuclear weapons on the Korean Peninsula."[25] Wang Yi, a vice minister in China's foreign ministry, stated in the chairman's statement that the parties had "expressed their commitment to a nuclear-weapon-free Korean Peninsula" through the establishment of a working group and "agreed to take coordinated steps to address the nuclear issue and related concerns."[26] The diplomatic formulations of these statements, although seemingly indicative of progress, concealed fundamental disagreements over both the range of issues to be addressed and the sequence of concessions to be required from each party.

While other participants concentrated on denuclearization, Japan interpreted the chairman's reference to "related concerns" as a diplomatic opportunity; its delegation construed this language as specifically pertaining to the abduction issue. Kelly also aligned himself with this perspective. Before traveling to the talks, he met with Director-General Mitoji Yabunaka of MOFA's Asian and Oceanic Affairs Bureau in Seoul on February 23 and voiced support for Japan's position on the abduction issue.[27] A meeting between Yabunaka and North Korean Deputy Foreign Minister Kim Kye-gwan after the talks revealed significant discord between the two parties. Yabunaka pressed for an investigation into the 10 abductees who remained unaccounted for, while Kim contended that "Japan broke its promise, and it must return the five abductees who returned to Japan from North Korea."[28] Japan asserted that it had no obligation to return the abductees, who had previously faced considerable challenges in their initial departure from North Korea. Despite this dispute, Koizumi's second visit to North Korea later that spring would facilitate the return of additional abductees.

Koizumi's Second Visit to North Korea

Following the mixed results of the second round of Six-Party Talks, Koizumi again pursued direct bilateral engagement with North Korea in an attempt to address the unresolved issues between the two nations. On May 22, he visited Pyongyang for his second meeting with Kim Jong-il; this occurred between the second and third rounds of the Six-Party Talks. This was their first encounter in 18 months, and the two leaders engaged in candid discussions of the abduction, nuclear, and missile issues. That same evening, another five Japanese nationals were repatriated to Japan. When Koizumi requested that North Korea investigate the cases of the abductees previously reported to be dead or missing (including Megumi Yokota), Kim promised to reevaluate their cases. Charles Jenkins, the spouse of one of the abductees, Hitomi Soga, opted to remain in North Korea with the couple's two children. Jenkins was a former US Army sergeant who had defected to North Korea in 1965. Kim indicated that he would leave the decision up to Jenkins, implying a reluctance to mitigate any potential legal challenges with the US. Koizumi was able to communicate with Jenkins and his daughters, but Jenkins remained apprehensive that returning to Japan could result in his extradition to the US for desertion. Because of this, Japan and North Korea negotiated terms for Jenkins and Soga to meet in a third country.[29]

The second segment of their discussions concerned disarmament. Koizumi asserted that North Korea's advancement of nuclear weapons was unequivocally unacceptable and emphasized that comprehensive nuclear disarmament, accompanied by international verification, was essential. He advocated for proactive measures to be implemented within the framework of the Six-Party Talks. Kim concurred that the ultimate objective was the denuclearization of the Korean Peninsula and acknowledged that a nuclear freeze would necessarily entail verification, as it represented the initial step toward denuclearization. He also declared that North Korea would pursue a peaceful resolution through the Six-Party Talks. The two leaders also reaffirmed the moratorium on missile launches. Koizumi expressed his conviction that diplomatic relations would be normalized once the various issues were thoroughly addressed. He pledged to provide 250,000 tons of food and $10 million worth of medicine as humanitarian assistance, to be administered through international organizations, contingent upon North Korea's compliance with the Japan–DPRK Pyongyang Declaration.[30] After the meeting, Koizumi stated at a press conference that the objective of his visit had been to reaffirm "the vital importance of sincerely implementing the Japan–DPRK Pyongyang Declaration."[31]

What were the implications of Koizumi's second diplomatic mission to North Korea, and how should its outcomes be assessed? The visit resulted in several concrete outcomes, including the repatriation of five abductees to Japan and Kim's renewed commitment to the denuclearization of the Korean Peninsula through peaceful negotiations within the framework of the Six-Party Talks. However, despite Kim's assurances that the cases of the 10 abductees previously reported deceased or missing would be investigated, no substantial progress was achieved on that front. Moreover, North Korea's nuclear weapons development program continued unabated in violation of the Pyongyang Declaration. Notably, Koizumi's emphasis on addressing both the abduction issue and security concerns through parallel diplomatic channels—the bilateral Japan–DPRK dialogue and the multilateral Six-Party Talks—ultimately complicated efforts to secure breakthrough agreements with North Korea.[32] And while Yabunaka's participation in the mission alongside Koizumi should have theoretically bolstered his position as Japan's representative in the Six-Party Talks, Japan increasingly relied on the US for security assurances against North Korea and assistance in resolving the abduction issue.[33]

In the wake of his Pyongyang visit, Koizumi aimed to cultivate international endorsement for Japan's approach to North Korea by engaging with other global leaders. On June 9, he met with Russian President Vladimir Putin during the G8 summit held at Sea Island and discussed North Korean issues. During the plenary session of the summit, Putin praised Koizumi's diplomatic initiative on North Korea. And when Koizumi expressed gratitude for Putin's "understanding and support," the Russian leader called the visit a "great achievement" and advocated for the revitalization of Japanese–Russian collaboration within the framework of the Six-Party Talks.[34] The specifics of the Sea Island summit will be examined further in this chapter.

THE THIRD ROUND OF THE SIX-PARTY TALKS

The third round of the Six-Party Talks, held in Beijing from June 23 to 26, marked another crucial phase in the ongoing negotiations over North Korea's nuclear program. Based on the positive outcomes of Koizumi's meeting with Kim a month earlier, the Japanese delegation approached this round with the intention of making significant contributions. However, the most prominent figures in these negotiations would be Assistant Secretary of State Kelly and Deputy Foreign Minister Kim rather than Yabunaka. The discord surrounding the nuclear weapon issue predominantly involved the US and North Korea, particularly after North Korea perplexed the American, Japanese, and South Korean representatives by indicating that it had potentially carried out a nuclear test. The divergence between North Korea's position and those of the other participating countries primarily centered on the extent of the verification procedures and which preliminary measures were to be implemented, specifically whether uranium enrichment was to be included or not. While North Korea hoped for an agreement that would only freeze its nuclear program, the US, Japan, and South Korea advocated for a comprehensive framework for that program's complete dismantlement.[35]

Yabunaka used Kim Jong-il's statements to Koizumi in May to robustly confront the North Korean representatives. He stressed that the leader of North Korea had committed to "the denuclearization of the Korean Peninsula" and acknowledged that the "first step" toward that would "naturally come with verification."[36] Deputy Foreign Minister Kim had little choice but to heed Yabunaka's remarks, as the latter had been present when Kim Jong-il had made them. However, Japan also complicated the situation by highlighting the abduction issue during the discussions, with Yabunaka reaffirming Japan's commitment to provide economic cooperation only once the nuclear, missile, and abduction issues had been comprehensively resolved (in accordance with the principles outlined in the Pyongyang Declaration).[37] Historically, Japan had supported North Korean energy assistance, but only indirectly through South Korea and other nations. It now expressed a willingness to participate directly in international energy assistance, but this was conditional on North Korea freezing its nuclear program, disclosing all relevant information, and undergoing verification.

Given the complex and contentious nature of the negotiations, the parties opted to forgo a joint communiqué in favor of a broadly worded chairman's statement. This statement merely acknowledged that the discussions had been "constructive, pragmatic and substantive" and reaffirmed the participants' commitment to "the goal of denuclearization of the Korean Peninsula," while underscoring the importance of taking initial steps toward this objective.[38] Notably, the statement did not reference a nuclear freeze or the dismantling of any weapons. Following the conclusion of the talks, Yabunaka held a press conference where he gave Japan's response to the round. In his remarks, he recognized that North Korea's proposal for a "nuclear freeze" as a preliminary measure marked the first instance where North Korea's "statements [were] finally beginning to align" with those of the other participants.[39] But he adopted a cautious stance overall, stressing that North Korea's genuineness would "depend on the extent of the freeze and the specific proposals they present in the forthcoming days concerning nuclear dismantlement."[40] In essence, while Yabunaka expressed a degree of approval regarding North Korea's response, he refrained from making any definitive judgments about their true intentions and the feasibility of any concrete measures. The adoption of a joint communiqué would have to wait until the fourth round of talks.

The UNSC and the Comprehensive Report on WMD

UNSC Resolution 1546 and the Iraqi Interim Government

At the same time that the multilateral negotiations over North Korea's nuclear program were making progress under the Six-Party framework, diplomatic initiatives aimed at addressing global security challenges increasingly came to utilize the UNSC's formal institutional channels. On June 8, the UNSC unanimously adopted Resolution 1546, which transferred Iraqi sovereignty from the CPA to the Iraqi Interim Government, thereby securing international recognition for the new government and concluding the occupation of Iraq by June 30 at the latest. Following the transfer of sovereignty, the CPA—previously responsible for guaranteeing the legal status of the SDF and other foreign military forces present in the country—would be dissolved. However, the newly established government had consented to the continued presence of a multinational force in Iraq. As such, it was advantageous for the US that each nation's garrison gain a new legal status by integrating with this force.[41]

The leaders of the US and Japan used the G8 summit at Sea Island, Georgia, as an opportunity to reinforce bilateral relations and carry out discussions over significant issues of mutual interest. When Bush and Koizumi met from 12:30 to 1:45 p.m. on June 8, Koizumi indicated that he would continue the SDF's deployment following the transfer of sovereignty in a manner that would be welcomed by the Iraqi Interim Government. This statement that the SDF would be joining the multinational force predated even the passage of UNSC Resolution 1546. They also discussed Koizumi's recent trip to North Korea and the case of Hitomi Soga, one of the abductees. Bush expressed his support for Koizumi's efforts regarding the abduction issue and was briefed on Soga's husband, Jenkins, who remained in North Korea. However, he did not clarify whether Jenkins would be granted immunity from prosecution should he enter Japan. Koizumi maintained that continued cooperation with the US in Iraq was essential for bringing resolution of the abduction issue closer. When

Koizumi turned to Security Council reform, linking the topic to Iraq, Bush unequivocally stated that Japan should be a permanent member, declaring, "We are for you."[42]

Koizumi's argument was based on the premise that Japan's substantial economic support for Iraq warranted a more prominent voice in UN decision-making processes, given the critical role of the UN in the reconstruction process. His use of the phrase "the right to speak at the UN" was salient in illustrating his attempt to connect Japan's financial commitments with the enhanced international authority that being a permanent member of the UNSC would provide.[43]

After speaking with Bush, Koizumi participated in a series of diplomatic engagements with other world leaders to secure their support for Japan's involvement in Iraq. Meeting with Tony Blair from 5:05 to 5:55 p.m. that same day, he expressed satisfaction with the recently approved Resolution 1546 and specifically commended Blair's role in facilitating its unanimous passage, remarking that it was a "tribute to your efforts."[44] Blair reciprocated by commending Koizumi for demonstrating "great courage and conviction" in his sustained support for the reconstruction of Iraq.[45] Koizumi then spoke with French President Chirac from 6:15 to 7:00 p.m. During their discussion, Chirac ascribed the resolution's unanimous approval to American diplomacy, particularly noting that the US's readiness to adopt "international cooperation" had been instrumental in attaining this consensus.[46]

Koizumi continued his diplomatic efforts in the following days, meeting with King Abdullah II of Jordan and Chancellor Schröder of Germany to promote collaboration on the reconstruction of Iraq. He met with the king for approximately half an hour at 8:30 a.m. on the 9th and outlined Japan's diplomatic approach, emphasizing its desire to build stronger ties with Arab nations, particularly in the context of Iraq. As he did so, he specifically highlighted the significance of Japan's "friendly relations" with Jordan as a foundation for broader regional engagement.[47] King Abdullah responded by affirming Jordan's commitment to supporting Japan's military presence, stressing his country's role as "a friend of Japan" and its readiness to offer any necessary assistance to facilitate the SDF deployment.[48] Jordan served as a base for Japanese operations supporting Iraqi reconstruction, including the provision of medical assistance and the training of Iraqis in electrical engineering.[49] When Koizumi met with German Chancellor Schröder at 9:30 a.m. on the following morning, Schröder expressed an interest in collaborating with Japan on Iraq's reconstruction. The two then discussed ongoing training programs for Iraqi police officers. Schröder also expressed a desire to address Iraq's debt through the Paris Club, to which Koizumi concurred. Thus, despite Japan and Germany's differing stances regarding the outbreak of the war, they were able to collaborate in the areas of policing and debt reduction.[50]

Bilateral meetings to build support for Japan's role in Iraqi reconstruction were not Koizumi's only focus during the summit, however; he also worked on North Korean issues. Having visited North Korea just a month earlier, he took the initiative in this area, securing support from other nations for comprehensive solutions to the nuclear and abduction issues.[51] As chair of the summit, Bush delivered a statement on June 10 that highlighted two key achievements. First, he emphasized that the G8 had collectively endorsed UNSC Resolution 1546 and given their unified support for Iraq's sovereignty and reconstruction efforts. Second, he invoked the group's endorsement of the Six-Party framework as a means for achieving a resolution to the North Korean nuclear crisis while also advocating for diplomatic efforts aimed at achieving "a comprehensive solution" to the nuclear issue and other security concerns, including "humanitarian issues, such as the abductions."[52] This statement demonstrated that Koizumi had successfully elevated Iraq's reconstruction and North Korean concerns—including the abduction issue—as priorities for coordinated international action.

The successful conclusion of the G8 summit was followed by a significant milestone in Iraq's political transition, as the nation prepared for the transfer of sovereignty. The Iraqi Interim Government was inaugurated on June 28, 2004, with President Ghazi al-Yawar, Prime Minister Ayad Allawi, and other officials taking their oaths of office during the ceremony.[53] As previously noted, the CPA had administered operations in Iraq since UNSC Resolution 1483 in May 2003. The Iraqi law enacted in March 2004, along with UNSC Resolution 1546 in June 2004, facilitated the transfer of governmental authority to the Iraqi Interim Government. Koizumi congratulated Allawi by letter on his appointment and outlined Japan's position regarding its involvement in Iraq. He stated that, in accordance with UNSC Resolution 1546 and the request from the Interim Government, Japan was dedicated to actively supporting Iraq's reconstruction efforts, both financially and through personnel, likening the two to essential components of a unified entity. He emphasized that the SDF would continue its role within the multinational force, concentrating on humanitarian and reconstruction efforts in accordance with Japan's specific legislation pertaining to activities in Iraq. He assured Allawi that there would be close collaboration with him and the Interim Government to ensure that the SDF's operations aligned with the expectations and approval of the Iraqi populace.[54]

Deputy Secretary of State Armitage also held a press conference at the National Press Club in Washington, DC, on June 28, during which he expressed his high regard for Japan's contributions to Iraq and reaffirmed that the US would persist in its role in coordination with the international community, including the UN.[55] These coordinated statements from both Tokyo and Washington reinforced the international legitimacy of Japan's ongoing military presence in Iraq while underscoring the robust bilateral support for Japan's enhanced role in the nation's reconstruction efforts.

The Global Posture Review and Japan

In response to growing global security concerns, President Bush outlined a strategy to reevaluate the US military presence worldwide, emphasizing collaboration with allied nations to address emerging threats. On November 25, 2003, he had announced plans to increase dialogue with Congress and America's allies over the deployment of American military forces overseas. His statement highlighted the need to adjust to emerging threats, specifically referencing "rogue nations, global terrorism, and weapons of mass destruction."[56] This announcement was part of a broader review of US global military deployments that took shape over the course of 2004. Formal discussions between the US and Japan on the issue were postponed until after Japan's House of Councillors election on July 11. Shortly after they began, however, tensions escalated when a US Marine Corps CH-53D helicopter crashed into the main building of Okinawa International University on August 13, eliciting widespread public outrage in Japan.

Notwithstanding this incident, Bush gave a speech on August 16 in which he spoke on the rationale behind his administration's reorganization and reduction of US forces stationed abroad. He outlined how the new strategy would enhance the US's military capabilities for contemporary warfare while fostering stronger international partnerships "to better preserve the peace."[57] He emphasized that the reorganization would alleviate burdens on service members and their families. The plan called for the repatriation of "60,000 to 70,000 uniformed personnel" over the following decade while still maintaining a robust overseas presence.[58] Despite the comprehensiveness of his address, he notably omitted any mention of a reduction of US forces in Japan, potentially due to their critical role in the American military deployment across Asia. The proposals put forth by the Bush administration in August 2004 on the transformation of American military deployments were designated as the Global Posture Review (GPR).[59]

The US planned to relocate a portion of its military headquarters to Japan in response to the "arc of instability" that extends from Africa to the Middle East and Southeast Asia. In an interview on strategic priorities, Admiral Blair of the US Pacific Command identified Japan as the foremost partner, followed by South Korea and subsequently other Asian nations. He underscored the importance of maintaining a "stable US military presence in Japan" as a means of serving America's persistent strategic interests, particularly in contexts where facilities were collaboratively utilized by US forces and the SDF, such as at "Yokosuka, Misawa, Sasebo, and Yokota."[60] He acknowledged that although the ongoing discussions regarding the realignment of US forces in Japan might not result in significant reductions of the US military presence in Okinawa, efforts to alleviate the burdens on Okinawa must persist, all while ensuring the operational readiness of US forces was maintained.[61]

Building on these developments in US military strategy, Koizumi took advantage of his attendance at the UNGA to meet with Bush to directly discuss bilateral security concerns with him. The two leaders' conversation on September 21 covered Iraq, the realignment of US military forces, North Korea, UN reform, and various other issues, thereby reaffirming the cooperation between the US and Japan on these matters. Of the topics addressed, the global reorganization of the US military was particularly significant. Bush stated that the realignment was intended to create a capable, robust, and efficient military. Koizumi expressed his commitment to closely collaborating with the US on the issue of realigning American forces and suggested that the US consider alleviating the burden on Okinawa and other local populations while still maintaining a deterrent capability. He also informed Bush that a recent helicopter crash had caused alarm among the residents of Okinawa, where the majority of US military facilities in Japan were situated. In response, Bush indicated that he would strive to achieve more effective deterrence through discussions concerning realignment, which would also alleviate the burden on local communities.[62]

Koizumi's security policy was not confined solely to relations with the US, however. Later that same day, he convened a G4 summit on UN reform with the leaders of Brazil, India, and Germany. During the summit, Koizumi advocated for UNSC reform, emphasizing that nations demonstrating both the commitment and capability to support global peace should be included in key decision-making processes. He specifically called for the number of "both permanent and non-permanent seats" on the Council to be increased.[63]

He lacked a comprehensive global strategy akin to the GPR, however, which effectively positioned tactics at the regional level. In Japan, there were two predominant schools of thought on the GPR: the "small package" and the "total package" perspectives.[64] The "small package" view, which was primarily held within MOFA, opposed extensive Japanese involvement in the reorganization of American forces, particularly the relocation of the Headquarters of the US Army I Corps to Camp Zama in Kanagawa Prefecture. This opposition stemmed from Japan's ongoing difficulties in deploying the SDF to Iraq. Conversely, the "total package" perspective, which advocated for enhanced cooperation with the US and supported the deployment of US forces in Japan, was championed by the Defense Agency. This viewpoint was further endorsed by the Council on Security and Defense Capabilities, an advisory body to the prime minister. Frequently overshadowed by MOFA in the policy-making process, the Defense Agency sought to elevate its status by collaborating with the American military realignment. Koizumi discussed the deployment levels of US troops in Japan with Bush on November 20 while the two were attending the APEC meeting in Chile. His position aligned more closely with the "total package" approach advocated by the Defense Agency.[65]

Japan's National Defense Program Outline for 2005, adopted by the Koizumi administration on December 10, notably explicitly referenced the modernization of Chinese military capabilities and maritime operations for the first time. The outline also addressed issues of terrorism and the North Korean threat, proposing measures to strengthen the US–Japan security framework and facilitate the regular overseas deployment of the SDF.[66] Overall, the outline indicated an intention for the SDF to be increasingly integrated into US military operations, signaling the development of a robust US–Japan global alliance. Should American and Japanese military forces become more closely integrated, Japan would face heightened challenges in declining to support US military engagements in which it might not wish to participate.

Table 4.5. Japanese Positions and Advocates of the Department of Defense's Global Posture Review

Position	"Small Package"	"Total Package"
Objectives	Opposition to the relocation of US Army I Corps headquarters to Camp Zama; unwillingness to relocate US forces in Japan	Strengthening cooperation with the US and promoting the relocations of US Forces in Japan
Politicians	Hosoda, Koizumi, Machimura, Ohno	Hosoda, Koizumi, Machimura, Ohno
Bureaucrats	Masahiro Futahashi (Deputy Chief Cabinet Secretary) Yukio Takeuchi (Vice-Minister for Foreign Affairs)	Takemasa Moriya (Vice-Minister of Defense) Tsuneo Nishida (Director-General, Foreign Policy Bureau)
Advisory Council	(nothing)	"Council on Security and Defense Capabilities" or "Araki Report"

Sources: Compiled from: Council on Security and Defense Capabilities, "'Anzen Hoshō to Bōeiryoku ni kan suru Kondankai' Hōkokusho: Mirai e no Anzen Hoshō Bōeiryoku Vision" [The Council on Security and Defense Capabilities Report: Japan's Visions for Future Security and Defense Capabilities], October 2004, www.kantei.go.jp/jp/singi/ampobouei/dai13/13siryou.pdf; Taketsugu Sato and Yoshiyuki Komurata, "Tsuyomaru Nichi-Bei 'Dōshō Imu' Bei Daiichi Gundan Shireibu Zama e Iten" [Growing Differences Between Japan and the US: US First Army Headquarters to Relocate to Zama], *Asahi Shimbun*, April 13, 2005; Yoshinori Ohno, *Warm Heart: Kozokaikaku no Ato ni Kurumono* [Warm Heart: What Comes After the Structural Reform] (Parade, 2006), 169–73; Tsuyoshi Sunohara, *Dōmei Henbō: Nichi–Bei Ittaika no Hikari to Kage* [Alliance Transformed: Light and Shadow of the Integration of Japan and the United States] (Nihon Keizai Shimbun Shuppansha, 2007); Takemasa Moriya, *"Futenma" Kosho Hiroku* [Secret Records of the "Futenma" Negotiations] (Shinchosha, 2012).

THE COMPREHENSIVE REPORT ON WMD

As Japan and the US worked to reinforce their military cooperation through the GPR, the two countries' relationship was challenged by a significant development concerning the original justification for the Iraq War. On September 30, 2004, the Special Advisor to the Director of Central Intelligence on Iraq's WMD released an in-depth report known as the Duelfer Report.[67] This report was named after Charles Duelfer, chief weapons inspector of the Iraq Survey Group (ISG), a team of American and British experts who had been dispatched to Iraq to search for the Hussein regime's WMD. This report concluded that the ISG found no evidence indicating that Iraq had possessed WMD at the time of the onset of the Iraq War in 2003.[68] Bush openly acknowledged the intelligence failures, admitting that the "accumulated body of 12 years of our intelligence" from both the US and its allies had been proven "wrong," and emphasized the necessity of identifying and addressing these systematic problems.[69] Similarly, Secretary of State Powell expressed regret regarding the inaccuracies of some information,[70] while Prime Minister Blair provided a conditional apology to the governing Labour Party, acknowledging that the evidence he had utilized to justify Britain's involvement in the war had been proven to be erroneous.[71]

Koizumi must have been taken aback by the Duelfer Report and its findings; he had maintained the conviction that "WMD will be found eventually," and Foreign Minister Kawaguchi had repeatedly asserted that "it is difficult to assume that there were no WMD in Iraq."[72] On October 13, he was questioned in the Diet by Democratic Party of Japan President Katsuya Okada as to whether his support for the Iraq War had been predicated on a misinterpretation of the facts. In his response, Koizumi defended Japan's position by shifting the focus from WMD to Iraq's consistent pattern of defiance against international authority. He emphasized that Iraq had "continued to violate successive UNSC resolutions for 12 years" and had rejected diplomatic solutions.[73] Referring back to his earlier statement from March 2003, Koizumi asserted that Japan's support for military action had been justified and not a "mistake."[74] The inconsistency in Koizumi's position is evident upon reviewing that statement, which specifically addressed the issue of WMD and underscored Japan's commitment to resolving "the problem of Iraq's WMD" through diplomatic channels and international cooperation.[75] Similarly, Bush had characterized the conflict as a defensive measure when initiating the war, asserting that Americans and their allies would not permit themselves to be endangered by an "outlaw regime" possessing "weapons of mass murder."[76] As such, Koizumi's argument may be interpreted as an instance of obstinate insistence.

Given the centrality of WMD to the Bush administration's casus belli, it appears improbable that military intervention in Iraq would have been pursued had definitive intelligence indicated the absence of such armaments. The WMD threat served as the primary justification for preemptive action within both domestic and international contexts. Richard Haass, who served as director of the State Department's policy planning staff, reflected that had he known at the time that Iraq lacked WMD, his opposition to the war would have been resolutely strong, to the extent that he would have contemplated resigning if Bush had chosen to proceed with military action. He speculated whether Bush would have opted for war given this knowledge, acknowledging that such a scenario is more appropriately examined by historians and novelists. When Bush was posed a similar question by ABC's Charles Gibson in 2008, he refrained from conjecturing about potential alternate outcomes. Haass expressed the belief that the absence of WMD would likely have dissuaded Bush from pursuing the war, as this rationale served as the principal justification for the conflict and that, without this justification, both international and domestic opposition would have been insurmountable unless Saddam Hussein had undertaken some new, provocative actions that might have warranted military intervention.[77]

The absence of WMD presented a considerable challenge for both Washington and Tokyo in the management of their diplomatic relationship and in the justification of their ongoing cooperation in Iraq. However, both governments seemed hesitant to directly address this uncomfortable reality in their bilateral discussions. On October 24, Powell met with Japanese Foreign Minister Nobutaka Machimura in Tokyo and expressed appreciation for the SDF's contributions in Samawah. The two discussed the potential extension of the SDF's deployment but, notably, neither man acknowledged the absence of WMD during their meeting.[78] Japan had been elected to a nonpermanent seat on the UNSC earlier in the month, and Powell affirmed his government's support for Japan's pursuit of permanent membership.[79] Powell also paid a courtesy visit to Koizumi on the same day. In his remarks, Koizumi reiterated the importance of "the Japan–US alliance in the world" and expressed his intent to address "new global threats such as terrorism and the proliferation of WMD," yet he failed to mention the final report that refuted the existence of such weapons in Iraq.[80]

Given the significant Japanese political and material investment in the Iraq coalition, it would have been diplomatically prudent for Koizumi and Machimura to pursue a substantive dialogue regarding the ISG's conclusive findings and to engage in thorough diplomatic discourse concerning the fundamental premises that precipitated the military intervention. Such diplomatic transparency could have served to strengthen bilateral strategic understanding and inform future policy coordination. But while Koizumi continued to invoke "the Japan–US alliance in the world," the telegrams summarizing the meetings indicate a superficiality in that alliance.[81]

Despite the absence of any verified WMD in Iraq, Bush was reelected on November 2, and inaugurated for a second term on January 20, 2005. He appointed National Security Advisor Rice to succeed Powell as secretary of state in his new administration. Throughout the Bush administration, the US was better positioned than Japan to independently verify the presence or absence of WMD in Iraq. It would not be until December 21, 2012—more than six years after Koizumi's resignation as prime minister and in the final days of the Democratic Party of Japan's control of the government—that the Japanese foreign ministry would issue a review of its response to the Iraq War, including considerations related to WMD. This concluded that "the fact that Iraq's WMD could not be confirmed must be accepted with the utmost solemnity by Japan," and emphasized the need for Japan to enhance its intelligence-gathering capabilities from a diverse array of sources and to foster cooperation not only with the US but also with the UK, France, Germany, and other nations to avert similar circumstances in the future.[82]

While increased diplomatic engagement may seem to provide safeguards against intelligence-based policy misjudgments reminiscent of those preceding the Iraq War, such measures are likely to prove inadequate in light of Japan's inherent security constraints. The enduring global alliance security dilemma indicates that Tokyo's strategic reliance on Washington for deterrence against regional threats, particularly from China and North Korea, structurally restricts its ability to conduct autonomous intelligence assessments and formulate independent policies. This dependency dynamic inherently subjects Japanese foreign policy to American strategic calculations, regardless of the strength of diplomatic channels. During the Koizumi administration, however, Japan had the potential to secure permanent membership on the UNSC, which could have empowered it to enhance its intelligence-gathering capabilities and increase its leverage over the US.

Conclusion

In 2004, Japan's strategic engagement through deployment of the SDF to Samawah and continued participation in the Six-Party Talks highlighted the complexities of the global alliance security dilemma. The SDF deployment to Iraq represented Japan's commitment to supporting US-led initiatives while attempting to maintain constitutional constraints, serving as a demonstration of how Japan found itself caught between supporting American military operations and maintaining its pacifist principles, particularly as the designation of Samawah as a "non-combat zone" proved problematic. The dilemma intensified further when the Iraq Survey Group's comprehensive report revealed no evidence of WMD in Iraq, undermining one of the primary justifications for Japan's support of the war. Yet neither Foreign Minister Machimura nor Secretary of State Powell acknowledged this finding in their October meeting, illustrating how the alliance relationship constrained Japan's ability to question US strategic decisions even when they proved faulty.

The inherent asymmetry of the US–Japan alliance was starkly demonstrated by the unilateral redeployment of US Marines from Okinawa to Iraq without prior consultation with Japanese authorities. Approximately 5,000 Marines were moved from Okinawa, nearly 20 percent of the Marine presence there, and yet MOFA classified this as a "move" rather than a "military combat operation" to avoid confrontation over the lack of the consultation required by treaty provisions. This highlighted Japan's limited influence over US force deployments, even when they directly affected Japan's security environment. Despite Foreign Minister Kawaguchi's assurances that deterrence would be maintained, the situation revealed Japan's fundamental inability to prevent the US from unilaterally deploying forces stationed in Japan for operations beyond the Far East.

The dual-structured security dilemma manifested as Japan attempted to balance its alliance commitments with regional security concerns, particularly those concerning North Korea. Japan's participation in the Six-Party Talks, concurrent with its efforts to support US operations in Iraq, illustrated how Tokyo had to simultaneously manage both internal alliance obligations and external regional relationships. Japan's insistence on including the abduction issue alongside nuclear concerns at the Six-Party Talks complicated the negotiations, while its increasing dependence on US support for addressing both the security and abduction issues demonstrated how regional challenges reinforced Japan's reliance on the alliance. This created a cyclical dynamic where addressing regional security concerns required stronger alliance commitments, which in turn affected regional relationships.

As will be shown in chapter 5, these themes would continue to evolve through the February 2005 SCC meeting, which would formally articulate the global nature of the US–Japan alliance and explicitly incorporate China as a strategic consideration for the first time. The failure of Japan's bid for permanent UNSC membership, despite its support for US operations in Iraq, would further highlight the limitations of the alliance relationship and demonstrate how Japan's global alliance security dilemma persisted even as the alliance expanded beyond its traditional geographic scope.

Chapter 5

Strategic Dialogues and the UN Reform Standstill

2005

US–Japan Security Talks

ELECTIONS IN IRAQ

The year 2005 saw several significant developments in international politics and US–Japan bilateral relations. Japan opened the year by supporting the January parliamentary elections for the Iraqi Transitional National Assembly, thereby demonstrating its alignment with international coalition efforts. A pivotal development then occurred in February when the Security Consultative Committee (SCC) formulated the globalization of the US–Japan alliance, notably incorporating China's influence as an explicit strategic consideration in its joint statement for the first time. The SCC's October interim report emphasized the restructuring of the US–Japan alliance with a particular focus on integrating the US military and SDF into the broader US global force realignment initiative. This globalization of the alliance presented Japan with an intensified alliance security dilemma that would only be further complicated by the failure of the country's attempt at UN Security Council reform. In the realm of regional security, while the Six-Party Talks achieved a milestone in their fourth round with the issuing of their first joint statement, the chairman's statement from the fifth round notably lacked specific provisions for dismantling North Korea's nuclear arsenal. Japan's position in these negotiations was characterized by its insistence on incorporating the abduction issue into a comprehensive solution, a stance that impeded the talks' progress.

The advancement of democratic governance in Iraq reached a historic milestone when the parliamentary elections for the Transitional National Assembly, the first post-Saddam elections, were held on January 30. Iraqis residing abroad were allowed to participate in the voting process, and the Japanese government directed representatives from its embassies in eight countries—France, Iran, Jordan, Sweden, Syria, Turkey, the United Arab Emirates, and the UK—to facilitate international monitoring of the elections in those regions. The International Organization for Migration (IOM) oversaw elections in an additional six countries: Australia, Canada, Denmark, Germany, the Netherlands, and the US. Japan also contributed $40 million to assist in the elections and provide Iraqi election officials with training.[1]

On the day of the elections, Bush commended the Iraqi populace for their engagement in their inaugural democratic vote. He emphasized that the journey toward a free Iraq was making progress and that the elections represented the first steps toward the creation and ratification of a new constitution, and with it, the groundwork for a fully democratic Iraqi government. Bush acknowledged that, despite this progress, terrorists and insurgents would continue their opposition to democracy, but he assured them that there would be ongoing support for the Iraqi people in their struggle against these adversarial forces and reiterated his commitment to training Iraqi security personnel. This training was deemed essential for empowering the nascent democracy to eventually manage its own security. While recognizing that the path to democracy remained a long one, he praised the Iraqi people for rising to the challenge: "On behalf of the American people, I congratulate the people of Iraq on this great and historic achievement."[2]

Despite the initial celebration of Iraq's democratic achievements, Bush's assessment proved overly optimistic, and the reality of sectarian divisions and political challenges soon became apparent. The electoral outcome reflected the demographic reality: The Shiite majority secured a decisive victory, while the Sunni minority, historically aligned with Saddam Hussein's regime, experienced a significant reduction in political influence. This electoral imbalance had profound implications for the constitutional drafting process, which ultimately lacked transparency and democratic inclusivity.[3] Within the US political sphere, the election results catalyzed divergent responses. Some within the Democratic Party advocated for a military withdrawal now that elections had been held. But the relatively peaceful execution of the electoral process, which had exceeded initial security expectations, bolstered the position of those favoring a continued military presence. Consequently, calls for immediate troop withdrawal failed to gain substantial political traction.[4]

SCC: A "Responsible and Constructive Role" for China

As the US navigated challenges in Iraq, it also sought to strengthen its alliance with Japan through diplomatic channels. On February 19, the Bush and Koizumi administrations convened a meeting of the SCC at the State Department. In attendance were Secretary of State Condoleezza Rice, Defense Secretary Donald Rumsfeld, Foreign Minister Nobutaka Machimura, and Defense Agency Director-General Yoshinori Ohno. This was the first gathering of the SCC since December 2002, and its primary focus was on the realignment of US forces in Japan and the enhancement of the US–Japan alliance in light of North Korea's cessation of participation in the Six-Party Talks and its declaration that it possessed nuclear weapons.

Rice and Machimura met briefly before the broader SCC meeting; most of their discussion was dedicated to North Korean issues rather than addressing matters related to UN reform or Middle Eastern peace. Machimura emphasized the need for North Korea's immediate and unconditional return to the Six-Party Talks, asserting that its nuclear arsenal constituted a threat to the security of Northeast Asia. He also said that Chinese Foreign Minister Li Zhaoxing needed to take a leadership role in engaging with North Korea and requested continued US support regarding the abduction issue. Rice concurred, stating that North Korea must dismantle its nuclear weapons and highlighting China's "special responsibility" in this context. While Machimura reassured Rice of his commitment to facilitating the resumption of the Six-Party Talks, he anticipated that the matter would ultimately be escalated to the UNSC if no progress was made, a prospect with which Rice agreed.[5]

The SCC convened in a 2+2 format following the foreign ministers' meeting and engaged in deliberations on several critical issues, including cooperation on global challenges (notably the reconstruction efforts in Iraq and Afghanistan), the provision of assistance in the aftermath of the Sumatra earthquake, and the need for North Korea's immediate and unconditional return to the Six-Party Talks and its verifiable nuclear disarmament. The discussions also encompassed East Asian security dynamics, including the situation in China and relations between China and Taiwan; the alleviation of the burden posed by US military bases in Okinawa; and the enhancement of the operational framework of the US–Japan SOFA, along with the implementation of the SACO Final Report.[6]

The SCC joint statement classified the shared strategic objectives of the two nations into two distinct categories: regional and global. The regional objectives comprised pursuit of a peaceful resolution to issues concerning North Korea; development of a cooperative relationship with China, encouraging the nation to assume a responsible and constructive role both regionally and globally; promotion of dialogue aimed at achieving a peaceful resolution of issues related to the Taiwan Strait; and encouraging China to enhance the transparency of its military affairs in Northeast Asia. The global objectives included promotion of fundamental values such as basic human rights, democracy, and the rule of law within the international community, and the coordination of efforts to enhance the effectiveness of the UNSC by taking advantage of the current momentum to fulfill Japan's aspiration for permanent membership.[7]

The SCC's 2005 deliberations are significant in three distinct ways. First, despite the absence of a legitimate justification for the initiation of the Iraq War and the ongoing instability within that country, the SCC redefined the US–Japan alliance as a global alliance that advocated for values such as democracy and the rule of law, including beyond the treaty-defined geographic parameters of the Far East. Second, for the first time, the joint statement explicitly identified China as being among the strategic objectives of the alliance and called for a peaceful resolution to the Taiwan Strait issue, thereby compelling Japan to align with the US in its defense strategy for Taiwan. Third, while China was encouraged to exhibit transparency in its military activities, the SCC also invited the nation to assume "a responsible and constructive role regionally as well as globally."[8] This invitation was an acknowledgment that Chinese influence over North Korea was deemed essential for resumption of the Six-Party Talks.

China's Military Power, Japan's Global Role

In its second term, the Bush administration's policy toward East Asia showed an increased focus on the military capabilities of China and Japan's expanding global role. On March 19, Secretary of State Rice met with Foreign Minister Machimura in Tokyo and discussed US–Japan relations, developments in Northeast Asia, issues related to the Middle East, and the prospect of Japanese permanent membership on the UNSC.

The emphasis placed by both leaders on the rise of China, particularly its naval capabilities, marked a notable divergence from the discussions held during Bush's first term. Machimura posited that China could become a "responsible partner" in global affairs, but that this would require reforms aimed at increasing transparency in both the political and security domains.[9] While recognizing China's considerable influence, he stressed the importance of promoting its engagement in a "constructive role within the international community."[10] After Rice identified China's emergence as a "major issue in international politics," Machimura emphasized the significance of closely monitoring China's expanding military capabilities, particularly its naval forces.[11] He asserted the necessity of realistically evaluating China's "real capabilities" rather than merely yielding to its contentions.[12] Rice expressed agreement and them stated her opposition to the EU's potential removal of its "arms embargo on China."[13] It can thus be seen that both officials acknowledged the importance of both engaging with China and remaining vigilant toward its military expansion.

Rice also paid a courtesy call to Koizumi later that day and commented that she had previously given lectures on American and Soviet military planning at the National Defense Academy in Yokosuka over a three-week period in 1986. Koizumi noted that he represented Yokosuka. Rice told Koizumi that she had wanted to visit Japan early in her tenure as secretary of state to underscore the significance of the US–Japan relationship, observing that while "Japan has long played an important role in the region," it was now "transforming into a global [power]," as evidenced by "its support for the reconstruction efforts in Iraq and Afghanistan, as well as by its efforts in the Indian Ocean."[14] She also expressed her support for Japanese membership in the UNSC. Koizumi reaffirmed that the US–Japan alliance was fundamental to Japanese diplomacy, asserting that "the Japan–US alliance in the world" had moved from conceptual framework to a tangible reality following the 2003 US–Japan agreement signed in Texas, as proven by their collaborative efforts in Afghanistan and Iraq.[15]

Notably, Koizumi made no explicit mention of China and, while Rice's visit was just a courtesy call, he also seemed to have less interest than Machimura in China's ascent; given that Rice was scheduled to be in Beijing the following day, it would have been prudent for Koizumi to raise the topic with her. Instead, he reiterated the phrase "the Japan–US alliance in the world," a slogan he had utilized since Bush's first term, without making any effort to explore the implications that China had for that alliance.

American and Japanese strategic priorities meant significant divergences in their approaches to the regional challenges of Northeast Asia. The Koizumi administration's primary concern remained the resolution of the North Korean abduction issue, and it held firm to the position that there could be no normalization of diplomatic relations until this issue was addressed, even though this emphasis meant a reduction of flexibility and created a rift in negotiations with North Korea. In contrast, the Bush administration was committed to revitalizing the Six-Party Talks with North Korea that had made little progress since beginning in 2003; Chinese cooperation was deemed essential for this endeavor. Despite its apprehensions regarding American intelligence on North Korea's nuclear program, after Rice met with President Hu in Beijing, China communicated to the US that it would endeavor to persuade North Korea to participate in the Six-Party Talks. Rice's visit to Northeast Asia illuminated a divergence between the positions of the US and Japan.[16]

"Significant Shift in US policy": The Fourth Round of the Six-Party Talks

With international tensions over North Korea's nuclear ambitions continuing to grow, diplomatic efforts successfully brought about the fourth round of Six-Party Talks, bringing multiple nations together in Beijing to address this complex security issue. The fourth round took place in two phases, the first from July 26 to August 7 and the second from September 13 to 19. A failure to reach a consensus, primarily over two key points, was responsible for the talks being temporarily suspended on August 7. The first of these points of dispute pertained to North Korea's assertion that it was entitled to pursue the peaceful application of nuclear energy; it thus sought to resume construction of light-water reactors. The US and Japan opposed this, contending that North Korea should first dismantle its nuclear program in a verifiable manner and fully adhere to its obligations under the NPT. The second point of dispute involved North Korea's uranium enrichment program. While the US and other concerned nations expressed significant apprehensions regarding this program, North Korea categorically denied that any such initiative existed.[17]

Despite these initial disagreements, the parties were able to achieve substantial progress once the negotiations resumed, and a joint statement was signed by Vice Minister of Foreign Affairs Wu Dawei, Vice Minister of Foreign Affairs Kim Kye-gwan, Director-General Ken'ichirō Sasae of the Japanese Foreign Ministry Bureau of Asian and Oceanic Affairs, Deputy Minister of Foreign Affairs and Trade Song Min-soon, Deputy Minister of Foreign Affairs Aleksandr Alekseyev, and Assistant Secretary of State for East Asian and Pacific Affairs Christopher Hill on September 19.[18]

The joint statement encompassed four principal commitments. First, North Korea committed to the complete abandonment of all nuclear weapons and existing nuclear programs, while also agreeing to promptly return to compliance with both the NPT and the IAEA. Second, North Korea asserted its right to the peaceful use of nuclear energy, and the other parties acknowledged this claim and agreed to engage in discussions regarding the provision of light-water reactors at an appropriate juncture. Third, the US confirmed that it possessed no nuclear weapons on the Korean Peninsula and had no intention of attacking or invading North Korea using either nuclear or conventional weapons. Fourth, Japan and North Korea pledged to undertake steps toward normalization in accordance with the Pyongyang Declaration, which included resolving the "unfortunate past and the outstanding issues of concern."[19]

In light of North Korea's denial of the existence of any uranium enrichment program, the statement incorporated a reference to the 1992 Joint Declaration, which had explicitly prohibited such activities. This statement represented the first agreement reached during the years-long negotiations; significantly, it also outlined provisions for the disposal of North Korea's nuclear arsenal, albeit under specific conditions. Nevertheless, the statement merely established objectives; the determination of concrete steps for the dismantlement of these weapons and the verification of such dismantlement were scheduled for subsequent discussions.[20]

This joint statement could not have been issued without the rapport established between the US and China at the opening of the 2005 UN General Assembly session. On September 13, Hu met Bush in New York and cautiously chose words to show that China was aligned with the US on "a nuclear-weapon-free Korean Peninsula."[21] Rice and Foreign Minister Li Zhaoxing were assigned the task of negotiating the terms, and Rice capitalized on the presence of the Chinese, Russian, South Korean, and Japanese foreign ministers at the UN. They reached an agreement under which the Chinese delegation at the talks would present a compromise proposal allowing North Korea to retain the non-threatening elements of its current infrastructure for peaceful nuclear energy purposes. In her memoirs, Rice noted that "the compromise . . . represented a significant shift in US policy. We [the Bush administration] had always refused to discuss, even mention, a light-water reactor."[22] There were thus two critical elements to the US's persuasion of North Korea to abandon its nuclear weapons program: a meeting between American and Chinese leaders and collaboration with America's allies, South Korea and Japan.

STALEMATE: THE FIFTH AND SIXTH ROUNDS OF THE SIX-PARTY TALKS

The fifth round of the Six-Party Talks attempted to follow up on the progress made in the prior round but encountered renewed tensions that highlighted the unresolved issues that would impede further diplomatic efforts. The first phase of the fifth round was held from November 9 to 11, but ended abruptly after the chairman issued a statement delineating guidelines for the implementation of the joint statement adopted during the fourth round. This statement asserted that the joint statement was to be fully executed in accordance with the principle of "commitment for commitment, action for action"; however, it notably lacked any language on the establishment of a working group, something that Japan had proposed as a concrete measure toward this objective.[23]

The negotiations between the US and North Korea over the implementation of the joint statement concluded in a stalemate, with North Korea issuing a strong condemnation of the economic sanctions that the US had imposed on a Macau bank for doing business with the country.[24] For its part, the Japanese delegation emphasized the "two wheels of a cart" concept in its own negotiations with North Korea. This approach argued that making progress in resolving bilateral issues (particularly the abductions issue) would positively influence the Six-Party Talks, and that success on the nuclear and missile issues within the Six-Party framework would in turn facilitate the normalization of diplomatic relations. North Korea exhibited only a limited degree of interest, however.[25]

Months after the end of the first phase, North Korea announced that it would not participate in further negotiations unless the US lifted its financial sanctions.[26] By the time the second phase of the fifth round was held from December 18 to 22, 2006, Koizumi had been succeeded as prime minister by Shinzō Abe. Even then, no significant progress toward denuclearization was achieved, as North Korea held firm to its stance of refusing to engage in discussions regarding the implementation of the joint statement until American financial sanctions were lifted. The Japanese delegation emphasized that the abduction issue was the foremost priority for the new Abe administration (thus maintaining the same position that Koizumi had). But North Korea's unwillingness to enter into a dialogue prevented any negotiations.[27] The third phase of the fifth round, conducted from February 8 to 13, 2007, resulted in the adoption of the "Initial Actions for the Implementation of the Joint Statement."[28] This document stipulated that, in exchange for North Korea's agreement to shut down its nuclear facilities in Yongbyon, the other parties (excluding Japan) would provide energy assistance amounting to 50,000 tons of heavy fuel oil (HFO). Japan opted not to participate in the agreement, as the abduction issue remained unresolved.

The Six-Party Talks had been designed to establish a framework for documenting nuclear verification measures, but despite convening for a sixth round of discussions from December 8 to 11, 2008, the participating parties remained unable to reach a consensus, primarily due to a disagreement between the US and North Korea over the verification of nuclear materials.[29] The statement issued by the Chinese chairman following the end of the round indicated that "the parties would welcome assistance and consultation from the IAEA in the course of verification," but included no details as to the timing or form of the process they were to assist with.[30] Speaking to the media afterward, Director-General Akitaka Saiki of MOFA's Asian and Oceanic Affairs Bureau commented that "it was very difficult to bridge the gap between North Korea's position and those of the others" and that "no substantial results were achieved this time."[31] By the end of the sixth round in 2008, Koizumi had already resigned, and Bush was in the final months of his administration. North Korea formally announced its withdrawal from the Six-Party Talks in 2009 and resumed its missile launches and nuclear tests. The abduction issue remains unresolved to this day.

Several significant conclusions can be drawn from an analysis of the six rounds of the Six-Party Talks. First, Japan's insistence under both the Koizumi and later Abe administrations to pursue a comprehensive solution that encompassed the abduction issue hindered progress in the negotiations. With the sole exception of the US, all other participants believed that Japan should have instead addressed the issue through bilateral discussions with North Korea. Nevertheless, the emphasis of the talks on achieving a peaceful resolution to the North Korean crisis aligned with Japan's broader strategic intentions. Koizumi had supported

Table 5.1 Outline of the Six-Party Talks

Round	Place	Last Date	Statement	Points of Agreement	Japan's Position
1	Beijing	August 29, 2003	not issued	Peaceful resolution of the nuclear problem through dialogue	Comprehensive solution including the abduction issue
2	Beijing	February 28, 2004	Chairman's Statement	Commitment to a nuclear-weapons-free Korean Peninsula	Resolution to the abduction issue at the earliest date possible
3	Beijing	June 26, 2004	Chairman's Statement	Denuclearization of the Korean Peninsula and first steps	Resolving the various concerns including the abduction issue
4	Beijing	September 19, 2005	Joint Statement	Abandonment of nuclear weapons and programs, prohibition of the uranium enrichment program, right to the peaceful use of nuclear energy, and economic cooperation	Take steps to normalize relations in accordance with the Pyongyang Declaration
5	Beijing	February 13, 2007	"Initial Actions for the Implementation of the Joint Statement"	In return for North Korea shutting down its nuclear facilities in Yongbyon, the countries involved (except Japan) would provide energy assistance	Refrain from participating in energy assistance for the time being because the abduction issue remained unresolved
6	Beijing	December 11, 2008	Chairman's Statement	Parties would welcome assistance and consultation from the IAEA in the course of verification	Resolution of the issues of concern and normalization of relations with North Korea

the Iraq War with the expectation that Bush would deter North Korea and facilitate a peaceful resolution. Although the more conservative faction within the Bush administration had opposed granting North Korea any form of legitimacy, key figures such as Bush, Rice, and Hill had managed to maintain a degree of control over this opposition.[32]

Second, North Korea was willing to remain unyielding and undermine the Chinese chairmanship by resisting the issuance of joint statements. Third, high-level cooperation between the US and China was essential for exerting pressure on North Korea. The only joint statement, produced during the fourth round of the talks, resulted from a meeting between Bush and Hu in New York, as well as a series of discussions involving five foreign ministers, notably including Rice and Li. The American focus on North Korea was one factor behind its decision to refrain from countering Chinese military expansion, something that helped contribute to China's rise as a global power. North Korea's independent stance would begin to overshadow Sino-American cooperation toward the end of the Bush administration, however, and by the sixth round of talks, Bush had effectively become a dormant leader.

SCC: "Transformation and Realignment for the Future"

Over the course of the Six-Party Talks, the US–Japan alliance was undergoing a process of globalization and integration. On October 28, 2005, Foreign Minister Machimura met with Secretary of State Rice in Washington, where they discussed North Korea, Iraq, and UN reform. He expressed gratitude to Rice for facilitating a meeting between the families of abductees and Jay Lefkowitz, Bush's special envoy on human rights in North Korea, during the families' visit to the US. Rice noted that the Bush administration had consistently upheld Japan's position on the abduction issue. When Machimura remarked that North Korea would only engage in the Six-Party Talks if discussions of economic support were included, Rice emphasized the necessity for collaboration among the US, Japan, and South Korea.[33]

Turning to Afghanistan, Rice expressed appreciation for Japan's decision to extend the Anti-Terrorism Special Measures Law for an additional year and indicated that the US and Japan should maintain their partnership to facilitate reconstruction efforts even following the conclusion of the Bonn Agreement. Machimura noted that the deadline for the Act on Special Measures Concerning Humanitarian Relief and Reconstruction

Work and Security Assistance in Iraq was set for December; however, he suggested that the Japanese government would make a proactive decision based on the prevailing circumstances in Iraq at that time. Rice argued that Iraq was progressing toward greater democracy and called for a unified commitment from the international community in support of the country.[34]

While this discussion addressed a range of topics, the SCC meeting that followed (attended by Rumsfeld, Rice, Machimura, and Ohno) was focused specifically on restructuring the US–Japan alliance. Rumsfeld commended Japan's contributions to various peacekeeping operations and emphasized key issues such as US–Japan interoperability, transportation cooperation, information sharing, enhanced joint training, missile defense, and capacity building for third countries. Ohno expressed that there was a need for an improved security environment, as this was seen as integral to the role of the SDF under the Koizumi administration's National Defense Program Guidelines. He also expressed a desire to address the joint utilization of bases. Machimura underscored the importance of strengthening security arrangements, positing that they served as the foundation for global coordination between Japan and the US.[35]

The presence of American military bases in Okinawa had been a significant concern for the Japanese government. Rumsfeld emphasized that the agreement to reduce the number of Marines stationed in the prefecture would occur simultaneously with the relocation of Marine Corps Air Station Futenma, arguing that this move would alleviate the burden on local residents while also enhancing the operational capabilities of US troops. Ohno expressed his appreciation for the planned reduction of 7,000 Marines and expressed a desire to foster regional understanding of the Futenma relocation. He also indicated a willingness to provide financial support for the relocation of the Marine Corps headquarters to Guam. Machimura advocated for the transfer of military training activities to SDF bases and Guam to mitigate the noise pollution originating from Kadena Air Base.[36] The ongoing operations in Iraq also played a role here; as discussed in the previous chapter, approximately 5,000 USMC combat troops and over 40 helicopters had been deployed from Okinawa to Iraq in 2004, and this had contributed to a reduction in noise and crime in the vicinity of the base.[37]

On October 29, 2005, the SCC released "U.S.-Japan Alliance: Transformation and Realignment for the Future," a pivotal interim assessment of the nature and trajectory of the US–Japan alliance. In this report, the US and Japan acknowledged recent advancements in their security and defense strategies, noting their bilateral cooperation in international endeavors such as counterterrorism, the Proliferation Security Initiative (PSI), support for Iraq, and the provision of disaster relief, as well as developments in the countries' collaboration on BMD. The document references Japanese initiatives including the National Defense Program Guidelines of December 2004 and developments, legislative measures for managing contingencies, and the planned transition of the SDF toward a new joint operations posture.[38] It also emphasizes the necessity of maintaining public support in both Japan and the US for the continued presence of US forces at Japanese facilities and in designated areas. To that end, it highlights the need to review the positioning of US forces in Japan in a way that recognizes the critical importance of maintaining deterrence and operational capabilities while also minimizing the impact on local communities, particularly in Okinawa.

The interim report delineated contingencies pertinent to Japan, the Far East, and broader global issues, alongside efforts to integrate the US military and the SDF within the overarching framework of American global realignment. It specified two facilities earmarked for enhanced integration and bilateral cooperation: Camp Zama and Yokota Air Base. Under the proposed command structure, Camp Zama was to be modernized into a deployable operational headquarters capable of supporting joint task forces. This was expected to augment its capacity to respond promptly to Japan's defense needs and other emergent contingencies. Adjustments to US facilities and areas would be implemented to facilitate this new Army command structure and its associated capabilities. The facility was also slated to serve as headquarters for a new GSDF Central Readiness Force Command, which would oversee nationwide mobile operations, thereby enhancing coordination between the two headquarters. The report also addressed the exploration of more effective and efficient utilization of Camp Zama (and the nearby Sagami General Depot) in light of these realignments.[39]

As part of Japan's initiative to transition the SDF toward a joint operations posture, a bilateral and joint operations coordination center was also to be created at Yokota Air Base to facilitate continuous connectivity, coordination, and interoperability between US forces stationed in Japan and the SDF. This move drew some criticism from civilian officials in Japan. Tokyo Governor Shintarō Ishihara, who had advocated for Yokota Air Base becoming a joint-use airport to alleviate congestion at Haneda Airport (Tokyo's busiest international airport), expressed considerable dissatisfaction with the report's decision to have base used solely by the US military and the ASDF: "It demonstrates the weakness of Japan's diplomatic power. It is very disagreeable to the Tokyo Metropolitan Government, which aims to have the base shared by the military and civilians."[40]

The globalization of the US–Japan alliance, driven by the conflicts in Afghanistan and Iraq and intensified by the realignment of US forces in Japan and the emergence of China, had led to a significant restructuring of the alliance. Although "U.S.-Japan Alliance: Transformation and Realignment for the Future" did not explicitly reference China, an SCC joint statement issued on February 19, 2005 did, stating that the two countries "[encouraged] the peaceful resolution of issues concerning the Taiwan Strait through dialogue," and "[encouraged] China to improve transparency of its military affairs."[41] The Japanese position adopted in the report lacked clear strategic direction, focusing mainly on three aspects: decreasing the military burden on Okinawa, moving Futenma, and maintaining deterrence—with this final point being the key reason for keeping Futenma's relocation within Okinawa itself. Japan pledged to maintain "seamless support to US operations" as it worked to decrease the military burden.[42] This support included providing bases and facilities, adapting to changing circumstances with appropriate measures including contingency-related legislative support, and cooperating with local communities to maintain stable US military operations and presence. The SCC report represented a significant evolution in the US–Japan security relationship.

Historically, Japan has functioned primarily as a recipient of US protection provided by American military forces at Japanese bases. But the alliance was now transitioning toward a more reciprocal and global partnership. In the words of Ohno, both nations were entering "a new era" characterized by active collaboration to enhance "the global security environment and peace," thereby moving beyond the traditional protector–protectee dynamic.[43] Not only was any sign of remorse for the Iraq War absent in the report, but some SCC participants even hinted at the possibility of Japan being placed in similar situations in the future; consequently, the security dilemma of the US–Japan global alliance persisted and arguably even intensified. The final report on the realignment of US forces in Japan, agreed to on May 1, 2006, will be discussed in chapter 6.

Setbacks in UNSC Reform

THE G4 AND THE US

Alongside its efforts to assert an increasingly prominent role within the US–Japan alliance, the Koizumi administration actively pursued a vision of UN reform aimed at enhancing Japan's stature in the realm of international security. Koizumi met with UN Secretary-General Annan on September 21, 2004, to announce Japan's intention to collaborate with Brazil, India, and Germany in advocating for Security Council reforms, expressing hope for "groundbreaking reforms" during Annan's tenure.[44] Annan offered a supportive yet diplomatic reply, stressing the need for member states to lead the UN toward "the appropriate conclusion on reform."[45]

2005 marked the 60th anniversary of the UN, and Annan presented a proposal for expansion of the Security Council to the UN General Assembly on March 21. On July 6, Japan submitted a draft resolution to the UNGA in collaboration with its G4 partners (Brazil, Germany, and India). This resolution—which sought to expand the Security Council by adding six permanent and four non-permanent seats—was supported by 32 co-sponsors and had numerous additional supporters. The proposal also encountered substantial opposition from various entities, however; the African Union introduced a competing resolution advocating for its own perspective on the expansion of permanent membership, while the Uniting for Consensus group (UFC) resisted these initiatives by promoting an expansion limited to non-permanent seats. Ultimately, none of these resolutions advanced to a vote, and all proposals were effectively rendered moot with the conclusion of the 59th session of the UNGA in September.[46]

UN reform was inextricably linked to the Iraq War; Annan's drive for institutional restructuring arose directly from the organization's demonstrated inability to prevent or effectively respond to the conflict. Following criticism that the UN had failed to adequately respond to American unilateral action, Annan had established the High-Level Panel, which included Sadako Ogata from Japan. There were numerous reasons that UNSC reform ultimately failed to materialize in 2005. According to Masaki Orita, special envoy for UN reform with a focus on Europe, European opinions on the matter were divided. While Britain and France expressed support for the G4 resolution, Italy and Spain exhibited reluctance at endorsing Germany as Europe's sole new permanent member. The US also harbored mistrust toward Germany due to its opposition to the Iraq War. Koizumi's continued visits to Yasukuni Shrine also provided China with a rationale to oppose Japan's permanent membership in the Council, and it advocated for no reform of the Security Council to be made without a consensus among member states. Coordination between the G4 nations and African representatives proved to be challenging as well.[47]

With continued diplomatic tensions with China and varying responses from European nations, Koizumi aimed to foster broader international support for UN reform by engaging directly with global leaders. During the G8 summit held in Gleneagles, Scotland, from July 6 to 8, he met individually with each of the G8 leaders to garner their support for the G4 proposal. Among those who responded favorably were Russian President Vladimir Putin and Canadian Prime Minister Paul Martin, with Putin notably voicing his endorsement of the initiative.[48] Koizumi addressed the issue of UN reform at the summit on its final day, recognizing the existing permanent members' concerns regarding their "vested interests" while also highlighting their transformed relationship with former adversaries Japan and Germany.[49] He asserted that reform efforts should extend beyond the UNSC to include broader objectives such as "peace and security, development, and human rights and humanitarianism."[50] Blair praised Koizumi's distinctive character in his memoirs, describing him as "a great leader, very lively, with an unusual personality" and noting his unique departure from the style typical of Japanese politicians.[51] This endorsement from Blair highlights how Koizumi's dynamic leadership style during this pivotal phase of UN reform negotiations was seen positively by foreign leaders.

Rice's diplomatic visit to Asia provided another crucial opportunity for Japan to advance its UN reform agenda. She met with Machimura and Chief Cabinet Secretary Hosoda in Tokyo on July 12 after paying a courtesy call to Koizumi. She had already traveled to China and Thailand on her trip and intended to visit South Korea after Japan. Discussing UN reform with Machimura, she noted, "The [G4] resolution was put up for discussion on [July] the 11th. We are currently in the process of deliberating on the draft resolution."[52] It had thus been added to the agenda the preceding day. During her diplomatic exchanges in Tokyo, Rice expressed "complete support" for Japan's bid for permanent membership on the UNSC, although her involvement in the discussions over the G4 proposal was limited.[53]

When she met Koizumi, he immediately brought up the subject, underscoring Japan's commitment to the G4 framework. He stressed that

"UN reform is gaining significant momentum" and advocated for its implementation within the year to facilitate Japan's aspiration for a permanent seat on the UNSC.[54] In advocating for the resolution, Koizumi strategically contextualized the initiative as an integral aspect of "Japan's foreign policy," which he characterized as being anchored in "the [US–Japan] alliance and international cooperation."[55] He pragmatically acknowledged that successful reform would necessitate both American backing and widespread international support, remarking that "any reform that does not have the support of the US will not be implemented."[56] But while Rice declared that "the US fully supports Japan's permanent membership on the Council," she avoided taking any position on the broader G4 initiative.[57]

Divergence Between the US and Japan

Despite the initial US support for Japan's UNSC bid, fundamental differences emerged between the American and Japanese positions on comprehensive UN reform, and the G4 resolution ultimately faced opposition from both the US and numerous African nations. The 59th UNGA adjourned on September 13, resulting in the dismissal of the G4 proposal without any consideration. Bush addressed the 60th UNGA's World Summit High-Level Plenary Meeting on Iraq and UN reform the next day. In his speech, he envisioned Iraq's transition to a constitutional government, supported by the UN, that served as a catalyst for inspiring democratic change in the region, creating what he referred to as "peace and hope and liberty" throughout the Middle East.[58] Despite this optimism, the actual prevailing conditions on the ground were far from satisfactory. Turning to UN reform, Bush acknowledged the initial progress that had been made while underscoring the US's commitment to lead further changes in the forthcoming UNGA meetings. He stressed that meaningful reform begins with member states "taking our responsibilities seriously."[59] In reality, however, the US, as a permanent member of the UNSC, consistently opposed any proposals that might erode its established privileges and vested interests within the UN system.

As Koizumi arrived in the US for the UNGA session, he had just led the LDP to victory in the September 11 general election, but he missed seeing Bush at the UN. He met with Annan in New York on September 15 and expressed his conviction that Japan should use the momentum generated by the 60th anniversary of the UN to advance its initiatives regarding UN reform, particularly reform of the Security Council. He acknowledged that the discussions over these reforms had reached an impasse but emphasized the necessity of collaboration with the US moving forward, as Japan's previous efforts had been concentrated on the G4.[60] Annan asserted that "Security Council reform should come to fruition by the end of this year."[61] Koizumi further remarked on the G4 resolution's dismissal, indicating that while their efforts thus far had not yielded the desired outcomes, they had not been in vain. He called for continued efforts to secure future results.[62]

During the afternoon session of the UNGA, Koizumi made use of his position as the 28th speaker to advocate Japan's case for Security Council reform and permanent membership.[63] In his speech, he emphasized how dramatically the world had evolved since the UN's founding, pointing to the emergence of formerly colonized Asian and African nations as key global actors. He highlighted Japan's six-decade journey as "a peace-loving nation" and its contributions to international stability and prosperity. Koizumi called for Security Council reform to reflect these global changes, advocating for the removal of the outdated "enemy state" clause and expressing Japan's readiness to "play a larger role as a permanent member."[64]

On September 16, the UNGA approved the 2005 World Summit Outcome, which encapsulated the results of the 2005 World Summit that had been held at the UN over the previous two days. MOFA regarded this document as a significant achievement, as it included a provision requesting that the UNGA evaluate progress on Security Council reform by the end of the year.[65] However, this likely exaggerates its significance, as the provision exerted only limited influence within the UN structure toward substantial reforms. Koizumi's visit to the US was notably brief, lasting only half a day, and he was unable to secure a meeting with Bush due to scheduling conflicts. This situation appeared to symbolize the ongoing discord between the two leaders over the reform of the UN.

Bush–Koizumi Discussions in Kyoto

Following the failure of the G4 resolution, the US–Japan relationship transitioned into a new phase in their discussions regarding Security Council reform. On October 29 in Washington, Machimura met with Rice in Washington and recognized that they had entered a "second stage" of Security Council reform initiatives.[66] He explained Japan's intent to develop new concrete proposals while maintaining its connections with the G4 but also stressed Japan's hope to "deepen our cooperation with the US"[67]

Rice responded by praising Japan's significant contributions to the UN and asserting that Japan was "qualified to be on the Security Council," thus reiterating the long-standing US position of endorsing Japan's bid for Security Council membership.[68] In short, this "second stage" was met with statements of support but no concrete proposals.[69]

Bush and Koizumi's summit in Kyoto provided an additional opportunity to discuss UNSC reform within the context of US–Japan relations. Bush arrived in Japan on November 15, and the two met in Kyoto on the following day. During the meeting, Bush expressed gratitude to Japan for its support in the "democratization in Iraq and Afghanistan" and praised its extensive global humanitarian aid efforts, emphasizing that such US–Japan cooperation was "essential for the long-term maintenance of peace and stability in the Far East region."[70] Koizumi replied that it had been his long-standing perspective that "U.S.–Japan relations must be strengthened rather than weakened in order to improve Japan's relations with China, South Korea, and the countries of Southeast Asia."[71]

Despite this statement, while US–Japan relations had made strides under Koizumi, Japan's diplomatic interactions with China and South Korea during the same period had been hindered by incidents such as Koizumi's visit to Yasukuni Shrine and issues related to the North Korean abductions.[72] Moving the discussion to North Korea, Koizumi emphasized that resolving "either the nuclear issue or the abduction issue alone" was insufficient, to which Bush replied by stressing that "this is not an issue that the US can or should deal with on its own."[73] According to Bush, it was essential to consider China's influence over North Korea, and he indicated that the North Korean abductions were not a priority issue. Koizumi also addressed the matter of Security Council reform. Although Bush reaffirmed that "we consistently support Japan's permanent membership in the Security Council," like Rice, he refrained from making any definitive statements regarding the reform process.[74] Bush's response effectively aimed to preclude Japan's ascendance to permanent membership in the UNSC.

Of the issues discussed, the reform of the Security Council appeared to be the one that most profoundly disappointed Koizumi, and he attempted to pursue reform by distancing himself from the G4 and aligning more closely with Bush. According to the account Rice gave in her memoirs, while the US supported Japan's bid for UNSC reform, numerous political obstacles made progress impossible. She identified several key issues: China's opposition to India's potential membership and concerns over Mexico's exclusion should Brazil join. The African situation proved challenging due to regional divisions between North and Sub-Saharan Africa, which prevented the selection of a single representative. Germany's bid for membership complicated matters by raising questions regarding European overrepresentation, particularly in light of the EU's commitment to a unified foreign policy approach. According to Rice, although the US had consistently supported Japan's aspirations, "the politics of UNSC reform were just too complicated to take on."[75]

This web of competing interests and regional dynamics ultimately made meaningful UNSC reform unattainable. The US was opposed to the expansion of the Security Council, and Koizumi's close relationship with Bush failed to alter American attitudes. Moreover, even if the US had been amenable to UN reform, granting Japan permanent membership would have been nearly impossible due to its dependence on other member states. As Secretary-General Annan noted in his memoirs, "Pakistan essentially said India would get a permanent seat over its dead body; China was deeply ambivalent about Japan."[76] Consequently, Japan lost an opportunity to establish its own intelligence network, enhance its standing in the US–Japan relationship, and address the global alliance security dilemma.

Conclusion

The SCC meetings of 2005 highlighted the intensification of Japan's global alliance security dilemma. Despite the lack of evidence for WMD in Iraq and the ongoing instability there, the February SCC meeting formally redefined the US–Japan alliance beyond its traditional geographic scope, emphasizing shared values like democracy and rule of law. The October interim report then further institutionalized this expanded alliance through concrete measures like establishing bilateral joint operations centers at Yokota Air Base and Camp Zama. Japan found itself increasingly committed to supporting US global strategy even as the original justification for the Iraq War proved false, demonstrating how the alliance's globalization constrained Japan's strategic autonomy. This dilemma was particularly evident in Japan's unsuccessful bid for UNSC permanent membership—despite supporting US actions in Iraq, Japan could not secure American backing for UN reform that would have enhanced its independent diplomatic capabilities.

The fundamental asymmetry of the US–Japan alliance was clearly evident in the details of "U.S.-Japan Alliance: Transformation and Realignment for the Future." While Japan committed to funding $6.09 billion of the $10.27 billion cost for relocating Marines from Okinawa to Guam and agreed to host new US command facilities, it had only limited input into the strategic direction of the alliance. This asymmetry was further demonstrated in the handling of China policy—although Japan raised concerns about Chinese military transparency in the SCC, the US maintained primary control over the alliance's approach to China, viewing it as a potential "responsible stakeholder" that could help address issues like North Korea. Even on basing issues directly affecting Japan, Tokyo Governor Ishihara's criticism of the Yokota Air Base arrangements highlighted Japan's limited ability to influence alliance decisions about facilities on its own territory.

The dual-structured security dilemma became more pronounced as the alliance explicitly incorporated China as a strategic consideration for the first time in the February SCC statement. Japan had to balance strengthening alliance integration through measures like the bilateral joint operations center while avoiding provocative moves that could acceler-ate regional tensions, particularly with China. This was evident in the careful language of the SCC statements, which called for China to play a "responsible and constructive role" while also expressing concerns about military transparency. The need to maintain deterrence through enhanced alliance capabilities while preventing an arms race with China emerged as a central challenge, especially as the US sought Chinese cooperation on North Korea even as Japan worried about growing Chinese military power.

As will be seen in chapter 6, these dilemmas would come to the fore in 2006 as the alliance faced critical tests, including the withdrawal of GSDF forces from Iraq and North Korea's missile tests. The joint state-ment on "The Japan-U.S. Alliance of the New Century" would attempt to reconcile these tensions, but the fundamental challenges of balancing alliance obligations, regional stability, and Japan's strategic autonomy would persist. The theoretical frameworks established in 2005 through the SCC's strategic realignment initiatives and Japan's thwarted UN reform efforts would prove essential for understanding how Japan navigated these challenges while maintaining its crucial security relationship with the US during the final months of the Koizumi administration.

Chapter 6

"Alliance of the New Century"

2006

Deepening the Strategic Dialogue

"Two Pillars": The Second National Security Strategy

Although Jun'ichirō Koizumi stepped down as prime minister in 2006, to be replaced in September of that year by Shinzō Abe, Koizumi implemented several consequential policy decisions in the final months of his administration that would significantly influence Japan's security framework and alliance relationships. He authorized the extension of the MSDF's Indian Ocean deployment, and the SCC established a framework for realigning US military installations in Japan, including a partial relocation of Marine units from Okinawa to Guam. And while the GSDF was withdrawn from Iraq, his administration maintained financial support to the country through continued yen loans. In June, Koizumi conducted a diplomatic visit to the US, where he informed Bush of Japan's commitment to sustaining ASDF support in Iraq and increasing official development assistance (ODA). Following these discussions, the leaders jointly issued a strategic document entitled "The Japan-U.S. Alliance of the New Century." In response to North Korea's missile launches in July, Bush and Koizumi engaged in direct telephone consultations and pursued a UNSC resolution through multiple diplomatic channels, circumventing traditional bureaucratic processes. This chapter examines the evolution of US–Japan bilateral relations during the final year of the Bush–Koizumi era.

On March 16, 2006, the White House publicly released the National Security Strategy (NSS) for the Bush administration's second term. Bush described this policy as being founded on two primary pillars. The first focused on the promotion of freedom, justice, and human dignity, with an objective of eliminating tyranny, fostering the establishment of effective democracies, and enhancing prosperity through equitable trade and sound development practices. Governments that were genuinely free were expected to be accountable to their citizens, manage their affairs with efficiency, and implement policies that served the interests of their populace without resorting to oppression or aggression against other free states. The principle of freedom was identified as the cornerstone of lasting peace and global stability. The second pillar underscored the necessity of addressing contemporary global challenges by leading an expanding alliance of democratic nations. Given that issues such as pandemic diseases, the proliferation of WMD, terrorism, human trafficking, and natural disasters transcended national borders, it was deemed imperative to engage in effective international collaboration to confront these challenges. The NSS asserted that "history has shown that only when we do our part will others do theirs. America must continue to lead."[1]

While the document stated that "the United States will, if necessary, act preemptively in exercising our inherent right of self-defense," thereby incorporating the Bush Doctrine of preemptive strikes against any adversary possessing WMD, it adopted a more subdued approach to unilateralism.[2] This emphasized the promotion of freedom and democracy, particularly in the case of North Korea, which was specifically urged to abandon all existing nuclear programs. The NSS concluded that "regional cooperation offers the best hope for a peaceful, diplomatic resolution of this problem."[3]

According to Stephen Hadley, assistant to the President for national security affairs and the principal author of the NSS, the document encompasses five key themes.

First, it asserts that America must be "strong and secure," recognizing the reality that the nation is engaged in a conflict where defeating terrorism represents the "most immediate challenge."[4]

Second, the strategy to combat terrorism necessitates countering "their hateful ideology" by advocating for "the promise of freedom and democracy."[5]

Third, the promotion of freedom and democracy is framed not merely as a strategic choice but as "the birthright of every human being," with the US historically endorsing the principle that every individual is entitled to freedom.[6] This advocacy extends to the belief that effective democracy is the optimal means for nations to guarantee their citizens' freedom, prosperity, and safety.

Fourth, the achievement of security and the fostering of effective democracy are deemed prerequisites for implementing intelligent development strategies that can enhance global quality of life.

Fifth, the formation of a coalition of effective democracies is viewed as the most efficacious approach to addressing "the regional and global challenges of our time."[7]

Acting in alignment with the Bush administration's NSS, in April the Koizumi administration extended the MSDF deployment to the Indian Ocean under the Anti-Terrorism Special Measures Law until November 1. The stated rationale for this extension was to "achieve the UN Charter's objectives in response to the terrorist attacks on the US on September 11, 2001, and other events."[8]

SCC: "ROADMAP FOR REALIGNMENT IMPLEMENTATION"

Building on the strategic priorities outlined in the NSS, the US and Japan advanced specific plans to restructure their military alliance. The two countries initiated comprehensive discussions on the reconfiguration of US military forces deployed within Japanese territories following the October 2005 SCC interim report. A watershed moment in this process occurred on May 1, when the "United States-Japan Roadmap for Realignment Implementation" was released alongside a joint statement from Secretary of State Condoleezza Rice, Secretary of Defense Donald Rumsfeld, Japanese Foreign Minister Taro Asō, and Defense Agency Director-General Fukushirō Nukaga. This joint statement characterized the US–Japan alliance as the "indispensable foundation" of Japan's security architecture and the "linchpin" of American security policy in the Asia-Pacific region, emphasizing the bilateral partnership's vital role in addressing global challenges and promoting shared values, including "basic human rights, freedom, democracy, and the rule of law."[9] The document acknowledged the alliance's demonstrated adaptability to evolving security dynamics while also stressing that its continued effectiveness would require sustained public support from both nations' constituencies.

It identified efforts being made toward several pressing "global challenges," including initiatives to fortify democratic institutions in Iraq and Afghanistan, diplomatic endeavors regarding Iran's nuclear enrichment activities, and multilateral negotiations concerning North Korea's nuclear program.[10] The nations mentioned here notably corresponded with those previously named in Bush's "axis of evil" rhetoric during his 2002 State of the Union address. The statement particularly emphasized the two countries' commitment to the Six-Party Talks framework, advocating for North Korea's return to negotiations for the "complete, verifiable and irreversible" dismantlement of its nuclear capabilities.[11] The ministerial approval of the implementation details for the roadmap signaled the two governments' anticipation for a "new phase in alliance cooperation" with enhanced regional capabilities.[12] The following are summarized excerpts from the roadmap's central section, which was the focus of the SCC's efforts:

1. Realignment on Okinawa

   a. Futenma Replacement Facility (FRF): The US and Japan will locate the FRF in a "V"-shaped configuration near Henoko-saki; it will include two 1,600-meter runways with additional overruns and aim for completion by 2014.

   b. Force Reductions and Relocation to Guam: Approximately 8,000 III Marine Expeditionary Force (MEF) personnel and their 9,000 dependents will move from Okinawa to Guam by 2014, with Japan funding $6.09 billion of the estimated $10.27 billion cost.

   c. Land Returns and Shared Use of Facilities: After relocation, significant land areas south of Kadena Air Base will be returned to Japan, including the total or partial return of six facilities, with a detailed consolidation plan to be developed by March 2007.

2. Improvement of US Army Command and Control Capability: The US Army's command and control structure at Camp Zama will be transformed by 2008, with the Ground SDF Central Readiness Force headquarters arriving by 2012 and SDF helicopters gaining access to Kastner Heliport.

3. Yokota Air Base and Air Space: The ASDF Air Defense Command (ADC) and relevant units will relocate to Yokota Air Base by 2010, establishing a bilateral joint operations coordination center (BJOCC). Measures will be taken to facilitate civilian aircraft movement through Yokota airspace, including returning portions to Japanese control by September 2008 and establishing a program in 2006 to inform commercial aviation entities of transit procedures.[13]

The roadmap outlined the construction of two runways at Henoko to replace Marine Corps Air Station Futenma, the relocation of approximately 8,000 Marines from Okinawa to Guam, and the promotion of cooperation between the American and Japanese commands, as exemplified by those at Camp Zama in Kanagawa Prefecture. The Marines' relocation to Henoko would ultimately be postponed until the 2020s, however. Despite its exclusion from the joint statement and roadmap, China emerged as a pivotal factor in the strengthening of the US–Japan partnership. At the SCC, Asō emphasized the necessity of encouraging China to assume a constructive role as a "responsible stakeholder" in addressing issues such as North Korea and Iran, while also advocating for increased transparency in the modernization of regional military forces.[14] Nukaga expressed concern over both the rapid expansion of Chinese military expenditures and, more critically, the "absence of transparency" in the development of their armed forces.[15] Rumsfeld responded by characterizing China's military expansion as a "challenge," and delineated several options available to the Department of Defense as part of their ongoing efforts to promote greater transparency from China, including naval port visits and military personnel exchanges.[16] At the press conference held afterward, Nukaga observed that China's "defense budget" was "paralleling their economic growth" and emphasized the necessity to "foster transparency" in their military capabilities for the sake of regional security.[17]

While the 2006 roadmap focused on realigning US forces in Japan, concerns over China's growing military power and lack of transparency ultimately underscored the need for a stronger US–Japan partnership. Cheney conveyed to Asō on May 1 that, during Hu's visit to the US, he had urged China to assume the role of a "responsible stakeholder" in addressing the nuclear challenges posed by both North Korea and Iran.[18] He concurred when Asō remarked that, throughout history, "the rise of great powers" had generated friction with their neighbors, citing the empires of Alexander, the Saracens, and the Mongols. Asō added that the US was also China's neighbor, albeit "across the Pacific."[19] Although the Six-Party Talks were a prominent focus overshadowing China's ascent, concerns regarding this rise were shared by both the US and Japan during this period. Had the US and Japan formed a coalition to counter China's rise, it is conceivable that China would have accelerated its military expansion, thus placing the US–Japan alliance and China in a security dilemma amidst a subsequent arms race. This situation exemplifies the dual-structured security dilemma inherent in the asymmetric triangle formed by the US, Japan, and China. There was a separate security dilemma between the US–Japan alliance and China in addition to the one arising from that alliance itself.

Figures 6.1a–b. Realignment of US Forces in Japan. Source: Source: Adapted from Ministry of Foreign Affairs, "Realignment of U.S. forces in Japan," March 6, 2020, www.mofa.go.jp/files/100029846.pdf.

Realignment of U.S. Forces in Japan (Okinawa)

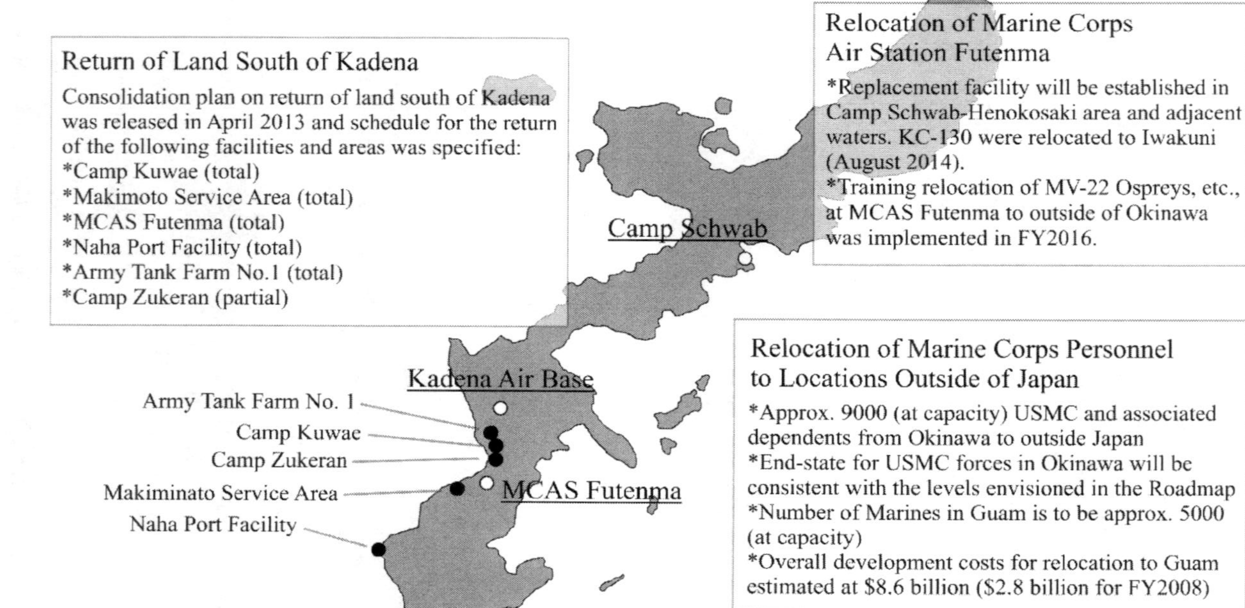

*In the April 2012 "2+2" Joint Statement, Japan and the U.S. decided to delink the relocation of USMC personnel to Guam and the return of land south of Kadena from the relocation of MCAS Futenma

Realignment of U.S. Forces in Japan (Mainland)

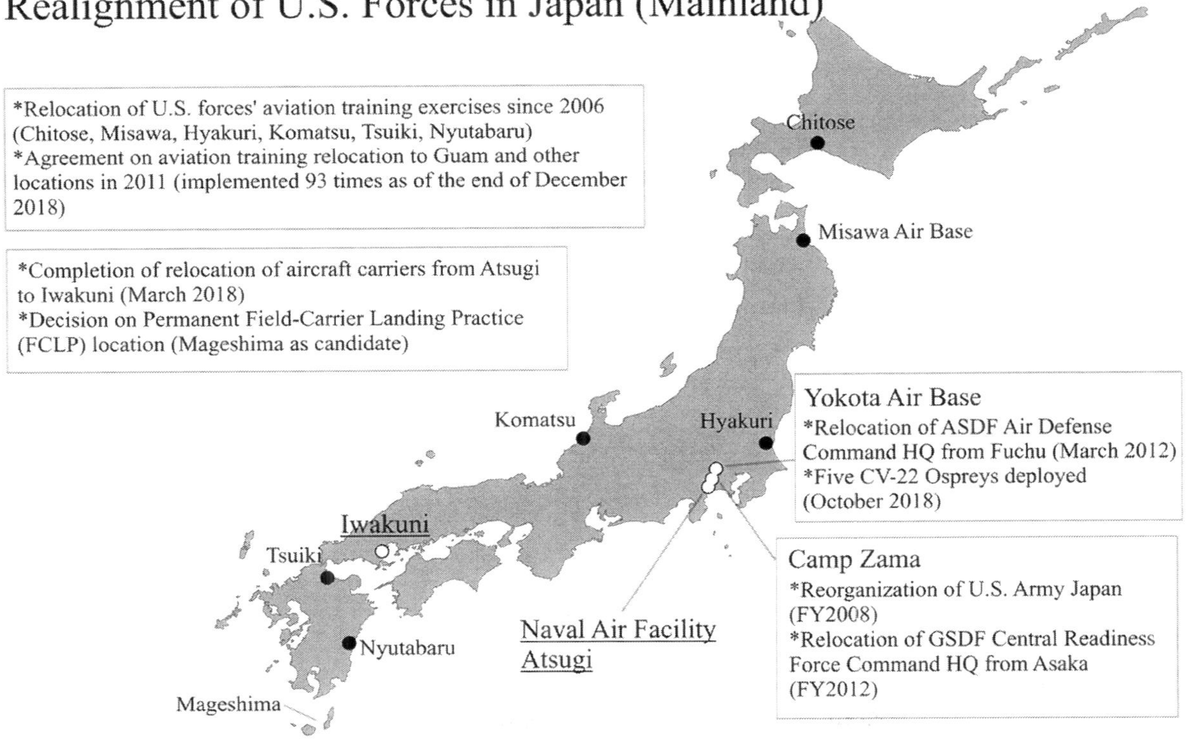

Despite these high-level diplomatic exchanges over regional security, the domestic implementation of the realignment plans encountered substantial challenges. On May 30, the Koizumi administration announced a strategic plan for the realignment of US military forces in Japan. Although the plan proposed a cost-sharing arrangement for the relocation of Marines to Guam, it merely indicated that the relocation site for the contentious Futenma Air Station would be established in accordance with the plan ratified by the SCC; no specific references were made to Henoko or any alternate locations. Furthermore, Koizumi exhibited a lack of enthusiasm for the implementation of the realignment of US bases in Okinawa, and his feud with Okinawa prefecture intensified as local officials and residents continued to resist the central government's base relocation proposals.[20]

The SDF's Withdrawal from Iraq

While a substantial portion of the bilateral agenda was taken up by military base realignment, another significant transformation in Japan's security posture also became apparent in the summer of 2006. On June 20, the Koizumi administration announced the withdrawal of the 600-man GSDF deployment from Samawah, Iraq; at the same time, it also expressed its intention to resume the construction of large power plants and bridges through the provision of yen loans.[21] The decision by the Koizumi administration to withdraw GSDF troops from Iraq represented a significant strategic shift in Japan's approach to supporting reconstruction efforts there, from a military presence to a focus on financial assistance.

At a press conference, Koizumi emphasized the impact of the GSDF units' humanitarian and reconstruction assistance activities and indicated that the withdrawal was necessary due to the transfer of authority over regional security to the newly established Iraqi government.[22] Koizumi's decision to withdraw the troops after two and a half years, even though security had yet to be fully restored, is commendable in that it precluded a permanent military presence in support of an unjust conflict. During a press conference, National Security Advisor Steve Hadley stated that "the missions of . . . the Japanese forces there have been successfully completed" because the Iraqi government had taken over control of security in the region from the coalition.[23] This transition in Samawah aligned with a broader strategy aimed at reducing the foreign military presence as Iraqi security capabilities continued to improve. The Japanese government adapted its role in Iraq by enhancing its air operations, including by offering C-130 transport services to Baghdad and supporting the Multi-National Force—Iraq and the UN's expanded regional efforts. Japan made a substantial contribution to Iraq's reconstruction, committing over $5 billion in aid.

Contradictions between official statements and realities on the ground caused the constitutional legitimacy of the deployment to be called into question. During the initial deployment, Koizumi had asserted that Samawah constituted a "non-combat zone" and that the military action could therefore not be classified as an act of force abroad nor as a violation of the Constitution. Numerous statements in the GSDF activity reports released by the Ministry of Defense in April 2018 cast doubt on the characterization of the region as a "non-combat zone," however. For example, a daily report dated January 22, 2006, detailing "the recent security situation in Samawah," included references to "a firefight between the British and an armed force."[24] This discrepancy between Koizumi's public assurances of the non-combat status of Samawah and the GSDF's operational records, which highlighted armed confrontations in the area, raises significant questions about the constitutional legitimacy of the deployment and the government's transparency in communicating security realities to the Japanese public.

Challenges to the constitutionality of the deployment would ultimately reach the Japanese judiciary, and the Nagoya High Court ruled in April 2008 that the ongoing conflicts in the vicinity breached the legal designation of a "non-combat zone." The case in question involved a petition for an injunction against the ASDF airlifts to Iraq and ultimately resulted in a favorable ruling for the government, which had contended that there had been no infringement of the plaintiffs' rights. Nevertheless, another significant outcome of the case was the court's determination that the SDF's activities contravened Article 9, Section 1 of the Japanese constitution. The High Court noted that, given the permanent instability in the area, the government's description of Baghdad Airport (the point of departure and arrival for the ASDF) as a "non-combat zone" was a misrepresentation. Unlike conventional interstate warfare, conflicts in Iraq were predominantly characterized by internal strife involving multinational forces and residual militias. Consequently, the application of the concept of "non-combat zones" was predicated on an erroneous assumption from the very beginning.[25] Attempting to sustain cooperation with the US while relying on a foundation of repeated misrepresentations could potentially undermine public trust in the government, thereby weakening the US–Japan alliance.

"The Japan-U.S. Alliance of the New Century"

Koizumi's visit to the US in the final months of his administration represented a pivotal moment in US–Japan relations, significantly shaping his legacy in terms of alliance strengthening, even as unresolved regional challenges persisted. Koizumi arrived in Washington on June 29. Rumsfeld described how Japan's "ebullient leader with a flamboyant persona and a passion for all things Elvis Presley" arrived at the White House.[26] After a welcome ceremony, Rumsfeld met with Bush and Koizumi for a two-hour discussion addressing various matters related to what he characterized as "one of America's most important bilateral relationships."[27] Judging from the duration of the meeting between Bush and Koizumi in the Oval Office, it resembled a summit. The length was presumably due to Koizumi's impending resignation as prime minister in the fall.[28]

During the extended meeting in the Oval Office, the two leaders reflected on the transformation of the US–Japan alliance and commemorated their shared accomplishments, particularly in Iraq. Bush praised Koizumi's "epoch-making" decision to deploy Japanese forces to Iraq, suggesting that, while this represented "a tremor for Japan," it meant that Koizumi acknowledged that "democracy brings peace."[29] In informing Bush of the withdrawal of the GSDF from Iraq, Koizumi pledged continued ASDF support and emphasized that since "the fight against terrorism is not over," Japan would continue to collaborate with its allies to provide "as much support as possible."[30] Bush valued Koizumi's support for the US; however, neither leader acknowledged the failure to find WMD in Iraq despite their use as a justification for initiating the war. The GSDF withdrew, but the ASDF continued to conduct airlifts to Baghdad and northern Iraq as part of a new operational initiative. The SDF was becoming an integral component of the US global strategy, as shown by the SCC roadmap. Notably, Koizumi's 2006 visit to the US marked the first instance in the history of US–Japan summits in which the prime minister was accompanied by the defense administrative vice-minister. Although Administrative Vice-Minister of Defense Takemasa Moriya did not attend the discussions, his presence symbolized the elevated status of the Defense Agency with the Japanese government—a consequence of the reorganization of US forces in Japan.[31]

Despite their mutual satisfaction with the level of alliance cooperation in Iraq, significant challenges in Northeast Asia remained a central focus in Bush and Koizumi's discussion, with the issue of North Korea taking up the majority of their time. When Bush remarked, "on the abductee issue, it was truly moving meeting with the mother of the abductee," Koizumi expressed gratitude for Bush's meeting with Sakie Yokota, the mother of Megumi Yokota.[32] Koizumi further added, "We are confidentially considering a range of sanctions against North Korea," to which Bush responded, "the flow of illegal funds must be cut off."[33] When the conversation turned to Japan's bid for permanent membership on the UNSC, Bush stated that "UNSC reform is necessary, but the right balance must be struck."[34] Koizumi did not inquire about the specifics of this "right balance." Bush's carefully worded response indicated that UNSC reform would require complex negotiations that extend beyond Japan's singular pursuit of permanent membership.

As their discussion concluded, the two leaders sought to formalize their vision for the future of the alliance and commemorate their unique partnership in an official declaration. This took the form of a joint statement titled "The Japan-U.S. Alliance of the New Century," which they issued following the meeting. This document highlights the distinctive character of the relationship between Japan and the US, characterizing it as "one of the most accomplished bilateral relationships in history."[35] It emphasizes that these two nations were united in two significant respects: They collaboratively confronted shared challenges and upheld a shared commitment to fundamental principles. These principles included the promotion of human rights and dignity, the maintenance of democratic values, the support of free market systems, and the establishment of legal frameworks to govern society. The statement positioned the alliance not merely as a defensive partnership, but rather as a proactive force advancing these universal ideals.

On the subject of Asia, the statement stressed that the robust cooperation between the two nations "embraces the dynamism of China" while also fostering regional stability in Northeast Asia.[36] The leaders underscored the significance of fortifying strategic partnerships with regional allies, particularly Australia. On North Korea, they advocated for adherence to prior commitments, specifically those articulated in "the September 2005 Joint Statement of the Six Party Talks," and called for ongoing compliance with the missile testing moratorium.[37] Concerning matters related to the UN, the statement recognized Japan's significant contributions and its importance within the organization. The two countries committed to enhancing their collaborative efforts, with the US expressing support for Japan's bid to become "a permanent membership at the Security Council."[38]

However, any reform proposal aimed at granting Japan individual permanent membership was unlikely to achieve international consensus, and Japan's prospects for securing a permanent seat remained minimal.

At the press conference following their meeting, Bush reflected on the significant transition of the US–Japan relationship over the previous 60 years, from a state of conflict to that of collaborative partners on contemporary global issues such as North Korea, Iran, Iraq, trade, and energy cooperation. He characterized this shift as a testament to the transformative power of liberty and democracy in converting former adversaries into allies and reshaping international relations. Bush commended Koizumi for his profound commitment to universal values and freedom, as well as his willingness to act in accordance with these principles. He lauded Koizumi's leadership and decisiveness, saying that they had greatly strengthened the partnership between Japan and the US and fostered closer collaboration in the 21st century. He also recognized Koizumi's contributions to the strategic realignment of troops in a way that not only addressed the needs of the Japanese populace but would "keep in position a relationship that will be necessary for peace and stability."[39]

Koizumi observed that his five-year friendship with Bush had cultivated an atmosphere in which they could speak to another candidly, and that this close relationship was needed for the future relationship between Japan and the US. He emphasized, "Japan and the United States is in a Japan-U.S. alliance in the world" and highlighted the importance of maintaining Japan's security and deterrence while also alleviating burdens on local communities.[40] He expressed gratitude for the significant agreements that had been reached on these critical matters. Noting that their discussions extended beyond bilateral relations to encompass global issues such as Afghanistan, North Korea, and poverty alleviation—particularly for individuals afflicted by disease—Koizumi stressed that "we shared a common perception," and that that had facilitated enhanced bilateral cooperation.[41] This meeting marked the thirteenth between Bush and Koizumi. With Koizumi poised to resign in the fall, Chief Cabinet Secretary Abe characterized the visit as the "final settlement of Koizumi diplomacy."[42] The subsequent focus would be on the implementation of the close relationship between the two countries in the post-Koizumi era and how Japan could normalize its relations with China. The US government had had low expectations for improvements in Sino-Japanese relations under the Koizumi administration and was looking ahead to the post-Koizumi landscape.

North Korea and the UN: From Koizumi to Abe

BALLISTIC MISSILES IN THE SEA OF JAPAN

The celebratory atmosphere surrounding Koizumi's final visit to the US was soon disrupted by a significant provocation that tested the crisis management capabilities of the alliance. The primary focus of Koizumi and Bush's meeting had been North Korea, and on July 5, less than one week later, North Korea launched seven missiles of various types without providing any advance warning to China or any other nation. Although the Taepodong-2 missile (which was capable of reaching the US West Coast) failed, both the short-range Scud-C missiles and intermediate-range Rodong missiles successfully landed in the Sea of Japan.[43] In his memoirs, Rumsfeld observed that the leadership of what he referred to as the "Hermit Kingdom" frequently engaged in provocative actions during American holidays, and US intelligence assessments leading up to July 4 had indicated a potential long-range missile launch, although North Korea's specific intent remained ambiguous—ranging from a mere "demonstration firing" to a potential satellite launch attempt.[44]

The international community, spearheaded by the US and Japan, acted promptly to coordinate a diplomatic response to North Korea's provocative missile launches. The situation generated particular concern for US allies South Korea and Japan, who feared being potential targets of these missiles and aimed to avoid being "ill prepared" for any eventuality.[45] On July 15, the UNSC unanimously adopted Resolution 1695, which condemned the missile launch and prohibited the transfer of missile supplies to North Korea. Japan and the US undertook several measures in response to the launches. The test prompted the Koizumi administration to establish a countermeasures office, convene a Security Council meeting at the Prime Minister's Office, and issue strong diplomatic protests to North Korea through Beijing. The Security Council subsequently implemented actions such as prohibiting the North Korean vessel *Man Gyong Bong 92* from entering Japanese waters and imposing restrictions on entry and exit from North Korea. Foreign Minister Asō spoke with the US secretary of state and the foreign ministers of South Korea, China, Russia, France, and the UK via telephone, confirming that they would continue to remain in close contact and discuss the relevant issues. Secretary of State Rice remarked, "North Korea's provocative actions are extremely regrettable, and it is important that the countries affected send a strong message in unison."[46]

At Japan's request, the UNSC addressed the issue of the missile launches.

Japan responded decisively, with senior officials delivering immediate and unequivocal condemnations. On July 5, Chief Cabinet Secretary Abe expressed strong objections to North Korea's missile activities, emphasizing that these actions transpired despite prior warnings issued by Japan and other nations. He characterized these developments as profoundly concerning for Japan's national security, international stability, and efforts to prevent the proliferation of WMD. He also raised concerns about violations of international aviation and maritime safety regulations, positing that these launches contravened the missile moratorium established in the Japan-DPRK Pyongyang Declaration and undermined the agreements reached during the Six-Party Talks. Japan formally lodged a protest, conveying its disappointment and urging North Korea to restore the moratorium, fulfill its commitments, and reengage in the Six-Party Talks without any preconditions.[47]

The missile launches prompted immediate high-level coordination between the US and Japan, illustrating the alliance's ability to respond rapidly to crises. Bush acted swiftly, speaking with Koizumi by phone on the evening of July 5. The two leaders concurred on the need for the international community, including key stakeholders, to present a unified message in response to North Korea's missile launch. They agreed on the importance of having the UNSC issue a strong statement and concluded that the US and Japan would maintain close collaboration on the issue.[48] Bush also communicated with President Hu Jintao. According to Bush, he informed Hu that "Kim Jong-Il had insulted China" and urged him to publicly condemn the missile launch.[49] Hu subsequently released a statement reaffirming his commitment to "peace and stability" while opposing "any actions that might intensify the situation."[50] Although Hu's remarks were measured, they represented a positive step forward.

The US and Japan established multiple diplomatic channels to coordinate their response to the crisis, which reflected the intricate nature of alliance communication during emergencies. In addition to working-level meetings, Bush and Koizumi used at least four distinct channels in presenting their "resolute message" at the Security Council: telephone conversations between Rice and Asō;[51] discussions between US Ambassador to Japan J. Thomas Schieffer and Asō; meetings between Schieffer and Abe; and phone calls between National Security Advisor Stephen J. Hadley and Abe. Table 6.1 provides examples of these interactions (all dates are in Japan time).

Table 6.1. Routes Between Bush and Koizumi for a "Resolute Message" at the UNSC

Japan Time	Rice–Asō	Schieffer–Asō	Schieffer–Abe	Hadley–Abe
July 5	○[a]			
July 7	○[b]			
July 10	○[c]	○[d]		○[e]
July 12	○[f]		○[g]	
July 14				○[h]
July 16	○[i]			
July 19		○[j]	○[k]	

Source: MOFA documents disclosed under the Information Disclosure Law.

Notes:

a. Tarō Asō to Ryōzō Katō, July 5, 2006, telegraph no. 82874, MOFA documents disclosed under the Information Disclosure Law, 2019–249–12.

b. First North America Division, "Asō Daijin to Rice Kokumu Chōkan tono Denwa Kaidan ni tsuite" [A Telephone Talk Between Minister Asō and Secretary of State Rice], July 7, 2006, MOFA documents disclosed under the Information Disclosure Law, 2019–126–18.

c. First North America Division, "Asō Daijin to Rice Kokumu Chōkan tono Denwa Kaidan ni tsuite" [A Telephone Talk Between Minister Asō and Secretary of State Rice], July 10, 2006, MOFA documents disclosed under the Information Disclosure Law, 2019–126–19.

d. Tarō Asō to Ryōzō Katō and Kenzō Ōshima, July 10, 2006, telegraphic proposal, MOFA documents disclosed under the Information Disclosure Law, 2019–249–38.

e. First North America Division and United Nations Policy Division, "Abe Kanbō Chōkan to Hadley Bei Kokka Anzen Hoshō Mondai Tantō Daitōryō Hosakan no Denwa Kaidan" [A Telephone Talk Between Chief Cabinet Secretary Abe and American Assistant to the President for National Security Affairs Hadley], July 10, 2006, MOFA documents disclosed under the Information Disclosure Law, 2019–126–26.

f. United Nations Policy Division and First North America Division, "Asō Gaimu Daijin to Rice Bei Kokumu Chōkan tono Denwa Kaidan" [A Telephone Talk Between Foreign Minister Asō and Secretary of State Rice], July 12, 2006, MOFA documents disclosed under the Information Disclosure Law, 2019–126–20.

g. United Nations Policy Division, "Abe Kanbō Chōkan to Schieffer Chūnichi Bei Taishi tono Kaidan" [Talk Between Chief Cabinet Secretary Abe and US Ambassador to Japan Schieffer], July 12, 2006, MOFA documents disclosed under the Information Disclosure Law, 2019–126–24; Abe, *Utsukushii Kuni e* [Toward a Beautiful Country] (Bungeishunjū, 2006), 53–54.

h. MOFA, "Abe Kanbō Chōkan to Hadley Bei Daitōryōfu Jiseki Hosakan tono Denwa Kaidan" [A Telephone Talk Between Chief Cabinet Secretary Abe and American Assistant to the President Hadley], July 14, 2006, MOFA documents disclosed under the Information Disclosure Law, 2019–249–47.

i. United Nations Policy Division, "Nichi–Bei Gaishō Denwa Kaidan" [A Telephone Talk Between Japanese Foreign Minister and US Secretary of State], July 16, 2006, MOFA documents disclosed under the Information Disclosure Law, 2019–126–22.

j. First North America Division, "Asō Daijin to Schieffer Zaikyo Bei Taishi tono Denwa Kaidan" [A Telephone Talk between Minister Asō and US Ambassador to Japan Schieffer], July 19, 2006, MOFA documents disclosed under the Information Disclosure Law, 2019–126–23.

k. United Nations Policy Division, "Abe Kanbō Chōkan to Schieffer Zaikōo Bei Taishi tono Denwa Kaidan" [A Telephone Talk Between Chief Cabinet Secretary Abe and US Ambassador to Japan Schieffer], July 19, 2006, MOFA documents disclosed under the Information Disclosure Law, 2019–126–21.

As a nonpermanent member of the UNSC, Japan proposed the resolution in conjunction with eight other countries, including the US, the UK, and France. This resolution, which was unanimously adopted as Resolution 1695 on July 15, demanded that North Korea cease its missile program and that the Six-Party Talks resume immediately and unconditionally. The US and Japan had agreed to omit a reference to Chapter 7 of the UN Charter (which permits sanctions) from the draft resolution as a compromise after Russian and Chinese opposition.[52] Immediately following the resolution's adoption, Parliamentary Vice-Minister for Foreign Affairs Shintarō Itō and US Ambassador to the UN John Bolton commended the Council's unanimous decision. Although North and South Korea were not members of the UNSC, they were present at the meeting as concerned states. The representative from North Korea was the only participant to state that they "totally rejected the resolution."[53]

The resolution was a significant development, as it was the first of its kind in several years; when North Korea had launched a Taepodong-1 missile in 1998 in a similar incident, the UNSC only issued a perfunctory press statement. In stark contrast, this UNSC resolution conveyed a robust message on behalf of the international community and established a decision with binding implications. It holds considerable significance for peace and stability in Northeast Asia, as well as for efforts to prevent the proliferation of missiles and WMD. During the negotiation process, China and Russia had proposed drafts for a chairperson's statement and a weakened resolution that employed the term "deplores." But Japan successfully garnered unanimous support for a more stringent resolution that used the term "condemns," backed by eight countries. Although the reference to Chapter 7 of the UN Charter was ultimately omitted, the US and Japan concurred that the resolution carried binding authority.[54]

North Korea's missile launches represented a significant turning point for South Korea. According to Ambassador Schieffer, ROK Ambassador Ra Jong-yil informed him on July 18 that public sentiment toward the North had reached a pivotal juncture in South Korea due to the missile launches and its unfavorable conduct during a recent South–North ministerial meeting. However, Ra expressed concern that a visit by Koizumi to Yasukuni Shrine on August 15 could "reverse that favorable trend."[55] Schieffer firmly rejected Ra's attempt to involve the US in the Yasukuni controversy, emphasizing that disputes between South Korea and Japan should be resolved bilaterally.[56] As Ra had anticipated, Koizumi did visit

Yasukuni Shrine on August 15, an event that ultimately did not improve relations between Japan and South Korea.

THE ST. PETERSBURG G8 SUMMIT

As the North Korean missile crisis unfolded, there was ongoing international diplomacy in multiple forums, creating opportunities for broader coordination among the global powers. Adoption of the North Korea resolution at the UNSC coincided with the St. Petersburg G8 summit held from July 15 to 17. Notably, it was during this summit that Koizumi chose to remove the reference to Chapter 7 in order to secure unanimous approval.[57]

During summit breaks, Koizumi informed Bush that "the Security Council resolution on North Korea was a commendable one" and expressed his appreciation for the collaboration, to which Bush responded favorably.[58] During his one-on-one meeting with Putin, Koizumi emphasized to him that Japan's priority was addressing issues related to "North Korea's nuclear weapons, missiles, and abductions." Putin acknowledged that these "concerns and anxieties" were "well-founded and understood."[59] Koizumi also asserted at the summit that North Korea should promptly and unconditionally resume its participation in the Six-Party Talks to comprehensively address missile, nuclear weapon, and abduction issues, a position that garnered the support of the summit's participants, including the chair, Putin.[60] The G8 statement on nonproliferation condemned North Korea's numerous ballistic missile launches and articulated "serious concerns as this jeopardizes peace, stability and security in the region and beyond."[61] The Chair's summary addressed nuclear and other security concerns, as well as humanitarian issues related to North Korea, and strongly urged the nation to relinquish all nuclear weapons and terminate existing nuclear programs.[62]

In his final assessment of the summit's achievements, given at a press conference, Koizumi emphasized the unified response of the international community to North Korea's provocations. He noted that the missile issue had significantly influenced discussions leading up to the summit and that two notable diplomatic achievements had been made: the unanimous passage of the UNSC resolution and the unified stance of the G8. With regard to the "nuclear issue, the missile issue, and the abduction issue," Koizumi stressed that "resolving all these matters necessitates international coordination" in managing the multifaceted challenges presented by North Korea.[63] This marked Koizumi's sixth G8 summit, the highest number ever attended by a single Japanese prime minister. He and Bush should be commended for achieving an international consensus on maintaining a hardline stance toward North Korea. Nevertheless, despite these efforts, the Six-Party Talks would conclude in December 2008, and North Korea has continued to carry out missile launches and nuclear tests.

The G8 summit provided a revealing window into Koizumi's nuanced stance on China, which balanced economic opportunity against security concerns. This was expressed most clearly during his bilateral meeting with German Chancellor Angela Merkel, during which he characterized China's development as an "opportunity" and welcomed its "increasingly constructive presence" in both regional and global affairs.[64] But while acknowledging the growing bilateral exchanges in trade and personnel, he also expressed serious reservations about lifting the EU's arms embargo, citing concerns over China's military expenditures, which were "rising at an annual rate of nearly 20 percent."[65] Merkel responded diplomatically, expressing understanding of Koizumi's concerns and agreeing that any potential lifting of the EU arms embargo on China would require a cautious approach. During the discussion, Koizumi reflected on the paradoxical state of Japan–China relations, noting that cultural, trade, and tourism exchanges between the countries had made progress over the previous five years. However, he found it "perplexing" that Beijing refused to hold summit meetings with him due to "differing opinions" regarding his visits to Yasukuni Shrine.[66]

From Koizumi to Abe

The final months of 2006 were a pivotal period for Japanese politics, marked by substantial changes and an innovative approach to addressing regional tensions. Chief among these changes was Shinzō Abe becoming prime minister on September 26. The US perspective on Japan's leadership transition was perhaps best captured in Secretary of State Rice's assessment following her October 18 visit to Tokyo. She characterized the shift from Koizumi to Abe as a marked change in leadership style and diplomatic approach. While Koizumi had been an "animated personality" and a "fierce defender of the US–Japan alliance," demonstrating his commitment through military support in Afghanistan and Iraq, Abe presented himself as a more "traditional and reserved leader."[67] She noted that despite Abe's occasional forcefulness, Japan faced significant regional trust deficits, not only with China but also with America's "South Korean friends."[68] She suggested that while some Japanese assertiveness could be beneficial, it needed careful calibration to avoid exacerbating regional tensions. Abe exhibited more conservative values than Koizumi, raising uncertainties regarding his ability to enhance Japan's diplomatic relations with China and South Korea.[69]

On October 9, North Korea carried out a nuclear test. This was followed by the unanimous adoption of Resolution 1718 by the UNSC on October 14, the first instance in which the UNSC imposed sanctions on North Korea. Both the Bush and Abe administrations supported this move. The North Korean challenge presented a complex diplomatic inheritance from Koizumi to the Abe administration. Rice observed that Tokyo feared that Washington might strike a nuclear deal with Pyongyang that sidelined the "tragic Japanese abduction cases."[70] She noted growing friction with Japanese officials, who perceived her as "too interested in resolving the North Korean nuclear issue" at the expense of the abductions matter.[71] Koizumi had established the precedent of prioritizing the abduction issue through his visits to Pyongyang, and the Abe government increased this focus out of concern that a US–North Korea nuclear agreement would diminish American leverage in pressing for resolution of the abductions.

Rumsfeld offered a different assessment of the lack of progress, focusing on China's role. He argued that Beijing prioritized preventing North Korean state collapse over denuclearization, fearing a refugee crisis and "failed Korean state" on its border.[72] In his view, China's protective stance toward North Korea undermined the prospects for successful Six-Party Talks. The failure to achieve denuclearization thus stemmed from multiple factors: Japan's insistence on linking the nuclear and abduction issues, China's prioritization of regime stability over denuclearization, and the resulting complications in multilateral negotiations.[73] Consequently, there would be no denuclearization of North Korea under either the Koizumi or Abe administrations.

A comparative analysis of the foreign policies of Prime Ministers Koizumi and Abe reveals fundamental differences in their strategic approaches to international relations. While Koizumi's diplomatic strategy predominantly focused on strengthening bilateral ties with the US, it lacked a comprehensive framework for broader regional engagement. This limitation becomes particularly apparent when contrasted with Abe's more sophisticated foreign policy architecture. As documented in Abe's memoirs, although Koizumi successfully reinforced the US–Japan alliance during the Bush administration, his diplomatic relationships with regional powers, particularly China, suffered significantly due to his controversial visits to Yasukuni Shrine. In contrast, Abe adopted a more balanced approach upon taking office, prioritizing regional diplomatic engagement alongside the US alliance. This was exemplified by his strategic decision to make Beijing his first overseas destination as prime minister, and his attempt to establish what he termed a "Mutually Beneficial Relationship Based on Common Strategic Interests."[74]

Abe further distinguished his foreign policy through the development of multilateral frameworks, notably the Quadrilateral Security Dialogue (Quad) with the US, India, and Australia, as well as the articulation of the Free and Open Indo-Pacific Strategy (FOIP). These initiatives represented a departure from the traditional pattern of US involvement in shaping Japan's strategic outlook. While Koizumi's foreign policy remained largely reactive and bilateral in nature, Abe constructed a more sophisticated and multidimensional strategic framework that expanded Japan's diplomatic options beyond the confines of the US–Japan alliance.

Conclusion

The final year of the Bush–Koizumi era exemplified the enduring nature of Japan's global alliance security dilemma. While the Koizumi administration withdrew the GSDF troops from Iraq, it maintained ASDF support and increased ODA commitments. This strategic approach highlighted Japan's need to sustain alliance solidarity, despite the absence of the WMD that had initially justified the intervention into Iraq. The dilemma intensified following North Korea's missile tests in July 2006, as these compelled Japan to coordinate its response through multiple diplomatic channels alongside the US. The joint statement, "The Japan-U.S. Alliance of the New Century," formalized the expanded alliance framework while underscoring Japan's challenging position; even as it withdrew from Iraq, it still felt obligated to maintain support for US objectives that extended beyond the alliance's original geographic scope to ensure continued American backing on North Korean issues.

The fundamental asymmetry of the alliance was apparent in both military and diplomatic dimensions throughout 2006. The May "Road-map for Realignment Implementation" mandated that Japan finance $6.09

billion of the $10.27 billion cost associated with relocating Marines to Guam while affording Japan limited input in strategic decisions. Japan's strategic response to North Korea's missile launches was significantly influenced by the need to align with the US and involved navigating various diplomatic channels to ensure a coordinated response. Although Japan actively supported the alliance, its strategic autonomy was constrained in a way that reflected the structural dependencies limiting Japan's capacity to operate independently, even in the face of pressing regional security threats. The greater flexibility shown by the US in its response highlighted the asymmetry between the two partners; the US was able to act independently, whereas Japan remained reliant on American deterrence and security guarantees.

The dual-structured security dilemma became increasingly pronounced as the alliance explicitly incorporated China as a strategic consideration. During SCC meetings, Japan was tasked with balancing the enhancement of alliance capabilities against the necessity of avoiding provocative actions that could exacerbate regional tensions with China. This balance was exemplified by Foreign Minister Asō's careful characterization of China as a potential "responsible stakeholder" even as he simultaneously raised concerns over military transparency. The May 2006 roadmap's enhancement of bilateral military coordination, which included the establishment of joint operations centers, had to be weighed against the risk of precipitating an arms race with China. This dilemma was further complicated by North Korea's missile tests, which underscored the necessity for alliance deterrence while potentially accelerating regional military competition.

These developments in 2006 laid the groundwork for the comprehensive examination of the broader implications of the US–Japan alliance of the Bush–Koizumi era that will be carried out in the next chapter, the conclusion. The arrangements established—from the realignment roadmap to the "Alliance of the New Century" framework—would significantly influence how later administrations navigated both global and regional security challenges. The transition from Koizumi to Abe would serve as a test of whether these newly established alliance structures could effectively address Japan's strategic needs while managing the inherent tensions between alliance obligations and regional relationships. The fundamental dilemmas that crystallized during the Bush–Koizumi period would continue to shape Japan's security choices well into the future, as it sought to balance alliance requirements against the imperative of regional stability.

Conclusion

The Dilemmas of the Alliance and Its Future

The Decline of "Pax Americana"

The contemporary US–Japan alliance has prioritized deterrence and regional stability over direct military intervention; this is why the analysis of the alliance in the early 21st century given in the preceding chapters has focused on diplomatic dimensions. In this chapter, I seek to synthesize the implications of US–Japan relations and Asian diplomatic initiatives during the Bush–Koizumi administration while situating this period in the context of broader historical developments. The conclusion of the Cold War, marked by the historic Malta Summit between US President George H. W. Bush and Soviet General Secretary Mikhail Gorbachev in 1989, heralded an era of anticipated global peace. The subsequent decade witnessed the emergence of American unipolarity, a paradigm that persisted throughout the 2001–2006 period analyzed in this study. However, this unipolar moment evolved into what scholars have characterized as the US–China Cold War, a transition precipitated by China's economic ascendancy later in the first decade of the 21st century and further solidified following Donald Trump's presidential victory in 2016. It is worth noting that the original Cold War's bipolar configuration, in which American influence, even by liberal estimates, did not encompass the majority of the global community, complicates the subsumption of this period within the broader framework of "Pax Americana."

The interregnum between the conclusion of the Cold War and the emergence of US–China strategic competition spanned approximately 25 years, a time that is more aptly characterized as a transitional phase than a distinct systemic epoch. During this period, the US exercised unprecedented hegemony across military, economic, and soft power domains. A strict definitional framework of Pax Americana as a unipolar system would confine it to the administrations of Clinton, Bush, and Obama. Throughout these post–Cold War decades, American preeminence coincided with China's developmental trajectory, positioning Beijing as an entity to be engaged rather than contained within the international order.

While the Iraq War represented the apex of Pax Americana, it paradoxically catalyzed America's relative decline. The military campaign initiated by the Bush administration, although tactically successful, exposed the limitations of unilateral power projection. Despite securing support from key allies such as Blair and Koizumi—who were persuaded by ultimately unfounded intelligence regarding WMD—the intervention generated significant friction within the G8, particularly from Russia, France, and Germany. This international discord amplified Bush's reliance on steadfast partners, notably precipitating an expanded scope for the US–Japan alliance beyond its traditional East Asian parameters during the Bush–Koizumi era.

The globalization of the US–Japan alliance emerged as a direct consequence of the legitimacy deficit associated with American unilateralism. However, the failure to uncover WMD or successfully implement democratization in Iraq undermined American credibility and expedited the erosion of the unipolar order. The very magnitude of American power appears to have fostered strategic overreach within the Bush administration, ultimately compromising the sustainability of the unipolar system. Despite well-intentioned objectives, the interventions in Afghanistan and Iraq revealed the limitations of American nation-building capabilities, highlighting a critical disjuncture between military superiority and post-conflict stabilization competencies.

Although the Bush–Koizumi partnership established an unprecedented level of intimacy in US–Japan diplomatic relations during the Iraq War, their collaboration should not be regarded as a paradigm for future bilateral engagement. The growing skepticism regarding democratization as a vehicle for peace, which emerged in the latter half of the Bush administration, foreshadowed a decline in America's global influence. This trajectory stands in stark contrast to former Japanese Prime Minister Yoshida Shigeru's astute observation following the San Francisco Peace Conference: "There are cases in history of winning by diplomacy after losing a war."[1] Paradoxically, while Bush and Koizumi attained military success, their diplomatic shortcomings ultimately undermined their credibility both domestically and internationally. This legacy influenced subsequent administrations—Obama, Trump, and Biden—to adopt a more circumscribed approach to American engagement, not only in the Middle East but across the global arena.

Global Alliance Security Dilemma

Aside from the personal relationship between Bush and Koizumi, three fundamental factors motivated Japan's support for the Iraq War. First, Japan lacked its own intelligence network and relied heavily on American assessments regarding WMD that ultimately proved to be erroneous. Koizumi's conviction in the existence of WMD in Iraq, stemming from his uncritical faith in the superiority of US intelligence, constituted a significant misjudgment of his administration. Bush's assumption that war and military occupation could facilitate the democratization of Iraq was similarly misguided. Both leaders were also overly optimistic regarding the stabilization of Afghanistan. These misconceptions proliferated within the US–Japan alliance, functioning as a mechanism that amplified erroneous beliefs through the resonance of American wishful thinking and a Japanese apprehension of potential abandonment.

The second critical factor was the enduring influence of "Gulf War Trauma"—a manifestation of both the "free rider complex" and a "misuse of history"—which prompted Japan's reflexive support for US initiatives in the Iraq War. In the context of recurring American characterizations of Japan as a beneficiary of the international order and the bilateral alliance without commensurate contributions, Koizumi's ability to transform these critical American perceptions through alliance enhancement was significant, as exemplified by the 2006 declaration of "The Japan-U.S. Alliance of the New Century." However, the absence of WMD in Iraq, which had served as the primary justification for military intervention, coupled with SDF field reports that exposed the conceptual inadequacy of "non-combat zone" designations, subsequently generated a new "Iraq War Trauma." This experiential legacy has constrained Japan's capacity for overseas SDF deployments while paradoxically intensifying its security dependence on the US.

Third, Japan's strategic calculus was fundamentally shaped by the dynamics of the global alliance security dilemma. Given Japan's reliance on US security guarantees against potential threats from North Korea and China, the apprehension regarding alliance abandonment compelled Japanese participation in what could be characterized as a problematic American agenda, despite the associated costs. This strategic reasoning is definitively evidenced in former Chief Cabinet Secretary Yasuo Fukuda's recollection that "There was the matter of North Korea; we continued to hope for American deterrence in that context."[2] The Koizumi administration assessed that preventing US diplomatic isolation over Iraq would secure heightened American engagement with Japanese concerns regarding North Korea, particularly by strengthening the influence of the Powell-Armitage faction over North Korea policy. The establishment of the Ruling Parties' Liaison Committee on Iraq–North Korea Affairs symbolically reflected this perceived quid pro quo arrangement within the alliance: Japanese support for American objectives in Iraq in exchange for US attention to Japanese priorities vis-à-vis North Korea. Thus, Japan strategically leveraged its support for the Iraq War as diplomatic capital to influence US policy orientation toward North Korea.

Despite Japan's substantial support for US military operations in Iraq and significant contributions to reconstruction efforts, its fundamental strategic vulnerabilities persisted unabated. Japan's support for the Iraq War failed to reduce its strategic dependence on the US; instead, Koizumi's decisions deepened Japan's reliance on American security guarantees while constraining its diplomatic autonomy, making Japan's position even more precarious in balancing alliance obligations against independent national interests. The conflict yielded several critical insights, particularly regarding Japan's need for enhanced independent intelligence capabilities and the risks associated with excessive reliance on US intelligence—lessons that contemporary policymakers must incorporate into strategic planning.

In Northeast Asia, the Bush–Koizumi era was characterized by the challenge of addressing North Korea's missile program and nuclear weapons development. In contrast to the military solution pursued in Iraq, Koizumi was successful in advocating for a diplomatic approach to the North Korean crisis, while also elevating the abduction issue through G8 summit diplomacy. In its final months, the Koizumi administration secured a unanimous UNSC resolution condemning North Korea's missile launches—an achievement that, while failing to prevent subsequent launches, represented a significant diplomatic milestone. As China's influence grew, the US sought to leverage it as an intermediary in dealings with North Korea. Although both Washington and Tokyo acknowledged China's ascending power during Bush's second term, the North Korean threat remained paramount in their strategic calculations. The US anticipated that Chinese mediation would prove crucial within the Six-Party Talks framework. Consequently, despite concerns regarding China's military opacity, its expanding defense expenditures were relegated to secondary importance, inadvertently fostering conditions conducive to China's military advancement. Had the US and Japan adopted a confrontational stance toward China, they might have accelerated its military modernization, potentially triggering a security dilemma and an ensuing arms race between the alliance and China.

While Japan linked the issues of Iraq and North Korea within the framework of the US–Japan alliance, this connection arose more from circumstantial pressures than from a deliberate strategic approach. The formal integration of these two challenges occurred during the SCC meeting on December 16, 2002, which was convened shortly after North Korea announced the resumption of its nuclear program. Japan's seemingly contradictory positions—supporting military intervention in Iraq while advocating for a peaceful resolution with North Korea—reflected a fundamental strategic constraint: Japan's reliance on American nuclear deterrence against North Korean threats necessitated support for US military initiatives, even when such support appeared to conflict with Japan's preferred diplomatic approaches.

The Iraq War significantly altered the US–Japan alliance and the dynamics of Asian security in two notable ways. First, Japan's substantial support for military operations in Iraq expanded the US–Japan alliance beyond its traditional regional parameters. Second, the prolonged deployment of American forces from Japan to Iraq resulted in a considerable reduction of US military presence in Japan, one that particularly affected Marine Corps units stationed in Okinawa. However, this substantial decrease in forward-deployed forces did not immediately undermine the alliance's deterrent capability; instead, Japan's commitment to the Iraq War and the cultivation of American trust ultimately served to reinforce US security commitments to Japan's defense.

Two theoretical frameworks elucidate this apparent paradox in deterrence. The first, drawing on Hans J. Morgenthau's classical realist perspective,[3] emphasizes the quantitative military balance, suggesting that the reduction of US forces in Japan temporarily enhanced North Korean and Chinese relative military capabilities, thereby diminishing the alliance's deterrent effect. The strength of this interpretation lies in its empirical measurement of force reductions during the Iraq deployment. The second framework, aligned with Stephen M. Walt's balance of threat theory,[4] focuses on psychological factors, arguing that the enhanced trust between American and Japanese leaders bolstered the alliance's credibility, thereby raising the perceived costs of aggression for the North Korean and Chinese leadership. While this psychological interpretation is more challenging to verify due to limited access to primary sources from North

Korea and China, it offers a more convincing explanation for long-term deterrence dynamics: Despite the temporary reduction in US forces, the overall deterrent effect of the alliance was strengthened through enhanced bilateral trust and demonstrated commitment.

Regardless of which interpretation of deterrence proves more accurate, the unilateral deployment of Marine Corps units from Okinawa to conduct combat operations in Fallujah—without the prior consultation required by treaty obligations—profoundly disturbed Okinawan residents and undermined Japanese public trust in the alliance. This erosion of trust was particularly acute among communities adjacent to US military installations, whose support had historically served as a cornerstone of the US–Japan security relationship. The decline in public confidence was further exacerbated by two factors: first, the failure to discover the WMD in Iraq that had served as the primary justification for Japanese support of the war; and second, the government's reliance on the legally dubious concept of "non-combat zones" to justify the deployment of the SDF. As evidenced by GSDF activity reports released in 2018 and the 2008 Nagoya High Court ruling that challenged the designation of these areas as "non-combat zones," the Koizumi administration's repeated misrepresentation of operational realities in Iraq inflicted lasting damage on the credibility of the government's alliance management. These developments suggest that while the Iraq War may have strengthened elite bilateral ties, it simultaneously weakened grassroots support for the alliance, particularly in communities most directly affected by the US military presence.

FAILED ATTEMPTS TO MITIGATE ALLIANCE ASYMMETRY

From the perspective of the global alliance security dilemma, Koizumi's diplomatic initiatives toward North Korea and his advocacy for UNSC reform represented strategic efforts aimed at reducing Japan's dependence on the US and enhancing its diplomatic autonomy. However, these endeavors ultimately reinforced, rather than diminished, Japan's subordinate position in the alliance. The September 2002 Pyongyang Declaration serves as a pertinent example of this dynamic; while Koizumi believed he had secured constraints on North Korea's nuclear program, North Korea's subsequent admission to Assistant Secretary James Kelly just weeks later regarding an active nuclear weapons program underscored the declaration's fundamental shortcomings. Koizumi miscalculated in two critical respects: first, by accepting North Korean commitments at face value, and second, by failing to recognize that Pyongyang perceived nuclear negotiations as exclusively bilateral with Washington.

The outcomes of Koizumi's visit further complicated Japan's strategic position. Rather than alleviating security concerns, it underscored the intractability of the abduction issue. Koizumi's subsequent policy of "no normalization of diplomatic relations without resolution of the abduction issue" effectively paralyzed direct Japan–North Korea negotiations. This diplomatic impasse heightened Japanese reliance on American leverage as North Korea continued to advance both its nuclear and missile capabilities. While the Bush administration shifted toward engaging North Korea through the Six-Party Talks framework, Japan's insistence on including abductions alongside denuclearization complicated multilateral diplomatic efforts. The paradoxical outcome of these initiatives intended to enhance Japanese diplomatic autonomy was an increase in its dependence on American security guarantees and diplomatic intermediation.

For Japan, permanent membership on the UNSC represented a critical pathway for mitigating the global alliance security dilemma, offering three strategic advantages. First, permanent membership would grant access to comprehensive intelligence and security information typically reserved for permanent members. Second, it would provide institutional leverage for addressing security challenges posed by North Korea and China. Third, permanent membership would enable Japan to align with European powers in moderating potentially unilateral American military initiatives. Given the absence of NATO-equivalent multilateral security frameworks in Asia, the UNSC represented Japan's most viable institutional opportunity for both accessing regional intelligence and employing multilateral diplomacy to balance US unilateralism and threats in Northeast Asia.

However, the US maintained a contradictory position; while publicly endorsing Japan's bid for permanent membership—particularly during Secretary Rice's visits to Tokyo—it actively opposed broader UNSC reforms that would facilitate Japan's accession. As Rice acknowledged in her memoirs, "the politics of UNSC reform were just too complicated to take on," citing concerns about Chinese opposition to India's inclusion and European overrepresentation.[5] The collapse of Japan's permanent membership aspirations, exemplified by the failure of the G4 resolution in 2005, effectively foreclosed this institutional path toward greater strategic autonomy. Notably, despite the close relationship between Bush and Koizumi, the US made no substantive effort to advance Japan's membership, suggesting a preference for maintaining the existing asymmetric alliance structure.

The global alliance security dilemma influenced American strategic calculations as well, albeit with a considerably less constraining effect than it exerted on Japanese policy choices. The US needed to accommodate Japan's advocacy for a peaceful resolution with North Korea in order to maintain Japanese support for military operations in Iraq, which constituted Washington's primary strategic priority. While Bush initially asserted that "all options were on the table" for North Korea, the alliance dynamics effectively precluded military action against Pyongyang. Although Koizumi's support for the Iraq War was not explicitly intended to obstruct American military action against North Korea, Japan's fundamental policy of supporting US initiatives would likely have remained consistent regardless of whether Shinzō Abe or Yasuo Fukuda held the position of prime minister. This consistency demonstrates how the global alliance security dilemma transcends individual leadership personalities.

The asymmetric nature of these constraints reflects the inherent power imbalance within the alliance. Japan faced a stark choice between potential entrapment in American military ventures and the risk of abandonment by its security guarantor. In contrast, the US encountered a less binding dilemma, between showing consideration for Japanese preferences and risking Japanese disapproval. Japan's fundamental dependence on American nuclear deterrence against North Korea effectively precluded any meaningful opposition to the Iraq War. Conversely, the US retained the capacity to pursue military action independently of Japanese support, illustrating how structural imbalances in alliance relationships generate correspondingly asymmetric strategic dilemmas for the partners involved.

DUAL-STRUCTURED SECURITY DILEMMA AND THE FUTURE OF THE ALLIANCE

This study has empirically elucidated the origins and structure of the US–Japan global alliance security dilemma through an examination of interconnected cases spanning the War in Afghanistan, the Iraq War, Northeast Asian issues, UN policy, and G8 summits. From a balance-of-power perspective, the threats posed by Iraq, North Korea, and China, coupled with the alliance security dilemma, necessitated the strengthening of the US–Japan alliance despite the potential drawbacks. However, this enhanced alliance partnership generated its own security dilemma for perceived adversaries, particularly China and North Korea, whose responses could ultimately undermine both US–Japan security interests and regional economic stability. Moreover, the strategic constraints operated in multiple directions. Had Japan pursued excessively close relations with China, Beijing could have leveraged that relationship to weaken Japan's alliance ties with the US amid US–China strategic competition. Thus, Japan faced not one but two interrelated security dilemmas: the first within its alliance relationship with the US, and the second in its interactions with China and North Korea. This dual-structured security dilemma fundamentally shaped the dynamics of the US–Japan–China asymmetric triangle.

The threat posed by China and North Korea intensified significantly during the 2010s. It was not until the Obama administration that the US, in concert with Japan, began actively working to constrain China's expanding influence.[6] In 2014, Japan undertook serious consideration of exercising CSD, and the second Abe administration enhanced Japan's international profile through the implementation of new security legislation. In the contemporary context of the 2020s, Japan's security dependence on the US has become increasingly pronounced, driven not only by North Korea's nuclear weapons and missile capabilities but also by China's territorial assertiveness in the East China Sea, which poses direct challenges to Japanese security interests. The alliance security dilemma—where Japan's reliance on American deterrence against potential adversaries in Northeast Asia effectively precludes opposition to American initiatives, even when their legitimacy may be questionable—continues to fundamentally shape Japanese defense policy. Japan has increased both its defense expenditures and its financial contributions toward maintaining US forces within its borders even though the SOFA remains unrevised. Concurrently, the security dynamic between the US–Japan alliance, China, and North Korea—the dual-structured security dilemma comprising both the alliance security dilemma and the traditional security dilemma that has historically characterized Northeast Asian international politics—persists unabated.

How might the US–Japan alliance evolve under the dual-structured security dilemma? Several potential scenarios warrant critical examination. The first, while theoretically conceivable but highly improbable, involves either Japan or the US withdrawing from the US–Japan Security Treaty, necessitating a substantial expansion of Japan's independent defense capabilities. This option, however, presents significant practical challenges for Japan: the dissolution of the security treaty, combined with an exclusively self-defense-oriented posture, would likely result in unsustainable military expenditures, economic instability, and diplomatic isolation. The ensuing reduction of Japan's national power would hinder its ability to independently address security challenges posed by China and North Korea. Even short of complete alliance termination, there is also the possibility of a Japanese variant of Gaullist independence—something similar to the notion of a "Security Treaty without permanent US military presence" as was proposed by Democratic Party of Japan leader Yukio Hatoyama prior to his 2009 ascension to the prime ministership.[7] As outlined in figure C.1, the implications of such a Japanese Gaullism would largely depend on whether the US pursued unilateralist policies or opted for accommodation with China.

The second scenario—maintaining the current alliance structure—represents the status quo baseline for US–Japan relations. This approach would necessitate careful alliance management to balance regional dynamics vis-à-vis an ascendant China and persistent North Korean threats. The third scenario envisions Japan developing a multilayered security architecture by strengthening partnerships with strategically aligned nations and regions—including Australia, India, and Europe—while preserving the US–Japan alliance as the coalition's cornerstone. This framework could potentially mitigate the dual-structured security dilemma through the establishment of a stratified security regime and the reinvigoration of the US–Japan alliance. Such an approach aligns with former prime minister Abe's FOIP vision and the Quadrilateral Security Dialogue (Quad) comprising the US, Japan, Australia, and India. This dynamic situation requires flexible analysis rather than static assessment. The traditional hub-and-spoke alliance system may need to evolve into a more distributed network of interconnected partnerships and quasi-alliances to address the vulnerabilities exposed during the Trump administration, when the US proved unreliable in exercising its function as the hub, and, more fundamentally, to adapt to America's relative power decline.

Nevertheless, even with the potential reinforcement of initiatives such as FOIP or the Quad, the US–Japan alliance will undoubtedly remain the cornerstone of Japan's defense architecture; partnerships with other democratic nations are likely to serve primarily as hedging mechanisms rather than viable alternatives to the alliance. Should the US again pursue contentious military actions beyond the Far East, as exemplified by the intervention in Iraq, Japan would face considerable pressure to provide support, particularly given that China's growing assertiveness, coupled with North Korea's persistent threats, has intensified Japan's reliance on American deterrence capabilities. However, the global alliance security dilemma has arguably diminished in significance over the course of the 2010s and 2020s, largely due to widespread opposition to Bush-era interventions in Iraq and Afghanistan and the notably isolationist tendencies of the Trump administration. Within this evolving strategic landscape, Japan must carefully calibrate its approach to the US–Japan alliance—maintaining sufficient commitment to prevent abandonment while avoiding entrapment in potentially destructive American military ventures or an escalating arms race with China.

The dual-structured security dilemma, which fundamentally shapes the triangular relationship between the US, Japan, and China, necessitates sophisticated multilayered trust-building initiatives and nuanced alliance-management strategies to address persistent vulnerabilities and strategic uncertainties in the Indo-Pacific theater. As regional power dynamics continue to evolve, particularly with China's growing influence and America's relative decline, Japanese policymakers must navigate an increasingly complex security environment while maintaining alliance cohesion and regional stability. This delicate balancing act will likely define the trajectory of both the US–Japan alliance and the broader Indo-Pacific security architecture in the decades ahead.

Figure C.1. The US–Japan Alliance Options and Their Expected Results. *Source:* Created by the author.

American Position	Japanese Position	Effect on Balance with China/North Korea
Unilateralism	Gaullism	Arms race/collision***
	Maintenance of the alliance	Japan needs to act as balancer/mediator
Committed to the alliance*		Alliance management is required to maintain balance and the status quo
Multilayered security regime in addition to the alliance		Restrictions on China/ North Korea**
Engagement with/ appeasement of China	Gaullism	G2 that would accelerate China's rise***
	Maintenance of the alliance	Triangle disadvantageous to Japan

* Baseline for U.S.-Japan relations

** Best scenario for Japan

*** Worst scenario for Japan

Notes

Introduction

1. Yasuaki Chijiwa, "Insights into Japan–U.S. Relations on the Eve of the Iraq War: Dilemmas over 'Showing the Flag,'" *Asian Survey* 45, no. 6 (November/December 2005): 843–64.

2. The only reference to Japan is "My blood pressure still goes up when I remember the cover of Newsweek, in October 1987. It pictured my dad, in his boat, with the caption: 'Fighting the Wimp Factor.' They were talking about George Bush, war hero, youngest pilot to earn his wings in the Navy, a pilot who had been shot down and rescued by a submarine near an island occupied by the Japanese." George W. Bush, *A Charge to Keep: My Journey to the White House* (Perennial, 2001), 180–81. See also Donald Rumsfeld, *Known and Unknown: A Memoir* (Sentinel, 2011), 37–39, 77, 301–2.

3. Steven Mufson, "Vietnam Era Shaped Two Different Worldviews: Gore Stresses 'Engagement,' U.S. Values; Bush Says Strategic Interests Are Central," *Washington Post*, October 27, 2000; Steven Mufson, "Vietnam Era Shaped Two Different Worldviews: Gore Stresses 'Engagement,' U.S. Values; Bush Says Strategic Interests Are Central," *New York Times*, October 30, 2000.

4. Makoto Iokibe, Motoshige Itō, and Katsuyuki Yakushiji, eds., *90 Nendai no Shōgen: Okamoto Yukio, Genbashugi o Tsuranuita Gaikōkan* [Testimony of the '90s: Yukio Okamoto, a Diplomat Who Pursued a Hands-On Approach] (Asahi Shimbun Shuppan, 2008), 298–99. On the historical transition of leadership in the Prime Minister's Office, see Tomoki Takeda, "Koizumi Naikakuki no Gaikō Seisaku Kettei no Rekishiteki Isō: 'Tsuyoi Shushō' no Gaikō no Katachi" [Historical Phase of Foreign Policy Making in the Koizumi Cabinet Period: The Diplomatic Shape of a "Strong Prime Minister"], in *Kantei Shudō to Jimintō Seiji: Koizumi Seiken no Shiteki Kenshō* [Prime Minister's Office Leadership and LDP Politics: A Historical Review of the Koizumi Administration] (Yoshida Shoten, 2022), ed. Kentarō Oku and Ryo Kurosawa, 399–444.

5. Ian E. Rinehart, "Collective Self-Defense and US–Japan Security Cooperation," *Politics, Governance, and Security Series*, no. 24 (October 2013): 2.

6. Akio Takahara and Hiroko Maeda, *Kaihatsu Shugi no Jidai e 1972–2014* [Toward the Era of Developmentalism] (Iwanami Shoten, 2014), 158–59; Shin Kawashima, *Chūgoku no Frontier: Yureugoku Kyokai kara Kangaeru* [China's Frontier: Considering from the Shifting Boundaries] (Iwanami Shoten, 2017), 1–7.

7. Akihiko Tanaka, *Fukuzatusei no Sekai: "Terror no Seiki" to Nihon* [The World of Complexity: Japan and the "Century of Terrorism"] (Keisō Shobō, 2003); James Mann, *Rise of the Vulcans: The History of Bush's War Cabinet* (Penguin Books, 2004); Shin'ichi Kitaoka, *Nihon no Jiritsu: Taibei Kyōchō to Asia Gaikō* [Japan's Independence: Cooperation with the United States and Diplomacy toward Asia] (Chūō Kōron Shinsha, 2004); Bob Woodward, *Plan of Attack* (Simon & Schuster, 2004); Chiyuki Aoi and Yozo Yokota, "Avoiding a Strategic Failure in the Aftermath of the Iraq War: Partnership in Peacebuilding," in *The Iraq Crisis and World Order: Structural, Institutional and Normative Challenges* (United Nations University Press, 2006), ed. Ramesh Thakur and Waheguru Pal Singh Sidhu, 282–97; Chiyuki Aoi, *Legitimacy and the Use of Armed Force: Stability Missions in the Post-Cold War Era* (Routledge, 2011), 104–215; Yee-Kuang Heng, *War as Risk Management: Strategy and Conflict in an Age of Globalised Risks* (Routledge, 2006), 87–143; Tomohito Shinoda, *Koizumi Diplomacy: Japan's Kantei Approach to Foreign and Defense Affairs* (University of Washington Press, 2007), 86–132; Richard J. Samuels, *Securing Japan: Tokyo's Grand Strategy and the Future of East Asia* (Cornell University Press, 2007), 5, 74–79, 83, 95–106, 112, 114, 119, 121, 124–27, 139–40, 146, 149, 154, 156, 165–66, 175, 177, 179–82, 191, 193, 196, 203–4; Tsuyoshi Sunohara, *Dōmei Henbō: Nichi–Bei Ittaika no Hikari to Kage* [Alliance Transformed: Light and Shadow of the Integration of Japan and the United States] (Nihon Keizai Shimbun Shuppansha, 2007); Andrew L. Oros, *Normalizing Japan: Politics, Identity, and the Evolution of Security Practice* (Stanford University Press, 2008), 180–87; Akihiro Sadō, "Koizumi Junichirō: Senryaku Naki Gaikō no Ketsudan to Jikkō" [Jun'ichirō Koizumi: Decisions and Execution of Diplomacy without Strategy], in *Jinbutsu de Yomu Gendai Nihon Gaikōshi: Konoe Fumimaro kara Koizumi Jun'ichirō made* [A History of Contemporary Japanese Diplomacy: From Fumimaro Konoe to Junichirō Koizumi], ed. Akihiro Sadō, Kazuo Komiya, and Ryuji Hattori (Yoshikawa Kobunkan, 2008), 320–34; Akihiro Sadō, "Koizumi Junichirō: Gekijōgata Seijika no 'Ketsudan' to 'Shisō'" [Jun'ichirō Koizumi: The "Decision" and "Thought" of a Theater-Style Politician], in *Sengo Nihon Shushō no Gaikō Shisō: Yoshida Shigeru kara Koizumi Jun'ichirō made* [The Diplomatic Thoughts of Japan's Postwar Prime Ministers: From Shigeru Yoshida to Jun'ichirō Koizumi], ed. Hiroshi Masuda (Minerva Shobō, 2016), 409–31; Yuichi Hosoya, *Rinriteki na Sensō: Tony Blair no Eikō to Zasetsu* [Ethical Wars: The Glories and Setbacks of Tony Blair] (Keio University Press, 2009), 169–388; Yu Uchiyama, *Koizumi and Japanese Politics: Reform Strategies and Leadership Style*, trans. Carl

Freire (Routledge, 2010); Sheila A. Smith, *Japan Rearmed: The Politics of Military Power* (Harvard University Press, 2019), 68–81, 100–7, 132–29, 163, 180–81; Wataru Yamaguchi, *Nichi–Bei Shunō Kaidan* [Japan–US Summit Meetings] (Chūō Kōron Shinsha, 2024), 241–61.

8. Rinehart, "Collective Self-Defense and US–Japan Security Cooperation," 2.

9. In particular, "The United States and the Two Koreas Part II, 1969–2010," Digital National Security Archive, proquest.libguides.com/dnsa/2koreasII.

10. Christopher W. Hughes maintains that "Japanese policy-makers dispatched the JSDF to the Indian Ocean and to Iraq to help their US ally combat terrorism, but they believed this was the price they had to pay in order to obtain the assistance of the US in facing down North Korea, and most especially China, over the longer term." See Christopher W. Hughes, "Not Quite the 'Great Britain of the Far East': Japan's Security, the US–Japan Alliance and the 'War on Terror' in East Asia," *Cambridge Review of International Affairs* 20, no. 2 (June 2007): 336; Ryō Sahashi, "Anzen Hoshō Seisaku no Henyo to Kodo Kukan no Kakudai" [Transforming Security Policy and the Expansion of the Space for Action], in *Henbō suru Nihon Seiji: 90 Nendai Ikō "Henkaku no Jidai" o Yomitoku* [The Changing Japanese Politics: Understanding the "Era of Transformation" since the 1990s], ed. Takashi Mikuriya (Keisō Shobō, 2009), 207.

11. For Japanese diplomatic records and their declassification, see Ryuji Hattori, *Gaikō o Kirokushi, Kōkaisuru: Naze Kōbunsho Kanri ga Jūyōnanoka* [Diplomatic Records and Their Declassification: Why Archives Management Is Important] (University of Tokyo Press, 2020).

12. Robert Jervis, "Images and the Gulf War," in *The Political Psychology of the Gulf War: Leaders, Publics, and the Process of Conflict*, ed. Stanley A. Renshon (University of Pittsburgh Press, 1993), 173. See also Robert Jervis, *Why Intelligence Fails: Lessons from the Iranian Revolution and the Iraq War* (Cornell University Press, 2010).

13. Jervis, "Images and the Gulf War," 173.

14. Robert Jervis, *Perception and Misperception in International Politics*, rev. ed. (Princeton University Press, 2017), 356–81.

15. Robert Draper, *To Start a War: How the Bush Administration Took America into Iraq* (Penguin Press, 2020), ix.

16. Masaki Orita, *Gaikō Shōgenroku: Wangan Sensō, Futenma Mondai, Iraq Sensō* [Diplomatic Testimony: The Gulf War, the Futenma Issue, and the Iraq War], ed. Ryuji Hattori and Jun'ichirō Shiratori (Iwanami Shoten, 2013); Kensaku Hōgen, *Moto Kokuren Jimujicho Hōgen Kensaku Kaikoroku* [Memoirs of Former UN Under-Secretary-General Kensaku Hōgen], ed. Hiroaki Katō, Ryuji Hattori, Kei Takeuchi, and Tomoaki Murakami (Yoshida Shoten, 2015); Masahiro Akiyama, *Moto Bōeijimujikan Akiyama Masahiro Kaikoroku: Reisengo no Anzen Hoshō to Bōei Koryu* [Memoirs of Former Administrative Vice-Minister of Defense Masahiro Akiyama], ed. Naotaka Sanada, Ryuji Hattori, and Yoshiyuki Kobayashi (Yoshida

Shoten, 2018); Terusuke Terada, *Gaikō Kaisōroku: Takeshita Gaikō, Peru Nihon Taishi Kotei Senkyo Jiken, Chōsen Hantō Mondai* [Diplomatic Memoirs: Takeshita Diplomacy, the Occupation of Japanese Ambassador's Residence in Peru, and the Korean Peninsula Issues], ed. Ryuji Hattori, Hidekazu Wakatsuki, and Takayuki Shōji (Yoshida Shoten, 2020).

17. Glenn H. Snyder, *Alliance Politics* (Cornell University Press, 1997), 4.

18. Stephen M. Walt, "Alliances in a Unipolar World," *World Politics* 61, no. 1 (January 2009): 86. See also Stephen M. Walt, *The Origins of Alliances* (Cornell University Press, 1987), 12.

19. Glenn H. Snyder, "Alliance Theory: A Neorealist First Cut," *Journal of International Affairs* 44, no. 1 (Spring/Summer 1990): 112–13. See also Michael Mandelbaum, *The Nuclear Revolution: International Politics Before and After Hiroshima* (Cambridge University Press, 1981), 151–52; Glenn H. Snyder, "The Security Dilemma in Alliance Politics," *World Politics* 36, no. 4 (July 1984): 461–95; Chijiwa, "Insights into Japan–U.S. Relations on the Eve of the Iraq War," 843–64; Daniel M. Kliman, *Japan's Security Strategy in the Post-9/11 World: Embracing a New Realpolitik* (Praeger, 2006), 8–19; Yasuhiro Izumikawa, "Explaining Japanese Antimilitarism: Normative and Realist Constraints on Japan's Security Policy," *International Security* 35, no. 2 (Fall 2010): 131–32, 156–57; Yasuhiro Izumikawa, "Network Connections and the Emergence of the Hub-and-Spokes Alliance System in East Asia," *International Security* 45, no. 2 (Fall 2020): 7–50; Natsuyo Ishibashi, *Alliance Security Dilemmas in the Iraq War: German and Japanese Responses* (Palgrave Macmillan, 2012), 8–11; Jitsuo Tsuchiyama, *Anzen Hoshō no Kokusai Seijigaku: Aseri to Ogori* [International Politics of Security: Anxiety and Hubris], 2nd ed. (Yuhikaku, 2014), 295–99; Nobuhiko Tamaki, "Dōmei Gainen Saikō: Yureugoku Kokusaijōsei to Nichi–Bei Dōmei" [Rethinking the Concepts of Alliance: The Shifting International Situation and the Japan–US Alliance], *Kanagawa Daigaku Asia Review* 3 (March 2016): 82–97; Nobuhiko Tamaki, *Teikoku America ga Yuzuru Toki: Jōho to Atsuryoku no Hitaishō Dōmei* [The Concessions of Imperial America: Asymmetric Alliances of Compromise and Pressure] (Iwanami Shoten, 2024), 19–31; Elena Atanassova-Cornelis and Yoichiro Sato, "The US-Japan Alliance Dilemma in the Asia-Pacific: Changing Rationales and Scope," *International Spectator* 54, no. 4 (November 2019): 78–93.

20. Hiroaki Katō defines the "Gulf War Trauma" as "the psychological scars that have been etched on the Japanese government in the wake of the US's criticism of Japan's efforts from the Gulf Crisis through the Gulf War" (my translation). See Hiroaki Katō, *Jieitai Kaigai Haken no Kigen* [The Origins of the Self-Defense Forces Overseas Deployment] (Keisō Shobō, 2020), 126; Yukio Takeuchi et al., *Gaikō Shōgenroku Kōdoseichōki kara Post Reisenki no Gaikō Anzenhoshō: Kokusai Chitsujo no Ninaite e no Michi* [Diplomatic Testimonials Diplomacy and Security from High Growth to Post–Cold War Era: Becoming a Leader of the International Order] (Iwanami Shoten, 2022), 348.

21. Ernest R. May, *"Lessons" of the Past: The Use and Misuse of History in American Foreign Policy* (Oxford University Press, 1973).

22. James D. Morrow, "Alliances and Asymmetry: An Alternative to the Capability Aggregation Model of Alliances," *American Journal of Political Science* 35, no. 4 (November 1991): 904–33.

23. Department of Defense, "Base Structure Report," Fiscal Year 2018, www.acq.osd.mil/eie/Downloads/BSI/Base%20Structure%20Report%20FY18.pdf.

There is also the concept of a "quasi-alliance" between Japan and South Korea via the US–Japan alliance and the US–ROK alliance. Nonetheless, while the US–Japan alliance responds to China, North Korea, and other countries, post–Cold War South Korea mainly perceives only North Korea as a threat. See Victor D. Cha, *Alignment Despite Antagonism: The United States-Korea-Japan Security Triangle* (Stanford University Press, 1999), 55, 57, 167–68, 197, 199, 201, 223, 228–29; Kim Sung Chull, *Partnership Within Hierarchy: The Evolving East Asian Security Triangle* (State University of New York Press, 2017), 12, 167–88.

24. John Gerard Ruggie, "Multilateralism: The Anatomy of an Institution," in *Multilateralism Matters: The Theory and Praxis of an Institutional Form*, ed. John Gerard Ruggie (Columbia University Press, 1993), 3–47.

25. Tōru Aketagawa, *Nichi–Bei Chii Kyōtei: Sono Rekishi to Genzai* [The US–Japan Status of Forces Agreement: Its History and Present] (Misuzu Shobo, 2017), 92–93; Akiko Yamamoto, *Nichi–Bei Chii Kyōtei* [The US–Japan Status of Forces Agreement] (Chūō Kōron Shinsha, 2019), 59–64, 173–74, 210–12.

26. Fumiaki Kubo, "America Gaikō ni totte no Dōmei to Nichi–Bei Dōmei: Hitotsu no Mitorizu" [The Alliances and the Japan–US Alliance for US Diplomacy: An Overview], in *America ni totte Dōmei to wa Nanika* [What Are the Alliances for the US?], ed. Fumiaki Kubo (Chūō Kōron Shinsha, 2013), 3–30.

27. Robert O. Keohane, "The Big Influence of Small Allies," *Foreign Policy*, no. 2 (Spring 1971): 161–82; David A. Lake, *Hierarchy in International Relations* (Cornell University Press, 2011), 67–71, 82–92, 138–40.

28. Walt, "Alliances in a Unipolar World," 99.

29. Yasuhiro Takeda, *Nichi–Bei Dōmei no Cost: Jishu Bōei to Jiritsu no Tsuikyū* [The Cost of the US–Japan Alliance: Self-Defense and the Pursuit of Autonomy] (Aki Shobo, 2019), 29–52.

30. Snyder, "The Security Dilemma in Alliance Politics," 468.

31. Snyder, "The Security Dilemma in Alliance Politics," 468–79.

Chapter 1

1. Koizumi told Canadian Prime Minister Jean Chrétien, "When I fought the presidential election in April, it was completely unpredictable, and I was not expected to win." Akira Hayashi (ambassador to Italy) to Makiko Tanaka (foreign

minister), July 20, 2001, telegraph no. 36, MOFA documents disclosed under the Information Disclosure Law, 2019–169–1.

2. Yoshirō Mori and Sōichirō Tahara, *Nihon Seiji no Ura no Ura: Shōgen Seikai 50 Nen* [The Dark Side of Japanese Politics: Testimonies on 50 Years in Political Circles] (Kōdansha, 2013), 294–95.

3. Makiko Tanaka to Shunji Yanai (ambassador to the US), May 9, 2001, telegraph no. 1873, MOFA documents disclosed under the Information Disclosure Law, 2019–127–1.

4. Makiko Tanaka to Shunji Yanai, May 9, 2001, telegraph no. 1874, MOFA documents disclosed under the Information Disclosure Law, 2019–127–2.

5. Tanaka to Yanai, telegraph no. 1874.

6. Tanaka to Yanai, telegraph no. 1874.

7. Tanaka to Yanai, telegraph no. 1874.

8. Tanaka to Yanai, telegraph no. 1874.

9. Tanaka to Yanai, telegraph no. 1874.

10. Shunji Yanai to Makiko Tanaka, July 1, 2001, telegraph no. 6757, MOFA documents disclosed under the Information Disclosure Law, 2019–128–11.

11. Yanai to Tanaka, telegraph no. 6757.

12. Yanai to Tanaka, telegraph no. 6757. While MOFA prioritized reducing the number of marines, the Defense Agency was cautious about making cuts so as to maintain deterrence against China and North Korea. See Orita, *Gaikō Shogenroku*, 192–200, 208–12; Akiyama, *Moto Bōeijimujikan Akiyama Masahiro Kaikoroku*, 134–53.

13. Yanai to Tanaka, telegraph no. 6757.

14. Yanai to Tanaka, telegraph no. 6757.

15. Yanai to Tanaka, telegraph no. 6757.

16. Yanai to Tanaka, telegraph no. 6757.

17. Shunji Yanai to Makiko Tanaka, July 1, 2001, telegraph no. 6769, MOFA documents disclosed under the Information Disclosure Law, 2019–128–14. For SACO, see also Orita, *Gaikō Shogenroku*, 187–89, 209–12; Akiyama, *Moto Bōeijimujikan Akiyama Masahiro Kaikoroku*, 131–34.

18. Yanai to Tanaka, telegraph no. 6769.

19. Ryuji Hattori, *Understanding History in Asia: What Diplomatic Documents Reveal*, trans. Tara Cannon (Japan Publishing Industry Foundation for Culture, 2019), 180–89.

20. MOFA, "Tanaka Gaimu Daijin to Powell Kokumu Chōkan tono Denwa Kaidan: Okinawa ni okeru Fujo Bōkō Jiken Higisha no Kisomae no Migara Hikiwatashi ni tsuite" [A Telephone Talk Between Foreign Minister Tanaka and Secretary of State Powell: Extradition of a Suspect in an Assault on Women Incident in Okinawa Prior to Indictment], July 5, 2001, MOFA documents disclosed under the Information Disclosure Law, 2020–287–1.

21. I requested the release of any Joint Committee documents related to this incident, but this was refused by MOFA on the grounds that "documents that

form part of the agreements and minutes of the meetings of the US–Japan Joint Committee are not to be disclosed without the agreement of both Japan and the US. We have decided not to reveal these documents because there is a risk that public disclosure may damage the relationship of trust with the US and unfairly impair the frank exchange of opinions within the government." The Japan–US Joint Committee, minutes (undisclosed), MOFA documents disclosed under the Information Disclosure Law, 2020–287–2; the Japan–US Joint Committee, minutes (undisclosed), MOFA documents disclosed under the Information Disclosure Law, 2020–287–3.

22. MOFA, "Genoa Summit Gaiyō" [Genoa Summit Overview], July 22, 2001, MOFA documents disclosed under the Information Disclosure Law, 2019–138–2.

23. G7 Statement, Genoa, July 20, 2001, MOFA documents disclosed under the Information Disclosure Law, 2019–138–4.

24. Akira Hayashi to Makiko Tanaka, July 22, 2001, telegraph no. 69, MOFA documents disclosed under the Information Disclosure Law, 2019–138–10.

25. G8, statement on regional issues, Genoa, July 21, 2001, MOFA documents disclosed under the Information Disclosure Law, 2019–138–6.

26. Makiko Tanaka to Shunji Yanai, July 24, 2001, telegraph no. 3157, MOFA documents disclosed under the Information Disclosure Law, 2019–129–2.

27. Tanaka to Yanai, telegraph no. 3157. Powell's memoirs, published in 1995, provide only fragmentary coverage of Japan and do not present an in-depth perception of Japan. Colin Powell with Joseph E. Persico, *My American Journey* (Ballantine Books, 1995), 13, 135, 170, 273, 288–89, 355–56, 397, 505.

28. Barton Gellman, *Angler: The Cheney Vice Presidency* (Penguin Press, 2008), 114–30.

29. Melvyn P. Leffler, *Confronting Saddam Hussein: George W. Bush and the Invasion of Iraq* (Oxford University Press, 2023), 242.

30. MOFA Task Force, "Beikoku ni okeru Renzoku Terror Jiken (Kokkai Sōtei Mondōshū)" [Serial Terrorist Incidents in the US (Likely Questions and Answers for the Diet)], September 13, 2001, MOFA documents disclosed under the Information Disclosure Law, 2019–130–1. For a comprehensive study of Japan's response to terrorism and counterterrorism, see Chiyuki Aoi and Yee-Kuang Heng, "Japan: Terrorism and Counterterrorism in Japan," in *Non-Western Responses to Terrorism*, ed. Michael J. Boyle (Manchester University Press, 2019), 81–102. See also Michael J. Green, *By More than Providence: Grand Strategy and American Power in the Asia Pacific Since 1783* (Columbia University Press, 2017), 491; Green, *Line of Advantage: Japan's Grand Strategy in the Era of Abe Shinzō* (Columbia University Press, 2022), 116–17.

31. MOFA Task Force, "Beikoku ni okeru Renzoku Terror Jiken (Kokkai Sōtei Mondōshū)."

32. MOFA Task Force, "Beikoku ni okeru Renzoku Terror Jiken (Kokkai Sōtei Mondōshū)."

33. George W. Bush, *Decision Points* (Crown Publishers, 2010), 141.

34. Katsuyoshi Seimiya, "Beikoku Dōji Tahatsu Tero Bei Kokumu Fukuchōkan Nihon ni Kōhōshien Dashin Jieitai o Sōtei: Tero Hōfuku" [Simultaneous Terrorist Attacks in the US: US Deputy Secretary of State Requests Logistical Support from Japan, Assuming Involvement of the SDF: Terrorist retaliation], *Mainichi Shimbun*, September 18, 2001, evening edition.

35. Howard W. French, "Japan Says Its Armed Forces Will Actively Back the U.S.," *New York Times*, September 19, 2001.

36. Makoto Iokibe, Motoshige Itō, and Katsuyuki Yakushiji, eds., *90 Nendai no Shogen: Gaikō Gekihen, Moto Gaimushō Jimujikan Yanai Shunji* [Testimony of the '90s: The Drastic Change in Diplomacy, Former Administrative Vice Minister of the Ministry of Foreign Affairs, Shunji Yanai] (Asahi Shimbun, 2005), 188–98. See also Katsuhiro Musashi, *Reisengo Nihon no Civilian Control no Kenkyū* [A Study of Civilian Control in Post-Cold War Japan] (Seibundoh, 2009), 117–45.

37. Gaku Shibata, "Bei Dōji Tero Kōhō Shien Rippō Isogu Hitsuyō Yanai Chūbei Taishi 'Nichi-Bei Dōmei no Shōnenba da'" [US Simultaneous Terrorist Attacks: Urgent Need for Legislation on Logistical Support; Ambassador to the US Yanai Says, "This Is a Critical Moment for the Japan–U.S. Alliance"], *Yomiuri Shimbun*, September 19, 2001, evening edition. See also Yōko Miyazaki, *"Terror to no Tatakai" to Nihon* ["The War on Terror" and Japan] (University of Nagoya Press, 2018), 38–39.

38. Iokibe et al., *90 Nendai no Shogen: Okamoto Yukio, Genbashugi o Tsuranuita Gaikōkan*, 281–85. See also Yukio Okamoto, "Japan and the United States: The Essential Alliance," *Washington Quarterly* 25, no. 2 (Spring 2002): 59–72.

39. Prime Minister's Office, "Statement by the Prime Minister (Provisional Translation)," September 19, 2001, japan.kantei.go.jp/koizumispeech/2001/0919tero-soti_e.html.

40. UNSC Resolution 1368, September 12, 2001, https://undocs.org/S/RES/1368(2001). See also Ken Jimbo, "'Tai Terror Sensō' to Nichi–Bei Dōmei: Bei Anzen Hoshō no Saikochiku to Dōmeikankei no Saiteigi?" [The "War on Terror" and the Japan–US Alliance: Restructuring US Security and Redefining the Alliance?] in *9/11 Terror Kōgeki Iko no Kokusai Jōsei to Nihon no Taiō* [The International Affairs after the 9/11 Terrorist Attacks and Japan's Response], ed. Japan Institute of International Affairs (Japan Institute of International Affairs, 2002), 144–47.

41. Prime Minister's Office, "Opening Statement by Prime Minister Junichiro Koizumi at the Press Conference (Provisional Translation)," September 19, 2001, japan.kantei.go.jp/koizumispeech/2001/0919sourikaiken_e.html.

42. Prime Minister's Office, "Opening Statement," September 19, 2001.

43. Prime Minister's Office, "Opening Statement," September 19, 2001.

44. Yasuo Fukuda and Akihiko Tanaka, "Seiken Chūsū kara Mita 'Tai Terror Sensō' to Nichi–Bei Kankei" [The "War against Terrorism" and Japan–US Relations from the Center of the Administration], *Gaikō*, no. 69 (September/October 2021): 7.

45. Yukio Satō (ambassador to the UN) to Makiko Tanaka, September 24, 2001, telegraph no. 5970, MOFA documents disclosed under the Information Disclosure Law, 2019–137–3.

46. Satō to Tanaka, telegraph no. 5970.

47. Satō to Tanaka, telegraph no. 5970.

48. Shunji Yanai to Makiko Tanaka, September 26, 2001, telegraph no. 9782, MOFA documents disclosed under the Information Disclosure Law, 2019–170–8.

49. Yanai to Tanaka, telegraph no. 9782.

50. Yanai to Tanaka, telegraph no. 9782.

51. Shunji Yanai to Makiko Tanaka, September 26, 2001, telegraph no. 9786, MOFA documents disclosed under the Information Disclosure Law, 2019–170–9.

52. Yanai to Tanaka, telegraph no. 9786.

53. Hisayoshi Ina, "Document 9/11 no Shogeki: Sonotoki Kantei wa, Gaimushō wa" [Document 9/11 Shock: At that Time, the Prime Minister's Office and MOFA], in *"Atarashii Sensō" Jidai no Anzen Hoshō: Ima Nihon no Gaikōryoku ga Towareteiru* [The Security of the "New War" Era: Japan's Diplomatic Power Now Questioned], ed. Akihiko Tanaka (Toshi Shuppan, 2020), 191. When Abe was prime minister, he would regularly meet with the Chief, Joint Staff, Admiral Katsutoshi Kawano.

54. Makiko Tanaka to Shunji Yanai, October 8, 2001, unnumbered telegraph, MOFA documents disclosed under the Information Disclosure Law, 2019–199–3.

55. Tanaka to Yanai, unnumbered telegraph, October 8, 2001.

56. Oren Harari, *The Leadership Secrets of Colin Powell* (McGraw-Hill, 2002), 2–3.

57. Shunji Yanai to Makiko Tanaka, October 7, 2001, telegraph no. 10327, MOFA documents disclosed under the Information Disclosure Law, 2019–199–2.

58. Countermeasures Headquarters, Ministry of Foreign Affairs, "Beikokutō ni yoru Taliban Gunji Shisetsutō ni tai suru Kōgeki" [Attacks on Taliban Military Facilities by the United States and other Countries], October 8, 2001, MOFA documents disclosed under the Information Disclosure Law, 2019–199–5.

59. Prime Minister's Office, "Emergency Response Measures (Provisional Translation)," October 8, 2001, japan.kantei.go.jp/koizumispeech/2001/1008taiou_e. html.

60. Yukio Okamoto, *Sabaku no Sensō: Iraq o Kakenuketa Tomo, Oku Katsuhiko e* [War in the Desert: To Katsuhiko Oku, the Friend Who Ran Through Iraq] (Bungeishunju, 2006), 197–202; Teijirō Furukawa, *Kasumigaseki Hanseiki* [Half of My Life in Kasumigaseki], new and rev. ed. (Saga Shimbun, 2011), 221–23; Teijirō Furukawa, *Watashi no Rirekisho* [My Resume] (Nihon Keizai Shimbun Shuppansha, 2015), 115–16.

61. Kiichi Fujiwara, "'Jindōteki na Kūbaku' wa Genso: Bei Ei no Afghan Kōgeki" ["Humanitarian Airstrikes" are Illusion: US–UK Attacks on Afghanistan], *Asahi Shimbun*, October 10, 2001, evening edition. See also Kiichi Fujiwara,

Shinpen Heiwa no Realism [New Edition, The Realism of Peace] (Iwanami Shoten, 2010), 224–27.

62. Shōtarō Yachi, "9/11 Terrorist Kōgeki no Keii to Nihon no Taiō" [The Process of the 9/11 Terrorist Attacks and Japan's Response], *Kokusai Mondai*, no. 503 (February 2002): 11–14.

63. Department of State, Office of the Spokesman, "Statement by Richard Boucher, Spokesman: Japan—New Counterterrorism Legislation," October 29, 2001, avalon.law.yale.edu/sept11/state_009.asp. See also Ryōzō Katō (ambassador to the US) to Makiko Tanaka, October 29, 2001, telegraph no. 11782, MOFA documents disclosed under the Information Disclosure Law, 2019-119-12.

64. Department of Defense, Office of Public Affairs, "International Contributions to the War Against Terrorism," June 14, 2002, 2001-2009.state.gov/coalition/cr/fs/12753.htm; Rumsfeld, *Known and Unknown*, 374.

65. Japan–US Security Treaty Division, "Mini SSC no Gaiyō" [The Overview of the Mini–SSC], November 1, 2001, MOFA documents disclosed under the Information Disclosure Law, 2019-119-13; Tanaka to Katō, November 2, 2001, fax no. F25557, MOFA documents disclosed under the Information Disclosure Law, 2019-119-20.

66. Japan–US Security Treaty Division, "Mini SSC no Gaiyō."

67. Ryōzō Katō to Makiko Tanaka, November 6, 2001, telegraph no. 11645, MOFA documents disclosed under the Information Disclosure Law, 2019-120-3; Katō to Tanaka, November 7, 2001, telegraph no. 11686, MOFA documents disclosed under the Information Disclosure Law, 2019-120-2; Security Council, "Jōhōshūshū no tame no Goeikantō no Haken ni tsuite" [Dispatch of Destroyers, etc. for Information Gathering], November 8, 2001, MOFA documents disclosed under the Information Disclosure Law, 2019-120-1; Minoru Shibuya (consul general to Honolulu) to Makiko Tanaka, November 8, 2001, telegraph no. 1106, MOFA documents disclosed under the Information Disclosure Law, 2019-120-4; Shibuya to Tanaka, November 8, 2001, telegraph no. 1108, MOFA documents disclosed under the Information Disclosure Law, 2019-120-5; Shibuya to Tanaka, November 9, 2001, telegraph no. 1124, MOFA documents disclosed under the Information Disclosure Law, 2019-120-6; Shibuya to Tanaka, November 9, 2001, telegraph no. 1125, MOFA documents disclosed under the Information Disclosure Law, 2019-120-7.

68. Makiko Tanaka, "Afghanistan Zantei Seiken Juritsu ni kan suru Gōibunshotō ni tsuite" [The Agreed Document, etc., on the Establishment of the Interim Government in Afghanistan], December 5, 2001, MOFA documents disclosed under the Information Disclosure Law, 2019-200-2. See also Rumsfeld, *Known and Unknown*, 483.

69. State Department, "The Bonn Agreement on the Future of Afghanistan," December 7, 2001, MOFA documents disclosed under the Information Disclosure Law, 2019-200-4.

70. Press Division, "Uetake Gaimufukudaijin no Afghanistan Hōmon ni tsuite" [Vice-Minister for Foreign Affairs Uetake's Visit to Afghanistan], December 21, 2001, MOFA documents disclosed under the Information Disclosure Law, 2019–200–1.

71. MOFA, *Gaikō Seisho* [Diplomatic Bluebook], no. 45 (Ministry of Foreign Affairs, 2002), 14.

Chapter 2

1. Takeshi Nobayashi and Masatsugu Naya, eds., *Kikigaki Ogata Sadako Kaikoroku* [Dictation Sadako Ogata Memoirs] (Iwanami Shoten, 2020), 276.

2. Sadako Ogata, *Watashi no Shigoto: Kokuren Nanmin Kotobenmukan no 10 Nen to Heiwa no Kochiku* [My Work: Ten Years of the United Nations High Commissioner for Refugees and Peacebuilding] (Asahi Shimbun Publications, 2017), 293–97. See also Sadako Ogata, *The Turbulent Decade: Confronting the Refugee Crises of the 1990s* (W.W. Norton, 2005), 276.

3. Ogata, *Watashi no Shigoto*, 298–302; "Afghan Shien Kaigi Kaimaku 'Shuyaku' Karoyaka, Gekiteki 'Dokuen'" [Afghanistan Assistance Conference Opens: "Leading Role" Lighthearted, Dramatic "Solo Performance"], *Asahi Shimbun*, January 22, 2002.

4. Yōichi Nishimura et al., "Kichō Tsuranuita Madam Ogata no Ishi: Kenshō Afghan Fukko Shien Kaigi" [Madame Ogata's Consistent Commitment: Verification of the Afghanistan Reconstruction Support Conference], *Asahi Shimbun*, January 26, 2002.

5. *Asahi Shimbun*, January 26, 2002.

6. Junichirō Koizumi, "Starting from Scratch . . . Again," *Newsweek* (Pacific ed.) 139, no. 3 (January 21, 2002): 11. MOFA responded to a request to disclose the documents related to Koizumi's paper by saying, "because the relevant documents had already been discarded due to the expiration of the retention period, they were not in possession of our ministry and were not disclosed (non-existent)." Thus, it is unclear who drafted Koizumi's manuscript and why they chose *Newsweek*. However, as noted above, the Middle Eastern and African Affairs Bureau is presumed to have been involved. Non-disclosure (non-existence), MOFA documents disclosed under the Information Disclosure Law, 2020–385.

7. Koizumi, "Starting from Scratch . . . Again."

8. MOFA, "International Conference on Reconstruction Assistance to Afghanistan," January 21–22, 2002, www.mofa.go.jp/region/middle_e/afghanistan/min0201/index.html.

9. Second Middle East Division, "Afghanistan Fukkōshien Kokusai Kaigi (Gaiyō to Hyōka)" [The International Conference on Reconstruction Assistance to Afghanistan (Overview and Evaluation)], January 24, 2002, MOFA documents disclosed under the Information Disclosure Law, 2019–201–1.

10. Jun'ichirō Koizumi, opening statement at the International Conference on Reconstruction Assistance to Afghanistan, January 21, 2002, www.mofa.go.jp/region/middle_e/afghanistan/min0201/pm0121.html.

11. Second Middle East Division, "Afghanistan Fukkōshien Kokusai Kaigi."

12. "Afghan Shien Kaigi Kaimaku 'Shuyaku" Karoyaka, Gekiteki 'Dokuen'" [Afghanistan Assistance Conference Opens: "Leading Role" Lighthearted, Dramatic "Solo Performance"], *Asahi Shimbun*, January 22, 2002.

13. Hamid Karzai (chairman of the Interim Administration of Afghanistan), statement, January 21, 2002, www.mofa.go.jp/region/middle_e/afghanistan/min0201/karzai0121.html.

14. Karzai, statement, January 21, 2002.

15. Sadako Ogata (special representative of the Japanese prime minister), opening statement at the International Conference on Reconstruction Assistance to Afghanistan, January 21, 2002, www.mofa.go.jp/region/middle_e/afghanistan/min0201/state0121.html. See also Ogata, *Watashi no Shigoto*, 333–37.

16. Ogata, opening statement at the International Conference on Reconstruction Assistance to Afghanistan, January 21, 2002.

17. International Conference on Reconstruction Assistance to Afghanistan co-chairs' summary of conclusions, January 21–22, 2002, www.mofa.go.jp/region/middle_e/afghanistan/min0201/summary.html.

18. Makiko Tanaka to Ryōzō Katō, etc., January 29, 2002, telegraph no. 2441 (draft), MOFA documents disclosed under the Information Disclosure Law, 2019-201-4; Ogata, *Watashi no Shigoto*, 302–4, 338–51, 363–70.

19. Bush, *Decision Points*, 207. See also Kensaku Hōgen (ambassador to Canada) to Yoriko Kawaguchi (foreign minister), June 26, 2002, MOFA documents disclosed under the Information Disclosure Law, 2020-258-4.

20. Second Middle East Division, "Afghanistan Fukkōshien Kokusai Kaigi."

21. Nobayashi and Naya, *Kikigaki Ogata Sadako Kaikoroku*, 280. See also Sadako Ogata and UNIFEM Japan, *Josei to Fukkōshien: Afghanistan no Genba kara* [Women and Reconstruction Assistance: From the Field in Afghanistan] (Iwanami Shoten, 2004), 4–5, 16–20.

22. President George W. Bush, State of the Union Address, January 29, 2002, www.whitehouse.gov/news/releases/2002/01/20020129-11.html.

23. Bush, *Decision Points*, 233.

24. Condoleezza Rice, *No Higher Honor: A Memoir of My Years in Washington* (Broadway Books, 2011), 150–51.

25. First North America Division, "Bush Daitōryō no Ippan Kyōsho Enzetsu" [President Bush's State of the Union Address], February 4, 2002, MOFA, 2019-131-1.

26. First North America Division, "Bush Daitōryō no Ippan Kyōsho Enzetsu."

27. Yoriko Kawaguchi to Ryōzō Katō, February 18, 2002, unnumbered telegraph, MOFA documents disclosed under the Information Disclosure Law, 2019-132-3.

28. Yoriko Kawaguchi to Ryōzō Katō, February 18, 2002, unnumbered telegraph, MOFA documents disclosed under the Information Disclosure Law, 2019-132-5.

29. Yoriko Kawaguchi to Ryōzō Katō, February 18, 2002, unnumbered telegraph, MOFA documents disclosed under the Information Disclosure Law, 2019-132-8.

30. Yoriko Kawaguchi to Ryōzō Katō, February 18, 2002, unnumbered telegraph, MOFA documents disclosed under the Information Disclosure Law, 2019-132-9.

31. Yoriko Kawaguchi to Ryōzō Katō, February 18, 2002, unnumbered telegraph, MOFA documents disclosed under the Information Disclosure Law, 2019-132-6.

32. Kawaguchi to Katō, unnumbered telegraph, February 18, 2002, 2019-132-6.

33. Kawaguchi to Katō, unnumbered telegraph, February 18, 2002, 2019-132-6.

34. Bush, *Decision Points*, 423-24.

35. Yoriko Kawaguchi to Ryōzō Katō, February 18, 2002, unnumbered telegraph, MOFA documents disclosed under the Information Disclosure Law, 2019-132-13.

36. Yoriko Kawaguchi to Ryōzō Katō, February 18, 2002, unnumbered telegraph, MOFA documents disclosed under the Information Disclosure Law, 2019-132-19.

37. Kawaguchi to Katō, unnumbered telegraph, February 18, 2002, 2019-132-19.

38. Kawaguchi to Katō, unnumbered telegraph, February 18, 2002, 2019-132-19.

39. Makiko Tanaka to Ryōzō Katō, December 17, 2001, telegraph no. 5303, MOFA documents disclosed under the Information Disclosure Law, 2019-111-12.

40. Ryōzō Katō to Makiko Tanaka, January 8, 2002, telegraph no. 112, MOFA documents disclosed under the Information Disclosure Law, 2019-111-13. See also Tetsuya Umemoto, "Ballistic Missile Defense and the U.S.-Japan Alliance," in *Reinventing the Alliance: U.S.-Japan Security Partnership in an Era of Change*, ed. G. John Ikenberry and Takashi Inoguchi (Palgrave Macmillan, 2003), 187-212.

41. Bush, *Decision Points*, 230-32, 239. See also Kazuto Suzuki, "Blair to Europe 1997-2007: 'Osekkai na Neokonsei'" [Blair and Europe 1997-2007: Meddling Neoconservatism], in *Igirisu to Europe: Koritsu to Tōgō no Nihyakunen* [Britain and Europe: Two Hundred Years of Isolation and Integration], ed. Yuichi Hosoya (Keisō Shobo, 2009), 299-326; Tony Blair, *A Journey* (Hutchinson, 2010), 399-403.

42. Bush, *Decision Points*, 232.

43. Chair's summary, Kananaskis Summit, June 27, 2002, MOFA documents disclosed under the Information Disclosure Law, 2020-252-1; G8 Leaders, "The G8 Global Partnership Against the Spread of Weapons and Materials of Mass

Destruction," June 27, 2002, www.mofa.go.jp/policy/economy/summit/2002/ state_g8.html#1; G8 Leaders, "The G8 Global Partnership: Principles to Prevent Terrorists, or Those That Harbour Them, from Gaining Access to Weapons or Materials of Mass Destruction," June 27, 2002, www.mofa.go.jp/policy/economy/ summit/2002/state_g8.html#2.

44. Hōgen to Kawaguchi, June 27, 2002, telegraph no. 67, MOFA documents disclosed under the Information Disclosure Law, 2020–252–10; Russia Division, European Affairs Bureau, Ministry of Foreign Affairs, "Kananaskis ni okeru Nichi–Ro Shunō Kaidan (Gaiyō)" [Japan–Russia Summit in Kananaskis (Overview)], June 27, 2002, MOFA documents disclosed under the Information Disclosure Law, 2020–256–1.

45. Isao Iijima, *Jitsuroku Koizumi Gaikō* [True Record of Koizumi's Diplomacy] (Nihon Keizai Shimbun Shuppansha, 2007), 307.

46. Bush, *Decision Points*, 349–50. See also Rice, *No Higher Honor*, 146; Hōgen, *Moto Kokuren Jimujicho Hōgen Kensaku Kaikoroku*, 286–93.

47. Bush, *Decision Points*, 349–50.

48. Defense Agency, "Armitage Kokumu Fukuchōkan Raichō Kanren Sōtei" [Assumption of a Visit to the Defense Agency by Deputy Secretary of State Armitage], August 27, 2002, MOFA documents disclosed under the Information Disclosure Law, 2019–133–1.

49. Kōichi Haraguchi (ambassador to the UN) to Yoriko Kawaguchi, September 13, 2002, telegraph no. 6412, MOFA documents disclosed under the Information Disclosure Law, 2019–202–1.

50. Kōichi Haraguchi to Yoriko Kawaguchi, September 13, 2002, telegraph no. 6412, MOFA documents disclosed under the Information Disclosure Law, 2019–202–1. See also Blair, *A Journey*, 407–8.

51. Prime Minister's Office, "Dai 57 Kai Kokuren Sōkai de Enzetsu" [Speech at the 57th Session of the UN General Assembly], September 13, 2002, www. kantei.go.jp/jp//koizumiphoto/2002/09/13nichibei.html.

52. Mitoji Yabunaka, *Gaikō Kōshō 40 Nen: Yabunaka Mitoji Kaikoroku* [Forty Years of Diplomatic Negotiations: A Memoir of Yabunaka Mitoji] (Minerva Shobō, 2021), 127–30.

53. Terada, *Gaikō Kaisōroku*, 375–79.

54. Hisayoshi Ina, "Tanaka Hitoshi Shi ga Nokosu Nicchō no Nazo" [The Mystery of Japan–North Korea Relations Left Behind by Mr. Hitoshi Tanaka], *Nihon Keizai Shimbun*, July 14, 2013; Takeuchi et al., *Gaikō Shōgenroku Kōdoseichōki kara Post Reisenki no Gaikō Anzenhoshō*, 399–416.

55. Yabunaka, *Gaikō Kōshō 40 Nen*, 127–28.

56. Hitoshi Tanaka and Sōichirō Tahara, *Kokka to Gaikō* [State and Diplomacy] (Kōdansha, 2005), 25–67; Yomiuri Shimbun Seijibu, *Gaikō o Kenka ni shita Otoko: Koizumi Gaikō 2000 Nichi no Shinjitsu* [The Man Who Made Diplomacy into a Fight: The Truth of 2000 Days of Koizumi Diplomacy] (Shinchosha, 2006), 28–30, 37–38.

57. Eiji Yamamoto, *Kitachōsen Gaikō Kaikoroku* [A Memoir of North Korean Diplomacy] (Chikuma Shobo, 2022), 212.

58. Northeast Asia Division, "Nicchō Shunō Kaidan (Gaiyō to Hyōka) [Japan–DPRK Summit Meeting (Overview and Evaluation)]," September 25, 2002, MOFA documents disclosed under the Information Disclosure Law, 2019–122-2. See also Iijima, *Jitsuroku Koizumi Gaikō*, 105–10.

59. Kenji Hiramatsu, "Sōri Hōchō to Nicchō Pyongyang Sengen Shomei e no Michi" [The Road to Signature of the Japan–DPRK Pyongyang Declaration], *Gaikō Forum*, no. 173 (December 2002): 23–29; Shinzō Abe, *Utsukushii Kuni e* [Toward a Beautiful Country] (Bungeishunjū, 2006), 46–52.

60. Nicchō Pyongyang Sengen [the Japan–DPRK Pyongyang Declaration], September 17, 2002, MOFA documents disclosed under the Information Disclosure Law, 2019–122-1, 6.

61. MOFA, "Koizumi Sōri Kaiken Yōshi" [Summary of Prime Minister Koizumi's Press Conference], September 17, 2002, MOFA documents disclosed under the Information Disclosure Law, 2019–122-3.

62. MOFA, "Basic Policy on Japan-Democratic People's Republic of Korea (DPRK) Normalization Talks," October 9, 2002, www.mofa.go.jp/region/asia-paci/n_korea/nt/bp0210.html.

63. "Koizumi Shushō Kyō Hōkan Tai Kitachōsen de Nichi-Bei-Kan Renkei Kakunin e" [Prime Minister Koizumi visits South Korea today to confirm Japan–US–South Korea cooperation on North Korea], *Yomiuri Shimbun*, March 21, 2002.

64. Yoichi Funabashi, *The Peninsula Question: A Chronicle of the Second Korean Nuclear Crisis* (Brookings Institution Press, 2007), 472.

65. Isao Iijima, *Koizumi Kantei Hiroku: Sōri towa Nanika* [Secret Records of the Prime Minister's Office: What Is the Prime Minister?] (Bungeishunjū, 2016), 183–84.

66. Kawaguchi to Katō, September 20, 2002, telegraph no. 3810, MOFA documents disclosed under the Information Disclosure Law, 2019–122–14.

67. James Dao, "The Pact That the Koreans Flouted," *New York Times*, October 17, 2002; Yomiuri Shimbun Seijibu, *Gaikō o Kenka ni shita Otoko*, 42–43; Rice, *No Higher Honor*, 160–63.

68. "Kitachōsen Kaku Kaihatsu Wakugumi Gōi Iji o Yōkyō e Seifu Seijōka Kōshō no Ba de" [Demanding Maintenance of Framework Agreement on North Korea's Nuclear Development], *Asahi Shimbun*, October 18, 2002.

69. Mitoji Yabunaka, *Kokka no Meiun* [The Fate of the Nation] (Shinchosha, 2010), 134–36.

70. "'Gonin no Sōkan o' Kitachōsen Gawa ga Henshin Rachi Hihan no Kokumin Kōkai ni" ["Return the Five," North Korea Replies to the National Association Criticizing Abductions], *Asahi Shimbun*, December 28, 2003.

71. Gorō Hashimoto, Hiroshi Oyama, and Shigeru Kitamura, eds., *Abe Shinzō Kaikoroku* [Memoirs of Shinzō Abe] (Chūō Kōron Shinsha, 2023), 141–42.

72. Japan–US Security Treaty Division, "Beikoku Kokka Anzen Hoshō Senryaku no Gaiyō" [Overview of the National Security Strategy of the United States of America], September 20, 2002, MOFA documents disclosed under the Information Disclosure Law, 2019-114-1.

73. White House, "The National Security Strategy of the United States of America," September 2002, georgewbush-whitehouse.archives.gov/nsc/nss/2002/.

74. White House, "The National Security Strategy," September 2002.

75. White House, "The National Security Strategy," September 2002.

76. G. John Ikenberry, "America's Imperial Ambition," *Foreign Affairs* 81, no. 5 (September/October 2002): 44–60. See also G. John Ikenberry, *Liberal Order and Imperial Ambition: Essays on American Power and International Order* (Polity Press, 2006), 214–28; Ikenberry, *After Victory: Institutions, Strategic Restraint, and the Rebuilding of Order after Major Wars*, new ed. (Princeton University Press, 2019), 273.

77. Bush, *Decision Points*, 396–97. See also Elisabeth Bumiller, *Condoleezza Rice: An American Life: A Biography* (Random House, 2007), 195; Condoleezza Rice, *No Higher Honor*, 326; Rice, *Democracy: Stories from the Long Road to Freedom* (Twelve, 2017), 277–78; Jeffrey J. Matthews, *Colin Powell: Imperfect Patriot* (University of Notre Dame Press, 2019), 265.

78. Ryuji Hattori, *Eisaku Satō, Japanese Prime Minister, 1964–72: Okinawa, Foreign Relations, Domestic Politics and the Nobel Prize*, trans. Graham B. Leonard (Routledge, 2021), 73–128.

79. David Wallis, "Occupation Preoccupation," *New York Times*, March 30, 2003.

80. Takeuchi et al., *Gaikō Shōgenroku Kōdoseichōki kara Post Reisenki no Gaikō Anzenhoshō*, 354.

81. Ryōzō Katō, *Nichi–Bei no Kizuna: Moto Chūbei Taishi Katō Ryōzō Kaikoroku* [Japan–US Ties: Memoirs of Ryōzō Katō, Former Ambassador to the US], ed. Norihide Miyoshi (Yoshida Shoten, 2021), 324. For Japanese-style democracy in the late 1940s, see Ryuji Hattori, *Japan at War and Peace: Shidehara Kijūro and the Making of Modern Diplomacy* (Australian National University Press, 2021), 257.

82. The National Security Strategy of the United States of America, September 2002.

83. Japan–US Security Treaty Division, "Beikoku Kokka Anzen Hoshō Senryaku no Gaiyō."

84. Jiang Zemin, *Jiang Zemin Wen Xuan* [Selected Works of Jiang Zemin], vol. 3 (Renmin Chubanshe, 2006), 525–57; Bush, *Decision Points*, 424.

85. Masanobu Takagi, "Chūgoku Kyōiron o Hitei Keizai Hokan o Mezasu Koizumi Shushō ga Enzetsu/Asia Forum" [Denying the Chinese Threat: Aiming for Economic Complementarity in Prime Minister Koizumi's Speech at the Asia Forum], *Yomiuri Shimbun*, April 12, 2002, evening edition.

86. Qian Qichen, *Waijiao Shiji* [Ten Diplomatic Memoirs], 2nd ed. (Sanlian Shudian, 2018), 272, 348–49, 352–55, 370–71.

87. Colin Powell with Tony Koltz, *It Worked for Me: In Life and Leadership* (Harper, 2012), 209–11.

88. Kōichi Haraguchi to Yoriko Kawaguchi, November 8, 2002, telegraph no. 8426, MOFA documents disclosed under the Information Disclosure Law, 2019–203-2. See also Christopher Meyer, *DC Confidential: The Controversial Memoirs of Britain's Ambassador to the U.S. at the Time of 9/11 and the Iraq War* (Weidenfeld & Nicolson, 2005), 256–59.

89. Tang Jiaxuan, *Jinyu Xufeng* [Heavy Rain and Warm Wind] (Shijie Zhishi Chubanshe, 2009), 104–8.

90. Yoriko Kawaguchi, statement on the adoption of UNSC Resolution 1441, November 9, 2002, MOFA documents disclosed under the Information Disclosure Law, 2019–203–3.

91. United Nations Policy Division, "Anporiketsugi 1441 Saitaku ni kan suru Taigai Ōtō Yōryō" [Outline for External Response on the Adoption of the Security Council Resolution 1441], November 9, 2002, MOFA documents disclosed under the Information Disclosure Law, 2019–203–3.

92. Bush, remarks on UNSC Resolution 1441, November 8, 2002, 2001-2009.state.gov/p/nea/rls/rm/15019.htm.

93. Bush, *Decision Points*, 241.

94. Ryōzō Katō to Yoriko Kawaguchi, November 8, 2002, telegraph no. 10250, MOFA documents disclosed under the Information Disclosure Law, 2019–203–4.

95. Yoriko Kawaguchi to Ryōzō Katō, December 11, 2002, telegraph no. 4950, MOFA documents disclosed under the Information Disclosure Law, 2019–134–5.

96. Kawaguchi to Katō, telegraph no. 4950.

97. Yoriko Kawaguchi to Ryōzō Katō, December 11, 2002, telegraph no. 4951, MOFA documents disclosed under the Information Disclosure Law, 2019–134–6; Kawaguchi to Katō, December 11, 2002, telegraph no. 4959, MOFA documents disclosed under the Information Disclosure Law, 2019–134–9.

98. Yoriko Kawaguchi to Ryōzō Katō, December 9, 2002, telegraph no. 4910, MOFA documents disclosed under the Information Disclosure Law, 2019–134–1.

99. Defense Policy Division, Bureau of Defense Policy, to the First North American Division, Ministry of Foreign Affairs, December 10, 2002, fax, MOFA documents disclosed under the Information Disclosure Law, 2019–134–13.

100. Defense Policy Division, Bureau of Defense Policy, to the First North American Division, Ministry of Foreign Affairs, December 10, 2002.

101. "'Nichi-Bei-Kan de Renkei o' Koizumi Shushō Kawaguchi Gaishō ni Shiji Kitachōsen Kaku Mondai" ["Cooperation Between Japan, the US, and South Korea" Prime Minister Koizumi Instructs Foreign Minister Kawaguchi on North Korea's Nuclear Issue], *Asahi Shimbun*, December 13 (evening edition), 2002.

102. Hirotoshi Sako and Toshiaki Miura, "Kitachōsen to Iraq 'Futatsu no Nandai' Nayamu Nichi-Bei 17 Nichi Anpo Kyōgii Kaisai" [North Korea and Iraq: Japan and the US Grapple with "Two Difficult Issues"; Security Council Meeting to Be Held on the 17th], *Asahi Shimbun*, December 15, 2002.

103. Joint statement of the Security Consultative Committee, December 16, 2002, MOFA documents disclosed under the Information Disclosure Law, 2020-199-1; Ministry of Foreign Affairs and Defense Agency, "Nichi-Bei Anzen Hoshō Kyōgi Iinkai ('2+2' Kaigō) Gaiyō" [The US-Japan Security Consultative Committee ("2+2" Meeting) Overview], December 17, 2002, MOFA documents disclosed under the Information Disclosure Law, 2020-199-1.

104. Shigeru Ishiba, remarks at a cabinet meeting, December 19, 2002, MOD documents disclosed under the Information Disclosure Law, 2021.4.2-HonHonB13-12.

105. Defense Policy Division, Defense Bureau, "Bōei Seisaku Kachō, Nichi-Bei Anzen Hoshō Jōyaku Kachō, Hōjin Kisha Briefing" [Briefing for Japanese Journalists by the Director of the Defense Policy Division and the Director of the Japan-US Security Treaty Division], December 17, 2002, MOD documents disclosed under the Information Disclosure Law, 2021.4.2-HonHonB13-1.

Chapter 3

1. Shunji Hiraiwa, *Chōsen Minshushugi Jinmin Kyōwakoku to Chūka Jinmin Kyōwakoku: "Shinshi no Kankei" no Kōzō to Hen'yō* [The Democratic People's Republic of Korea and the People's Republic of China: The Structure and Transformation of "Lip-Tooth Relations"] (Seori Shobō, 2010), 233–69; Hideya Kurata, "Bei-Chu 'Taikokukan no Kyōchō' toshiteno Chōsen Hantō Rokusha Kyodan: Kakufukakusan Seisaku to Chiiki Anzen Hoshō no Kosaku" [The Six-Party Talks on the Korean Peninsula as the US-China "Cooperation Among Great Powers": The Intersection of Nuclear Non-proliferation Policy and Regional Security Policy], in *Bōchōsuru Chūgoku no Taigai Kankei: Pax Sinica to Shūhenkoku* [Expanding China's Foreign Relations: Pax Sinica and Neighboring Countries], ed. Satoshi Amako and Emi Mifune (Keisō Shobō, 2010), 131–83; Narushige Michishita, *North Korea's Military-Diplomatic Campaigns, 1966-2008* (Routledge, 2010), 93–167; Don Oberdorfer and Robert Carlin, *The Two Koreas: A Contemporary History*, 3rd ed. (Basic Books, 2014), 215–19, 239, 276, 394.

2. Department of State, Bureau of Intelligence and Research, "The Secretary's Morning Intelligence Summary," March 12, 1993, search.proquest.com/docview/1679129205?accountid=26790.

3. Department of State, "The Secretary's Morning Intelligence Summary," March 12, 1993.

4. Department of State, Bureau of Intelligence and Research, "The Secretary's Morning Intelligence Summary," June 18, 1993, search.proquest.com/docview/1679129946?accountid=26790.

5. "Agreed Framework between the United States of America and the Democratic People's Republic of Korea," October 21, 1994, search.proquest.com/docview/1679080933?accountid=26790.

6. Government of the Democratic People's Republic of Korea, "Statement of the Government of the Democratic People's Republic of Korea," January 10, 2003, MOFA documents disclosed under the Information Disclosure Law, 2019–112–3.

7. Arms Control and Disarmament Division, "Kitachōsen no NPT (Kakuheiki Kakusanbōshi Jōyaku) Dattai Hyōmei" [North Korean Announcement of Withdrawal from the NPT (Nuclear Non-proliferation Treaty)], January 16, 2003, MOFA documents disclosed under the Information Disclosure Law, 2019–112–1.

8. Northeast Asia Division, "Nichi–Bei Gaishō Denwa Kaidan" [A Telephone Talk Between Japanese Foreign Minister and US Secretary of State], January 10, 2003, MOFA documents disclosed under the Information Disclosure Law, 2019–112–3.

9. Bush, *Decision Points*, 424. See also Akio Takahara, "Chūgoku no Takaku Gaikō: Shin Anzen Hoshōkan no Shodo to Shuhen Gaikō no Shintenkai" [China's Multilateral Diplomacy: The New Security View and New Developments in Peripheral Diplomacy], *Kokusai Mondai*, no. 527 (February 2004): 28.

10. Bush, *Decision Points*, 424.

11. Hideya Kurata, "Rokusha Kaidan no Seiritsu Katei to Bei–Chu Kankei: 'Hikakuka' to 'Anpojo no Kenen' o meguru Sogosayo" [The Formation Process of the Six–Party Talks and the US–China Relationship: Interaction on 'Denuclearization' and 'Security Concerns'], in *Bei–Chū Kankei: Reisengo no Kōzō to Tenkai* [The US–China Relations: Structure and Development after the Cold War], ed. Seiichirō Takagi (Japan Institute of International Affairs, 2007), 69–92; Yabunaka, *Gaikō Kōshō 40 Nen*, 130–33.

12. Northeast Asia Division, "Kitachōsen Hodo 'Yokushiryoku no Motsukoto o Kesshin' (Gaimushō Spokesman Danwa)" [North Korea Report "Determined to Have Deterrent" (Foreign Ministry Spokesman's Statement)], April 30, 2003, MOFA documents disclosed under the Information Disclosure Law, 2019–123–1.

13. Northeast Asia Division, "Kitachōsen Hodo 'Yokushiryoku no Motsukoto o Kesshin.'"

14. Ministry of Foreign Affairs of China, "Lizhaoxing Fenbie yu Chaoemei Sanfang jiu Beijing Liufang Huitan Jiaohuan Yijian" [Li Zhaoxing Exchanges Views with DPRK, Russia, and the US on Beijing Six–Party Talks], August 22, 2003, www.fmprc.gov.cn/web/wjb_673085/zzjg_673183/yzs_673193/dqzz_673197/cxbdhwt_673311/xgxw_673317/t25294.shtml. See also Chisako Masuo, "Rokusha Kyōgi to Chūgoku no Kitachōsen Mondai" [The Six–Party Talks and China's

North Korea Policy], in *Hokutō Asia no Anzen Hoshō to Nihon* [Northeast Asian Security and Japan], ed. Japan Institute of International Affairs (Japan Institute of International Affairs, 2004), 64–78.

15. Taku Yamasaki, *YKK Hiroku* [YKK Secret Notes] (Kōdansha, 2004), 305. See also Li Zhaoxing, *Shuobujinde Waijiao* [Untold Stories of My Diplomatic Life] (Sanlian Shudian, 2014), 148–53.

16. Yamasaki, *YKK Hiroku*, 305.

17. Yamasaki, *YKK Hiroku*, 305.

18. Dick Cheney with Liz Cheney, *In My Time: A Personal and Political Memoir* (Threshold Editions, 2011), 473–74, 490, 492. See also Rice, *No Higher Honor*, 248–49.

19. Northeast Asia Division, "Rokusha Kaigō (Gaiyō to Hyōka)" [the Six-Party Talks (Overview and Evaluation)], September 1, 2003, MOFA documents disclosed under the Information Disclosure Law, 2019–124–1; Yabunaka, *Kokka no Meiun*, 138–40; Mitoji Yabunaka, *Sekai ni Makenai Nihon: Kokka to Nihonjin ga Ima Nasubekikoto* [Japan Unbeatable in the World: What the Nation and the Japanese Should Do Now] (PHP Kenkyujo, 2016), 97–101; Yabunaka, *Gaikō Kōshō 40 Nen*, 133–36; Mori and Tahara, *Nihon Seiji no Ura no Ura*, 296–97.

20. Northeast Asia Division, "Rokusha Kaigō."

21. Office of the Press Secretary, "President Bush Meets with President of China: Remarks by President Bush and President Hu Jintao of China," October 19, 2003, georgewbush-whitehouse.archives.gov/news/releases/2003/10/20031019-6.html; Office of the Press Secretary, "President Bush Meets with President Roh Moo-Hyun: Joint Statement Between the United States and the Republic of Korea," October 20, 2003, georgewbush-whitehouse.archives.gov/news/releases/2003/10/20031020-2.html.

22. On UNMOVIC and the IAEA, see Hans Blix, *Disarming Iraq* (Pantheon Books, 2004).

23. Bush, *Decision Points*, 252–53. See also Condoleezza Rice, "Why We Know Iraq is Lying," *New York Times*, January 23, 2003, 25; Meyer, *DC Confidential*, 279–281; Blair, *A Journey*, 412.

24. Tang, *Jinyu Xufeng*, 109–34; Hu Jintao, *Hu Jintao Wen Xuan* [Selected works of Hu Jintao], vol. 2 (Renmin Chubanshe, 2016), 92–93. See also Kiyotaka Kawabata, *Iraq Kiki wa Naze Fusegenakattanoka: Kokuren Gaikō no Roppyakunichi* [Why Was the Iraqi Crisis Not Prevented? Six Hundred Days of UN Diplomacy] (Iwanami Shoten, 2007), 21–55.

25. Powell, *It Worked for Me*, 217–18.

26. Powell, *It Worked for Me*, 219.

27. Powell, *It Worked for Me*, 222.

28. Prime Minister's Office, "Koizumi Sōri Interview (Iraq Mondai ni tsuite)" [Interview with Prime Minister Koizumi (On the Iraq Issue)], March 18, 2003, www.kantei.go.jp/jp//koizumispeech/2003/03/18interview.html. See also Junichirō

Koizumi, *Ketsudan no Toki: Tomodachi Sakusen to Namida no Kikin* [The Time for Decisions: Operation Tomodachi and the Tearful Fund] (Shūeisha, 2018), 53.

29. UNSC Resolution 1441, November 8, 2002, www.un.org/depts/unmovic/documents/1441.pdf.

30. UNSC Resolution 678, November 29, 1990, unscr.com/en/resolutions/678.

31. Shigeru Ishiba, *Kokubō* [National Defense] (Sinchosha, 2011), 51–53.

32. Yoriko Kawaguchi to Ryōzō Katō, March 20, 2003, telegraph no. 1215, MOFA documents disclosed under the Information Disclosure Law, 2019-204-6.

33. Press conference by Jun'ichirō Koizumi, March 20, 2003, MOFA documents disclosed under the Information Disclosure Law, 2019-204-2. See also Jun'ichirō Koizumi, "Kaikaku ni Owari wa nai" [Reform Has No End], in *Ketsudan! Anotoki Watashi wa Koushita: Jiminto Sōri, Sosai, Kanbō Chōkan ga Kataru* [Decision! At That Time, I Did This: The Prime Ministers, Presidents and Chief Cabinet Secretaries of the LDP Talk], ed. Liberal Democratic Party (Chūō Kōron Jigyō Shuppan, 2006), 319.

34. Press conference by Koizumi, March 20, 2003.

35. "Iraq Sensō Koizumi Shushō Kaiken no Yōshi" [Summary of Prime Minister Koizumi's Press Conference on the Iraq War], *Yomiuri Shimbun*, March 21, 2003; Iijima, *Koizumi Kantei Hiroku*, 207.

36. Prime Minister's Office, "Statement by Prime Minister Junichiro Koizumi," March 20, 2003, japan.kantei.go.jp/koizumispeech/2003/03/20danwa_e.html.

37. Prime Minister's Office, "Statement by Prime Minister Junichiro Koizumi," March 20, 2003.

38. Prime Minister's Office, "Iraq Mondai ni kan suru Taisho Hōshin no Ketteitō" [Determination of Policy on the Iraqi Issue and Others], March 20, 2003, www.kantei.go.jp/jp//koizumiphoto/2003/03/20kettei.html.

39. Yoriko Kawaguchi to Ryōzō Katō, March 21, 2003, telegraph no. 1234, MOFA documents disclosed under the Information Disclosure Law, 2019-204-8; Kawaguchi to Katō, April 16, 2003, unnumbered telegraph (draft), MOFA documents disclosed under the Information Disclosure Law, 2019-204-12.

40. Ryōzō Katō to Yoriko Kawaguchi, March 20, 2003, telegraph no. 2787, MOFA documents disclosed under the Information Disclosure Law, 2019-204-7.

41. Yoriko Kawaguchi to Ryōzō Katō, February 23, 2003, telegraph no. 742 (draft), MOFA documents disclosed under the Information Disclosure Law, 2020-437-3.

42. Orita, *Gaikō Shogenroku*, 228–36.

43. Yamasaki, *YKK Hiroku*, 283.

44. Yamasaki, *YKK Hiroku*, 283. Yamasaki indicated that his meeting with Powell occurred on February 24; however, according to MOFA, it took place on the 23rd. See Yoriko Kawaguchi to Ryōzō Katō, February 23, 2003, telegraph no. 739 (draft), MOFA documents disclosed under the Information Disclosure Law, 2020-437-19.

45. Yamasaki, *YKK Hiroku*, 283. See also Kawaguchi to Katō, February 23, 2003, telegraph no. 739 (draft). UNSC Resolution 678, adopted on November 29, 1990, authorized member states cooperating with the Kuwaiti government to use all means unless Iraq on or before January 15, 1991, fully implemented the relevant resolutions. In response to this, the Multinational Force decided to use force against Iraq on January 17, 1991. UNSC Resolution 1441 strongly urged Iraq to fulfill its obligations, including acceptance of inspections, on November 8, 2002. See UNSC Resolution 678; UNSC Resolution 1441.

46. Yamasaki, *YKK Hiroku*, 283–84.

47. Yamasaki, *YKK Hiroku*, 284–86.

48. "Iraq to Kitachōsen Kirihanasazu Kyōgi: Yotō San Tō Hatsu Kaigō" [Iraq and North Korea to Be Discussed Together: The First Meeting of Three Ruling Parties], *Mainichi Shimbun*, March 13, 2003.

49. "Heiwa Rikkoku no Shiren" [Challenges of the Peaceful Nation], *Mainichi Shimbun*, December 10, 2003.

50. Nanae Kurashige and Naotaka Fujita, "Shiji no Senkō Hyōmei Eikoku ga Yōsei: Iraq Kaisen 10 Nen Fukuda Moto Shushō Interview" [The UK Requested Early Statement of Support: Ten Years since the Start of the Iraq War, Interview with Former Prime Minister Fukuda], *Asahi Shimbun*, March 20, 2013.

51. Fukuda and Tanaka, "Seiken Chūsū kara Mita 'Tai Terror Sensō' to Nichi–Bei Kankei," 9.

52. Fukuda and Tanaka, "Seiken Chūsū kara Mita 'Tai Terror Sensō' to Nichi–Bei Kankei," 9.

53. Fukuda and Tanaka, "Seiken Chūsū kara Mita 'Tai Terror Sensō' to Nichi–Bei Kankei," 9.

54. Fukuda and Tanaka, "Seiken Chūsū kara Mita 'Tai Terror Sensō' to Nichi–Bei Kankei," 9.

55. Nanae Kurashige and Naotaka Fujita, "Tairyō Hakai Heiki 'Wareware ni Jōhō Nakatta' Tōji no Kanbō Chōkan Fukuda Moto Shushō Iraq Kaisen 10 Nen" [We Had No Information About WMDs, Says Former Chief Cabinet Secretary and Prime Minister Fukuda, 10 Years after the Start of the Iraq War], *Asahi Shimbun*, March 20, 2013. See also Blair, *A Journey*, 414, 423–40; Patrick Porter, *Blunder: Britain's War in Iraq* (Oxford University Press, 2018), 61–70.

56. Kurashige and Fujita, "Shiji no Senkō Hyōmei Eikoku ga Yōsei: Iraq Kaisen 10 Nen Fukuda Moto Shushō Interview."

57. *Asahi Shimbun*, March 20, 2013.

58. Fukuda and Tanaka, "Seiken Chūsū kara Mita 'Tai Terror Sensō' to Nichi–Bei Kankei," 10.

59. Fukuda and Tanaka, "Seiken Chūsū kara Mita 'Tai Terror Sensō' to Nichi–Bei Kankei," 10.

60. Kurashige and Fujita, "Shiji no Senkō Hyōmei Eikoku ga Yōsei: Iraq Kaisen 10 Nen Fukuda Moto Shushō Interview."

61. *Asahi Shimbun*, March 20, 2013.

62. *Asahi Shimbun*, March 20, 2013.

63. *Asahi Shimbun*, March 20, 2013. See also Nobutaka Machimura, *Hoshu no Ronri: "Rintoshite Utsukushii Nihon" o Tsukuru* [Conservatism's Logic: Creating a "Dignified and Beautiful Japan"] (PHP Kenkyūjo, 2005), 88–104.

64. Iokibe et al., *90 Nendai no Shogen*, 300–4. See also Keiko Sakai, *Iraq: Sensō to Senryō* [Iraq: War and Occupation] (Iwanami Shoten, 2004), 117–66; Kawabata, *Iraq Kiki wa Naze Fusegenakattanoka*, 71–100; Toby Dodge, *Iraq: From War to a New Authoritarianism* (International Institute for Strategic Studies, 2012), 26–57.

65. Lewis Paul Bremer III, *My Year in Iraq: The Struggle to Build a Future of Hope* (Simon and Schuster, 2006), 2; Bob Woodward, *State of Denial* (Simon & Schuster, 2006), 173–74, 180–86, 190–203.

66. UNSC Resolution 1483, May 22, 2003, undocs.org/S/RES/1483(2003).

67. Ryōzō Katō to Yoriko Kawaguchi, May 26, 2003, telegraph no. 5420, MOFA documents disclosed under the Information Disclosure Law, 2019–135–2. See also Laura Bush, *Spoken from the Heart* (Scribner, 2010), 291.

68. Ryōzō Katō to Yoriko Kawaguchi, May 26, 2003, telegraph no. 5421, MOFA documents disclosed under the Information Disclosure Law, 2019–135–3.

69. Ryōzō Katō to Yoriko Kawaguchi, May 26, 2003, telegraph no. 5422, MOFA documents disclosed under the Information Disclosure Law, 2019–135–4.

70. Katō to Kawaguchi, telegraph no. 5422.

71. Katō to Kawaguchi, telegraph no. 5422.

72. Katō to Kawaguchi, telegraph no. 5422.

73. Ryōzō Katō to Yoriko Kawaguchi, May 26, 2003, telegraph no. 5424, MOFA documents disclosed under the Information Disclosure Law, 2019–135–6.

74. Katō to Kawaguchi, telegraph no. 5424.

75. Katō to Kawaguchi, telegraph no. 5424.

76. Katō to Kawaguchi, telegraph no. 5424.

77. Ryōzō Katō to Yoriko Kawaguchi, May 26, 2003, telegraph no. 5425, MOFA documents disclosed under the Information Disclosure Law, 2019–135–7.

78. Katō to Kawaguchi, telegraph no. 5425.

79. Katō to Kawaguchi, telegraph no. 5425.

80. Katō to Kawaguchi, telegraph no. 5425.

81. Katō to Kawaguchi, telegraph no. 5425.

82. Katō to Kawaguchi, telegraph no. 5425.

83. Katō to Kawaguchi, telegraph no. 5425.

84. Katō to Kawaguchi, telegraph no. 5425.

85. Katō to Kawaguchi, telegraph no. 5425.

86. Katō to Kawaguchi, telegraph no. 5425.

87. Katō to Kawaguchi, telegraph no. 5425. See also Yomiuri Shimbun Seijibu, *Gaikō o Kenka ni shita Otoko*, 45–50.

88. Ryōzō Katō to Yoriko Kawaguchi, May 26, 2003, telegraph no. 5427, MOFA documents disclosed under the Information Disclosure Law, 2019–135–9.

89. Katō to Kawaguchi, telegraph no. 5427.

90. Katō to Kawaguchi, telegraph no. 5427.

91. Ryōzō Katō to Yoriko Kawaguchi, May 26, 2003, telegraph no. 10, MOFA documents disclosed under the Information Disclosure Law, 2019–135–10. See also Hideki Kan, *America no Sekai Senryaku* [US World Strategy] (Chūō Kōron Shinsha, 2008), 63.

92. Keizo Nabeshima, "U.S.–Japan Global Alliance," *Japan Times*, June 2, 2003. See also Takashi Inoguchi and Paul Bacon, "Rethinking Japan as an Ordinary Country," in *The United States and Northeast Asia: Debates, Issues, and New Order*, ed. G. John Ikenberry and Chung-in Moon (Rowman & Littlefield, 2008), 79–98; Yoshihide Soeya, Masayuki Tadokoro, and David A. Welch, eds., *Japan as a "Normal Country"?: A Nation in Search of Its Place in the World* (University of Toronto Press, 2011).

93. Ministry of Foreign Affairs, "G8 Evian Summit (Gaiyō to Hyōka)" [G8 Evian Summit (Overview and Assessment)], June 4, 2003, MOFA documents disclosed under the Information Disclosure Law, 2019–113–2.

94. Chair's summary, Evian Summit, June 3, 2003, MOFA documents disclosed under the Information Disclosure Law, 2019–113–1.

95. Hiroshi Hirabayashi (ambassador to France) to Yoriko Kawaguchi, June 3, 2003, telegraph no. 26, MOFA documents disclosed under the Information Disclosure Law, 2019–113–22.

96. Hirabayashi to Kawaguchi, telegraph no. 26.

97. Hirabayashi to Kawaguchi, telegraph no. 26.

98. Hiroshi Hirabayashi to Yoriko Kawaguchi, June 3, 2003, telegraph no. 27, MOFA documents disclosed under the Information Disclosure Law, 2019–113–22.

99. Hiroshi Hirabayashi to Yoriko Kawaguchi, June 3, 2003, telegraph no. 34, MOFA documents disclosed under the Information Disclosure Law, 2019–113–22; Hiroshi Hirabayashi, *Shunō Gaikōryoku: Shushō, Anata Jishin ga Message desu!* [Summit Diplomacy: Prime Minister, You Yourself Are the Message!] (NHK Publishing, 2008), 22–23.

100. Ministry of Foreign Affairs, "Nichi–Bei Shunō Kaidan Gaiyō" [Overview of the Japan–US Summit], March 20, 2001, MOFA documents disclosed under the Information Disclosure Law, 2019–182–14; Defense Agency, *Nihon no Bōei: Bōei Hakusho* [Defense of Japan: Defense White Paper] (National Printing Bureau, 2004), 150–56. See also Musashi, *Reisengo Nihon no Civilian Control no Kenkyū*, 146–296.

101. Iijima, *Koizumi Kantei Hiroku*, 205, 209.

102. George W. Bush, "Statement on the Establishment of the Iraqi Governing Council," July 14, 2003, www.govinfo.gov/content/pkg/PPP-2003-book2/html/PPP-2003-book2-doc-pg873.htm.

103. Second Middle East Division, "Saikin no Iraq Jōsei ni tsuite" [The Recent Situation in Iraq], July 25, 2003, MOFA documents disclosed under the Information Disclosure Law, 2019–205–1.

104. Cabinet Secretariat, "Iraq ni okeru Jindō Fukkō Shien Katsudō oyobi Anzen Kakuho Shien Katsudō no Jissi ni kan suru Tokubetsu Sochihō Sekōreian ni tsuite" [A Draft for the Act on Special Measures Concerning Humanitarian Relief and Reconstruction Work and Security Assistance in Iraq], July 2003, MOFA documents disclosed under the Information Disclosure Law, 2019–205–4; "'Dokoga Sentō Chiiki ka Wakaru Wakenai' Jieitai Haken de Koizumi Shushō Honne?" ["There Is No Way to Know Where the Combat Zone Is." Is This Prime Minister Koizumi's True Opinion on Dispatching the Self-Defense Forces?], *Asahi Shimbun*, July 24, 2003. See also Takayuki Shōji, *Jieitai Kaigai Haken to Nihon Gaikō: Reisengo ni okeru Jinteki Kōken no Mosaku* [SDF Overseas Missions and Japanese Diplomacy: The Search for Human Contribution in the Post–Cold War Era] (Nihon Keizai Hyōronsha, 2015), 236–46.

105. Kyōji Yanagisawa, *Kenshō Kantei no Iraq War: Moto Bōeikanryo ni yoru Hihan to Jisei* [An Examination of the Iraq War: Criticism and Self-reflection by Former Defense Bureaucrat] (Iwanami Shoten, 2013), 91–93. See also Yamasaki, *YKK Hiroku*, 24–36, 234–43, 269, 283–86, 289.

106. "Rikuji Iraq Haken Anpo Seisaku Girigiri no Issen: Waga Taikenteki Seikairon Yamasaki Taku Shi Hen" [The Ground Self-Defense Force Dispatch to Iraq, the Fine Line of Security Policy: My Experiential Political Analysis by Taku Yamazaki], *Nihon Keizai Shimbun*, April 28, 2011, electronic edition.

107. "Iraq Fukkō de 1000 Nin Kibo no Haken Motomeru: Bei Kōkan Nihon Seifu ni Hikōshiki no Dashin" [US Official Informally Asks the Japanese Government to Dispatch 1,000 Personnel for Iraq Reconstruction], *Mainichi Shimbun*, May 27, 2003; Masaru Honda, "Bei Tsuizui to Dokujisei no Aida de (Iraq to Jieitai Tokuso Hōan ha Tou: Jō)" [Between Following the US and Maintaining Independence (Iraq and the Self-Defense Forces: The Special Measures Bill in Question: Part 1)], *Asahi Shimbun*, June 25, 2003.

108. Joseph S. Nye Jr., *Soft Power: The Means to Success in World Politics* (Public Affairs, 2004), 140.

109. Yoshinobu Yamamoto, *"Teikoku" no Kokusai Seijigaku: Reisengo no Kokusai System to America* [International Politics of "Empire": The International System after the Cold War and the United States] (Toshindo, 2004), 73–84. See also Robert Jervis, "The Compulsive Empire," *Foreign Policy*, no. 137 (July/August 2003): 83–87; Robert Kagan, *Of Paradise and Power: America and Europe in the New World Order* (Vintage Books, 2004); Francis Fukuyama, *America at the Crossroads: Democracy, Power, and the Neoconservative Legacy* (Yale University Press, 2006).

110. Powell, *It Worked for Me*, 211–12. See also Chiyuki Aoi, "Kokka Kensetsu to Chianbumon Kaikaku: Iraq no Jirei ni miru Anteika Paradigm kara

no Kairi to Kaiki" [State Building and Security Sector Reform: Departure from and Return to the Stabilization Paradigm in Iraq], *Aoyama Kokusai Seikei Ronshū* 88 (September 2012): 169.

111. Powell, *It Worked for Me*, 211–12.

112. Robert Jervis, "Understanding the Bush Doctrine," *Political Science Quarterly* 118, no. 3 (Fall 2003): 388. See also John J. Mearsheimer and Stephen M. Walt, "An Unnecessary War," *Foreign Policy*, no. 134 (January/February 2003): 51–59; Robert Jervis, *American Foreign Policy in a New Era* (Routledge, 2005), 79–102; Jervis, "An Empire, But We Can't Keep It," in *Imbalance of Power: US Hegemony and International Order*, ed. I. William Zartman (Lynne Rienner, 2009), 45–53.

113. Jervis, "Understanding the Bush Doctrine," 388.

114. UNSC Resolution 1511, October 16, 2003, undocs.org/S/RES/1511(2003). See also Kawabata, *Iraq Kiki wa Naze Fusegenakattanoka*, 131–36.

115. Yoriko Kawaguchi, "On the Adoption of the United Nations Security Council Resolution on Iraq," October 16, 2003, MOFA documents disclosed under the Information Disclosure Law, 2019–206–2.

116. Yoriko Kawaguchi to Ryōzō Katō, October 19, 2003, telegraph no. 4392, MOFA documents disclosed under the Information Disclosure Law, 2019–140–4.

117. Kawaguchi to Katō, telegraph no. 4392.

118. Kawaguchi to Katō, telegraph no. 4392.

119. Kawaguchi to Katō, telegraph no. 4392.

120. Yoriko Kawaguchi to Ryōzō Katō, October 19, 2003, telegraph no. 4393, MOFA documents disclosed under the Information Disclosure Law, 2019–140–5.

121. Kawaguchi to Katō, telegraph no. 4393.

122. Kawaguchi to Katō, telegraph no. 4393.

123. Kawaguchi to Katō, telegraph no. 4393.

124. Yoriko Kawaguchi to Ryōzō Katō, October 19, 2003, telegraph no. 4395, MOFA documents disclosed under the Information Disclosure Law, 2019–140–7.

125. Kawaguchi to Katō, telegraph no. 4395.

126. Yoriko Kawaguchi to Ryōzō Katō, October 19, 2003, telegraph no. 4396, MOFA documents disclosed under the Information Disclosure Law, 2019–140–8.

127. Yoriko Kawaguchi to Ryōzō Katō, November 15, 2003, telegraph no. 4820, MOFA documents disclosed under the Information Disclosure Law, 2019–115–4.

128. Kawaguchi to Katō, telegraph no. 4820.

129. Kawaguchi to Katō, telegraph no. 4820.

130. Department of Defense, "U.S.–Japan Security Arrangements Remain Vital," November 15, 2003, archive.defense.gov/news/newsarticle.aspx?id=27782.

131. Yomiuri Shimbun Seijibu, *Gaikō o Kenka ni shita Otoko*, 187–89. See also Keiichi Inamine, *Ware Igai Mina Waga Shi: Inamine Keiichi Kaikoroku* [Everyone Is My Mentor Except Me: Memoirs of Keiichi Inamine], ed. Ryūkyū Shinpōsha (Ryūkyū Shinpōsha, 2011), 305–11, 363.

132. MOFA, "Iraq ni okeru Gaimushō Shokuin Satsugai Jiken (Jiken no Jokyo, Keiito)" [The Murder of the Ministry of Foreign Affair's Employees in Iraq (Situation and Background of the Incident)], May 12, 2004, MOFA documents disclosed under the Information Disclosure Law, 2019–207–5. See also Okamoto, *Sabaku no Sensō*, 16–50.

133. National Security Policy Division, "Iraq e no Jieitai Haken (Jisshi Yōryō no Gaiyō)" [Deployment of the Self-Defense Forces to Iraq (Overview of the Implementation Guideline)], December 13, 2003, MOFA documents disclosed under the Information Disclosure Law, 2019–208–1.

134. "Heiwa Rikkoku no Shiren" [Challenges of the Peaceful Nation], *Mainichi Shimbun*, December 10, 2003.

135. "Heiwa Rikkoku no Shiren," *Mainichi Shimbun*.

136. "Heiwa Rikkoku no Shiren," *Mainichi Shimbun*.

137. Yomiuri Shimbun Seijibu, *Gaikō o Kenka ni shita Otoko*, 171–77; Iokibe et al., *90 Nendai no Shōgen*, 311–13.

138. Yanagisawa, *Kenshō Kantei no Iraq Sensō*, 94–97.

139. Yoriko Kawaguchi to Ryōzō Katō, December 15, 2003, unnumbered telegraph, MOFA documents disclosed under the Information Disclosure Law, 2019–209–5.

140. Kawaguchi to Katō, unnumbered telegraph, December 15, 2003.

141. MOFA, press release, December 14, 2003, MOFA documents disclosed under the Information Disclosure Law, 2019–209–2.

142. MOFA, press release, December 14, 2003.

143. MOFA, press release, December 14, 2003.

144. John Nixon, *Debriefing the President: The Interrogation of Saddam Hussein* (Blue Rider Press, 2016), 10, 40, 137, 194, 222–23. See also "Saddam Hussein Talks to the FBI: Twenty Interviews and Five Conversations with 'High Value Detainee #1' in 2004," National Security Archive Electronic Briefing Book no. 279, ed. Joyce Battle, assisted by Brendan McQuade, July 1, 2009, nsarchive2.gwu.edu/NSAEBB/NSAEBB279/.

145. Nixon, *Debriefing the President*, 222–23.

146. Koizumi Cabinet, Security Council and Cabinet Decision, "Dandō Missile Bōei System no Seibitō ni tsuite" [On the Adjustment of Ballistic MD Systems and Others], December 19, 2003, MOFA documents disclosed under the Information Disclosure Law, 2019–198–1.

147. Security Council and Cabinet Decision, "Dandō Missile Bōei System no Seibitō ni tsuite."

148. Yoriko Kawaguchi to Ryōzō Katō, December 29, 2003, telegraph no. 5459, MOFA documents disclosed under the Information Disclosure Law, 2019–210–2.

149. MOFA, "Iraq Fukkō Shien ni okeru Nichi-Doku Kyōryoku" [Japan–Germany Cooperation in Iraqi Reconstruction Assistance], June 2004, MOFA documents disclosed under the Information Disclosure Law, 2019–153–1.

150. Kawaguchi to Katō, telegraph no. 5459.

Chapter 4

1. MOFA, "Samawah ni okeru Rikujō Jieitai no Ninmu to Gaimushō tono Renkei" [The Ground Self-Defense Force's Mission in Samawah and Cooperation with the Ministry of Foreign Affairs], January 8, 2004, MOFA documents disclosed under the Information Disclosure Law, 2019–211–1. See also Masahisa Satō, *Iraq Jieitai "Sentoki"* [The SDF in Iraq "Battle Records"] (Kōdansha, 2007).

2. Cabinet Secretariat, "Iraq ni okeru Jindō Fukkō Shien Katsudō oyobi Anzen Kakuho Shien Katsudō no Jisshi ni kan suru Tokubetsu Shochihō ni motozuku Taiō Sochi no Kekka" [Results of Response Measures Based on the Act on Special Measures Concerning the Implementation of Humanitarian and Reconstruction Assistance Activities and Security Assistance Activities in Iraq], July 2009, MOD documents disclosed under the Information Disclosure Law, 2021.4.2–HonHonB15.

3. MOD, "Zai–Oki Kaiheitai no Jitsudō (Shuyō Jisseki)" [Actual Operations of Marines in Okinawa (Major Achievements)], undated, MOD documents disclosed under the Information Disclosure Law, 2021.4.2–HonHonB14–1; Japan–US Security Treaty Division, "Zai–Oki Kaiheitai no Iraq Haken Jōkyo (Shuyō Butai)" [Deployment of Marines in Okinawa to Iraq (Major Units)], May 12, 2007, MOD documents disclosed under the Information Disclosure Law, 2021.4.2–HonHonB14–3. According to MOD, "Zai–Oki Kaiheitai no Jitsudō," the Marines from Okinawa had previously been deployed to Iraq (1991, 1996, 1998, 2004), East Timor (1999), and Sumatra (2005).

4. Chinen Seicho, "Zai Oki Kaiheitai Daikibo Iraq Hahei/16,000 Nin Chūryū ni Gimon/Katsudō no Hadome Miezu" [Large-Scale Deployment of Marines to Iraq/Questions Raised over 16,000-troop Presence/No End in Sight for Activities], *Okinawa Times*, January 12, 2004.

5. Seicho, "Zai Oki Kaiheitai Daikibo Iraq Hahei/16,000 Nin Chūryū ni Gimon/Katsudō no Hadome Miezu."

6. Japan–US Security Treaty Division, "Taigai Ōtō Yōryō: Zai Okinawa Kaiheitai no Iraq Haken ni tsuite" [Outline of Foreign Correspondence: Deployment of Marines in Okinawa to Iraq], February 19, 2004, MOFA documents disclosed under the Information Disclosure Law, 2020–628–24; Japan–US Security Treaty Division, "Taigai Ōtō Yōryō: Zai Okinawa Kaiheitai no Iraq Haken ni tsuite" [Outline of Foreign Correspondence: Deployment of Marines in Okinawa to Iraq], August 19, 2004, MOD documents disclosed under the Information Disclosure Law, 2021.4.2–HonHonB14–11.

7. Shūgiin Anzen Hoshō Iinkai [House of Representatives Committee on Security], February 26, 2004, MOD documents disclosed under the Information Disclosure Law, 2021.4.2–HonHonB14–2.

8. Shūgiin Anzen Hoshō Iinkai, February 26, 2004.

9. Strategic Information Analysis Office, Defense Intelligence Division and Japan–US Defense Cooperation Division, Bureau of Defense Policy, "Number of U.S. Troops Stationed outside the U.S. in Operation Iraqi Freedom (OIF), Operation New Dawn (OND), and Operation Enduring Freedom (OEF) from Their Respective Destination Countries," March 17, 2015, MOD documents disclosed under the Information Disclosure Law, 2021.4.2–HonHonB14–12.

10. Inamine, *Ware Igai Mina Waga Shi*, 325–27, 362–66.

11. Sengo 60 Nen Shuzaihan, "Sentaku no Toki/Q: Chikai Shōrai Okinawa ha Sensō ni Makikomareruka?" [The Moment of Choice/Q: Will Okinawa Be Drawn into War in the Near Future?], *Okinawa Times*, December 7, 2004.

12. Minutes of the House of Representatives Committee on Security, May 14, 2010, MOD documents disclosed under the Information Disclosure Law, 2021.4.2–HonHonB14–12.

13. MOFA, "Saikin no Afghanistan Jōsei" [Recent Situations in Afghanistan], May 27, 2004, MOFA documents disclosed under the Information Disclosure Law, 2019–153–1.

14. MOFA, "Afghanistan ni kan suru Kokusai Kaigi no Gaiyō to Hyōka" [Overview and Evaluation of the International Conference on Afghanistan], April 1, 2004, MOFA documents disclosed under the Information Disclosure Law, 2019–153–1.

15. Second Middle East Division, "Wagakuni no Afghanistan Shien" [Japan's Support for Afghanistan], May 20, 2004, MOFA documents disclosed under the Information Disclosure Law, 2019–153–1.

16. Yoriko Kawaguchi to Ryōzō Katō, April 13, 2004, telegraph no. 1670, MOFA documents disclosed under the Information Disclosure Law, 2019–141–9.

17. Yoriko Kawaguchi to Ryōzō Katō, April 13, 2004, telegraph no. 1672, MOFA documents disclosed under the Information Disclosure Law, 2019–141–11.

18. Rice, *No Higher Honor*, 204.

19. Rice, *No Higher Honor*, 204.

20. James Risen, "G.I.'s Are Accused of Abusing Iraqi Captives," *New York Times*, April 29, 2004.

21. Joseph Kahn, "U.S. and North Korea Agree to More Talks: A Lack of Progress on Nuclear Issues, but Signs of Conciliation," *New York Times*, February 29, 2004; Northeast Asia Division, "Dainikai Rokusha Kaigō (Gaiyō to Hyōka)" [The Second Round of Six–Party Talks (Overview and Assessment)], March 1, 2004, MOFA documents disclosed under the Information Disclosure Law, 2020–359–1.

22. Ministry of Foreign Affairs of China, "Dierlun Liufanghuitan Zhongguo Daibiaotuan Tuanyuan, Waijiaobu Xinwen Sifusichang Liu Jianchao Jizhe Zhaodaihui Jilu" [Record of the Press Conference by Liu Jianchao, Deputy Director-General of the Department of Information of the Ministry of Foreign Affairs, Member of the Chinese Delegation to the Second Round of the Six–Party Talks],

February 27, 2004, www.fmprc.gov.cn/web/wjb_673085/zzjg_673183/yzs_673193/dqzz_673197/cxbdhwt_673311/xgxw_673317/t69562.shtml.

23. Ministry of Foreign Affairs of China, "Dierlun Liufanghuitan Zhongguo Daibiaotuan Tuanyuan, Waijiaobu Xinwen Sifusichang Liu Jianchao Jizhe Zhaodaihui Jilu."

24. Yabunaka, *Kokka no Meiun*, 129–31.

25. James Kelly, opening remarks before the Senate Foreign Relations Committee, March 2, 2004, 2001-2009.state.gov/p/eap/rls/rm/2004/30093.htm.

26. Six-Party Talks Chairman's statement, the Second Round of Six-Party Talks, February 28, 2004, www.mofa.go.jp/region/asia-paci/n_korea/state0402.html.

27. Toshiyuki Takano (ambassador to South Korea) to Yoriko Kawaguchi, February 23, 2004, telegraph no. 1323, MOFA documents disclosed under the Information Disclosure Law, 2020–359–3; Koreshige Anami (ambassador to China) to Yoriko Kawaguchi, February 26, 2004, telegraph no. 855, MOFA documents disclosed under the Information Disclosure Law, 2020–359–28.

28. Hayami Ichikawa, "Sagyō Bukai Towareru Yakuwari Kakkoku Kyōtsū Rikainaku Rokusha Kyōgi ga Heimaku" [Working Groups' Role Questioned: Six-Party Talks Conclude Without Common Understanding Among Countries], *Asahi Shimbun*, February 29, 2004; Yabunaka, *Gaikō Kōshō 40 Nen*, 145.

29. Charles Robert Jenkins with Jim Frederick, *The Reluctant Communist: My Desertion, Court-Martial, and Forty-Year Imprisonment in North Korea* (University of California Press, 2008), 153–80.

30. Northeast Asia Division, "Nicchō Shunō Kaidan (Gaiyō)" [Japan–DPRK Summit Meeting (Overview)], May 26, 2004, MOFA documents disclosed under the Information Disclosure Law, 2019–125–1.

31. MOFA, "Koizumi Sōri Kaiken Yōshi" [Summary of Prime Minister Koizumi's Press Conference], May 26, 2004, MOFA documents disclosed under the Information Disclosure Law, 2019–125–2.

32. Tanaka and Tahara, *Kokka to Gaikō*, 67–82; Yomiuri Shimbun Seijibu, *Gaikō o Kenka ni shita Otoko*, 59–73; Iijima, *Jitsuroku Koizumi Gaikō*, 172–78.

33. Yabunaka, *Gaikō Kōshō 40 Nen*, 146–49.

34. Ryōzō Katō to Yoriko Kawaguchi, June 10, 2004, telegraph no. 86, MOFA documents disclosed under the Information Disclosure Law, 2019–151–3.

35. MOFA, "Third Round of Six-Party Talks Concerning North Korean Nuclear Issues," June 27, 2004, www.mofa.go.jp/region/asia-paci/n_korea/6party/talk0406.html; Northeast Asia Division, "Kitachōsen no Kakumondai ni kan suru Daisankai Rokusha Kaigō (Gaiyō to Hyōka)" [the Third Round of Six-Party Talks concerning North Korean Nuclear Issues (Overview and Evaluation)], June 27, 2004, MOFA documents disclosed under the Information Disclosure Law, 2020–360–1.

36. Nobuyoshi Sakajiri, "Bei Koritsu o Nogare Andokan" [US Avoids Isolation, Breathes Sigh of Relief], *Asahi Shimbun*, June 27, 2004; Yabunaka, *Gaikō Kōshō 40 Nen*, 149–51.

37. MOFA, "Third Round of Six-Party Talks concerning North Korean Nuclear Issues"; Northeast Asia Division, "Kitachōsen no Kakumondai ni kan suru Daisankai Rokusha Kaigō (Gaiyō to Hyōka)."

38. Six-Party Talks Chairman's statement of the Third Round of the Six-Party Talks, June 26, 2004, www.chinaembassy.org.nz/eng/xw/t140647.htm.

39. Koreshige Anami to Yoriko Kawaguchi, June 26, 2004, telegraph no. 803, MOFA documents disclosed under the Information Disclosure Law, 2020–360–22.

40. Anami to Kawaguchi, June 26, 2004, telegraph no. 803.

41. Kōichi Haraguchi to Yoriko Kawaguchi, June 8, 2004, telegraph no. 282, MOFA documents disclosed under the Information Disclosure Law, 2020–163–3; UNSC Resolution 1546, June 8, 2004, undocs.org/S/RES/1546(2004).

42. North American Affairs Bureau, "Nichi–Bei Shunō Kaidan no Gaiyō" [Overview of the JapanU.S. Summit], June 9, 2004, MOFA documents disclosed under the Information Disclosure Law, 2019–171–1; Ryōzō Katō to Yoriko Kawaguchi, June 9, 2004, telegraph no. 46, MOFA documents disclosed under the Information Disclosure Law, 2019–171–6; Katō to Kawaguchi, June 9, 2004, telegraph no. 47, MOFA documents disclosed under the Information Disclosure Law, 2019–171–7; Katō to Kawaguchi, June 9, 2004, telegraph no. 48, MOFA documents disclosed under the Information Disclosure Law, 2019–171–8; Katō to Kawaguchi, June 9, 2004, telegraph no. 51, MOFA documents disclosed under the Information Disclosure Law, 2019–171–11; Yomiuri Shimbun Seijibu, *Gaikō o Kenka ni shita Otoko*, 181–82; Satō, Iraq Jieitai "Sentoki," 206–10. Jenkins later moved to Japan, where he lived the rest of his life. See Austin Ramzy, "Charles Jenkins, 77, G.I. Who Fled to North Korea," *New York Times*, December 13, 2017.

43. North American Affairs Bureau, "Nichi–Bei Shunō Kaidan no Gaiyō."

44. Second Western Europe Division, "Nichi–Ei Shunō Kaidan no Gaiyō" [Overview of the JapanU.K. Summit], June 9, 2004, MOFA documents disclosed under the Information Disclosure Law, 2019–156–2. See also Ryōzō Katō to Yoriko Kawaguchi, June 9, 2004, telegraph no. 41, MOFA documents disclosed under the Information Disclosure Law, 2019–156–1.

45. Second Western Europe Division, "Nichi–Ei Shunō Kaidan no Gaiyō."

46. Katō to Kawaguchi, June 9, 2004, telegraph no. 41. See also First Western Europe Division, "Nichi–Futsu Shunō Kaidan no Gaiyō" [Overview of the Japan-France Summit], June 9, 2004, MOFA documents disclosed under the Information Disclosure Law, 2019–157–2.

47. MOFA, "Nihon Jordan Shunō Kaidan" [Japan-Jordan Summit (Overview)], June 10, 2004, www.mofa.go.jp/mofaj/kaidan/s_koi/g8_04/jjo_kaidan.html. See also First Middle East Division, "Nichi–Jordan Shunō Kaidan" [Japan-Jordan Summit], June 10, 2004, MOFA documents disclosed under the Information Disclosure Law, 2019–168–2.

48. MOFA, "Nihon Jordan Shunō Kaidan."

49. First Middle East Division, "Nichi–Jordan Shunō Kaidan no Igi" [The Significance of the Japan–Jordan Summit], June 4, 2004, MOFA documents disclosed under the Information Disclosure Law, 2019–168–3.

50. Ryōzō Katō to Yoriko Kawaguchi, June 10, 2004, telegraph no. 95, MOFA documents disclosed under the Information Disclosure Law, 2019–153–11.

51. Ryōzō Katō to Yoriko Kawaguchi, June 10, 2004, telegraph no. 99, MOFA documents disclosed under the Information Disclosure Law, 2020–314–20; MOFA, "Sea Island Summit (Overview)," June 11, 2004, MOFA documents disclosed under the Information Disclosure Law, 2020–314–2.

52. Chair's summary, Sea Island Summit, June 10, 2004, MOFA documents disclosed under the Information Disclosure Law, 2020–314–1.

53. Tsukasa Uemura (chargé d'affaires to Iraq) to Yoriko Kawaguchi, June 28, 2004, telegraph no. 128, MOFA documents disclosed under the Information Disclosure Law, 2019–212–3.

54. Yoriko Kawaguchi to Tsukasa Uemura, June 28, 2004, telegraph no. 14149, MOFA documents disclosed under the Information Disclosure Law, 2019–212–4.

55. Ryōzō Katō to Yoriko Kawaguchi, June 28, 2004, telegraph no. 1126, MOFA documents disclosed under the Information Disclosure Law, 2019–212–5.

56. Office of the Press Secretary, "Statement by the President," November 25, 2003, georgewbush-whitehouse.archives.gov/news/releases/2003/11/20031125-11.html.

57. George W. Bush, remarks to Veterans of Foreign Wars Convention, August 16, 2004, georgewbush-whitehouse.archives.gov/news/releases/2004/08/20040816-12.html.

58. Bush, remarks to Veterans of Foreign Wars Convention.

59. According to Kent E. Calder, "The 2004 proposals involved returning 60,000–70,000 service members and their families to the United States over the ensuing decade—two-thirds from Europe, with the majority returning from Germany. Over the ensuing three years, 12,500 soldiers were also scheduled to return from Korea, with many of those remaining in Korea repositioned." See Calder, *Embattled Garrisons: Comparative Base Politics and American Globalism* (Princeton University Press, 2007), 34–35, 263–64. See also Takashi Kawakami, *Beigun no Zenpo Tenkai to Nichi–Bei Dōmei* [US Forces Forward Deployment and the US-Japan Alliance] (Dobunkan Shuppan, 2004), 193–216; Nina Silove, "The Pivot Before the Pivot: U.S. Strategy to Preserve the Power Balance in Asia," *International Security* 40, no. 4 (Spring 2016): 75–76.

60. Yuki Tatsumi, "Blair Moto Bei Taiheiyōgun Shireikan ni Kiku" [Interview with Blair, Former Commander of US Pacific Command], *Ronza*, No. 124 (September 2005): 180–81.

61. Tatsumi, "Blair Moto Bei Taiheiyōgun Shireikan ni Kiku," 182.

62. Kōichi Haraguchi to Yoriko Kawaguchi, September 22, 2004, telegraph no. 3681, MOFA documents disclosed under the Information Disclosure Law, 2020–

478–11; MOFA, "Nichi–Bei Shunō Kaidan no Gaiyō" [Overview of the Japan–US Summit], September 22, 2004, www.mofa.go.jp/mofaj/area/usa/kaidan_040922.html; North American Affairs Bureau, "Nichi–Bei Shunō Kaidan no Gaiyō" [Overview of the Japan–US Summit], September 27, 2004, MOFA documents disclosed under the Information Disclosure Law, 2020–478–6. See also Masahiko Hisae, *Beigun Saihen: Nichi–Bei "Himitsu Kosho" de Nani ga Attaka* [US Military Realignment: What Happened in the Japan–US "Secret Negotiations"?] (Kōdansha, 2005), 128–35.

63. Kōichi Haraguchi to Yoriko Kawaguchi, September 23, 2004, telegraph no. 3756, MOFA documents disclosed under the Information Disclosure Law, 2020–478–18.

64. Council on Security and Defense Capabilities, "'Anzen Hoshō to Bōeiryoku ni kan suru Kondankai' Hōkokusho: Mirai e no Anzen Hoshō Bōeiryoku Vision" [The Council on Security and Defense Capabilities Report: Japan's Visions for Future Security and Defense Capabilities], October 2004, www.kantei.go.jp/jp/singi/ampobouei/dai13/13siryou.pdf; Taketsugu Sato and Yoshiyuki Komurata, "Tsuyomaru Nichi-Bei 'Dōshō Imu' Bei Daiichi Gundan Shireibu Zama e Iten" [Growing Differences between Japan and the US: US First Army Headquarters to Relocate to Zama], *Asahi Shimbun*, April 13, 2005; Tsuyoshi Sunohara, *Dōmei Henbō*; Takemasa Moriya, *"Futenma" Kōshō Hiroku* [Secret Records of the "Futenma" Negotiations] (Shinchosha, 2012).

65. Hajime Ogawa (ambassador to Chile) to Nobutaka Machimura, November 20, 2004, telegraph no. 966, MOFA documents disclosed under the Information Disclosure Law, 2020–553–7. See also Hisae, *Beigun Saihen*, 157–61.

66. Security Council and Cabinet, "National Defense Program Guideline, FY 2005–," December 10, 2004, japan.kantei.go.jp/policy/2004/1210taikou_e.html.

67. Special Advisor to the DCI on Iraq's WMD, "Comprehensive Report," September 30, 2004, www.cia.gov/library/reports/general-reports-1/iraq_wmd_2004/.

68. Charles Duelfer, *Hide and Seek: The Search for Truth in Iraq* (Public Affairs, 2009), 441–60. See also Charles A. Duelfer and Stephen Benedict Dyson, "Chronic Misperception and International Conflict: The U.S.-Iraq Experience," *International Security* 36, no. 1 (Summer 2011): 73–100.

69. George W. Bush, departure remarks, "Topic: The Duelfer Report on Iraqi Weapons Programs," October 7, 2004, in Ryōzō Katō to Nobutaka Machimura (foreign minister), October 7, 2004, telegraph no. 4985, MOFA documents disclosed under the Information Disclosure Law, 2019–213–2.

70. Ryōzō Katō to Nobutaka Machimura, October 7, 2004, telegraph no. 4988, MOFA documents disclosed under the Information Disclosure Law, 2019–213–3.

71. Patrick E. Tyler, "Blair Offers an Apology, of Sorts, Over Iraq," *New York Times*, September 29, 2004.

72. MOFA, "Iraq Taryō Hakai Heiki (Sōteimondō: Set Ban)" [WMD in Iraq (Supposed Questions and Answers: Set Version)], October 7, 2004, MOFA documents disclosed under the Information Disclosure Law, 2019–213–1.

73. Minutes of the Plenary Session of the House of Representatives, October 13, 2004, kokkai.ndl.go.jp/#/detail?minId=116105254X00220041013&spkNum=4¤t=1.

74. Minutes of the Plenary Session of the House of Representatives, October 13, 2004.

75. Koizumi Cabinet, "Naikaku Sōridajin Danwa" [Prime Minister's Statement], March 20, 2003, MOFA documents disclosed under the Information Disclosure Law, 2019–204–1.

76. Office of the Press Secretary, "President Bush Addresses the Nation," March 19, 2003. georgewbush-whitehouse.archives.gov/news/releases/2003/03/20030319-17.html.

77. Richard N. Haass, *War of Necessity: War of Choice* (Simon & Schuster, 2009), 247–8.

78. Nobutaka Machimura to Ryōzō Katō, October 25, 2004, telegraph no. 66423, MOFA documents disclosed under the Information Disclosure Law, 2019–142–7.

79. Nobutaka Machimura to Ryōzō Katō, October 25, 2004, telegraph no. 66425, MOFA documents disclosed under the Information Disclosure Law, 2019–142–11.

80. Nobutaka Machimura to Ryōzō Katō, October 24, 2004, telegraph no. 66415, MOFA documents disclosed under the Information Disclosure Law, 2019–142–15; Machimura to Katō, October 24, 2004, telegraph no. 66416, MOFA documents disclosed under the Information Disclosure Law, 2019–142–16.

81. Machimura to Katō, October 24, 2004, telegraph No. 66415; Machimura to Katō, October 24, 2004, telegraph No. 66416.

82. MOFA, "Tai Iraq Buryoku Kōshi ni kan suru Wagakuni no Taiō (Kenshō Kekka)" [Japan's Response to the Use of Force Against Iraq (Verification Result)], December 21, 2012, www.mofa.go.jp/mofaj/area/iraq/taiou_201212.html.

Chapter 5

1. MOFA, "Iraqi Kokumin Gikai Zaigai Senkyo ni okeru Kokusai Kanshi e no Wagakuni Seifu no Sanka ni tsuite" [On the Government's Participation in International Monitoring of the Iraqi National Assembly Overseas Elections], January 28, 2005, MOFA documents disclosed under the Information Disclosure Law, 2019–214–1.

2. Office of the Press Secretary, "President Congratulates Iraqis on Election," January 30, 2005, georgewbush-whitehouse.archives.gov/news/releases/2005/01/20050130-2.html.

3. Dodge, *Iraq*, 35–36.

4. Ryōzō Katō to Nobutaka Machimura, January 31, 2005, telegraph no. 998, MOFA documents disclosed under the Information Disclosure Law, 2019–214–5.

5. Ryōzō Katō to Nobutaka Machimura, February 19, 2005, telegraph no. 1989, MOFA documents disclosed under the Information Disclosure Law, 2019–172–1; Katō to Machimura, February 19, 2005, telegraph no. 1994, MOFA documents disclosed under the Information Disclosure Law, 2019–172–5; Katō to Machimura, February 19, 2005, telegraph no. 1996, MOFA documents disclosed under the Information Disclosure Law, 2019–172–8; Katō to Machimura, February 19, 2005, telegraph no. 1997, MOFA documents disclosed under the Information Disclosure Law, 2019–172–9.

6. MOFA, "Nichi–Bei Anzen Hoshō Kyōgi Iinkai ('2+2') no Kaisai" [The Japan–US Security Consultative Committee ("2+2") Meeting], February 19, 2005, MOFA documents disclosed under the Information Disclosure Law, 2019–178–1.

7. US–Japan Security Consultative Committee, "Joint Statement," February 19, 2005, www.mofa.go.jp/region/n-america/us/security/scc/joint0502.html.

8. Ryōzō Katō to Nobutaka Machimura, February 20, 2005, telegraph no. 2014, MOFA documents disclosed under the Information Disclosure Law, 2019–178–2.

9. Nobutaka Machimura to Ryōzō Katō, March 20, 2005, telegraph no. 36222, MOFA documents disclosed under the Information Disclosure Law, 2019–144–17.

10. Machimura to Katō, telegraph no. 36222.

11. Machimura to Katō, telegraph no. 36222.

12. Machimura to Katō, telegraph no. 36222.

13. Machimura to Katō, telegraph no. 36222.

14. Nobutaka Machimura to Ryōzō Katō, March 19, 2005, telegraph no. 36192, MOFA documents disclosed under the Information Disclosure Law, 2019–144–19. See also Condoleezza Rice, *Extraordinary, Ordinary People: A Memoir of Family* (Three Rivers Press, 2010), 226–28; Condoleezza Rice, *Condoleezza Rice: A Memoir of My Extraordinary, Ordinary Family and Me* (Ember, 2012), 224–25.

15. Machimura to Katō, telegraph no. 36192.

16. Rice, *No Higher Honor*, 346–52. See also Michael W. Michalak (US chargé d'affaires to Japan) to Condoleezza Rice (US secretary of state), March 10, 2005, cable no. 1415, search.proquest.com/docview/1679131347?accountid=26790.

17. Northeast Asia Division, "Daiyonkai Rokusha Kaigō (Gaiyō to Hyōka)" [The Fourth Round of Six-Party Talks (Overview and Assessment)], August 2005, MOFA documents disclosed under the Information Disclosure Law, 2020–361–1; MOFA, "Daiyonkai Rokusha Kaigō (Gaiyō to Hyōka)" [The Fourth Round of Six-Party Talks (Overview and Evaluation)], September 2005, www.mofa.go.jp/mofaj/area/n_korea/6kaigo/6kaigo4_gh.html.

18. Six-Party Talks Joint Statement of the Fourth Round-Party, September 19, 2005, www.mofa.go.jp/region/asia-paci/n_korea/6party/joint0509.html.

19. Six-Party Talks Joint Statement of the Fourth Round-Party, September 19, 2005.

20. Asian and Oceanian Affairs Bureau, "Daiyonkai Rokusha Kaigō Dainiji Kaigō (Gaiyō to Hyōka)" [The Second Meeting of the Fourth Round of Six-Party Talks (Overview and Assessment)], September 27, 2005, MOFA documents disclosed under the Information Disclosure Law, 2020–361–61; MOFA, "Daiyonkai Rokusha Kaigō Dainiji Kaigō (Gaiyō to Hyōka)" [The Second Meeting of the Fourth Round of Six-Party Talks (Overview and Assessment)], September 2005, www.mofa.go.jp/mofaj/area/n_korea/6kaigo/6kaigo4_2gh.html.

21. David Sanger, "Bush Puts Iraq, China and Iran on Agenda," *New York Times*, September 14, 2005.

22. Rice, *No Higher Honor*, 400–1, 704.

23. Six-Party Talks Chairman's statement, the First Phase of the Fifth Round of the Six-Party Talks, November 11, 2005, mu.china-embassy.gov.cn/eng/sgxw/200511/t20051111_6483111.htm.

24. Yabunaka, *Gaikō Kōshō 40 Nen,* 156–58.

25. MOFA, "Daigokai Rokusha Kaigō Daiichiji Kaigō (Gaiyō to Tenbō)" [The First Phase of the Fifth Round of Six-Party Talks (Overview and Prospects)], November 2005, MOFA documents disclosed under the Information Disclosure Law, 2020–362–1.

26. J. Thomas Schieffer to Condoleezza Rice, April 12, 2006, cable no. 1985, search.proquest.com/docview/1679131369?accountid=26790.

27. Six-Party Talks Chairman's statement, the Second Phase of the Fifth Round of the Six-Party Talks, December 22, 2006, www.mofa.go.kr/viewer/skin/doc.html?fn=file_20131008185240480_0&rs=/viewer/result/202010; MOFA, "Daigokai Rokusha Kaigō Dainiji Kaigō (Gaiyō to Tenbō)" [The Second Phase of the Fifth Round of Six-Party Talks (Overview and Prospects)], December 2006, www.mofa.go.jp/mofaj/area/n_korea/6kaigo/6kaigo5_2gt.html.

28. Six-Party Talks, "Initial Actions for the Implementation of the Joint Statement," February 13, 2007, www.mofa.go.jp/region/asia-paci/n_korea/6party/action0702.html; MOFA, "Daigokai Rokusha Kaigō Daisan Session no Gaiyō" [Overview of the Third Session of the Fifth Round of Six-Party Talks], February 2007, www.mofa.go.jp/mofaj/area/n_korea/6kaigo/6kaigo5_3g.html.

29. Six-Party Talks Chairman's statement, December 11, 2008, www.mofa.go.jp/region/asia-paci/n_korea/6party/state0812.html; Ministry of Foreign Affairs, "Dairokkai Rokusha Kaigō ni kan suru Shuseki Daihyō Kaigō (Gaiyō)" [The Meeting of Heads of Delegations of the Sixth Round of Six-Party Talks (Overview)], December 2008, www.mofa.go.jp/mofaj/area/n_korea/6kaigo/6kaigo6_skg3.html.

30. Six-Party Talks Chairman's statement, December 11, 2008.

31. Akihiro Ito and Jun Kato, "Rokkakoku Kyōgi ga Heimaku Kaku Bunshoka ni Gōi sezu: Bei Jiki Seiken e Sakiokuri" [Six-Party Talks Concluded Without Agreement on Nuclear Document: Decision Postponed to Next US Administration], *Yomiuri Shimbun*, December 12, 2008.

32. Christopher R. Hill, *Outpost: A Diplomat at Work* (Simon and Schuster, 2014), 234–37.

33. First North America Division, "Nichi–Bei Gaishō Kaidan no Gaiyō" [Overview of the U.S.-Japan Foreign Ministers' Talks], October 29, 2005, MOFA documents disclosed under the Information Disclosure Law, 2019–173–1. See also First North America Division, "Machimura Daijin to Hadley Beikoku Kokka Anzen Hoshō Tantō Daitōryō Hosakan tono Kaidan no Gaiyō" [Overview of Talks between Minister Machimura and Hadley, Assistant to the President for National Security Affairs], October 29, 2005, MOFA documents disclosed under the Information Disclosure Law, 2019–173–11.

34. First North America Division, "Nichi–Bei Gaishō Kaidan no Gaiyō", October 29, 2005.

35. Security Council and Cabinet, "National Defense Program Guideline, FY 2005–"; MOFA and Defense Agency, "Nichi–Bei Anzen Hoshō Kyōgi Iinkai ('2+2') no Kaisai" [Japan–US Security Consultative Committee ("2+2") Meeting], October 29, 2005, MOFA documents disclosed under the Information Disclosure Law, 2019–177–1.

36. MOFA and Defense Agency, "Nichi–Bei Anzen Hoshō Kyōgi Iinkai ('2+2') no Kaisai." The 2005 proposal to package Futenma Air Station's relocation with the Marines' relocation to Guam never came to fruition. In 2012, the Futenma Air Station relocation and the Marine Corps relocation to Guam were delinked, with the Marine Corps relocation to Guam to be implemented first. See Kosuke Saito, "Zaigai Kichi Saihen o meguru Beikokunai Seiji to Sono Senryakuteki Hakyū: Futenma—Guam Package to Sono Kirihanashi" [The US Domestic Politics over Overseas Base Realignment and Its Strategic Spillover: The Futenma—Guam Package and Its Detachment], in *Okinawa to Kaiheitai: Churyu no Rekishiteki Tenkai* [Okinawa and the Marine Corps: Historical Development of Stationing], ed. Tomohiro Yara et al. (Junposha, 2016), 143–71.

37. Kuniich Tanida, "Zaioki Kaiheitai nado Sentō Butai ha Onzon—Tōi Jimoto Futan Keigen: Beigun Saihen 'Chūkan Hōkoku' Happyō" [Combat Units Including Okinawa-Based Marines Preserved—Alleviation of Local Burden Remains Distant: US Military Reorganization "Interim Report" Released], *Asahi Shimbun*, October 30, 2005.

38. US–Japan Security Consultative Committee, "U.S.-Japan Alliance: Transformation and Realignment for the Future," October 29, 2005, www.mofa.go.jp/region/n-america/us/security/scc/doc0510.html.

39. US–Japan Security Consultative Committee, "U.S.-Japan Alliance: Transformation and Realignment for the Future."

40. Jun Ikai, "Zainichi Beigun Saihen: Yokota Kichi 'Gun-Gun Kyōyō Hanashi ga Chigau' Ishihara Chiji Ikari Arawa" [US Forces Reorganization in Japan: "Joint Military Use Contradicts Previous Agreements"—Governor Ishihara Expresses Overt Indignation Regarding Yokota Air Base], *Mainichi Shimbun*, October 29, 2005.

41. US–Japan Security Consultative Committee, "Joint Statement," February 19, 2005, www.mofa.go.jp/region/n-america/us/security/scc/joint0502.html.

42. US–Japan Security Consultative Committee, "U.S.-Japan Alliance: Transformation and Realignment for the Future."

43. Taketsugu Sato and Yoshiyuki Komurata, "Takokusekigun Sanka Kōkyūhō mo: Jieitai Zainichi Beigun to Yūgō Kasoku" [Participation in Multinational Forces and Permanent Law: Accelerating Integration of Japan Self-Defense Forces with US Forces in Japan], *Asahi Shimbun*, October 31, 2005.

44. Yoriko Kawaguchi to Kōichi Haraguchi, September 23, 2004, telegraph no. 3761, MOFA documents disclosed under the Information Disclosure Law, 2020–478–1.

45. Kawaguchi to Haraguchi, telegraph no. 3761.

46. MOFA, "Anpori Kaikaku no Ikistasu to Genjō" [The Evolution and Current Status of Security Council Reform], April 27, 2022, www.mofa.go.jp/mofaj/gaiko/un_kaikaku/kaikaku2.html.

47. Orita, *Gaikō Shogenroku*, 252–61.

48. Shūhei Takahashi (consul general in Edinburgh) to Nobutaka Machimura, July 8, 2005, telegraph no. 419, MOFA documents disclosed under the Information Disclosure Law, 2020–322–8; Nobutaka Machimura to Sadaaki Numata (ambassador to Canada), July 13, 2005, telegraph no. 89778, MOFA documents disclosed under the Information Disclosure Law, 2020–323–1.

49. Shūhei Takahashi to Nobutaka Machimura, July 8, 2005, unnumbered telegraph (draft), MOFA documents disclosed under the Information Disclosure Law, 2020–353–18. Koizumi's remarks were made at the G8 meeting on African issues. See also Clarence Lusane, foreword by Kwame Dixon, *Colin Powell and Condoleezza Rice: Foreign Policy, Race, and the New American Century* (Praeger, 2006), 132–33.

50. Takahashi to Machimura, unnumbered telegraph (draft), July 8, 2005.

51. Blair, *A Journey*, 562.

52. Nobutaka Machimura to Ryōzō Katō, July 12, 2005, unnumbered telegraph (draft), MOFA, 2019–145–19. For a study of the "cold" relationship between the US and UN in the broader context of structural realism, exceptionalism, and organizational factors, see Chiyuki Aoi, "America to Kokuren: Takakushugi no Kongo" [America and UN: The future of Multilateralism], in *America Seijigaikō no Anatomy* [Anatomy of American Politics and Diplomacy], eds. Yoshinobu Yamamoto and Okiyoshi Takeda (Kokusai Shoin, 2006), 89–113.

53. Machimura to Katō, unnumbered telegraph (draft), July 12, 2005.

54. Nobutaka Machimura to Ryōzō Katō, July 13, 2005, unnumbered telegraph (draft), MOFA documents disclosed under the Information Disclosure Law, 2019–145–4.

55. Machimura to Katō, unnumbered telegraph (draft), July 13, 2005.

56. Machimura to Katō, unnumbered telegraph (draft), July 13, 2005.

57. Machimura to Katō, unnumbered telegraph (draft), July 13, 2005.

58. George W. Bush, statement, 2005 World Summit High Level Plenary Meeting, September 14, 2005, www.un.org/webcast/summit2005/statements/usa050914.pdf.

59. Bush, statement, 2005 World Summit High Level Plenary Meeting, September 14, 2005.

60. Kenzō Ōshima (ambassador to the UN) to Nobutaka Machimura, September 16, 2005, telegraph no. 10587, MOFA documents disclosed under the Information Disclosure Law, 2019–217–8. Senior Deputy Minister for Foreign Affairs Tsuneo Nishida briefed Koizumi on the plane for his meeting with Annan. Ministry of Foreign Affairs, "Koizumi Sōri to Annan Jimusōchō no Kaidan" [Talk between Prime Minister Koizumi and Secretary-General Annan], September 15, 2005, MOFA documents disclosed under the Information Disclosure Law, 2019–217–4.

61. Ōshima to Machimura, telegraph no. 10587.

62. Ōshima to Machimura, telegraph no. 10587.

63. Kenzō Ōshima to Nobutaka Machimura, September 19, 2005, telegraph no. 10719, MOFA documents disclosed under the Information Disclosure Law, 2019–217–11.

64. Koizumi's address at the High–Level Plenary Meeting of the 60th session of the General Assembly of the United Nations, "Turning Words into an Action," September 15, 2005, www.un.org/webcast/summit2005/statements15/jap050915eng.pdf.

Negotiations over the International Convention for the Suppression of Acts of Nuclear Terrorism began at the United Nations in February 1997 and it was adopted by the UN General Assembly in April 2005. Disarmament, Non–proliferation and Science Department, "Kaku ni yoru Terrorism no Koi no Bōshi ni kan suru Kokusai Jōyaku (Kashō) ni tsuite" [About the International Convention for the Suppression of Acts of Nuclear Terrorism (Provisional Name)], September 2005, MOFA documents disclosed under the Information Disclosure Law, 2019–248–5.

65. United Nations Policy Division, "Koizumi Sōridaijin no Kokusairengō Shunōkaigo Shusseki (Toriaezuno Gaiyō to Hyōka)" [Prime Minister Koizumi's Attendance at the United Nations Summit (Present Overview and Evaluation)], September 20, 2005, MOFA documents disclosed under the Information Disclosure Law, 2019–217–15.

66. First North America Division, "Nichi–Bei Gaishō Kaidan no Gaiyō."

67. First North America Division, "Nichi–Bei Gaishō Kaidan no Gaiyō."

68. First North America Division, "Nichi–Bei Gaishō Kaidan no Gaiyō."

69. First North America Division, "Nichi–Bei Gaishō Kaidan no Gaiyō."

70. Tarō Asō (foreign minister) to Ryōzō Katō, November 17, 2005, telegraph no. 143969 (draft), MOFA documents disclosed under the Information Disclosure Law, 2019–146–4.

71. Asō to Katō, telegraph no. 143969 (draft).

72. Asō to Katō, telegraph no. 143969 (draft).

73. Tarō Asō to Ryōzō Katō, November 17, 2005, telegraph no. 143971 (draft), MOFA documents disclosed under the Information Disclosure Law, 2019–146–7.

74. Tarō Asō to Ryōzō Katō, November 17, 2005, telegraph no. 143970 (draft), MOFA documents disclosed under the Information Disclosure Law, 2019–146–6.

75. Rice, *No Higher Honor*, 441–42.

76. Kofi Annan with Nader Mousavizadeh, *Interventions: A Life in War and Peace* (Penguin Books, 2012), 143.

Chapter 6

1. National Security Strategy of the United States of America, March 2006, georgewbush-whitehouse.archives.gov/nsc/nss/2006/. See also Ryōzō Katō to Tarō Asō, March 16, 2006, telegraph no. 2980, MOFA documents disclosed under the Information Disclosure Law, 2019–116–2.

2. National Security Strategy of the United States of America, March 2006.

3. National Security Strategy of the United States of America, March 2006.

4. Stephen Hadley (national security advisor), "Remarks to the United States Institute of Peace on the President's National Security Strategy," March 16, 2006, georgewbush-whitehouse.archives.gov/news/releases/2006/03/20060316-8.html. See also Ryōzō Katō to Tarō Asō, March 16, 2006, telegraph No. 2984, MOFA documents disclosed under the Information Disclosure Law, 2019–116–1; David Sanger, "Report Backs Iraq Strike and Cites Iran Peril," *New York Times*, March 16, 2006.

5. Hadley, "Remarks to the United States Institute of Peace on the President's National Security Strategy."

6. Hadley, "Remarks to the United States Institute of Peace on the President's National Security Strategy."

7. Hadley, "Remarks to the United States Institute of Peace on the President's National Security Strategy."

8. Ministry of Foreign Affairs, "Terror Taisaku Tokusoho ni motozuku Taiō Sochi ni kan suru Kihon Keikaku no Henkō ni tsuite" [Changes to the Master Plan for Response Measures Under the Anti-Terrorism Special Measures Law], April 2006, MOFA documents disclosed under the Information Disclosure Law, 2019–121–1.

9. US–Japan Security Consultative Committee, "Joint Statement," May 1, 2006, www.mod.go.jp/e/d_act/us/dp12.html.

10. US–Japan Security Consultative Committee, "Joint Statement," May 1, 2006.

11. US–Japan Security Consultative Committee, "Joint Statement," May 1, 2006.

12. US–Japan Security Consultative Committee, "Joint Statement," May 1, 2006.

13. US–Japan Security Consultative Committee, "United States–Japan Roadmap for Realignment Implementation," May 1, 2006, www.mofa.go.jp/region/n-america/us/security/scc/doc0605.html.

14. Ryōzō Katō to Tarō Asō, May 2, 2006, telegraph no. 4842, MOFA documents disclosed under the Information Disclosure Law, 2019–121–4. On China as "a responsible stakeholder," see also Robert B. Zoellick (deputy secretary of state), "Whither China: From Membership to Responsibility?" September 21, 2005, 2001-2009.state.gov/s/d/former/zoellick/rem/53682.htm; Department of Defense, "Quadrennial Defense Review Report," 29, February 6, 2006, archive.defense.gov/pubs/pdfs/QDR20060203.pdf.

15. Katō to Asō, telegraph no. 4842.

16. Katō to Asō, telegraph no. 4842.

17. Condoleezza Rice (secretary of state), "Remarks with Secretary of Defense Donald Rumsfeld, Japanese Foreign Minister Taro Aso, and Japanese Defense Minister of State for Defense Fukushirō Nukaga—Japan Security Consultative Committee," May 1, 2006, 2001-2009.state.gov/secretary/rm/2006/65528.htm.

18. Ryōzō Katō to Tarō Asō, May 4, 2006, telegraph no. 4945, MOFA documents disclosed under the Information Disclosure Law, 2019–174–1.

19. Katō to Asō, telegraph no. 4945.

20. "Zainichi Beigun Saihen Kihon Hōshin o Kakugi Kettei: 'Futenma' Isetsu Chimei Kisai sezu" [Cabinet Approves Basic Policy for US Military Realignment in Japan: Futenma Relocation Plan Omits Specific Location], *Yomiuri Shimbun*, May 30, 2006, evening edition. See also Inamine, *Ware Igai Mina Waga Shi*, 321–24, 358–59, 368–88; Taizo Miyagi and Tsuyoshi Watanabe, *Futenma, Henoko: Yugamerareta 20 Nen* [Futenma, Henoko: Distorted 20 Years] (Shūeisha, 2016), 96–120; Fumiaki Nozoe, *Okinawa Beigun Kichi Zenshi* [The Comprehensive History of US Bases in Okinawa] (Yoshikawa Kōbunkan, 2020), 158–70; Hiroshi Hashimoto, *Futenma Hikōjo Dou Torimodosu? Tairitsu ka Kyōchō ka no Sentakushi* [How to Reclaim Futenma Air Station? A Choice Between Confrontation and Cooperation] (Jiji Tsūshin Shuppankyoku, 2020), 32; Kyōji Yanagisawa et al., *Henoko ni Kawaru Yutakana Sentakushi: "Beigun Kichi Mondai ni kan suru Bankoku Shinryō Kaigi" no Teigen o Yomu* [Rich Alternatives to Henoko: Read the Proposals of "the Bankoku Shinryō Council on US Military Base Issues"] (Kamogawa Shuppan, 2020), 29–33.

21. Second Middle East Division, "Rikujō Jieitai Iraq Fukkō Gyōmu Shien Taichō oyobi Zai Samawah Gaimushō Renraku Jimushochō no Iraq Muthanna Kenchiji tono Kaidan" [Meeting of the Commander of the Ground Self-Defense Force's Iraq Reconstruction Operations Support Unit and the Head of MOFA Liaison

Office in Samawah, the Governor of Muthanna Province, Iraq], June 20, 2006, MOFA documents disclosed under the Information Disclosure Law, 2019–215–1. See also Joel D. Rayburn and Frank K. Sobchak, eds., *The U.S. Army in the Iraq War*, vol. 1: *Invasion, Insurgency, Civil War, 2003–2006* (Strategic Studies Institute and United Stages Army War College Press, 2019), 577.

22. Koizumi's press conference, "Iraq Haken no Jieitai Tesshutō" [Withdrawal of Self-Defense Forces from Iraq, etc.], June 20, 2006, www.kantei.go.jp/jp//koizumispeech/2006/06/20kaiken.html.

23. Tony Snow and Steve Hadley, "Press Gaggle by Tony Snow and National Security Advisor Steve Hadley," June 20, 2006, georgewbush-whitehouse.archives.gov/news/releases/2006/06/20060620-2.html.

24. Japanese Iraq Reconstruction and Support Group, "Iraq Fukkō Shiengun Katsudō Hōkoku" [The Japanese Iraq Reconstruction and Support Group Activity Report], January 22, 2006, www.asahicom.jp/news/esi/ichikijiatesi/iraq-nippo-list/20180416/370/060122.pdf.

25. Yanagisawa, *Kenshō Kantei no Iraq War*, 98, 152–55.

26. Rumsfeld, *Known and Unknown*, 591. See also Bush, *Spoken from the Heart*, 373.

27. Rumsfeld, *Known and Unknown*, 591.

28. Ryōzō Katō to Tarō Asō, June 30, 2006, telegraph no. 7301, MOFA documents disclosed under the Information Disclosure Law, 2019–118–1.

29. Ryōzō Katō to Tarō Asō, June 30, 2006, telegraph no. 7360, MOFA documents disclosed under the Information Disclosure Law, 2019–118–4.

30. Katō to Asō, telegraph no. 7360.

31. Katō to Asō, June 30, 2006, telegraph no. 7301. See also Sunohara, *Dōmei Henbō*, 229–32; Moriya, *"Futenma" Kōshō Hiroku*, 247–56.

32. Ryōzō Katō to Tarō Asō, June 30, 2006, telegraph no. 7361, MOFA documents disclosed under the Information Disclosure Law, 2020–164–4.

33. Katō to Asō, telegraph no. 7361.

34. Ryōzō Katō to Tarō Asō, June 30, 2006, telegraph no. 7365, MOFA documents disclosed under the Information Disclosure Law, 2020–164–8.

35. Office of the Press Secretary, "Joint Statement: The Japan-U.S. Alliance of the New Century," June 29, 2006, georgewbush-whitehouse.archives.gov/news/releases/2006/06/text/20060629-2.html.

36. Office of the Press Secretary, "Joint Statement: The Japan-U.S. Alliance of the New Century."

37. Office of the Press Secretary, "Joint Statement: The Japan-U.S. Alliance of the New Century."

38. Office of the Press Secretary, "Joint Statement: The Japan-U.S. Alliance of the New Century."

39. Office of the Press Secretary, "President Bush and Japanese Prime Minister Koizumi Participate in a Joint Press Availability," June 29, 2006, georgewbush-whitehouse.archives.gov/news/releases/2006/06/20060629-3.html; Ryōzō Katō to

Tarō Asō, June 30, 2006, telegraph no. 7307, MOFA documents disclosed under the Information Disclosure Law, 2019–118–6.

40. Office of the Press Secretary, "President Bush and Japanese Prime Minister Koizumi Participate in a Joint Press Availability." See also Katō to Asō, June 30, 2006, telegraph no. 7307.

41. Office of the Press Secretary, "President Bush and Japanese Prime Minister Koizumi Participate in a Joint Press Availability."

42. Hiroshi Ito, "Nichi-Bei Kankei 'Mottomo Seijuku': Kyōdō Bunsho 'Shinseiki no Dōmei' Happyō Shunō Kaidan" [Japan–US Relations "Most Mature": Joint Document "Alliance for the New Century" Announced at Summit Meeting], *Asahi Shimbun*, June 30, 2006.

43. Norimitsu Onishi and David Sanger, "6 Missiles Fired By North Korea: Tests Protested: Long-Range Rocket Fails Launchings Over Sea Defy Warnings From Bush, Japan and China," *New York Times*, July 5, 2006.

44. Rumsfeld, *Known and Unknown*, 613.

45. Rumsfeld, *Known and Unknown*, 613.

46. Ministry of Foreign Affairs, "Kitachōsen ni yoru Dandō Missile Hassha" [Ballistic Missile Launches by North Korea], July 6, 2006, MOFA documents disclosed under the Information Disclosure Law, 2019–126–4; Tarō Asō to Ryōzō Katō, July 5, 2006, telegraph no. 82509, MOFA documents disclosed under the Information Disclosure Law, 2019–126–11.

47. Shinzō Abe, Chief Cabinet Secretary Shinzō Abe's statement, July 5, 2006, MOFA documents disclosed under the Information Disclosure Law, 2019–126–1.

48. First North America Division, "Nichi–Bei Shunō Denwa Kaidan" [A Japan–US Summit Telephone Talk], July 6, 2006, MOFA documents disclosed under the Information Disclosure Law, 2019–126–15.

49. Bush, *Decision Points*, 425. See also Akio Takahara, "America kara Mita Nicchu Kankei" [Sino-Japanese Relations from the US Perspective], *Tōa*, no. 471 (September 2006): 11–12.

50. Bush, *Decision Points*, 425.

51. For Rice–Asō, see: Tarō Asō to Ryōzō Katō, July 5, 2006, telegraph no. 82874, MOFA documents disclosed under the Information Disclosure Law, 2019–249–12; First North America Division, "Asō Daijin to Rice Kokumu Chōkan tono Denwa Kaidan ni tsuite" [A Telephone Talk Between Minister Asō and Secretary of State Rice], July 7, 2006, MOFA documents disclosed under the Information Disclosure Law, 2019–126–18; First North America Division, "Asō Daijin to Rice Kokumu Chōkan tono Denwa Kaidan ni tsuite" [A Telephone Talk Between Minister Asō and Secretary of State Rice], July 10, 2006, MOFA documents disclosed under the Information Disclosure Law, 2019–126–19; United Nations Policy Division and First North America Division, "Asō Gaimu Daijin to Rice Bei Kokumu Chōkan tono Denwa Kaidan" [A Telephone Talk Between Foreign Minister Asō and Secretary of State Rice], July 12, 2006, MOFA documents disclosed under the Information Disclosure Law, 2019–126–20; United Nations Policy Division,

"Nichi–Bei Gaishō Denwa Kaidan" [A Telephone Talk Between Japanese Foreign Minister and US Secretary of State], July 16, 2006, MOFA documents disclosed under the Information Disclosure Law, 2019-126-22. For Schieffer–Asō, see Tarō Asō to Ryōzō Katō and Kenzō Ōshima, July 10, 2006, telegraphic proposal, MOFA documents disclosed under the Information Disclosure Law, 2019-249-38; First North America Division, "Asō Daijin to Schieffer Zaikyo Bei Taishi tono Denwa Kaidan" [A Telephone Talk Between Minister Asō and US Ambassador to Japan Schieffer], July 19, 2006, MOFA documents disclosed under the Information Disclosure Law, 2019-126-23. For Schieffer–Abe, see: United Nations Policy Division, "Abe Kanbō Chōkan to Schieffer Chūnichi Bei Taishi tono Kaidan" [Talk Between Chief Cabinet Secretary Abe and US Ambassador to Japan Schieffer], July 12, 2006, MOFA documents disclosed under the Information Disclosure Law, 2019-126-24; Abe, *Utsukushii Kuni e*, 53–54; United Nations Policy Division, "Abe Kanbō Chōkan to Schieffer Zaikōo Bei Taishi tono Denwa Kaidan" [A Telephone Talk Between Chief Cabinet Secretary Abe and US Ambassador to Japan Schieffer], July 19, 2006, MOFA documents disclosed under the Information Disclosure Law, 2019-126-21. For Hadley–Abe, see: First North America Division and United Nations Policy Division, "Abe Kanbō Chōkan to Hadley Bei Kokka Anzen Hoshō Mondai Tantō Daitōryō Hosakan no Denwa Kaidan" [A Telephone Talk Between Chief Cabinet Secretary Abe and American Assistant to the President for National Security Affairs Hadley], July 10, 2006, MOFA documents disclosed under the Information Disclosure Law, 2019-126-26; Ministry of Foreign Affairs, "Abe Kanbō Chōkan to Hadley Bei Daitōryōfu Jiseki Hosakan tono Denwa Kaidan" [A Telephone Talk Between Chief Cabinet Secretary Abe and American Assistant to the President Hadley], July 14, 2006, MOFA documents disclosed under the Information Disclosure Law, 2019-249-47.

52. Kenzō Ōshima to Tarō Asō, July 17, 2006, telegraph no. 7157, MOFA documents disclosed under the Information Disclosure Law, 2019-249-1. See also Rice, *No Higher Honor*, 473–75.

53. UNSC, 5490th meeting, July 15, 2006, www.un.org/press/en/2006/sc8778.doc.htm; Kenzō Ōshima to Tarō Asō, July 18, 2006, telegraph no. 7197, MOFA documents disclosed under the Information Disclosure Law, 2019-249-57.

54. Tarō Asō to Ryōzō Katō, etc., July 16, 2006, telegraph no. 87828, MOFA documents disclosed under the Information Disclosure Law, 2019-249-63; Kenzō Ōshima to Tarō Asō, July 16, 2006, telegraph no. 7152, MOFA documents disclosed under the Information Disclosure Law, 2019-249-58; Ōshima to Asō, July 17, 2006, telegraph no. 7157.

55. J. Thomas Schieffer (US ambassador to Japan) to Condoleezza Rice (US secretary of state), July 18, 2006, cable no. 3988, search.proquest.com/docview/1679141652?accountid=26790.

56. Schieffer to Rice, cable no. 3988.

57. Asō to Katō, etc., telegraph no. 87828.

58. Takuo Kidokoro (consul general in St. Petersburg) to Tarō Asō, July 16, 2006, telegraph no. 738, MOFA documents disclosed under the Information Disclosure Law, 2019–249–60.

59. Takuo Kidokoro to Tarō Asō, July 16, 2006, telegraph no. 733, MOFA documents disclosed under the Information Disclosure Law, 2019–152–4.

60. Ministry of Foreign Affairs, "St. Petersburg Summit: Gaiyō" [St. Petersburg Summit: An Overview], July 18, 2006, MOFA documents disclosed under the Information Disclosure Law, 2019–139–2.

61. G8, "Statement on Non-proliferation," July 16, 2006, www.mofa.go.jp/policy/economy/summit/2006/non_pro.html.

62. G8 Chair's summary, St. Petersburg, July 17, 2006, www.mofa.go.jp/policy/economy/summit/2006/summary.html.

63. Takuo Kidokoro to Tarō Asō, July 18, 2006, telegraph no. 756, MOFA documents disclosed under the Information Disclosure Law, 2019–139–30.

64. Takuo Kidokoro to Tarō Asō, July 17, 2006, telegraph no. 746, MOFA documents disclosed under the Information Disclosure Law, 2019–155–4.

65. Kidokoro to Asō, telegraph no. 746.

66. Kidokoro to Asō, telegraph no. 746.

67. Rice, *No Higher Honor*, 527–28.

68. Rice, *No Higher Honor*, 528.

69. Giulio Pugliese, "Kantei Diplomacy? Japan's Hybrid Leadership in Foreign and Security Policy," *Pacific Review* 30, no. 2 (July 2016): 155–58.

70. Rice, *No Higher Honor*, 528.

71. Rice, *No Higher Honor*, 648–49, 707, 713.

72. Rumsfeld, *Known and Unknown*, 642.

73. Rumsfeld, *Known and Unknown*, 642.

74. Hashimoto, et al., eds., *Abe Shinzō Kaikoroku*, 79–80, 314–18.

Conclusion

1. Masataka Kōsaka, *Saishō Yoshida Shigeru* [Prime Minister Shigeru Yosida] (Chūō Kōron Shinsha, 2004), 6.

2. Nanae Kurashige and Naotaka Fujita, "Shiji no Senkō Hyōmei Eikoku ga Yōsei: Iraq Kaisen 10 Nen Fukuda Moto Shushō Interview" [The UK Requested Early Statement of Support: Ten Years since the Start of the Iraq War, Interview with Former Prime Minister Fukuda], *Asahi Shimbun*, March 20, 2013.

3. Hans J. Morgenthau, *Politics among Nations: The Struggle for Power and Peace*, 6th ed., revised by Kenneth W. Thompson (McGraw-Hill, 1985), 187–240.

4. Walt, *The Origins of Alliances*, 5, 21–26.

5. Rice, *No Higher Honor*, 441.

6. For a discussion by a member of the Bush administration, see Condoleezza Rice and Amy Zegart, *Political Risk: Facing the Threat of Global Insecurity in the Twenty-First Century* (Weidenfeld & Nicolson, 2018), 43.

7. Hiroshi Ito, Shinji Muramatsu, and Akira Uchida, "Kaidan Chokuzen Kishimu Nichi-Bei: Obama Daitōryō 12 Nichi Hatsurainich" [US–Japan Relations Under Strain: President Obama's First Visit to Japan on 12th], *Asahi Shimbun*, November 7, 2009.

Bibliography

Primary Sources

MINISTRY OF FOREIGN AFFAIRS OF JAPAN (MOFA) DOCUMENTS DISCLOSED UNDER THE INFORMATION DISCLOSURE LAW

Abe, Shinzō. Chief Cabinet Secretary Shinzō Abe's statement. July 5, 2006. MOFA documents disclosed under the Information Disclosure Law, 2019–126–1.

Anami, Koreshige (ambassador to China) to Yoriko Kawaguchi (foreign minister). February 26, 2004. Telegraph no. 855. MOFA documents disclosed under the Information Disclosure Law, 2020–359–28.

Anami, Koreshige, to Yoriko Kawaguchi. June 26, 2004. Telegraph no. 803. MOFA documents disclosed under the Information Disclosure Law, 2020–360–22.

Arms Control and Disarmament Division. "Kitachōsen no NPT (Kakuheiki Kakusanbōshi Jōyaku) Dattai Hyōmei" [North Korean Announcement of Withdrawal from the NPT (Nuclear Non-proliferation Treaty)]. January 16, 2003. MOFA documents disclosed under the Information Disclosure Law, 2019–112–1.

Asian and Oceanian Affairs Bureau. "Daiyonkai Rokusha Kaigō Dainiji Kaigō (Gaiyō to Hyōka)" [The Second Meeting of the Fourth Round of Six-Party Talks (Overview and Assessment)]. September 27, 2005. MOFA documents disclosed under the Information Disclosure Law, 2020–361–61.

Asō, Tarō (foreign minister), to Ryōzō Katō (ambassador to the US). November 17, 2005. Telegraph no. 143969 (draft). MOFA documents disclosed under the Information Disclosure Law, 2019–146–4.

Asō, Tarō, to Ryōzō Katō. November 17, 2005. Telegraph no. 143970 (draft). MOFA documents disclosed under the Information Disclosure Law, 2019–146–6.

Asō, Tarō, to Ryōzō Katō. November 17, 2005. Telegraph no. 143971 (draft). MOFA documents disclosed under the Information Disclosure Law, 2019–146–7.

Asō, Tarō, to Ryōzō Katō. July 5, 2006. Telegraph no. 82509. MOFA documents disclosed under the Information Disclosure Law, 2019–126–11.

Asō, Tarō, to Ryōzō Katō. July 5, 2006. Telegraph no. 82874. MOFA documents disclosed under the Information Disclosure Law, 2019-249-12.

Asō, Tarō, to Ryōzō Katō and Kenzō Ōshima (ambassador to the UN). July 10, 2006. Telegraphic proposal. MOFA documents disclosed under the Information Disclosure Law, 2019-249-38.

Asō, Tarō, to Ryōzō Katō, etc., July 16, 2006. Telegraph no. 87828. MOFA documents disclosed under the Information Disclosure Law, 2019-249-63.

Bush, George W. Departure remarks. "Topic: The Duelfer Report on Iraqi Weapons Programs." October 7, 2004. In Ryōzō Katō to Nobutaka Machimura (foreign minister). October 7, 2004. Telegraph no. 4985. MOFA documents disclosed under the Information Disclosure Law, 2019-213-2.

Cabinet Secretariat. "Iraq ni okeru Jindō Fukkō Shien Katsudō oyobi Anzen Kakuho Shien Katsudō no Jissi ni kan suru Tokubetsu Sochihō Sekōreian ni tsuite" [A Draft for the Act on Special Measures Concerning Humanitarian Relief and Reconstruction Work and Security Assistance in Iraq]. July 2003. MOFA documents disclosed under the Information Disclosure Law, 2019-205-4.

Chair's summary, Evian Summit. June 3, 2003. MOFA documents disclosed under the Information Disclosure Law, 2019-113-1.

Chair's summary, Kananaskis Summit, June 27, 2002. MOFA documents disclosed under the Information Disclosure Law, 2020-252-1.

Chair's summary, Sea Island Summit. June 10, 2004. MOFA documents disclosed under the Information Disclosure 2020-314-1.

Countermeasures Headquarters, Ministry of Foreign Affairs. "Beikokutō ni yoru Taliban Gunji Shisetsutō ni tai suru Kōgeki" [Attacks on Taliban Military Facilities by the United States and Other Countries]. October 8, 2001. MOFA documents disclosed under the Information Disclosure Law, 2019-199-5.

Defense Agency. "Armitage Kokumu Fukuchōkan Raichō Kanren Sōtei" [Assumption of a Visit to the Defense Agency by Deputy Secretary of State Armitage]. August 27, 2002. MOFA documents disclosed under the Information Disclosure Law, 2019-133-1.

Defense Policy Division, Bureau of Defense Policy, to the First North American Division, MOFA. December 10, 2002. Fax. MOFA documents disclosed under the Information Disclosure Law, 2019-134-13.

Disarmament, Non-proliferation and Science Department. "Kaku ni yoru Terrorism no Koi no Bōshi ni kan suru Kokusai Jōyaku (Kashō) ni tsuite" [About the International Convention for the Suppression of Acts of Nuclear Terrorism (Provisional Name)]. September 2005. MOFA documents disclosed under the Information Disclosure Law, 2019-248-5.

First Middle East Division. "Nichi–Jordan Shunō Kaidan no Igi" [The Significance of the Japan–Jordan Summit]. June 4, 2004. MOFA documents disclosed under the Information Disclosure Law, 2019-168-3.

First Middle East Division. "Nichi–Jordan Shunō Kaidan" [Japan–Jordan Summit]. June 10, 2004. MOFA documents disclosed under the Information Disclosure Law, 2019–168–2.

First North America Division. "Bush Daitōryō no Ippan Kyōsho Enzetsu" [President Bush's State of the Union Address]. February 4, 2002. MOFA documents disclosed under the Information Disclosure Law, 2019–131–1.

First North America Division. "Machimura Daijin to Hadley Beikoku Kokka Anzen Hoshō Tantō Daitōryō Hosakan tono Kaidan no Gaiyō" [Overview of Talks Between Minister Machimura and Hadley, Assistant to the President for National Security Affairs]. October 29, 2005. MOFA documents disclosed under the Information Disclosure Law, 2019–173–11.

First North America Division. "Nichi–Bei Gaishō Kaidan no Gaiyō" [Overview of the US–Japan Foreign Ministers' Talks]. October 29, 2005. MOFA documents disclosed under the Information Disclosure Law, 2019–173–1.

First North America Division. "Nichi–Bei Shunō Denwa Kaidan" [A Japan–US Summit Telephone Talk]. July 6, 2006. MOFA documents disclosed under the Information Disclosure Law, 2019–126–15.

First North America Division. "Asō Daijin to Rice Kokumu Chōkan tono Denwa Kaidan ni tsuite" [A Telephone Talk Between Minister Asō and Secretary of State Rice]. July 7, 2006. MOFA documents disclosed under the Information Disclosure Law, 2019–126–18.

First North America Division. "Asō Daijin to Rice Kokumu Chōkan tono Denwa Kaidan ni tsuite" [A Telephone Talk Between Minister Asō and Secretary of State Rice]. July 10, 2006. MOFA documents disclosed under the Information Disclosure Law, 2019–126–19.

First North America Division. "Asō Daijin to Schieffer Zaikyo Bei Taishi tono Denwa Kaidan" [A Telephone Talk Between Minister Asō and US Ambassador to Japan Schieffer]. July 19, 2006. MOFA documents disclosed under the Information Disclosure Law, 2019–126–23.

First North America Division and United Nations Policy Division. "Abe Kanbō Chōkan to Hadley Bei Kokka Anzen Hoshō Mondai Tantō Daitōryō Hosakan no Denwa Kaidan" [A Telephone Talk Between Chief Cabinet Secretary Abe and American Assistant to the President for National Security Affairs Hadley]. July 10, 2006. MOFA documents disclosed under the Information Disclosure Law, 2019–126–26.

First Western Europe Division. "Nichi–Futsu Shunō Kaidan no Gaiyō" [Overview of the Japan–France Summit]. June 9, 2004. MOFA documents disclosed under the Information Disclosure Law, 2019–157–2.

G7 Statement, Genoa. July 20, 2001. MOFA documents disclosed under the Information Disclosure Law, 2019–138–4.

G8 statement on regional issues, Genoa. July 21, 2001. MOFA documents disclosed under the Information Disclosure Law, 2019–138–6.

Government of the Democratic People's Republic of Korea. "Statement of the Government of the Democratic People's Republic of Korea." January 10, 2003. MOFA documents disclosed under the Information Disclosure Law, 2019–112–3.

Haraguchi, Kōichi (ambassador to the UN), to Yoriko Kawaguchi. September 13, 2002. Telegraph no. 6412. MOFA documents disclosed under the Information Disclosure Law, 2019–202–1.

Haraguchi, Kōichi, to Yoriko Kawaguchi. November 8, 2002. Telegraph no. 8426. MOFA documents disclosed under the Information Disclosure Law, 2019–203–2.

Haraguchi, Kōichi, to Yoriko Kawaguchi. June 8, 2004. Telegraph no. 282. MOFA documents disclosed under the Information Disclosure Law, 2020–163–3.

Haraguchi, Kōichi, to Yoriko Kawaguchi. September 22, 2004. Telegraph no. 3681. MOFA documents disclosed under the Information Disclosure Law, 2020–478–11.

Haraguchi, Kōichi, to Yoriko Kawaguchi. September 23, 2004. Telegraph no. 3756. MOFA documents disclosed under the Information Disclosure Law, 2020–478–18.

Hayashi, Akira (ambassador to Italy), to Makiko Tanaka (foreign minister). July 20, 2001. Telegraph no. 36. MOFA documents disclosed under the Information Disclosure Law, 2019–169–1.

Hayashi, Akira, to Makiko Tanaka. July 22, 2001. Telegraph no. 69. MOFA documents disclosed under the Information Disclosure Law, 2019–138–10.

Hirabayashi, Hiroshi (ambassador to France), to Yoriko Kawaguchi. June 3, 2003. Telegraph no. 26. MOFA documents disclosed under the Information Disclosure Law, 2019–113–22.

Hirabayashi, Hiroshi, to Yoriko Kawaguchi. June 3, 2003. Telegraph no. 27. MOFA documents disclosed under the Information Disclosure Law, 2019–113–22.

Hirabayashi, Hiroshi, to Yoriko Kawaguchi. June 3, 2003. Telegraph no. 34. MOFA documents disclosed under the Information Disclosure Law, 2019–113–22.

Hōgen, Kensaku (ambassador to Canada), to Yoriko Kawaguchi. June 26, 2002. MOFA documents disclosed under the Information Disclosure Law, 2020–258–4.

Hōgen, Kensaku, to Yoriko Kawaguchi. June 27, 2002. Telegraph no. 67. MOFA documents disclosed under the Information Disclosure Law, 2020–252–10.

Japan–US Joint Committee. Minutes (undisclosed). MOFA documents disclosed under the Information Disclosure Law, 2020–287–2.

Japan–US Joint Committee. Minutes (undisclosed). MOFA documents disclosed under the Information Disclosure Law, 2020–287–3.

Japan–US Security Treaty Division. "Mini SSC no Gaiyō" [The Overview of the Mini-SSC]. November 1, 2001. MOFA documents disclosed under the Information Disclosure Law, 2019–119–13.

Japan–US Security Treaty Division. "Beikoku Kokka Anzen Hoshō Senryaku no Gaiyō" [Overview of the National Security Strategy of the United States of America]. September 20, 2002. MOFA documents disclosed under the Information Disclosure Law, 2019-114-1.

Japan–US Security Treaty Division. "Taigai Ōtō Yōryō: Zai Okinawa Kaiheitai no Iraq Haken ni tsuite" [Outline of Foreign Correspondence: Deployment of Marines in Okinawa to Iraq]. February 19, 2004. MOFA documents disclosed under the Information Disclosure Law, 2020-628-24.

Katō, Ryōzō (ambassador to the US), to Makiko Tanaka (foreign minister). October 29, 2001. Telegraph no. 11782. MOFA documents disclosed under the Information Disclosure Law, 2019-119-12.

Katō, Ryōzō, to Makiko Tanaka. November 6, 2001. Telegraph no. 11645. MOFA documents disclosed under the Information Disclosure Law, 2019-120-3.

Katō, Ryōzō, to Makiko Tanaka. November 7, 2001. Telegraph no. 11686. MOFA documents disclosed under the Information Disclosure Law, 2019-120-2.

Katō, Ryōzō, to Makiko Tanaka. January 8, 2002. Telegraph no. 112. MOFA documents disclosed under the Information Disclosure Law, 2019-111-13.

Katō, Ryōzō, to Yoriko Kawaguchi (foreign minister). November 8, 2002. Telegraph no. 10250. MOFA documents disclosed under the Information Disclosure Law, 2019-203-4.

Katō, Ryōzō, to Yoriko Kawaguchi. March 20, 2003. Telegraph no. 2787. MOFA documents disclosed under the Information Disclosure Law, 2019-204-7.

Katō, Ryōzō, to Yoriko Kawaguchi. May 26, 2003. Telegraph no. 10. MOFA documents disclosed under the Information Disclosure Law, 2019-135-10.

Katō, Ryōzō, to Yoriko Kawaguchi. May 26, 2003. Telegraph no. 5420. MOFA documents disclosed under the Information Disclosure Law, 2019-135-2.

Katō, Ryōzō, to Yoriko Kawaguchi. May 26, 2003. Telegraph no. 5421. MOFA documents disclosed under the Information Disclosure Law, 2019-135-3.

Katō, Ryōzō, to Yoriko Kawaguchi. May 26, 2003. Telegraph no. 5422. MOFA documents disclosed under the Information Disclosure Law, 2019-135-4.

Katō, Ryōzō, to Yoriko Kawaguchi. May 26, 2003. Telegraph no. 5424. MOFA documents disclosed under the Information Disclosure Law, 2019-135-6.

Katō, Ryōzō, to Yoriko Kawaguchi. May 26, 2003. Telegraph no. 5425. MOFA documents disclosed under the Information Disclosure Law, 2019-135-7.

Katō, Ryōzō, to Yoriko Kawaguchi. May 26, 2003. Telegraph no. 5427. MOFA documents disclosed under the Information Disclosure Law, 2019-135-9.

Katō, Ryōzō, to Yoriko Kawaguchi. June 9, 2004. Telegraph no. 41. MOFA documents disclosed under the Information Disclosure Law, 2019-156-1.

Katō, Ryōzō, to Yoriko Kawaguchi. June 9, 2004. Telegraph no. 46. MOFA documents disclosed under the Information Disclosure Law, 2019-171-6.

Katō, Ryōzō, to Yoriko Kawaguchi. June 9, 2004. Telegraph no. 47. MOFA documents disclosed under the Information Disclosure Law, 2019-171-7.

Katō, Ryōzō, to Yoriko Kawaguchi. June 9, 2004. Telegraph no. 48. MOFA documents disclosed under the Information Disclosure Law, 2019-171-8.

Katō, Ryōzō, to Yoriko Kawaguchi. June 9, 2004. Telegraph no. 51. MOFA documents disclosed under the Information Disclosure Law, 2019-171-11.

Katō, Ryōzō, to Yoriko Kawaguchi. June 10, 2004. Telegraph no. 86. MOFA documents disclosed under the Information Disclosure Law, 2019-151-3.

Katō, Ryōzō, to Yoriko Kawaguchi. June 10, 2004. Telegraph no. 95. MOFA documents disclosed under the Information Disclosure Law, 2019-153-11.

Katō, Ryōzō, to Yoriko Kawaguchi. June 10, 2004. Telegraph no. 99. MOFA documents disclosed under the Information Disclosure Law, 2020-314-20.

Katō, Ryōzō, to Yoriko Kawaguchi. June 28, 2004. Telegraph no. 1126. MOFA documents disclosed under the Information Disclosure Law, 2019-212-5.

Katō, Ryōzō, to Nobutaka Machimura (foreign minister). October 7, 2004. Telegraph no. 4988. MOFA documents disclosed under the Information Disclosure Law, 2019-213-3.

Katō, Ryōzō, to Nobutaka Machimura. January 31, 2005. Telegraph no. 998. MOFA documents disclosed under the Information Disclosure Law, 2019-214-5.

Katō, Ryōzō, to Nobutaka Machimura. February 19, 2005. Telegraph no. 1989. MOFA documents disclosed under the Information Disclosure Law, 2019-172-1.

Katō, Ryōzō, to Nobutaka Machimura. February 19, 2005. Telegraph no. 1994. MOFA documents disclosed under the Information Disclosure Law, 2019-172-5.

Katō, Ryōzō, to Nobutaka Machimura. February 19, 2005. Telegraph no. 1996. MOFA documents disclosed under the Information Disclosure Law, 2019-172-8.

Katō, Ryōzō, to Nobutaka Machimura. February 19, 2005. Telegraph no. 1997. MOFA documents disclosed under the Information Disclosure Law, 2019-172-9.

Katō, Ryōzō, to Nobutaka Machimura. February 20, 2005. Telegraph no. 2014. MOFA documents disclosed under the Information Disclosure Law, 2019-178-2.

Katō, Ryōzō, to Tarō Asō. March 16, 2006. Telegraph no. 2980. MOFA documents disclosed under the Information Disclosure Law, 2019-116-2.

Katō, Ryōzō, to Tarō Asō. March 16, 2006. Telegraph no. 2984. MOFA documents disclosed under the Information Disclosure Law, 2019-116-1.

Katō, Ryōzō, to Tarō Asō. May 2, 2006. Telegraph no. 4842. MOFA documents disclosed under the Information Disclosure Law, 2019-121-4.

Katō, Ryōzō, to Tarō Asō. May 4, 2006. Telegraph no. 4945. MOFA documents disclosed under the Information Disclosure Law, 2019-174-1.

Katō, Ryōzō, to Tarō Asō. June 30, 2006. Telegraph no. 7301. MOFA documents disclosed under the Information Disclosure Law, 2019-118-1.

Katō, Ryōzō, to Tarō Asō. June 30, 2006. Telegraph no. 7307. MOFA documents disclosed under the Information Disclosure Law, 2019-118-6.

Katō, Ryōzō, to Tarō Asō. June 30, 2006. Telegraph no. 7360. MOFA documents disclosed under the Information Disclosure Law, 2019-118-4.

Katō, Ryōzō, to Tarō Asō. June 30, 2006. Telegraph no. 7361. MOFA documents disclosed under the Information Disclosure Law, 2020-164-4.

Katō, Ryōzō, to Tarō Asō. June 30, 2006. Telegraph no. 7365. MOFA documents disclosed under the Information Disclosure Law, 2020-164-8.

Kawaguchi, Yoriko (foreign minister). Statement on the adoption of the UNSC Resolution on Iraq. November 9, 2002. MOFA documents disclosed under the Information Disclosure Law, 2019-203-3.

Kawaguchi, Yoriko. "On the Adoption of the United Nations Security Council Resolution on Iraq." October 16, 2003. MOFA documents disclosed under the Information Disclosure Law, 2019-206-2.

Kawaguchi, Yoriko, to Ryōzō Katō. February 18. 2002. Unnumbered telegraph. MOFA documents disclosed under the Information Disclosure Law, 2019-132-3.

Kawaguchi, Yoriko, to Ryōzō Katō. February 18, 2002. Unnumbered telegraph. MOFA documents disclosed under the Information Disclosure Law, 2019-132-5.

Kawaguchi, Yoriko, to Ryōzō Katō. February 18, 2002. Unnumbered telegraph. MOFA documents disclosed under the Information Disclosure Law, 2019-132-6.

Kawaguchi, Yoriko, to Ryōzō Katō. February 18, 2002. Unnumbered telegraph. MOFA documents disclosed under the Information Disclosure Law, 2019-132-8.

Kawaguchi, Yoriko, to Ryōzō Katō. February 18, 2002. Unnumbered telegraph. MOFA documents disclosed under the Information Disclosure Law, 2019-132-9.

Kawaguchi, Yoriko, to Ryōzō Katō. February 18, 2002. Unnumbered telegraph. MOFA documents disclosed under the Information Disclosure Law, 2019-132-13.

Kawaguchi, Yoriko, to Ryōzō Katō. February 18, 2002. Unnumbered telegraph. MOFA documents disclosed under the Information Disclosure Law, 2019-132-19.

Kawaguchi, Yoriko, to Ryōzō Katō. September 20, 2002. Telegraph no. 3810. MOFA documents disclosed under the Information Disclosure Law, 2019-122-14.

Kawaguchi, Yoriko, to Ryōzō Katō. December 9, 2002. Telegraph no. 4910. MOFA documents disclosed under the Information Disclosure Law, 2019-134-1.

Kawaguchi, Yoriko, to Ryōzō Katō. December 11, 2002. Telegraph no. 4950. MOFA documents disclosed under the Information Disclosure Law, 2019-134-5.

Kawaguchi, Yoriko, to Ryōzō Katō. December 11, 2002. Telegriph no. 4951. MOFA documents disclosed under the Information Disclosure Law, 2019-134-6.

Kawaguchi, Yoriko, to Ryōzō Katō. December 11, 2002. Telegraph no. 4959. MOFA documents disclosed under the Information Disclosure Law, 2019-134-9.

Kawaguchi, Yoriko, to Ryōzō Katō. February 23, 2003. Telegraph no. 739 (draft). MOFA documents disclosed under the Information Disclosure Law, 2020-437-19.

Kawaguchi, Yoriko, to Ryōzō Katō. February 23, 2003. Telegraph no. 742 (draft). MOFA documents disclosed under the Information Disclosure Law, 2020-437-3.

Kawaguchi, Yoriko, to Ryōzō Katō. March 20, 2003. Telegraph no. 1215. MOFA documents disclosed under the Information Disclosure Law, 2019-204-6.

Kawaguchi, Yoriko, to Ryōzō Katō. March 21, 2003. Telegraph no. 1234. MOFA documents disclosed under the Information Disclosure Law, 2019-204-8.

Kawaguchi, Yoriko, to Ryōzō Katō. April 16, 2003. Unnumbered telegraph (draft). MOFA documents disclosed under the Information Disclosure Law, 2019-204-12.

Kawaguchi, Yoriko, to Ryōzō Katō. October 19, 2003. Telegraph no. 4392. MOFA documents disclosed under the Information Disclosure Law, 2019-140-4.

Kawaguchi, Yoriko, to Ryōzō Katō. October 19, 2003. Telegraph no. 4393. MOFA documents disclosed under the Information Disclosure Law, 2019-140-5.

Kawaguchi, Yoriko, to Ryōzō Katō. October 19, 2003. Telegraph no. 4395. MOFA documents disclosed under the Information Disclosure Law, 2019-140-7.

Kawaguchi, Yoriko, to Ryōzō Katō. October 19, 2003. Telegraph no. 4396. MOFA documents disclosed under the Information Disclosure Law, 2019-140-8.

Kawaguchi, Yoriko, to Ryōzō Katō. November 15, 2003. Telegraph no. 4820. MOFA documents disclosed under the Information Disclosure Law, 2019-115-4.

Kawaguchi, Yoriko, to Ryōzō Katō. December 15, 2003. Unnumbered telegraph. MOFA documents disclosed under the Information Disclosure Law, 2019-209-5.

Kawaguchi, Yoriko, to Ryōzō Katō. December 29, 2003. Telegraph no. 5459. MOFA documents disclosed under the Information Disclosure Law, 2019-210-2.

Kawaguchi, Yoriko, to Ryōzō Katō. April 13, 2004. Telegraph no. 1670. MOFA documents disclosed under the Information Disclosure Law, 2019-141-9.

Kawaguchi, Yoriko, to Ryōzō Katō. April 13, 2004. Telegraph no. 1672. MOFA documents disclosed under the Information Disclosure Law, 2019-141-11.

Kawaguchi, Yoriko, to Tsukasa Uemura (chargé d'affaires to Iraq). June 28, 2004. Telegraph no. 14149. MOFA documents disclosed under the Information Disclosure Law, 2019-212-4.

Kawaguchi, Yoriko, to Kōichi Haraguchi. September 23, 2004. Telegraph no. 3761. MOFA documents disclosed under the Information Disclosure Law, 2020-478-1.

Kidokoro, Takuo (consul general in St. Petersburg), to Tarō Asō (foreign minister). July 16, 2006. Telegraph no. 733. MOFA documents disclosed under the Information Disclosure Law, 2019-152-4.

Kidokoro, Takuo, to Tarō Asō. July 16, 2006. Telegraph no. 738. MOFA documents disclosed under the Information Disclosure Law, 2019-249-60.

Kidokoro, Takuo, to Tarō Asō. July 17, 2006. Telegraph no. 746. MOFA documents disclosed under the Information Disclosure Law, 2019-155-4.

Kidokoro, Takuo, to Tarō Asō. July 18, 2006. Telegraph no. 756. MOFA documents disclosed under the Information Disclosure Law, 2019-139-30.

Koizumi, Jun'ichirō. Press conference. March 20, 2003. MOFA documents disclosed under the Information Disclosure Law, 2019-204-2.

Koizumi Cabinet. "Naikaku Sōridajin Danwa" [Prime Minister's Statement]. March 20, 2003. MOFA documents disclosed under the Information Disclosure Law, 2019-204-1.

Koizumi Cabinet. Security Council and Cabinet Decision. "Dandō Missile Bōei System no Seibitō ni tsuite" [On the Adjustment of Ballistic Missile Defense Systems and Others]. December 19, 2003. MOFA documents disclosed under the Information Disclosure Law, 2019-198-1.

Machimura, Nobutaka (foreign minister), to Ryōzō Katō. October 24, 2004. Telegraph no. 66415. MOFA documents disclosed under the Information Disclosure Law, 2019-142-15.

Machimura, Nobutaka, to Ryōzō Katō. October 24, 2004. Telegraph no. 66416. MOFA documents disclosed under the Information Disclosure Law, 2019-142-16.

Machimura, Nobutaka, to Ryōzō Katō. October 25, 2004. Telegraph no. 66423. MOFA documents disclosed under the Information Disclosure Law, 2019-142-7.

Machimura, Nobutaka, to Ryōzō Katō. October 25, 2004. Telegraph no. 66425. MOFA documents disclosed under the Information Disclosure Law, 2019-142-11.

Machimura, Nobutaka, to Ryōzō Katō. March 19, 2005. Telegraph no. 36192. MOFA documents disclosed under the Information Disclosure Law, 2019-144-19.

Machimura, Nobutaka, to Ryōzō Katō. March 20, 2005. Telegraph no. 36222. MOFA documents disclosed under the Information Disclosure Law, 2019-144-17.

Machimura, Nobutaka, to Ryōzō Katō. July 12, 2005. Unnumbered telegraph (draft). MOFA documents disclosed under the Information Disclosure Law, 2019-145-19.

Machimura, Nobutaka, to Ryōzō Katō. July 13, 2005. Unnumbered telegraph (draft). MOFA documents disclosed under the Information Disclosure Law, 2019-145-4.

Machimura, Nobutaka, to Sadaaki Numata (ambassador to Canada). July 13, 2005. Telegraph no. 89778. MOFA documents disclosed under the Information Disclosure Law, 2020-323-1.

Ministry of Foreign Affairs. "Nichi–Bei Shunō Kaidan Gaiyō" [Overview of the Japan-US Summit]. March 20, 2001. MOFA documents disclosed under the Information Disclosure Law, 2019-182-14.

Ministry of Foreign Affairs. "Tanaka Gaimu Daijin to Powell Kokumu Chōkan tono Denwa Kaidan: Okinawa ni okeru Fujo Bōkō Jiken Higisha no Kisomae no Migara Hikiwatashi ni tsuite" [A Telephone Talk Between Foreign Minister Tanaka and Secretary of State Powell: Extradition of a Suspect in an Assault on Women Incident in Okinawa Prior to Indictment]. July 5, 2001. MOFA documents disclosed under the Information Disclosure Law, 2020–287–1.

Ministry of Foreign Affairs. "Genoa Summit Gaiyō" [Genoa Summit Overview]. July 22, 2001. MOFA documents disclosed under the Information Disclosure Law, 2019–138–2.

Ministry of Foreign Affairs. "Koizumi Sōri Kaiken Yōshi" [Summary of Prime Minister Koizumi's Press Conference]. September 17, 2002. MOFA documents disclosed under the Information Disclosure Law, 2019–122–3.

Ministry of Foreign Affairs. "G8 Evian Summit (Gaiyō to Hyōka)" [G8 Evian Summit (Overview and Assessment)]. June 4, 2003. MOFA documents disclosed under the Information Disclosure Law, 2019–113–2.

Ministry of Foreign Affairs. Press release. December 14, 2003. MOFA documents disclosed under the Information Disclosure Law, 2019–209–2.

Ministry of Foreign Affairs. "Samawah ni okeru Rikujō Jieitai no Ninmu to Gaimushō tono Renkei" [The Ground Self-Defense Force's Mission in Samawah and Cooperation with the Ministry of Foreign Affairs]. January 8, 2004. MOFA documents disclosed under the Information Disclosure Law, 2019–211–1.

Ministry of Foreign Affairs. "Afghanistan ni kan suru Kokusai Kaigi no Gaiyō to Hyōka" [Overview and Evaluation of the International Conference on Afghanistan]. April 1, 2004. MOFA documents disclosed under the Information Disclosure Law, 2019–153–1.

Ministry of Foreign Affairs. "Iraq ni okeru Gaimushō Shokuin Satsugai Jiken (Jiken no Jokyo, Keiito)" [The Murder of the Ministry of Foreign Affair's Employees in Iraq (Situation and Background of the Incident)]. May 12, 2004. MOFA documents disclosed under the Information Disclosure Law, 2019–207–5.

Ministry of Foreign Affairs. "Koizumi Sōri Kaiken Yōshi" [Summary of Prime Minister Koizumi's Press Conference]. May 26, 2004. MOFA documents disclosed under the Information Disclosure Law, 2019–125–2.

Ministry of Foreign Affairs. "Saikin no Afghanistan Jōsei" [Recent Situations in Afghanistan]. May 27, 2004. MOFA documents disclosed under the Information Disclosure Law, 2019–153–1.

Ministry of Foreign Affairs. "Sea Island Summit (Overview)." June 11, 2004. MOFA documents disclosed under the Information Disclosure Law, 2020–314–2.

Ministry of Foreign Affairs. "Iraq Fukkō Shien ni okeru Nichi–Doku Kyōryoku" [Japan–Germany Cooperation in Iraqi Reconstruction Assistance]. June 2004. MOFA documents disclosed under the Information Disclosure Law, 2019–153–1.

Ministry of Foreign Affairs. "Iraq Taryo Hakai Heiki (Sōteimondō: Set Ban)" [WMD in Iraq (Supposed Questions and Answers: Set Version)]. October 7, 2004. MOFA documents disclosed under the Information Disclosure Law, 2019-213-1.

Ministry of Foreign Affairs. "Iraqi Kokumin Gikai Zaigai Senkyo ni okeru Kokusai Kanshi e no Wagakuni Seifu no Sanka ni tsuite" [On the Government's Participation in International Monitoring of the Iraqi National Assembly Overseas Elections]. January 28, 2005. MOFA documents disclosed under the Information Disclosure Law, 2019-214-1.

Ministry of Foreign Affairs. "Nichi–Bei Anzen Hoshō Kyōgi Iinkai ('2+2') no Kaisai" [The Japan–US Security Consultative Committee ("2+2") Meeting]. February 19, 2005. MOFA documents disclosed under the Information Disclosure Law, 2019-178-1.

Ministry of Foreign Affairs. "Koizumi Sōri to Annan Jimusōchō no Kaidan" [Talk Between Prime Minister Koizumi and Secretary-General Annan]. September 15, 2005. MOFA documents disclosed under the Information Disclosure Law, 2019-217-4.

Ministry of Foreign Affairs. "Daigokai Rokusha Kaigō Daiichiji Kaigō (Gaiyō to Tenbō)" [The First Phase of the Fifth Round of Six-Party Talks (Overview and Prospects)]. November 2005. MOFA documents disclosed under the Information Disclosure Law, 2020-362-1.

Ministry of Foreign Affairs. "Terror Taisaku Tokusoho ni motozuku Taiō Sochi ni kan suru Kihon Keikaku no Henkō ni tsuite" [Changes to the Master Plan for Response Measures Under the Anti-Terrorism Special Measures Law]. April 2006. MOFA documents disclosed under the Information Disclosure Law, 2019-121-1.

Ministry of Foreign Affairs. "Kitachōsen ni yoru Dandō Missile Hassha" [Ballistic Missile Launches by North Korea]. July 6, 2006. MOFA documents disclosed under the Information Disclosure Law, 2019-126-4.

Ministry of Foreign Affairs. "Abe Kanbō Chōkan to Hadley Bei Daitōryōfu Jiseki Hosakan tono Denwa Kaidan" [A Telephone Talk Between Chief Cabinet Secretary Abe and American Assistant to the President Hadley]. July 14, 2006. MOFA documents disclosed under the Information Disclosure Law, 2019-249-47.

Ministry of Foreign Affairs. "St. Petersburg Summit: Gaiyō" [St. Petersburg Summit: An Overview]. July 18, 2006. MOFA documents disclosed under the Information Disclosure Law, 2019-139-2.

MOFA and the Defense Agency. "Nichi–Bei Anzen Hoshō Kyōgi Iinkai ('2+2' Kaigō) Gaiyō" [The US–Japan Security Consultative Committee ("2+2" Meeting) Overview]. December 17, 2002. MOFA documents disclosed under the Information Disclosure Law, 2020-199-1.

MOFA and the Defense Agency. "Nichi–Bei Anzen Hoshō Kyōgi Iinkai ('2+2') no Kaisai" [Japan–US Security Consultative Committee ("2+2") Meeting]. October 29, 2005. MOFA documents disclosed under the Information Disclosure Law, 2019–177–1.

MOFA Task Force. "Beikoku ni okeru Renzoku Terror Jiken (Kokkai Sōtei Mondōshū)" [Serial Terrorist Incidents in the US (Likely Questions and Answers for the Diet)]. September 13, 2001. MOFA documents disclosed under the Information Disclosure Law, 2019–130–1.

National Security Policy Division. "Iraq e no Jieitai Haken (Jisshi Yōryō no Gaiyō)" [Deployment of the Self-Defense Forces to Iraq (Overview of the Implementation Guideline)]. December 13, 2003. MOFA documents disclosed under the Information Disclosure Law, 2019–208–1.

Nicchō Pyongyang Sengen [the Japan–DPRK Pyongyang Declaration]. September 17, 2002. MOFA documents disclosed under the Information Disclosure Law, 2019–122–1, 6.

North American Affairs Bureau. "Nichi–Bei Shunō Kaidan no Gaiyō" [Overview of the Japan–US Summit]. June 9, 2004. MOFA documents disclosed under the Information Disclosure Law, 2019–171–1.

North American Affairs Bureau. "Nichi–Bei Shunō Kaidan no Gaiyō" [Overview of the Japan–US Summit]. September 27, 2004. MOFA documents disclosed under the Information Disclosure Law, 2020–478–6.

Northeast Asia Division. "Nicchō Shunō Kaidan (Gaiyō to Hyōka)" [Japan–DPRK Summit Meeting (Overview and Evaluation)]. September 25, 2002. MOFA documents disclosed under the Information Disclosure Law, 2019–122–2.

Northeast Asia Division. "Nichi–Bei Gaishō Denwa Kaidan" [A Telephone Talk Between Japanese Foreign Minister and US Secretary of State]. January 10, 2003. MOFA documents disclosed under the Information Disclosure Law, 2019–112–3.

Northeast Asia Division. "Kitachōsen Hodo 'Yokushiryoku no Motsukoto o Kesshin' (Gaimushō Spokesman Danwa)" [North Korea Report "Determined to Have Deterrent" (Foreign Ministry Spokesman's Statement)]. April 30, 2003. MOFA documents disclosed under the Information Disclosure Law, 2019–123–1.

Northeast Asia Division. "Rokusha Kaigō (Gaiyō to Hyōka)" [The Six-Party Talks (Overview and Evaluation)]. September 1, 2003. MOFA documents disclosed under the Information Disclosure Law, 2019–124–1.

Northeast Asia Division. "Dainikai Rokusha Kaigō (Gaiyō to Hyōka)" [The Second Round of Six-Party Talks (Overview and Assessment)]. March 1, 2004. MOFA documents disclosed under the Information Disclosure Law, 2020–359–1.

Northeast Asia Division. "Nicchō Shunō Kaidan (Gaiyō)" [Japan–DPRK Summit Meeting (Overview)]. May 26, 2004. MOFA documents disclosed under the Information Disclosure Law, 2019–125–1.

Northeast Asia Division. "Kitachōsen no Kakumondai ni kan suru Daisankai Rokusha Kaigō (Gaiyō to Hyōka)" [The Third Round of Six-Party Talks concerning North Korean Nuclear Issues (Overview and Evaluation)]. June 27, 2004. MOFA documents disclosed under the Information Disclosure Law, 2020–360–1.

Northeast Asia Division. "Daiyonkai Rokusha Kaigō (Gaiyō to Hyōka)" [The Fourth Round of Six-Party Talks (Overview and Assessment)]. August 2005. MOFA documents disclosed under the Information Disclosure Law, 2020–361–1.

Ogawa, Hajime (ambassador to Chile), to Nobutaka Machimura. November 20, 2004. Telegraph no. 966. MOFA documents disclosed under the Information Disclosure Law, 2020–553–7.

Ōshima, Kenzō (ambassador to the UN), to Nobutaka Machimura. September 16, 2005. Telegraph no. 10587. MOFA documents disclosed under the Information Disclosure Law, 2019–217–8.

Ōshima, Kenzō, to Nobutaka Machimura. September 19, 2005. Telegraph no. 10719. MOFA documents disclosed under the Information Disclosure Law, 2019–217–11.

Ōshima, Kenzō, to Tarō Asō. July 16, 2006. Telegraph no. 7152. MOFA documents disclosed under the Information Disclosure Law, 2019–249–58.

Ōshima, Kenzō, to Tarō Asō. July 17, 2006. Telegraph no. 7157. MOFA documents disclosed under the Information Disclosure Law, 2019–249–1.

Ōshima, Kenzō, to Tarō Asō. July 18, 2006. Telegraph no. 7197. MOFA documents disclosed under the Information Disclosure Law, 2019–249–57.

Press Division. "Uetake Gaimufukudaijin no Afghanistan Hōmon ni tsuite" [Vice Minister for Foreign Affairs Uetake's Visit to Afghanistan]. December 21, 2001. MOFA documents disclosed under the Information Disclosure Law, 2019–200–1.

Russia Division, European Affairs Bureau, MOFA. "Kananaskis ni okeru Nichi–Ro Shunō Kaidan (Gaiyō)" [Japan–Russia Summit in Kananaskis (Overview)]. June 27, 2002. MOFA documents disclosed under the Information Disclosure Law, 2020–256–1.

Satō, Yukio (ambassador to the UN) to Tanaka. September 24, 2001. Telegraph no. 5970. MOFA documents disclosed under the Information Disclosure Law, 2019–137–3.

Second Middle East Division. "Afghanistan Fukkōshien Kokusai Kaigi (Gaiyō to Hyōka)" [The International Conference on Reconstruction Assistance to Afghanistan (Overview and Evaluation)]. January 24, 2002. MOFA documents disclosed under the Information Disclosure Law, 2019–201–1.

Second Middle East Division. "Saikin no Iraq Jōsei ni tsuite" [The Recent Situation in Iraq]. July 25, 2003. MOFA documents disclosed under the Information Disclosure Law, 2019–205–1.

Second Middle East Division. "Wagakuni no Afghanistan Shien" [Japan's Support for Afghanistan]. May 20, 2004. MOFA documents disclosed under the Information Disclosure Law, 2019–153–1.

Second Western Europe Division. "Nichi–Ei Shunō Kaidan no Gaiyō" [Overview of the Japan–UK Summit]. June 9, 2004. MOFA documents disclosed under the Information Disclosure Law, 2019–156–2.

Second Middle East Division. "Rikujō Jieitai Iraq Fukkō Gyōmu Shien Taichō oyobi Zai Samawah Gaimushō Renraku Jimushochō no Iraq Muthanna Kenchiji tono Kaidan" [Meeting of the Commander of the Ground Self-Defense Force's Iraq Reconstruction Operations Support Unit and the Head of the Ministry of Foreign Affairs Liaison Office in Samawah, the Governor of Muthanna Province, Iraq]. June 20, 2006. MOFA documents disclosed under the Information Disclosure Law, 2019–215–1.

Security Council. "Jōhōshūshū notameno Goeikantō no Haken ni tsuite" [Dispatch of Destroyers, etc. for Information Gathering]. November 8, 2001. MOFA documents disclosed under the Information Disclosure Law, 2019–120–1.

Shibuya, Minoru (consul general to Honolulu), to Makiko Tanaka. November 8, 2001. Telegraph no. 1106. MOFA documents disclosed under the Information Disclosure Law, 2019–120–4.

Shibuya, Minoru, to Makiko Tanaka. November 8, 2001. Telegraph no. 1108. MOFA documents disclosed under the Information Disclosure Law, 2019–120–5.

Shibuya, Minoru, to Makiko Tanaka. November 9, 2001. Telegraph no. 1124. MOFA documents disclosed under the Information Disclosure Law, 2019–120–6.

Shibuya, Minoru, to Makiko Tanaka. November 9, 2001. Telegraph no. 1125. MOFA documents disclosed under the Information Disclosure Law, 2019–120–7.

State Department. "The Bonn Agreement on the Future of Afghanistan." December 7, 2001. MOFA documents disclosed under the Information Disclosure Law, 2019–200–4.

Takahashi, Shūhei (consul general in Edinburgh), to Nobutaka Machimura. July 8, 2005. Telegraph no. 419. MOFA documents disclosed under the Information Disclosure Law, 2020–322–8.

Takahashi, Shūhei, to Nobutaka Machimura. July 8, 2005. Unnumbered telegraph (draft). MOFA documents disclosed under the Information Disclosure Law, 2020–353–18.

Takano, Toshiyuki (ambassador to South Korea), to Yoriko Kawaguchi. February 23, 2004. Telegraph no. 1323. MOFA documents disclosed under the Information Disclosure Law, 2020–359–3.

Tanaka, Makiko (foreign minister). "Afghanistan Zantei Seiken Juritsu ni kan suru Gōibunshotō ni tsuite" [The Agreed Document, etc. on the Establishment of the Interim Government in Afghanistan]. December 5, 2001. MOFA documents disclosed under the Information Disclosure Law, 2019–200–2.

Tanaka, Makiko, to Shunji Yanai (ambassador to the US). May 9, 2001. Telegraph no. 1873. MOFA documents disclosed under the Information Disclosure Law, 2019–127–1.

Tanaka, Makiko, to Shunji Yanai. May 9, 2001. Telegraph no. 1874. MOFA documents disclosed under the Information Disclosure Law, 2019–127–2.

Tanaka, Makiko, to Shunji Yanai. July 24, 2001. Telegraph no. 3157. MOFA documents disclosed under the Information Disclosure Law, 2019–129–2.

Tanaka, Makiko, to Shunji Yanai. October 8, 2001. Unnumbered telegraph. MOFA documents disclosed under the Information Disclosure Law, 2019–199–3.

Tanaka, Makiko, to Ryōzō Katō. November 2, 2001. Fax no. F25557. MOFA documents disclosed under the Information Disclosure Law, 2019–119–20.

Tanaka, Makiko, to Ryōzō Katō. December 17, 2001. Telegraph no. 5303. MOFA documents disclosed under the Information Disclosure Law, 2019–111–12.

Tanaka, Makiko, to Ryōzō Katō, etc. January 29, 2002. Telegraph no. 2441 (draft). MOFA documents disclosed under the Information Disclosure Law, 2019–201–4.

Uemura, Tsukasa, to Yoriko Kawaguchi. June 28, 2004. Telegraph no. 128. MOFA documents disclosed under the Information Disclosure Law, 2019–212–3.

United Nations Policy Division. "Anpori Ketsugi 1441 Saitaku ni kan suru Taigai Ōtō Yōryō" [Outline for External Response on the Adoption of Security Council Resolution 1441]. November 9, 2002. MOFA documents disclosed under the Information Disclosure Law, 2019–203–3.

United Nations Policy Division. "Koizumi Sōridaijin no Kokusairengō Shunōkaigo Shusseki (Toriaezuno Gaiyō to Hyōka)" [Prime Minister Koizumi's Attendance at the United Nations Summit (Present Overview and Evaluation)]. September 20, 2005. MOFA documents disclosed under the Information Disclosure Law, 2019–217–15.

United Nations Policy Division. "Abe Kanbō Chōkan to Schieffer Chuniti Bei Taishi tono Kaidan" [Talk Between Chief Cabinet Secretary Abe and US Ambassador to Japan Schieffer]. July 12, 2006. MOFA documents disclosed under the Information Disclosure Law, 2019–126–24.

United Nations Policy Division. "Nichi–Bei Gaishō Denwa Kaidan" [A Telephone Talk Between Japanese Foreign Minister and US Secretary of State]. July 16, 2006. MOFA documents disclosed under the Information Disclosure Law, 2019–126–22.

United Nations Policy Division. "Abe Kanbō Chōkan to Schieffer Zaikyo Bei Taishi tono Denwa Kaidan" [A Telephone Talk Between Chief Cabinet Secretary Abe and US Ambassador to Japan Schieffer]. July 19, 2006. MOFA documents disclosed under the Information Disclosure Law, 2019–126–21.

United Nations Policy Division and the First North America Division. "Asō Gaimu Daijin to Rice Bei Kokumu Chōkan tono Denwa Kaidan" [A Telephone

Talk Between Foreign Minister Asō and Secretary of State Rice]. July 12, 2006. MOFA documents disclosed under the Information Disclosure Law, 2019–126–20.

US–Japan Security Consultative Committee. Joint statement. December 16, 2002. MOFA documents disclosed under the Information Disclosure Law, 2020–199–1.

Yanai, Shunji (ambassador to the US), to Makiko Tanaka. July 1, 2001. Telegraph no. 6757. MOFA documents disclosed under the Information Disclosure Law, 2019–128–11.

Yanai, Shunji, to Makiko Tanaka. July 1, 2001. Telegraph no. 6769. MOFA documents disclosed under the Information Disclosure Law, 2019–128–14.

Yanai, Shunji, to Makiko Tanaka. September 26, 2001. Telegraph no. 9782. MOFA documents disclosed under the Information Disclosure Law, 2019–170–8.

Yanai, Shunji, to Makiko Tanaka. September 26, 2001. Telegraph no. 9786. MOFA documents disclosed under the Information Disclosure Law, 2019–170–9.

Yanai, Shunji, to Makiko Tanaka. October 7, 2001. Telegraph no. 10327. MOFA documents disclosed under the Information Disclosure Law, 2019–199–2.

MINISTRY OF DEFENSE OF JAPAN (MOD) DOCUMENTS DISCLOSED UNDER THE INFORMATION DISCLOSURE LAW

Cabinet Secretariat. "Iraq ni okeru Jindō Fukkō Shien Katsudō oyobi Anzen Kakuho Shien Katsudō no Jisshi ni kan suru Tokubetsu Shochihō ni motozuku Taiō Sochi no Kekka" [Cabinet Secretariat, "Results of Response Measures Based on the Act on Special Measures Concerning the Implementation of Humanitarian and Reconstruction Assistance Activities and Security Assistance Activities in Iraq]. July 2009. MOD documents disclosed under the Information Disclosure Law, 2021.4.2–HonHonB15.

Defense Policy Division, Defense Bureau. "Bōei Seisaku Kachō, Nichi–Bei Anzen Hoshō Jōyaku Kachō, Hōjin Kisha Briefing" [Briefing for Japanese Journalists by the Director of the Defense Policy Division and the Director of the Japan–US Security Treaty Division]. December 17, 2002. MOD documents disclosed under the Information Disclosure Law, 2021.4.2–HonHonB13–1.

Ishiba, Shigeru (director general of the Defense Agency). Remarks at a cabinet meeting. December 19, 2002. MOD documents disclosed under the Information Disclosure Law, 2021.4.2–HonHonB13–12.

Japan–US Security Treaty Division. "Taigai Ōtō Yōryō: Zai Okinawa Kaiheitai no Iraq Haken ni tsuite" [Outline of Foreign Correspondence: Deployment of Marines in Okinawa to Iraq]. August 19, 2004. MOD documents disclosed under the Information Disclosure Law, 2021.4.2–HonHonB14–11.

Japan–US Security Treaty Division. "Zai-Oki Kaiheitai no Iraq Haken Jōkyō (Shuyō Butai)" [Deployment of Marines in Okinawa to Iraq (Major Units)]. May

12, 2007. MOD documents disclosed under the Information Disclosure Law, 2021.4.2–HonHonB14–3.

Minutes of the House of Representatives Committee on Security. May 14, 2010. MOD documents disclosed under the Information Disclosure Law, 2021.4.2–HonHonB14–12.

Ministry of Defense. "Zai-Oki Kaiheitai no Jitsudō (Shuyō Jisseki)" [Actual Operations of Marines in Okinawa (Major Achievements)]. Undated, MOD documents disclosed under the Information Disclosure Law, 2021.4.2–HonHonB14–1.

Shūgiin Anzen Hoshō Iinkai [House of Representatives Committee on Security]. February 26, 2004. MOD documents disclosed under the Information Disclosure Law, 2021.4.2–HonHonB14–2.

Strategic Information Analysis Office, the Defense Intelligence Division and the Japan–US Defense Cooperation Division, the Bureau of Defense Policy. "Number of U.S. Troops Stationed outside the U.S. in Operation Iraqi Freedom (OIF), Operation New Dawn (OND), and Operation Enduring Freedom (OEF) from Their Respective Destination Countries." March 17, 2015. MOD documents disclosed under the Information Disclosure Law, 2021.4.2–HonHonB14–12.

Documents on the Internet

English Documents

"Agreed Framework Between the United States of America and the Democratic People's Republic of Korea." October 21, 1994. search.proquest.com/docview/1679080933?accountid=26790.

Bush, George W. (president of the United States). State of the Union Address. January 29, 2002. www.whitehouse.gov/news/releases/2002/01/20020129-11.html.

Bush, George W. Remarks on UNSC Resolution 1441. November 8, 2002. 2001-2009.state.gov/p/nea/rls/rm/15019.htm.

Bush, George W. "Statement on the Establishment of the Iraqi Governing Council." July 14, 2003. www.govinfo.gov/content/pkg/PPP-2003-book2/html/PPP-2003-book2-doc-pg873.htm.

Bush, George W. Remarks to Veterans of Foreign Wars Convention. August 16, 2004. georgewbush-whitehouse.archives.gov/news/releases/2004/08/20040816-12.html.

Bush, George W. Statement, 2005 World Summit High-Level Plenary Meeting. September 14, 2005. www.un.org/webcast/summit2005/statements/usa050914.pdf.

Department of Defense. "U.S.–Japan Security Arrangements Remain Vital." November 15, 2003. archive.defense.gov/news/newsarticle.aspx?id=27782.

Department of Defense. "Quadrennial Defense Review Report." February 6, 2006. archive.defense.gov/pubs/pdfs/QDR20060203.pdf.

Department of Defense. "Base Structure Report." Fiscal year 2018. www.acq.osd.mil/eie/Downloads/BSI/Base%20Structure%20Report%20FY18.pdf.

Department of Defense, Office of Public Affairs. "International Contributions to the War Against Terrorism." June 14, 2002. 2001-2009.state.gov/coalition/cr/fs/12753.htm.

Department of State. Bureau of Intelligence and Research. "The Secretary's Morning Intelligence Summary." March 12, 1993. search.proquest.com/docview/1679129205?accountid=26790.

Department of State. "The Secretary's Morning Intelligence Summary." June 18, 1993. search.proquest.com/docview/1679129946?accountid=26790.

Department of State, Office of the Spokesman. "Statement by Richard Boucher, Spokesman: Japan—New Counterterrorism Legislation." October 29, 2001. avalon.law.yale.edu/sept11/state_009.asp.

G8. "Statement on Non-proliferation." July 16, 2006. www.mofa.go.jp/policy/economy/summit/2006/non_pro.html.

G8 Chair's summary. St. Petersburg. July 17, 2006. www.mofa.go.jp/policy/economy/summit/2006/summary.html.

G8 Leaders. "The G8 Global Partnership: Principles to Prevent Terrorists, or Those That Harbour Them, from Gaining Access to Weapons or Materials of Mass Destruction." June 27, 2002. www.mofa.go.jp/policy/economy/summit/2002/state_g8.html#2.

G8 Leaders. "The G8 Global Partnership Against the Spread of Weapons and Materials of Mass Destruction." June 27, 2002. www.mofa.go.jp/policy/economy/summit/2002/state_g8.html#1.

Hadley, Stephen (national security advisor). Remarks to the United States Institute of Peace on the President's National Security Strategy. March 16, 2006. georgewbush-whitehouse.archives.gov/news/releases/2006/03/20060316-8.html.

Hussein, Saddam. "Saddam Hussein Talks to the FBI: Twenty Interviews and Five Conversations with 'High Value Detainee #1' in 2004," National Security Archive Electronic Briefing Book no. 279. Edited by Joyce Battle, assisted by Brendan McQuade. July 1, 2009. nsarchive2.gwu.edu/NSAEBB/NSAEBB279/.

International Conference on Reconstruction Assistance to Afghanistan co-chairs' summary of conclusions. January 21–22, 2002. www.mofa.go.jp/region/middle_e/afghanistan/min0201/summary.html.

Karzai, Hamid. Statement. January 21, 2002. www.mofa.go.jp/region/middle_e/afghanistan/min0201/karzai0121.html.

Kelly, James. Opening remarks before the Senate Foreign Relations Committee. March 2, 2004. 2001-2009.state.gov/p/eap/rls/rm/2004/30093.htm.

Koizumi, Junichirō. Opening statement at the International Conference on Reconstruction Assistance to Afghanistan. January 21, 2002. www.mofa.go.jp/region/middle_e/afghanistan/min0201/pm0121.html.

Koizumi, Junichirō. Address at the High-Level Plenary Meeting of the 60th Session of the UNGA. "Turning Words into an Action." September 15, 2005. www.un.org/webcast/summit2005/statements15/jap050915eng.pdf.

Koizumi, Junichirō. Press conference, "Iraq Haken no Jieitai Tesshutō" [Withdrawal of Self-Defense Forces from Iraq, etc.]. June 20, 2006. www.kantei.go.jp/jp//koizumispeech/2006/06/20kaiken.html.

Michalak, Michael W. (US chargé d'affaires to Japan), to Condoleezza Rice (US secretary of state). March 10, 2005. Cable no. 1415. search.proquest.com/docview/1679131347?accountid=26790.

Ministry of Foreign Affairs. "International Conference on Reconstruction Assistance to Afghanistan." January 21–22, 2002. www.mofa.go.jp/region/middle_e/afghanistan/min0201/index.html.

Ministry of Foreign Affairs. "Basic Policy on Japan-Democratic People's Republic of Korea (DPRK) Normalization Talks." October 9, 2002. www.mofa.go.jp/region/asia-paci/n_korea/nt/bp0210.html.

Ministry of Foreign Affairs. "Third Round of Six-Party Talks Concerning North Korean Nuclear Issues." June 27, 2004. www.mofa.go.jp/region/asia-paci/n_korea/6party/talk0406.html.

Ministry of Foreign Affairs. "Realignment of U.S. forces in Japan." March 6, 2020. www.mofa.go.jp/files/100029846.pdf.

Ministry of Foreign Affairs. "Anpori Kaikaku no Ikistasu to Genjō" [The Evolution and Current Status of Security Council Reform]. April 27, 2022. www.mofa.go.jp/mofaj/gaiko/un_kaikaku/kaikaku2.html.

Office of the Press Secretary. "President Bush Addresses the Nation." March 19, 2003. georgewbush-whitehouse.archives.gov/news/releases/2003/03/20030319-17.html.

Office of the Press Secretary. "President Bush Meets with President of China: Remarks by President Bush and President Hu Jintao of China." October 19, 2003. georgewbush-whitehouse.archives.gov/news/releases/2003/10/20031019-6.html.

Office of the Press Secretary. "President Bush Meets with President Roh Moo-Hyun: Joint Statement Between the United States and the Republic of Korea." October 20, 2003. georgewbush-whitehouse.archives.gov/news/releases/2003/10/20031020-2.html.

Office of the Press Secretary. "Statement by the President." November 25, 2003. georgewbush-whitehouse.archives.gov/news/releases/2003/11/20031125-11.html.

Office of the Press Secretary. "President Congratulates Iraqis on Election." January 30, 2005. georgewbush-whitehouse.archives.gov/news/releases/2005/01/20050130-2.html.

Office of the Press Secretary. "President Bush and Japanese Prime Minister Koizumi Participate in a Joint Press Availability." June 29, 2006. georgewbush-whitehouse.archives.gov/news/releases/2006/06/20060629-3.html.

Office of the Press Secretary. "Joint Statement: The Japan-U.S. Alliance of the New Century." June 29, 2006. georgewbush-whitehouse.archives.gov/news/releases/2006/06/text/20060629-2.html.

Ogata, Sadako. Opening statement by at the International Conference on Reconstruction Assistance to Afghanistan. January 21, 2002. www.mofa.go.jp/region/middle_e/afghanistan/min0201/state0121.html.

Prime Minister's Office. "Statement by the Prime Minister (Provisional Translation)." September 19, 2001. japan.kantei.go.jp/koizumispeech/2001/0919terosoti_e.html.

Prime Minister's Office. "Opening Statement by Prime Minister Junichirō Koizumi at the Press Conference (Provisional Translation)." September 19, 2001. japan.kantei.go.jp/koizumispeech/2001/0919sourikaiken_e.html.

Prime Minister's Office. "Emergency Response Measures (Provisional Translation)." October 8, 2001. japan.kantei.go.jp/koizumispeech/2001/1008taiou_e.html.

Prime Minister's Office. "Statement by Prime Minister Junichiro Koizumi." March 20, 2003. japan.kantei.go.jp/koizumispeech/2003/03/20danwa_e.html.

Rice, Condoleezza. "Remarks with Secretary of Defense Donald Rumsfeld, Japanese Foreign Minister Taro Aso, and Japanese Defense Minister of State for Defense Fukushirō Nukaga—Japan Security Consultative Committee." May 1, 2006. 2001-2009.state.gov/secretary/rm/2006/65528.htm.

Schieffer, J. Thomas (US ambassador to Japan), to Condoleezza Rice (US secretary of state). April 12, 2006. Cable no. 1985. search.proquest.com/docview/1679131369?accountid=26790.

Schieffer, J. Thomas, to Condoleezza Rice. July 18, 2006. Cable no. 3988. search.proquest.com/docview/1679141652?accountid=26790.

Security Council and Cabinet. "National Defense Program Guideline, FY 2005–." December 10, 2004. japan.kantei.go.jp/policy/2004/1210taikou_e.html.

Six-Party Talks. "Initial Actions for the Implementation of the Joint Statement." February 13, 2007. www.mofa.go.jp/region/asia-paci/n_korea/6party/action0702.html.

Six-Party Talks Chairman's statement. The Second Round of Six-Party Talks. February 28, 2004. www.mofa.go.jp/region/asia-paci/n_korea/state0402.html.

Six-Party Talks Chairman's statement. The Third Round of the Six-Party Talks. June 26, 2004, www.chinaembassy.org.nz/eng/xw/t140647.htm.

Six-Party Talks Chairman's statement. The First Phase of the Fifth Round of the Six-Party Talks. November 11, 2005. mu.china-embassy.gov.cn/eng/sgxw/200511/t20051111_6483111.htm.

Six-Party Talks Chairman's statement. The Second Phase of the Fifth Round of the Six-Party Talks. December 22, 2006. www.mofa.go.kr/viewer/skin/doc.html?fn=file_20131008185240480_0&rs=/viewer/result/202010.

Six-Party Talks Chairman's statement. December 11, 2008. www.mofa.go.jp/region/asia-paci/n_korea/6party/state0812.html.

Six-Party Talks Joint Statement of the Fourth Round. September 19, 2005. www.mofa.go.jp/region/asia-paci/n_korea/6party/joint0509.html.

Snow, Tony, and Steve Hadley. "Press Gaggle by Tony Snow and National Security Advisor Steve Hadley." June 20, 2006. georgewbush-whitehouse.archives.gov/news/releases/2006/06/20060620-2.html.

Special Advisor to the DCI on Iraq's WMD. "Comprehensive Report." September 30, 2004. www.cia.gov/library/reports/general-reports-1/iraq_wmd_2004/.

United Nations Security Council. Resolution 678. November 29, 1990. unscr.com/en/resolutions/678.

United Nations Security Council. Resolution 1368. September 12, 2001. undocs.org/S/RES/1368(2001).

United Nations Security Council. Resolution 1441. November 8, 2002. www.un.org/depts/unmovic/documents/1441.pdf.

United Nations Security Council. Resolution 1483. May 22, 2003. undocs.org/S/RES/1483(2003).

United Nations Security Council. Resolution 1511. October 16, 2003. undocs.org/S/RES/1511(2003).

United Nations Security Council. Resolution 1546. June 8, 2004. undocs.org/S/RES/1546(2004).

United Nations Security Council. 5490th meeting. July 15, 2006. www.un.org/press/en/2006/sc8778.doc.htm.

US–Japan Security Consultative Committee. "Joint Statement." February 19, 2005. www.mofa.go.jp/region/n-america/us/security/scc/joint0502.html.

US–Japan Security Consultative Committee. "U.S.-Japan Alliance: Transformation and Realignment for the Future." October 29, 2005. www.mofa.go.jp/region/n-america/us/security/scc/doc0510.html.

US–Japan Security Consultative Committee. "Joint Statement." May 1, 2006. www.mod.go.jp/e/d_act/us/dp12.html.

US–Japan Security Consultative Committee. "United States-Japan Roadmap for Realignment Implementation." May 1, 2006. www.mofa.go.jp/region/n-america/us/security/scc/doc0605.html.

White House. "The National Security Strategy of the United States of America." September 2002. georgewbush-whitehouse.archives.gov/nsc/nss/2002/.

White House. "The National Security Strategy of the United States of America." March 2006. georgewbush-whitehouse.archives.gov/nsc/nss/2006/.

Zoellick, Robert B. "Whither China: From Membership to Responsibility?" September 21, 2005. 2001-2009.state.gov/s/d/former/zoellick/rem/53682.htm.

Japanese Documents

Council on Security and Defense Capabilities. "'Anzen Hoshō to Bōeiryoku ni kan suru Kondankai' Hōkokusho: Mirai e no Anzen Hoshō Bōeiryoku Vision" [The Council on Security and Defense Capabilities Report: Japan's Visions for Future Security and Defense Capabilities]. October 2004. www.kantei. go.jp/jp/singi/ampobouei/dai13/13siryou.pdf.

Japanese Iraq Reconstruction and Support Group. "Iraq Fukkō Shiengun Katsudō Hōkoku" [Japanese Iraq Reconstruction and Support Group Activity Report]. January 22, 2006. www.asahicom.jp/news/esi/ichikijiatesi/iraq-nippo-list/20180416/370/060122.pdf.

Ministry of Foreign Affairs. "Nihon Jordan Shunō Kaidan (Gaiyō)" [Japan–Jordan Summit (Overview)]. June 10, 2004. www.mofa.go.jp/mofaj/kaidan/s_koi/g8_04/jjo_kaidan.html.

Ministry of Foreign Affairs. "Nichi–Bei Shunō Kaidan no Gaiyō" [Overview of the Japan–US Summit]. September 22, 2004. www.mofa.go.jp/mofaj/area/usa/kaidan_040922.html.

Ministry of Foreign Affairs. "Daiyonkai Rokusha Kaigō (Gaiyō to Hyōka)" [The Fourth Round of Six-Party Talks (Overview and Evaluation)]. September 2005. www.mofa.go.jp/mofaj/area/n_korea/6kaigo/6kaigo4_gh.html.

Ministry of Foreign Affairs. "Daiyonkai Rokusha Kaigō Dainiji Kaigō (Gaiyō to Hyōka)" [The Second Meeting of the Fourth Round of Six-Party Talks (Overview and Assessment)]. September 2005. www.mofa.go.jp/mofaj/area/n_korea/6kaigo/6kaigo4_2gh.html.

Ministry of Foreign Affairs. "Daigokai Rokusha Kaigō Dainiji Kaigō (Gaiyō to Tenbō)" [The Second Phase of the Fifth Round of Six-Party Talks (Overview and Prospects)]. December 2006. www.mofa.go.jp/mofaj/area/n_korea/6kaigo/6kaigo5_2gt.html.

Ministry of Foreign Affairs. "Daigokai Rokusha Kaigō Daisan Session no Gaiyō" [Overview of the Third Session of the Fifth Round of Six-Party Talks]. February 2007. www.mofa.go.jp/mofaj/area/n_korea/6kaigo/6kaigo5_3g.html.

Ministry of Foreign Affairs. "Nihon no Gunshuku/Fukakusan Gaikō" [Japan's Disarmament and Non-Proliferation Diplomacy]. May 2008. www.mofa.go.jp/mofaj/gaiko/gun_hakusho/2008/pdfs/shi2_17.pdf.

Ministry of Foreign Affairs. "Dairokkai Rokusha Kaigō ni kan suru Shuseki Daihyō Kaigō (Gaiyō)" [The Meeting of Heads of Delegations of the Six Round of Six-Party Talks (Overview)]. December 2008. www.mofa.go.jp/mofaj/area/n_korea/6kaigo/6kaigo6_skg3.html.

Ministry of Foreign Affairs. "Tai Iraq Buryoku Kōshi ni kan suru Wagakuni no Taiō (Kenshō Kekka)" [Japan's Response to the Use of Force Against Iraq (Verification Result)]. December 21, 2012. www.mofa.go.jp/mofaj/area/iraq/taiou_201212.html.

National Diet. Minutes of the Plenary Session of the House of Representatives. October 13, 2004. kokkai.ndl.go.jp/#/detail?minId=116105254X00220041013&spkNum=4¤t=1.

Prime Minister's Office. "Dai 57 Kai Kokuren Sōkai de Enzetsu" [Speech at the 57th session of the UNGA]. September 13, 2002. www.kantei.go.jp/jp//koizumiphoto/2002/09/13nichibei.html.

Prime Minister's Office. "Koizumi Sōri Interview (Iraq Mondai ni tsuite)" [Interview with Prime Minister Koizumi (On the Iraq Issue)]. March 18, 2003. www.kantei.go.jp/jp//koizumispeech/2003/03/18interview.html.

Prime Minister's Office. "Iraq Mondai ni kan suru Taisho Hōshin no Ketteitō" [Determination of Policy on the Iraqi Issue and Others]. March 20, 2003. www.kantei.go.jp/jp//koizumiphoto/2003/03/20kettei.html.

Chinese Documents

Ministry of Foreign Affairs of China. "Lizhaoxing Fenbie yu Chaoemei Sanfang jiu Beijing Liufang Huitan Jiaohuan Yijian" [Li Zhaoxing Exchanges Views with DPRK, Russia, and the US on Beijing Six-Party Talks]. August 22, 2003. www.fmprc.gov.cn/web/wjb_673085/zzjg_673183/yzs_673193/dqzz_673197/cxbdhwt_673311/xgxw_673317/t25294.shtml.

Ministry of Foreign Affairs of China. "Dierlun Liufanghuitan Zhongguo Daibiaotuan Tuanyuan, Waijiaobu Xinwen Sifusichang Liu Jianchao Jizhe Zhaodaihui Jilu" [Record of the Press Conference by Liu Jianchao, Deputy Director-General of the Department of Information of the Ministry of Foreign Affairs, Member of the Chinese Delegation to the Second Round Six-Party Talks]. February 27, 2004. www.fmprc.gov.cn/web/wjb_673085/zzjg_673183/yzs_673193/dqzz_673197/cxbdhwt_673311/xgxw_673317/t69562.shtml.

Secondary Sources

ENGLISH SOURCES

Annan, Kofi, with Nader Mousavizadeh. *Interventions: A Life in War and Peace.* Penguin Books, 2012.

Aoi, Chiyuki. *Legitimacy and the Use of Armed Force: Stability Missions in the Post-Cold War Era.* Routledge, 2011.

Aoi, Chiyuki, and Yee-Kuang Heng. "Japan: Terrorism and Counterterrorism in Japan." In *Non-Western Responses to Terrorism*, edited by Michael J. Boyle, 81–102. Manchester University Press, 2019.

Aoi, Chiyuki, and Yozo Yokota. "Avoiding a Strategic Failure in the Aftermath of the Iraq War: Partnership in Peacebuilding." In *The Iraq Crisis and World Order: Structural, Institutional and Normative Challenges*, edited by Ramesh Thakur and Waheguru Pal Singh Sidhu, 282–97. United Nations University Press, 2006.

Atanassova-Cornelis, Elena, and Yoichiro Sato. "The US-Japan Alliance Dilemma in the Asia-Pacific: Changing Rationales and Scope." *International Spectator* 54, no. 4 (November 2019): 78–93.

Blair, Tony. *A Journey.* Hutchinson, 2010.

Blix, Hans. *Disarming Iraq*. Pantheon Books, 2004.

Bremer, Lewis Paul III. *My Year in Iraq: The Struggle to Build a Future of Hope*. Simon and Schuster, 2006.

Bumiller, Elisabeth. *Condoleezza Rice: An American Life: A Biography*. Random House, 2007.

Bush, George W. *A Charge to Keep: My Journey to the White House*. Perennial, 2001.

Bush, George W. *Decision Points*. Crown Publishers, 2010.

Bush, Laura. *Spoken from the Heart*. Scribner, 2010.

Calder, Kent E. *Embattled Garrisons: Comparative Base Politics and American Globalism*. Princeton University Press, 2007.

Cha, Victor D. *Alignment Despite Antagonism: The United States-Korea-Japan Security Triangle*. Stanford University Press, 1999.

Cheney, Dick, with Liz Cheney. *In My Time: A Personal and Political Memoir*. Threshold Editions, 2011.

Chijiwa, Yasuaki. "Insights into Japan–U.S. Relations on the Eve of the Iraq War: Dilemmas over 'Showing the Flag.'" *Asian Survey* 45, no. 6 (November/December 2005): 843–64.

Dodge, Toby. *Iraq: From War to a New Authoritarianism*. International Institute for Strategic Studies, 2012.

Dower, John W. *Embracing Defeat: Japan in the Wake of World War II*. W.W. Norton, 1999.

Draper, Robert. *To Start a War: How the Bush Administration Took America into Iraq*. Penguin Press, 2020.

Duelfer, Charles. *Hide and Seek: The Search for Truth in Iraq*. Public Affairs, 2009.

Duelfer, Charles A., and Stephen Benedict Dyson. "Chronic Misperception and International Conflict: The U.S.-Iraq Experience." *International Security* 36, no. 1 (Summer 2011): 73–100.

Fukuyama, Francis. *America at the Crossroads: Democracy, Power, and the Neoconservative Legacy*. Yale University Press, 2006.

Funabashi, Yoichi. *The Peninsula Question: A Chronicle of the Second Korean Nuclear Crisis*. Brookings Institution Press, 2007.

Gellman, Barton. *Angler: The Cheney Vice Presidency*. Penguin Press, 2008.

Green, Michael J. *By More than Providence: Grand Strategy and American Power in the Asia Pacific Since 1783*. Columbia University Press, 2017.

Green, Michael J. *Line of Advantage: Japan's Grand Strategy in the Era of Abe Shinzō*. Columbia University Press, 2022.

Haass, Richard N. *War of Necessity: War of Choice*. Simon & Schuster, 2009.

Harari, Oren. *The Leadership Secrets of Colin Powell*. McGraw-Hill, 2002.

Hattori, Ryuji. *Understanding History in Asia: What Diplomatic Documents Reveal*. Translated by Tara Cannon. Japan Publishing Industry Foundation for Culture, 2019.

Hattori, Ryuji. *Eisaku Satō, Japanese Prime Minister, 1964–72: Okinawa, Foreign Relations, Domestic Politics and the Nobel Prize.* Translated by Graham B. Leonard. Routledge, 2021.

Hattori, Ryuji. *Japan at War and Peace: Shidehara Kijūro and the Making of Modern Diplomacy.* Australian National University Press, 2021.

Heng, Yee-Kuang. *War as Risk Management: Strategy and Conflict in an Age of Globalised Risks.* Routledge, 2006.

Hill, Christopher R. *Outpost: A Diplomat at Work.* Simon and Schuster, 2014.

Hughes, Christopher W. "Not Quite the 'Great Britain of the Far East': Japan's Security, the US–Japan Alliance and the 'War on Terror' in East Asia." *Cambridge Review of International Affairs* 20, no. 2 (June 2007): 325–38.

Ikenberry, G. John. "America's Imperial Ambition," *Foreign Affairs* 81, no. 5 (September/October 2002): 44–60.

Ikenberry, G. John. *Liberal Order and Imperial Ambition: Essays on American Power and International Order.* Polity Press, 2006.

Ikenberry, G. John. *After Victory: Institutions, Strategic Restraint, and the Rebuilding of Order after Major Wars,* new ed. Princeton University Press, 2019.

Inoguchi, Takashi, and Paul Bacon. "Rethinking Japan as an Ordinary Country." In *The United States and Northeast Asia: Debates, Issues, and New Order,* edited by G. John Ikenberry and Chung-in Moon, 79–98. Rowman & Littlefield, 2008.

Ishibashi, Natsuyo. *Alliance Security Dilemmas in the Iraq War: German and Japanese Responses.* Palgrave Macmillan, 2012.

Izumikawa, Yasuhiro. "Explaining Japanese Antimilitarism: Normative and Realist Constraints on Japan's Security Policy." *International Security* 35, no. 2 (Fall 2010): 123–60.

Izumikawa, Yasuhiro. "Network Connections and the Emergence of the Hub-and-Spokes Alliance System in East Asia." *International Security* 45, no. 2 (Fall 2020): 7–50.

Jenkins, Charles Robert, with Jim Frederick. *The Reluctant Communist: My Desertion, Court-Martial, and Forty-Year Imprisonment in North Korea.* University of California Press, 2008.

Jervis, Robert. "Images and the Gulf War." In *The Political Psychology of the Gulf War: Leaders, Publics, and the Process of Conflict,* edited by Stanley A. Renshon, 173–79. University of Pittsburgh Press, 1993.

Jervis, Robert. "The Compulsive Empire." *Foreign Policy,* no. 137 (July/August 2003): 83–87.

Jervis, Robert. "Understanding the Bush Doctrine." *Political Science Quarterly* 118, no. 3 (Fall 2003): 365–88.

Jervis, Robert. *American Foreign Policy in a New Era.* Routledge, 2005.

Jervis, Robert. "An Empire, But We Can't Keep It." In *Imbalance of Power: US Hegemony and International Order*, edited by I. William Zartman, 37–59. Lynne Rienner, 2009.

Jervis, Robert. *Why Intelligence Fails: Lessons from the Iranian Revolution and the Iraq War*. Cornell University Press, 2010.

Jervis, Robert. *Perception and Misperception in International Politics*, rev. ed. Princeton University Press, 2017.

Kagan, Robert. *Of Paradise and Power: America and Europe in the New World Order*. Vintage Books, 2004.

Keohane, Robert O. "The Big Influence of Small Allies." *Foreign Policy*, no. 2 (Spring 1971): 161–82.

Kim Sung Chull. *Partnership Within Hierarchy: The Evolving East Asian Security Triangle*. State University of New York Press, 2017.

Kliman, Daniel M. *Japan's Security Strategy in the Post-9/11 World: Embracing a New Realpolitik*. Praeger, 2006.

Koizumi, Junichirō. "Starting from Scratch . . . Again." *Newsweek* (Pacific ed.) 139, no. 3 (January 21, 2002): 11.

Lake, David A. *Hierarchy in International Relations*. Cornell University Press, 2011.

Leffler, Melvyn P. *Confronting Saddam Hussein: George W. Bush and the Invasion of Iraq*. Oxford University Press, 2023.

Lusane, Clarence. *Colin Powell and Condoleezza Rice: Foreign Policy, Race, and the New American Century*. Foreword by Kwame Dixon. Praeger, 2006.

Mandelbaum, Michael. *The Nuclear Revolution: International Politics Before and After Hiroshima*. Cambridge University Press, 1981.

Mann, James. *Rise of the Vulcans: The History of Bush's War Cabinet*. Penguin Books, 2004.

Matthews, Jeffrey J. *Colin Powell: Imperfect Patriot*. University of Notre Dame Press, 2019.

May, Ernest R. *"Lessons" of the Past: The Use and Misuse of History in American Foreign Policy*. Oxford University Press, 1973.

Mearsheimer, John J., and Stephen M. Walt. "An Unnecessary War." *Foreign Policy*, no. 134 (January/February 2003): 51–59.

Meyer, Christopher. *DC Confidential: The Controversial Memoirs of Britain's Ambassador to the U.S. at the Time of 9/11 and the Iraq War*. Weidenfeld & Nicolson, 2005.

Michishita, Narushige. *North Korea's Military-Diplomatic Campaigns, 1966–2008*. Routledge, 2010.

Morgenthau, Hans J. *Politics Among Nations: The Struggle for Power and Peace*. 6th ed., revised by Kenneth W. Thompson. McGraw-Hill, 1985.

Morrow, James D. "Alliances and Asymmetry: An Alternative to the Capability Aggregation Model of Alliances." *American Journal of Political Science* 35, no. 4 (November 1991): 904–33.

Nabeshima, Keizo. "U.S.-Japan Global Alliance." *Japan Times*, June 2, 2003.

Nixon, John. *Debriefing the President: The Interrogation of Saddam Hussein*. Blue Rider Press, 2016.

Nye, Joseph S. Jr. *Soft Power: The Means to Success in World Politics*. Public Affairs, 2004.

Oberdorfer, Don, and Robert Carlin. *The Two Koreas: A Contemporary History*, 3rd ed. Basic Books, 2014.

Ogata, Sadako. *The Turbulent Decade: Confronting the Refugee Crises of the 1990s*. W.W. Norton, 2005.

Okamoto, Yukio. "Japan and the United States: The Essential Alliance." *Washington Quarterly* 25, no. 2 (Spring 2002): 59–72.

Oros, Andrew L. *Normalizing Japan: Politics, Identity, and the Evolution of Security Practice*. Stanford University Press, 2008.

Porter, Patrick. *Blunder: Britain's War in Iraq*. Oxford University Press, 2018.

Powell, Colin, with Tony Koltz. *It Worked for Me: In Life and Leadership*. Harper, 2012.

Powell, Colin, with Joseph E. Persico. *My American Journey*. Ballantine Books, 1995.

Pugliese, Giulio. "Kantei Diplomacy? Japan's Hybrid Leadership in Foreign and Security Policy." *Pacific Review* 30, no. 2 (July 2016): 152–68.

Rayburn, Joel D., and Frank K. Sobchak, eds. *The U.S. Army in the Iraq War*, vol. 1: *Invasion, Insurgency, Civil War, 2003–2006*. Strategic Studies Institute and United States Army War College Press, 2019.

Rice, Condoleezza. "Why We Know Iraq is Lying." *New York Times*, January 23, 2003.

Rice, Condoleezza. *Extraordinary, Ordinary People: A Memoir of Family*. Three Rivers Press, 2010.

Rice, Condoleezza. *No Higher Honor: A Memoir of My Years in Washington*. Broadway Books, 2011.

Rice, Condoleezza. *Condoleezza Rice: A Memoir of My Extraordinary, Ordinary Family and Me*. Ember, 2012.

Rice, Condoleezza. *Democracy: Stories from the Long Road to Freedom*. Twelve, 2017.

Rice, Condoleezza, and Amy Zegart. *Political Risk: Facing the Threat of Global Insecurity in the Twenty-First Century*. Weidenfeld & Nicolson, 2018.

Rinehart, Ian E. "Collective Self-Defense and US–Japan Security Cooperation." *Politics, Governance, and Security Series*, no. 24 (October 2013): 1–20.

Ruggie, John Gerard. "Multilateralism: The Anatomy of an Institution." In *Multilateralism Matters: The Theory and Praxis of an Institutional Form*, edited by John Gerard Ruggie, 3–47. Columbia University Press, 1993.

Rumsfeld, Donald. *Known and Unknown: A Memoir*. Sentinel, 2011.

Samuels, Richard J. *Securing Japan: Tokyo's Grand Strategy and the Future of East Asia*. Cornell University Press, 2007.

Shinoda, Tomohito. *Koizumi Diplomacy: Japan's Kantei Approach to Foreign and Defense Affairs*. University of Washington Press, 2007.

Silove, Nina. "The Pivot Before the Pivot: U.S. Strategy to Preserve the Power Balance in Asia." *International Security* 40, no. 4 (Spring 2016): 45–88.

Smith, Sheila A. *Japan Rearmed: The Politics of Military Power.* Harvard University Press, 2019.

Snyder, Glenn H. "The Security Dilemma in Alliance Politics." *World Politics* 36, no. 4 (July 1984): 461–95.

Snyder, Glenn H. "Alliance Theory: A Neorealist First Cut." *Journal of International Affairs* 44, no. 1 (Spring/Summer 1990): 103–23.

Snyder, Glenn H. *Alliance Politics.* Cornell University Press, 1997.

Soeya, Yoshihide, Masayuki Tadokoro, and David A. Welch, eds. *Japan as a "Normal Country"?: A Nation in Search of Its Place in the World.* University of Toronto Press, 2011.

Uchiyama, Yu. *Koizumi and Japanese Politics: Reform Strategies and Leadership Style.* Translated by Carl Freire. Routledge, 2010.

Umemoto, Tetsuya. "Ballistic Missile Defense and the U.S.-Japan Alliance." In *Reinventing the Alliance: U.S.-Japan Security Partnership in an Era of Change,* edited by G. John Ikenberry and Takashi Inoguchi, 187–212. Palgrave Macmillan, 2003.

Walt, Stephen M. *The Origins of Alliances.* Cornell University Press, 1987.

Walt, Stephen M. "Alliances in a Unipolar World." *World Politics* 61, no. 1 (January 2009): 86–120.

Woodward, Bob. *Plan of Attack.* Simon & Schuster, 2004.

Woodward, Bob. *State of Denial.* Simon & Schuster, 2006.

JAPANESE SOURCES

Abe, Shinzō. *Utsukushii Kuni e* [Toward a Beautiful Country]. Bungeishunjū, 2006.

Abe, Shinzō. *Abe Shinzō Kaikoroku* [Memoirs of Shinzō Abe]. Edited by Gorō Hashimoto, Hiroshi Oyama, and Shigeru Kitamura. Chūō Kōron Shinsha, 2023.

Aketagawa, Tōru. *Nichi–Bei Chii Kyōtei: Sono Rekishi to Genzai* [The US–Japan Status of Forces Agreement: Its History and Present]. Misuzu Shobō, 2017.

Akiyama, Masahiro. *Moto Bōeijimujikan Akiyama Masahiro Kaikoroku: Reisengo no Anzen Hoshō to Bōei Koryu* [Memoirs of Former Administrative Vice-Minister of Defense Masahiro Akiyama]. Edited by Naotaka Sanada, Ryuji Hattori, and Yoshiyuki Kobayashi. Yoshida Shoten, 2018.

Aoi, Chiyuki. "America to Kokuren: Takakushugi no Kongo" [America and UN: The Future of Multilateralism]. In *America Seijigaikō no Anatomy* [Anatomy of American Politics and Diplomacy], edited by Yoshinobu Yamamoto and Okiyoshi Takeda, 89–113. Kokusai Shoin, 2006.

Aoi, Chiyuki. "Kokka Kensetsu to Chianbumon Kaikaku: Iraq no Jirei ni miru Anteika Paradigm kara no Kairi to Kaiki" [State Building and Security

Sector Reform: Departure from and Return to the Stabilization Paradigm in Iraq]. *Aoyama Kokusai Seikei Ronshu* 88 (September 2012): 165–80.

Defense Agency. *Nihon no Bōei: Bōei Hakusho* [Defense of Japan: Defense White Paper]. Gyōsei, 2003.

Defense Agency. *Nihon no Bōei: Bōei Hakusho* [Defense of Japan: Defense White Paper]. National Printing Bureau, 2004.

Fujiwara, Kiichi. "'Jindōteki na Kūbaku' wa Genso: Bei Ei no Afghan Kōgeki" ["Humanitarian Airstrikes" are Illusion: US-UK Attacks on Afghanistan]. *Asahi Shimbun*, October 10, 2001 (evening edition).

Fujiwara, Kiichi. *Shinpen Heiwa no Realism* [New Edition the Realism of Peace]. Iwanami Shoten, 2010.

Fukuda, Yasuo, and Akihiko Tanaka. "Seiken Chūsū kara Mita 'Tai Terror Sensō' to Nichi–Bei Kankei" [The "War Against Terrorism" and Japan US Relations from the Center of the Administration]. *Gaikō*, no. 69 (September/October 2021): 6–11.

Furukawa, Teijirō. *Kasumigaseki Hanseiki* [Half of My Life in Kasumigaseki], new and rev. ed. Saga Shimbun, 2011.

Furukawa, Teijirō. *Watashi no Rirekisho* [My Resume]. Nihon Keizai Shimbun Shuppansha, 2015.

Hashimoto, Hiroshi. *Futenma Hikōjo Dou Torimodosu? Tairitsu ka Kyōchō kano Sentakushi* [How to Reclaim Futenma Air Station? A Choice Between Confrontation and Cooperation]. Jiji Tsūshin Shuppankyoku, 2020.

Hattori, Ryuji. *Gaikō o Kirokushi, Kōkaisuru: Naze Kōbunsho Kanri ga Jūyōnanoka* [Diplomatic Records and Their Declassification: Why Archives Management Is Important]. University of Tokyo Press, 2020.

Hirabayashi, Hiroshi. *Shunō Gaikōryoku: Shushō, Anata Jishin ga Message desu!* [Summit Diplomacy: Prime Minister, You Yourself Are the Message!]. NHK Publishing, 2008.

Hiraiwa, Shunji. *Chōsen Minshushugi Jinmin Kyōwakoku to Chūka Jinmin Kyōwakoku: "Shinshi no Kankei" no Kōzō to Hen'yō* [The Democratic People's Republic of Korea and the People's Republic of China: The Structure and Transformation of "Lip-Tooth Relations"]. Seori Shobō, 2010.

Hiramatsu, Kenji. "Sōri Hōchō to Nicchō Pyongyang Sengen Shomei e no Michi" [The Road to Signature of the Japan–DPRK Pyongyang Declaration]. *Gaikō Forum*, no. 173 (December 2002): 23–29.

Hisae, Masahiko. *Beigun Saihen: Nichi–Bei "Himitsu Kosho" de Nani ga Attaka* [US Military Realignment: What Happened in the Japan–US "Secret Negotiations"?]. Kōdansha, 2005.

Hōgen, Kensaku. *Moto Kokuren Jimujicho Hōgen Kensaku Kaikoroku* [Memoirs of Former UN Under-Secretary-General Kensaku Hōgen]. Edited by Hiroaki Katō, Ryuji Hattori, Kei Takeuchi, and Tomoaki Murakami. Yoshida Shoten, 2015.

Hosoya, Yuichi. *Rinriteki na Sensō: Tony Blair no Eikō to Zasetsu* [Ethical Wars: The Glories and Setbacks of Tony Blair]. Keio University Press, 2009.

Iijima, Isao. *Jitsuroku Koizumi Gaikō* [True Record of Koizumi's Diplomacy]. Nihon Keizai Shimbun Shuppansha, 2007.

Iijima, Isao. *Koizumi Kantei Hiroku: Sōri towa Nanika* [Secret Records of the Prime Minister's Office: What Is the Prime Minister?]. Bungeishunjū, 2016.

Ina, Hisayoshi. "Document 9/11 no Shōgeki: Sonotoki Kantei wa, Gaimushō wa" [Document 9/11 Shock: At that Time, the Prime Minister's Office and MOFA]. In *"Atarashii Sensō" Jidai no Anzen Hoshō: Ima Nihon no Gaikōryoku ga Towareteiru* [The Security of the "New War" Era: Japan's Diplomatic Power Now Questioned], edited by Akihiko Tanaka, 171–206. Toshi Shuppan, 2020.

Inamine, Keiichi. *Ware Igai Mina Waga Shi: Inamine Keiichi Kaikoroku* [Everyone Is My Mentor Except Me: Memoirs of Keiichi Inamine]. Edited by Ryūkyū Shinpōsha. Ryūkyū Shinpōsha, 2011.

Iokibe, Makoto, Motoshige Itō, and Katsuyuki Yakushiji, eds. *90 Nendai no Shogen: Gaikō Gekihen, Moto Gaimushō Jimujikan Yanai Shunji* [Testimony of the '90s: The Drastic Change in Diplomacy, Former Administrative Vice Minister of the Ministry of Foreign Affairs, Shunji Yanai]. Asahi Shimbun, 2005.

Iokibe, Makoto, Motoshige Itō, and Katsuyuki Yakushiji, eds. *90 Nendai no Shōgen: Okamoto Yukio, Genbashugi o Tsuranuita Gaikōkan* [Testimony of the '90s: Yukio Okamoto, a Diplomat Who Pursued a Hands-on Approach]. Asahi Shimbun Shuppan, 2008.

Ishiba, Shigeru. *Kokubō* [National Defense]. Shinchosha, 2011.

Jimbo, Ken. "'Tai Terror Sensō' to Nichi–Bei Dōmei: Bei Anzen Hoshō no Saikochiku to Dōmeikankei no Saiteigi?" [The "War on Terror" and the Japan–US Alliance: Restructuring U.S. Security and Redefining the Alliance?]. In *9/11 Terror Kōgeki Iko no Kokusai Jōsei to Nihon no Taiō* [The International Affairs after the 9/11 Terrorist Attacks and Japan's Response], edited by Japan Institute of International Affairs, 142–53. Japan Institute of International Affairs, 2002.

Kan, Hideki. *America no Sekai Senryaku* [US World Strategy]. Chūō Kōron Shinsha, 2008.

Katō, Hiroaki. *Jieitai Kaigai Haken no Kigen* [The Origins of the Self-Defense Forces Overseas Deployment]. Keisō Shobō, 2020.

Katō, Ryōzō. *Nichi–Bei no Kizuna: Moto Chūbei Taishi Katō Ryōzō Kaikoroku* [Japan–US Ties: Memoirs of Ryōzō Katō, Former Ambassador to the US]. Edited by Norihide Miyoshi. Yoshida Shoten, 2021.

Kawabata, Kiyotaka. *Iraq Kiki wa Naze Fusegenakattanoka: Kokuren Gaikō no Roppyakunichi* [Why Was the Iraqi Crisis Not Prevented? Six Hundred Days of UN Diplomacy]. Iwanami Shoten, 2007.

Kawakami, Takashi. *Beigun no Zenpo Tenkai to Nichi–Bei Dōmei* [US Forces Forward Deployment and the US–Japan Alliance]. Dōbunkan Shuppan, 2004.

Kawashima, Shin. *Chūgoku no Frontier: Yureugoku Kyokai kara Kangaeru* [China's Frontier: Considering from the Shifting Boundaries]. Iwanami Shoten, 2017.

Kitaoka, Shin'ichi. *Nihon no Jiritsu: Taibei Kyōchō to Asia Gaikō* [Japan's Independence: Cooperation with the United States and Diplomacy toward Asia]. Chūō Kōron Shinsha, 2004.

Koizumi, Jun'ichirō. "Kaikaku ni Owari wa nai" [Reform Has No End]. In *Ketsudan! Anotoki Watashi wa Koushita: Jiminto Sōri, Sosai, Kanbō Chōkan ga Kataru* [Decision! At That Time, I Did This: The Prime Ministers, Presidents and Chief Cabinet Secretaries of the LDP Talk], edited by Liberal Democratic Party, 313–36. Chūō Kōron Jigyō Shuppan, 2006.

Koizumi, Jun'ichirō. *Ketsudan no Toki: Tomodachi Sakusen to Namida no Kikin* [The Time for Decisions: Operation Tomodachi and the Tearful Fund]. Shūeisha, 2018.

Kōsaka, Masataka. *Saishō Yoshida Shigeru* [Prime Minister Shigeru Yoshida]. Chūō Kōron Shinsha, 2004.

Kubo, Fumiaki. "America Gaikō ni totte no Dōmei to Nichi–Bei Dōmei: Hitotsu no Mitorizu" [The Alliances and the Japan–US Alliance for US Diplomacy: An Overview]. In *America ni totte Dōmei toha Nanika* [What Are the Alliances for the US?], edited by Fumiaki Kubo, 3–30. Chūō Kōron Shinsha, 2013.

Kurata, Hideya. "Rokusha Kaidan no Seiritsu Katei to Bei–Chū Kankei: 'Hikakuka' to 'Anpojo no Kenen' o meguru Sogosayo" [The Formation Process of the Six-Party Talks and the US–China Relationship: Interaction on "Denuclearization" and "Security Concerns"]. In *Bei–Chū Kankei: Reisengo no Kōzō to Tenkai* [The US–China Relations: Structure and Development after the Cold War], edited by Seiichirō Takagi, 69–92. Japan Institute of International Affairs, 2007.

Kurata, Hideya. "Bei–Chū 'Taikokukan no Kyōchō' toshiteno Chōsen Hantō Rokusha Kyōdan: Kakufukakusan Seisaku to Chiiki Anzen Hoshō no Kōsaku" [The Six-Party Talks on the Korean Peninsula as the US–China "Cooperation Among Great Powers": The Intersection of Nuclear Non-proliferation Policy and Regional Security Policy]. In *Bōchōsuru Chūgoku no Taigai Kankei: Pax Sinica to Shūhenkoku* [Expanding China's Foreign Relations: Pax Sinica and Neighboring Countries], edited by Satoshi Amako and Emi Mifune, 131–83. Keisō Shobō, 2010.

Machimura, Nobutaka. *Hoshu no Ronri: "Rintoshite Utsukushii Nihon" o Tsukuru* [Conservatism's Logic: Creating a "Dignified and Beautiful Japan"]. PHP Kenkyūjo, 2005.

Masuo, Chisako. "Rokusha Kyōgi to Chūgoku no Kitachōsen Mondai" [The Six-Party Talks and China's North Korea Policy]. In *Hokuto Asia no Anzen Hoshō to Nihon* [Northeast Asian Security and Japan], edited by the Japan Institute of International Affairs, 64–78. Japan Institute of International Affairs, 2004.

Ministry of Foreign Affairs of Japan. *Gaikō Seisho* [Diplomatic Bluebook]. No. 45. Ministry of Foreign Affairs, 2002.

Miyagi, Taizō, and Tsuyoshi Watanabe. *Futenma, Henoko: Yugamerareta 20 Nen* [Futenma, Henoko: A Distorted 20 Years]. Shūeisha, 2016.

Miyazaki, Yoko. *"Terror tono Tatakai" to Nihon* ["The War on Terror" and Japan]. University of Nagoya Press, 2018.

Mori, Yoshirō, and Sōichirō Tahara. *Nihon Seiji no Ura no Ura: Shogen Seikai 50 Nen* [The Dark Side of Japanese Politics: Testimonies on 50 Years in Political Circles]. Kōdansha, 2013.

Moriya, Takemasa. *"Futenma" Kosho Hiroku* [Secret Records of the "Futenma" Negotiations]. Shinchosha, 2012.

Musashi, Katsuhiro. *Reisengo Nihon no Civilian Control no Kenkyū* [A Study of Civilian Control in Post-Cold War Japan]. Seibundoh, 2009.

Nozoe, Fumiaki. *Okinawa Beigun Kichi Zenshi* [The Comprehensive History of US Bases in Okinawa]. Yoshikawa Kōbunkan, 2020.

Ogata, Sadako. *Watashi no Shigoto: Kokuren Nanmin Kōtōbenmukan no 10 Nen to Heiwa no Kochiku* [My Work: Ten Years of the United Nations High Commissioner for Refugees and Peacebuilding]. Asahi Shimbun Publications, 2017.

Ogata, Sadako. *Kikigaki Ogata Sadako Kaikoroku* [Dictation Sadako Ogata Memoirs]. Edited by Takeshi Nobayashi and Masatsugu Naya. Iwanami Shoten, 2020.

Ogata, Sadako, and UNIFEM Japan. *Josei to Fukkōshien: Afghanistan no Genba kara* [Women and Reconstruction Assistance: From the Field in Afghanistan]. Iwanami Shoten, 2004.

Ohno, Yoshinori. *Warm Heart: Kozokaikaku no Ato ni Kurumono* [Warm Heart: What Comes after the Structural Reform]. Parade, 2006.

Okamoto, Yukio. *Sabaku no Sensō: Iraq o Kakenuketa Tomo, Oku Katsuhiko e* [War in the Desert: To Katsuhiko Oku, the Friend Who Ran Through Iraq]. Bungeishunjū, 2006.

Orita, Masaki. *Gaikō Shogenroku: Wangan Sensō, Futenma Mondai, Iraq Sensō* [Diplomatic Testimony: The Gulf War, the Futenma Issue, and the Iraq War], edited by Ryuji Hattori and Jun'ichiro Shiratori. Iwanami Shoten, 2013.

Sadō, Akihiro. "Koizumi Jun'ichirō: Senryaku Naki Gaikō no Ketsudan to Jikkō" [Jun'ichirō Koizumi: Decisions and Execution of Diplomacy Without Strategy]. In *Jinbutsu de Yomu Gendai Nihon Gaikōshi: Konoe Fumimaro kara Koizumi Jun'ichirō made* [A History of Contemporary Japanese Diplomacy: From Fumimaro Konoe to Jun'ichirō Koizumi], edited by Akihiro Sadō, Kazuo Komiya, and Ryuji Hattori, 320–34. Yoshikawa Kōbunkan, 2008.

Sadō, Akihiro. "Koizumi Jun'ichirō: Gekijōgata Seijika no 'Ketsudan' to 'Shisō'" [Jun'ichirō Koizumi: The "Decision" and "Thought" of a Theater-Style Politician]. In *Sengo Nihon Shushō no Gaikō Shisō: Yoshida Shigeru kara Koizumi Junichirō made* [The Diplomatic Thoughts of Japan's Post-war Prime

Ministers: From Shigeru Yoshida to Jun'ichirō Koizumi], edited by Hiroshi Masuda, 409–31. Minerva Shobō, 2016.

Sahashi, Ryō. "Anzen Hoshō Seisaku no Hen'yō to Kōdō Kūkan no Kakudai" [Transforming Security Policy and the Expansion of the Space for Action]. In *Henbō suru Nihon Seiji: 90 Nendai Iko "Henkaku no Jidai" o Yomitoku* [The Changing Japanese Politics: Understanding the "Era of Transformation" Since the 1990s], edited by Takashi Mikuriya, 189–219. Keisō Shobō, 2009.

Saito, Kosuke. "Zaigai Kichi Saihen o meguru Beikokunai Seiji to Sono Senryakuteki Hakyū: Futenma—Guam Package to Sono Kirihanashi" [The US Domestic Politics over Overseas Base Realignment and Its Strategic Spillover: The Futenma—Guam Package and Its Detachment]. In *Okinawa to Kaiheitai: Chūryū no Rekishiteki Tenkai* [Okinawa and the Marine Corps: Historical Development of Stationing], edited by Tomohiro Yara et al., 143–71. Junpōsha, 2016.

Sakai, Keiko. *Iraq: Sensō to Senryō* [Iraq: War and Occupation]. Iwanami Shoten, 2004.

Satō, Masahisa. *Iraq Jieitai "Sentoki"* [The SDF in Iraq "Battle Records"]. Kōdansha, 2007.

Shōji, Takayuki. *Jieitai Kaigai Haken to Nihon Gaikō: Reisengo ni okeru Jinteki Kōken no Mosaku* [SDF Overseas Missions and Japanese Diplomacy: The Search for Human Contribution in the Post-Cold War Era]. Nihon Keizai Hyōronsha, 2015.

Sunohara, Tsuyoshi. *Dōmei Henbō: Nichi–Bei Ittaika no Hikari to Kage* [Alliance Transformed: Light and Shadow of the Integration of Japan and the United States]. Nihon Keizai Shimbun Shuppansha, 2007.

Suzuki, Kazuto. "Blair to Europe 1997–2007: 'Osekkai na Neokonsei'" [Blair and Europe 1997–2007: Meddling Neoconservatism]. In *Igirisu to Europe: Koritsu to Togo no Nihyakunen* [Britain and Europe: Two Hundred Years of Isolation and Integration], edited by Yuichi Hosoya, 299–326. Keisō Shobō, 2009.

Takahara, Akio. "Chūgoku no Takaku Gaikō: Shin Anzen Hoshōkan no Shodo to Shuhen Gaikō no Shintenkai" [China's Multilateral Diplomacy: The New Security View and New Developments in Peripheral Diplomacy]. *Kokusai Mondai*, no. 527 (February 2004): 17–30.

Takahara, Akio. "America kara Mita Nicchū Kankei" [Sino–Japanese Relations from the US Perspective]. *Tōa*, No. 471 (September 2006): 10–23.

Takahara, Akio, and Hiroko Maeda. *Kaihatsu Shugi no Jidai he 1972–2014* [Toward the Era of Developmentalism, 1972–2014]. Iwanami Shoten, 2014.

Takeda, Tomoki. "Koizumi Naikakuki no Gaikō Seisaku Kettei no Rekishiteki Isō: 'Tsuyoi Shushō' no Gaikō no Katachi" [Historical Phase of Foreign Policy Making in the Koizumi Cabinet Period: The Diplomatic Shape of a "Strong Prime Minister"]. In *Kantei Shudō to Jimintō Seiji: Koizumi Seiken no Shiteki Kenshō* [Prime Minister's Office Leadership and LDP Politics: A

Historical Review of the Koizumi Administration], edited by Kentaro Oku and Ryo Kurosawa, 399–444. Yoshida Shoten, 2022.

Takeda, Yasuhiro. *Nichi–Bei Dōmei no Cost: Jishu Bōei to Jiritsu no Tsuikyū* [The Cost of the US–Japan Alliance: Self-Defense and the Pursuit of Autonomy]. Aki Shobō, 2019.

Takeuchi, Yukio, Kōji Nakakita, Hidekazu Wakatsuki, and Katsuhisa Kuramae. *Gaikō Shōgenroku Kōdoseichōki kara Post Reisenki no Gaikō Anzenhoshō: Kokusai Chitsujo no Ninaite e no Michi* [Diplomatic Testimonials Diplomacy and Security from High Growth to Post-Cold War Era: Becoming a Leader of the International Order]. Iwanami Shoten, 2022.

Tamaki, Nobuhiko. "Dōmei Gainen Saikō: Yureugoku Kokusaijōsei to Nichi–Bei Dōmei" [Rethinking the Concepts of Alliance: The Shifting International Situation and the Japan–US Alliance]. *Kanagawa Daigaku Asia Review*, no. 3 (March 2016): 82–97.

Tamaki, Nobuhiko. *Teikoku America ga Yuzuru Toki: Jōho to Atsuryoku no Hitaishō Dōmei* [The Concessions of Imperial America: Asymmetric Alliances of Compromise and Pressure]. Iwanami Shoten, 2024.

Tanaka, Akihiko. *Fukuzatusei no Sekai: "Terror no Seiki" to Nihon* [The World of Complexity: Japan and the "Century of Terrorism"]. Keisō Shobō, 2003.

Tanaka, Hitoshi, and Sōichirō Tahara. *Kokka to Gaikō* [State and Diplomacy]. Kōdansha, 2005.

Tatsumi, Yuki. "Blair Moto Bei Taiheiyōgun Shireikan ni Kiku" [Interview with Blair, Former Commander of US Pacific Command]. *Ronza*, no. 124 (September 2005), 178–83.

Terada, Terusuke. *Gaikō Kaisōroku: Takeshita Gaikō, Peru Nihon Taishi Kotei Senkyo Jiken, Chōsen Hantō Mondai* [Diplomatic Memoirs: Takeshita Diplomacy, the Occupation of Japanese Ambassador's Residence in Peru, and the Korean Peninsula Issues], edited by Ryuji Hattori, Hidekazu Wakatsuki, and Takayuki Shoji. Yoshida Shoten, 2020.

Tsuchiyama, Jitsuo. *Anzen Hoshō no Kokusai Seijigaku: Aseri to Ogori* [International Politics of Security: Anxiety and Hubris], 2nd ed. Yūhikaku, 2014.

Yabunaka, Mitoji. *Kokka no Meiun* [The Fate of the Nation]. Shinchosha, 2010.

Yabunaka, Mitoji. *Sekai ni Makenai Nihon: Kokka to Nihonjin ga Ima Nasubekikoto* [Japan Unbeatable in the World: What the Nation and the Japanese Should Do Now]. PHP Kenkyūjo, 2016.

Yabunaka, Mitoji. *Gaikō Kōshō 40 Nen: Yabunaka Mitoji Kaikoroku* [Forty Years of Diplomatic Negotiations: A Memoir of Yabunaka Mitoji]. Minerva Shobō, 2021.

Yachi, Shōtarō. "9/11 Terrorist Kōgeki no Keii to Nihon no Taiō" [The Process of the 9/11 Terrorist Attacks and Japan's Response]. *Kokusai Mondai*, no. 503 (February 2002): 2–20.

Yamaguchi, Wataru. *Nichi–Bei Shunō Kaidan* [Japan–US Summit Meetings]. Chūō Kōron Shinsha, 2024.

Yamamoto, Akiko. *Nichi–Bei Chii Kyōtei* [The US–Japan Status of Forces Agreement]. Chūō Kōron Shinsha, 2019.

Yamamoto, Eiji. *Kitachōsen Gaikō Kaikoroku* [A Memoir of North Korean Diplomacy]. Chikuma Shobo, 2022.

Yamamoto, Yoshinobu. *"Teikoku" no Kokusai Seijigaku: Reisengo no Kokusai System to America* [International Politics of "Empire": The International System after the Cold War and the United States]. Toshindo, 2004.

Yamasaki, Taku. *YKK Hiroku* [YKK Secret Notes]. Tokyo: Kōdansha, 2004.

Yanagisawa, Kyōji. *Kenshō Kantei no Iraq Sensō: Moto Bōeikanryo ni yoru Hihan to Jisei* [An Examination of the Iraq War: Criticism and Self-Reflection by Former Defense Bureaucrat]. Iwanami Shoten, 2013.

Yanagisawa, Kyōji, et al. *Henoko ni Kawaru Yutakana Sentakushi: "Beigun Kichi Mondai ni kan suru Bankoku Shinryō Kaigi" no Teigen o Yomu* [Rich Alternatives to Henoko: Read the Proposals of "the Bankoku Shinryō Council on US Military Base Issues"]. Kamogawa Shuppan, 2020.

Yomiuri Shimbun Seijibu. *Gaikō o Kenka ni shita Otoko: Koizumi Gaikō 2000 Nichi no Shinjitsu* [The Man Who Made Diplomacy into a Fight: The Truth of 2000 Days of Koizumi Diplomacy]. Shinchosha, 2006.

Chinese Sources

Hu Jintao. *Hu Jintao Wen Xuan* [Selected Works of Hu Jintao], vol. 2. Renmin Chubanshe, 2016.

Jiang Zemin. *Jiang Zemin Wen Xuan* [Selected Works of Jiang Zemin], vol. 3. Beijing: Renmin Chubanshe, 2006.

Li Zhaoxing. *Shuobujinde Waijiao* [Untold Stories of My Diplomatic Life]. Sanlian Shudian, 2014.

Qian Qichen. *Waijiao Shiji* [Ten Diplomatic Memoirs], 2nd ed. Sanlian Shudian, 2018.

Tang Jiaxuan. *Jinyu Xufeng* [Heavy Rain and Warm Wind]. Shijie Zhishi Chubanshe, 2009.

Index